From Renaissance to Renaissance

Hebrew Literature from 1492-1970

From Renaissance to Renaissance

Hebrew Literature from 1492-1970

Part One
by
EISIG SILBERSCHLAG

KTAV PUBLISHING HOUSE, INC.

NEW YORK

CONTENTS

Preface

NEW APPROACHES TO THE STUDY
OF HEBREW LITERATURE

Two problems vitiate the study of modern Hebrew literature: An arbitrary beginning has been accepted by most historians of Hebrew literature; it has been studied by itself and for itself rather than in contextual comparison with other literatures, and it has been reduced to the status of a parochial literature.

What is the reason, the effect, and the possible remedy of this perplexing situation?

The authority of Bialik, buttressed by traditions of enlightenment and by Slouschz's pioneering studies, encouraged erroneous views on the origins of modern Hebrew literature. In two articles "Our Recent Poetry"[1] and "The Young Man from Padua",[2] the best-known Hebrew poet of our century acknowledged Moses Hayyim Luzzatto (1707–1746) not only as the innovator in modern Hebrew poetry but also as the redeemer of modern Hebrew literature and the founder of three new orientations which were represented respectively by the Gaon of Vilna, the Baal Shem Tov and Moses Mendelssohn. In his view Luzzatto was not only the father of modern Hebrew literature but the progenitor of the ethical movement which stemmed from the great rabbinic schools of Eastern Europe, the ancestral saint of Hasidism and the prototype of enlightenment among the Jews of Germany.

Historians of Hebrew literature—Lachower and Zinberg—have more or less concurred in this view. Klausner has chosen the period of Naphtali Herz Wessely (1725–1805) rather than the period of Luzzatto as the beginning of modern Hebrew literature. The reason for that slight deviation from current theory was this: though Luzzatto, in Klausner's view, was intellectually superior to Wessely, the latter was modern and aggressive in the good fight on behalf of enlightenment and secular education. Since his *Words of Peace and Truth*[3] was published in 1781 and the pre-Zionist movement *Hibbat Zion* was initiated in 1881 and marked the end of the era of enlightenment, it conveniently provided Klausner with an exact century for the study of modern Hebrew literature.[4] Abraham Shaanan, a disciple of Klausner, accepts the master's view with slight modifications and reservations: the two central events in modern Jewish history—in his evaluation—are the Edict of Toleration and the French Revolution. Hence the eighties of the eighteenth century are the proper *terminus a quo* for modern Hebrew literature. Though conscious of secularism in the literature of the Hebrew renaissance in the sixteenth century, Shaanan is unwilling to deviate from the traditional century for the beginning of modern Hebrew literature.[5] Dov Sadan uses the term "modern Hebrew literature" and "Hebrew literature in recent times" interchangeably. This fluid terminology frees him from setting dates for the beginnings of modern Hebrew literature. But Sadan feels that historians of Hebrew literature in the last two hundred years—from Moses Mendelssohn or from Moses Hayyim Luzzatto onward—have concentrated on the phenomemon of enlightenment to the exclusion of Hasidism and rabbinic traditionalism. And, in his estimation, these three main trends make up modern Hebrew literature.[6]

The deeper reason for the divergencies in the beginnings of Hebrew literature is to be sought in the fact that all literary classifications are more or less arbitrary attempts to introduce order into chaotic and unmanageable masses of heterogeneous material. And a scattered people experiences dissimilar levels of development in the dissimilar countries of their dispersion. Italian Jewry of the sixteenth century differs markedly from Yemenite Jewry of that period. The former contributed to the renaissance of Europe, the latter continued in petrified medievalism. It is axiomatic, therefore, that modern Hebrew literature has different beginnings in different countries.

What is the criterion of modernity in Hebrew literature? Most scholars say: secularism. But the principal of secularism is a weak principle: the Hebrew middle ages had a thriving secular literature in spite of their religious orientation.

Besides, secularism may have been only an episode—and not a felicitous episode at that—of Hebrew literature. Already Franz Delitzsch observed in the first half of the nineteenth century that Hebrew poetry "struggles like its poets for emancipation, and the emancipation of Hebrew poetry will mean its self-destruction (*Selbstvernichtung*). Hebrew poetry of the middle ages is a document of a people's freedom in slavery, contemporary Hebrew poetry—a document of a people's slavery in freedom, and future Hebrew poetry may yet be a living image of a people's freedom living in freedom."[7] Another historian of Hebrew literature, Hayyim Nahman Schapiro, also disputed the validity of secularism as a criterion of modernity. But like many scholars before him, he accepted enlightenment as the beginning of modern Hebrew literature and resigned himself to the middle of the eighteenth century as a *terminus a quo* for modern Hebrew literature. He viewed the contributors to the periodical *ha-Meassef* as the pioneers of modern Hebrew literature.[8] Extreme spirituality, he thought, was the mark of our national literature up to the middle of the eighteenth century; an earth-centered vigor and vitality distinguished it from that time onward. A similar view was maintained by Baruch Kurzweil: modern Hebrew literature has broken with it sacral past. The break inaugurated a new and a superficial epoch.[9]

The great event in the last few centuries of Jewish history is the exile from Spain. It is the root of a mystical and—subsequently—rationalist revolution in Hebrew literature. It colors the first blush of dawn in the cultural regeneration of Jewry in Turkey and in Palestine, in Italy and in Holland—in the countries which absorbed the influx of Jewish refugees from the Iberian peninsula. That cultural regeneration reaches its full fruition in Italy in the eighteenth century, blossoms again in Germany in the eighteenth century, later in Eastern Europe in the nineteenth century, and in Israel and in America in the twentieth century. Luzzatto is not the beginning but the end of an epoch, not the progenitor, but the descendant.

Parochialism hampers the study of modern Hebrew literature. Ghetto and ghettoism shriveled the cultural vitality of Jewry and turned it inward. Criticism of Hebrew literature became a study in isolation. The time is ripe for broader outlooks. Comparative literature has developed into an important discipline. Special periodicals are devoted to its study, special chairs have been created for it at well-known universities. The makers of literature, novelists and poets, essayists and dramatists, no longer create their works in ignorance of foreign literatures. It is no mere accident of fate that many of them have become excellent translators. And the best of them are animated by a new sense of unity of all literatures.

The disappearance of geographical distances in this century induced a greater rapprochement between literatures. Rilke and Eliot, Joyce and Hemingway have not only contributed to their respective literatures but influenced other literatures including Hebrew. It is to the great credit of Klausner that he recognized the close ties between Hebrew and non-Hebrew literary movements in modern times. In the wake of German *Kulturhistoriker* he hunted influences and imitations with enormous diligence. But he was deficient in perceptive insights and evaluative powers of literary works.

The history of Hebrew literature must be written on a four-dimensional scale. It must encompass internal development, comparison with other literatures, esthetic judgment which is not afraid of generalities and generalizations, sensibility and sensitivity which accompanies thorough and precise analyses of literary works or passages as well as geneses of literary genes, philosophical themes and major currents in the arts. Sociological, economic and even religious research of literature can never be more than ancillary disciplines. Literature is interested in the immediacy of human experience and its adequate expression. What Robert Frost said of poetry applies to the whole of literature: it is "experience in search of meaning." Only incidentally does literature reflect the state of society during a certain period. This does not mean that it cannot profit from the enormous progress of historical studies in our time. But the modernist mathematization of history can be of very limited help to the study of literature. And what can be harmful is recourse to fashionable isms such as the new criticism which is no longer new or perhaps never was new or to Jean-Paul Weber's "monothematicism" which ascribes to each author a major obsession from early experience and an artistic expression of that experience in many guises.

The beginning of the end of the exile and the establishment of the State of Israel have prepared the historian of Hebrew literature for wider vistas of research. The fifteen chapters of the present volume have surveyed movements and personalities in Hebrew literature from 1492 to recent times. The second volume will be devoted to the literature of former Palestine and present-day Israel from 1890 to 1967.

ACKNOWLEDGMENTS

The author wishes to express his thanks and gratitude to Harvard University Press for permission to use material from his essay "Parapoetic Attitudes and Values in Early Nineteenth-Century Hebrew Poetry", Philip W. Lown Institute of Advanced and Judaic Studies, Brandeis University, *Studies and Texts* II ed. Alexander Altmann (Cambridge, Massachusetts, 1964); East and West Library of London and Cornell University Press in the standard credit line: Reprinted from Eisig Silberschlag: *Saul Tschernichowsky: Poet of Revolt,* © 1968 by Eisig Silberschlag. Used by permission of Cornell University Press. The author appreciates the courtesies of East and West Library for permission to use quotations from F. Thieberger, *The Great Rabbi Loew Of Prague* (London, 1955); *The Autobiography of Solomon Maimon* tr. J. Clark Murray (London, 1954); D. Patterson, *Abraham Mapu: The Creator of the Modern Hebrew Novel* (London, 1964); The Pennsylvania State University Press for material from his essay "Interpretations and Reinterpretations of Hasidism in Hebrew Literature" from *Anagogic Qualities of Literature (Yearbook of Comparative Criticism,* Vol. 4; edited by Joseph P. Strelka). Published by The Pennsylvania State University Press, University Park and London. Copyright © 1971 by The Pennsylvania State University. Reprinted by permission. The author is indebted to Bloch Publishing Company for permission to use quotations from Abraham J. Mesch's translation of *Abyss of Despair;* to Jewish Book Council of the National Jewish Welfare Board for the use of his essays "Two Progenitors of Hebrew Literature in America" and "Bialik at the Centenary", *Jewish Book Annual* 18 (1960/61) and *Jewish Book Annual* 30 (1972/3) respectively; to Schocken Books Inc. for a lengthy quotation reprinted by permission of Schocken Books Inc. from *A Jewish Reader* edited by Nahum N. Glatzer. Copyright © 1946, 1961; to Valentine, Mitchell & Co. Ltd. Publishers for permission to quote from Moses Cordovero's *The Palm Tree of Deborah* tr. Louis Jacobs (London, 1960); to *Jewish Frontier* for permission to use Milka Silberschlag's translation of Schoffmann's story "In the Circle," (1939); to *Judaism* for permission to use material from his essays "The Swan Song of Polish Jewry" (1954) and Naphtali Herz Imber" (1956).

Finally, a word of deep gratitude to Dr. M. Nadav, Head of the Department of Manuscripts and Archives, The Jewish National and University Library of Jerusalem, Mr. Dov ben Yaakov, Director of the Bio-Bibliographical Institute *Genazim* in Tel Aviv and Mr. M. Tuchman, Librarian of Hebrew College in Brookline, Massachusetts.

1
Humanism and Mysticism
1492–1750

Year of Agony: Cultural Consequences

The year 1492 is an end and a beginning in the history of the world: an end of the so-called middle ages and a beginning of the so-called modern era. Though the terms "middle ages" and "modern era" are imprecise, they are useful because they are roughly synonymous with a god-centered and man-centered age.

The man-centered age was ushered in by humanists. During the renaissance the Latin word *humanista* denoted the teacher or student of the humanities which comprised grammar, rhetoric, history, poetry and moral philosophy. Much Latin, less Greek and even less Hebrew formed an integral part of humanistic studies during the renaissance, for these classical languages were regarded as fountainheads of wisdom and ethical norms of social behavior.

The humanists believed that they were making a clean break with the past and that they were replacing barbarism with civilization through learning. The pithy epigram of an English scholar sheds a brilliant light upon their age: "Our legend of the Renaissance is a Renaissance legend."[1]

Most modern literatures—Italian and French, Spanish and Portuguese, German and English—have their roots and origins in the renaissance—*renascentia* in Latin. The chronological limits of the age are hotly debated and conceded to be the years 1300–1600.[2] If these rough limits are accepted, modern Hebrew literature may be said to coincide with the final rather than the initial century of the great efflorescence of literary and plastic arts in Italy which attained unquestioned and undisputed leadership and preeminence in the West.

1

But that final phase—early in sixteenth century Florence and Rome—marks the apogee of human reach in the arts.

For the Jews the year 1492 had the effect of a seismic shock. It was a sort of a third exile for them,[3] the end of their sojourn in Spain where they had lived for over a thousand years and where they made substantial achievements in philosophy, in poetry, in the sciences. Don Isaac Abrabanel, who had pleaded unsuccessfully with Ferdinand and Isabella to rescind the edict of expulsion, referred to the disaster in his works. In the commentary on *Daniel* he maintains that he had undertaken the work in order "to strengthen weak hands and tottering knees."[4] In modern paraphrase: to give courage to the desperate refugees. And in the commentary on *Kings* he mentioned his attempts to avert the catastrophe.[5]

Thirty years after the expulsion from Spain Solomon Ibn Verga wrote *The Scourge of Judah*[6] which is mainly a search for the causes of the disaster of 1492.[7] He pays a debt to the traditional view: ethical excellence of Jews brings severe punishment for their iniquities. But he also indicates that Jewish separatism, the crucifixion, the moral decline of Jewry in Spain caused the expulsion. And, what is especially important from the literary point of view, in a mixture of fact and fancy he emphasizes the poignancy of the expulsion as it affected the individual Jew:

> I heard from some of the elders who came out of Spain that one of the boats was infested with the plague, and the captain of the boat put the passengers ashore at some uninhabited place. And there most of them died of starvation, while some of them gathered up all their strength to set out on foot in search of some settlement.
>
> There was one Jew among them who struggled on foot together with his wife and two children. The wife grew faint and died, because she was not accustomed to so much difficult walking. The husband carried his children along until both he and they fainted from hunger. When he regained consciousness, he found that his two children had died.
>
> In great grief he rose to his feet and said: "O Lord of all the universe, you are doing a great deal that I might even desert my faith. But know you of a certainty that—even against the will of heaven—a Jew I am and a Jew I shall remain. And neither that which you have brought upon me nor that which you will bring upon me will be of any avail."
>
> Thereupon he gathered some earth and some grass, and covered

the boys, and went in search of a settlement.[8]

Joseph ha-Cohen, the historian, says explicitly that the expulsions from France and the expulsion from Spain induced him to write his famous chronicle *The Valley of Tears*,[9] "so that Jews may know what has been done to us. . ." As for the expulsion from Spain, he notes with pathos that Jews sailed in ships "wherever the winds carried them: to Africa, Asia, Greece and Turkey. They live there to this very day and they have suffered a great deal. . ."[10] The misery and the despair— these were also the burdens of Elijah Kapsali's account of the expulsion in his chronicle *Of The House of Elijah.*[11]

The need for a new home was the immediate necessity of the exiles. Many of them settled in Italy though Jews of Rome tried to bribe Pope Alexander VI to deny admission of Jewish exiles from Spain to Rome. Many of them had converted and continued to live in insecurity as Marranos. Whether these crypto-Jews were Jews inside and Christians outside—as Hayyim Beinart claims on the basis of a study of the Marrano community of Ciudad Real—or whether they were loyal Christians—as B. Netanyahu claims on the basis of a study of contemporary responsa—is immaterial as far as Judaism is concerned; they were lost to Jewry unless they were permitted to revert to Judaism.

The forced emigration of Jews to countries bordering on the Mediterranean Sea contributed in no small measure to the cultural and economic advancement of Italy and Palestine, Turkey and North Africa. Even the renaissance owes the Jews an unacknowledged or grudged debt. For some of them were the cultural middlemen par excellence: Baruch of Benevento translated parts of the *Zohar* into Latin, Abraham de Balmes translated Aristotle's *Posterior Analytics* with the *Major Commentary* of Averroes from Hebrew versions into Latin, the physician Moses Alatino translated Galen and even Aristotle's *De Coelo* from a Hebrew version into Latin. And they taught Christians Hebrew—the language, the grammar, the literature.

Many outstanding teachers who taught some eminent Christians were in the forefront of their age: Manuele da S. Miniato, the erudite banker and teacher of the Florentine statesman Giannozzo Manetti; the philosophical scholars Elijah del Medigo and Yohanan Alemanno, teachers of Giovanni Pico della Mirandola; Obadiah Sforno, the physician, the commentator on the Pentateuch and the teacher of Johannes Reuchlin;[12] Elijah Levita, the itinerant scholar, grammarian and teacher to such eminent personalities as Egidio da Viterbo, the General of the Order of the Hermits of Saint Augustine who became cardinal in 1517, Mario Grimani, the patriarch of Aquila, George de Selve, bishop of Lavaur, Sebastian Münster, the humanist of Basle and Paul Fagius, the reformed minister; Leone Modena who taught Giovanni Vislingio, professor of anatomy in Padua, Vincenzo Noghera, the scholarly theologian.[13]

The Christian scholars and sages did not study Hebrew for its own sake. Giovanni Pico della Mirandola (1463–1494) aimed at a reconciliation of Greek thought and Hebrew mysticism. In the Kabbalah he sought proofs for the messianism of Christ and confirmation of Christian dogmas. Reuchlin regarded Hebrew as the source of all theology. But even he sought to demonstrate christological tenets of faith by manipulating letters of the Hebrew alphabet. Thus, the three Hebrew letters of the second word in *Genesis* 1, 1: *Bet, Resh, Aleph* were, in his opinion, an indication of the trinity: *Bet,* an initial for *Ben*–son, *Resh,* an initial for *Ruah*–[holy] ghost, *Aleph,* an initial for *Ab*–father. Yet Giovanni Pico della Mirandola and Reuchlin were the important Christian pioneers of Hebrew studies in the West. Their enthusiasm for Hebrew letters led to a sympathetic attitude toward Jews. Reuchlin thwarted a cultural and physical disaster of Jewry in German lands. His spirited fight in word and deed against the calumnies of Johann Pfefferkorn, the nefarious convert, prevented the burning of the Talmud and other books as well as a series of potentially severe persecutions. That he also paved the way for the reformatory work of Martin Luther is an incontestable fact of world history.

Both Giovanni Pico della Mirandola and Reuchlin were courageous men to associate with Jews, the so-called "enemies of Christ." And it required audacity on the part of Jews to associate with Christians. Rabbis feared such associations as possible causes of persecution or conversion.

But more than the Jews contributed *to* the renaissance, they borrowed *from* the renaissance. The heady atmosphere of neoclassicism in Italy, the critical and even skeptical approach to secular and religious institutions, the revolution in the plastic arts agitated all inhabitants—including Jews—in the Appenine peninsula.The ghetto walls in Italy had many chinks: the strong light of the new learning, painting and sculpture penetrated into the narrow streets where Jews lived and generated a Jewish renaissance in Italy. There was no Michelangelo nor a Leonardo da Vinci among them. But they admired the works of the artists. Giorgio Vasari, the contemporary biographer of painters, sculptors and architects, tells us that the unexcelled statue of Moses drew crowds of Jews to the masterpiece: "Jews are to be seen every Saturday . . . hurrying like a flight of swallows, men and women, to visit and worship this figure not as a work of the human hand, but as something divine."[14] Some Jews acquired minor fame as miniaturists, illustrators and engravers. On the whole they were passive rather than active participants in art. The intimate connection between art and Christianity almost precluded growth of Jewish movements in art. But humanists, interested in Hebrew learning, established contacts with Jewish scholars. Both revered tradition, both modeled themselves on a past literature. Instead of inventing new philosophies, new types of wisdom, new literary genres, they borrowed from ancient sources and imitated them with abandon. Their ideas—both on the Jewish and non-Jewish side of the ghetto walls—were often restatements of classical ideas. It is no exaggeration to say that cultural ghettos were disappearing centuries before actual ghettos were abolished in Europe.

Four Trends in Hebrew Literature

Bias, based on rationalist prejudices of the eighteenth and nineteenth centuries, contributed to a slanted evaluation of Jewish literature in and after the renaissance. In his famous essay for Ersch and Gruber's Encyclopaedia the unexcelled Jewish bibliographer, Moritz Steinschneider, divided Jewish literature from the time of Ezra to the time of Mendelssohn into three periods. The last period—from the sixteenth to the end of the eighteenth century—he characterized as a period of decay.[15] He was right in his assumption that no other literary center of Jewry rivaled the Iberian center in range and scope of achievement. But for his rationalist mind Lurianism, Sabbatianism and Hasidism were, of course, emotion-laden movements and, as such, not particularly significant for the development of Judaism. Besides, the brief flash of dramatic activity which is one of the glories of Hebrew literature in the sixteenth century was an unforeseeable event of cultural magnitude: it was discovered by Cassuto and Schirmann in our century. Yet Steinschneider identified an incontrovertible fact of modern Jewish literature: it was written in almost all languages of Europe. He also underlined its continuity which, sometimes, was mere transplantation of Spanish-Jewish literature in new European centers. Thus, Leone Ebreo, author of *Dialoghi d'Amore*, continued the tradition of Jewish philosophy in Italy; Isaac Arama transferred a sort of philosophical homileticism to Salonika; David Yahya (c. 1440–1504), the Portuguese, brought a cult of grammar and poetics to Turkey; Joseph Karo emigrated to Palestine where he became the pillar of the mystic and halakic center in Safed; and Moses Alashkar re-established talmudic, philosophical and mystical studies in Egypt.

In the light of modern research it is best to indicate in the last demimillenium four main trends which are easily discernible and distinguishable from each other: pre-enlightenment, enlightenment, nationalism and Israelism. The pre-enlightenment period extends roughly from the end of the fifteenth to the middle of the eighteenth century—some two hundred and fifty years. But modern Hebrew literature boasts no single figure who has inaugurated the modern age. Leone da Sommo was a true man of the renaissance: as dramatist he had no modern precursor or parallel in Hebrew literature. Azariah de Rossi was also a true man of the renaissance in boldness of historical approach and critical evaluation of historical sources. And so is Leone Modena in his multiplicity of interests and in his self-doubt: a Hebrew Aretino with a rabbi's skullcap. These men togther, as a composite figure, might have done on an infinitely more modest scale what the genius of Petrarch did single-handedly. For Petrarch *is* the father of modern world literature—if such an entity exists. His link with the past as a cleric is weakened by his bold inauguration of a future. Not only did he advocate the worth of secular sciences, the dignity of the "vulgar tongue," the ennobling erudition through study of classical authors; he created the *Canzoniere*—the collection of 366 poems, mostly sonnets to Laura which were the prototype of the love lyric for the next six hundred years; he delighted in introspection as his 600 essay-letters abundantly show; and he created the prototype of intimate autobiography with his *Secretum*—the dialogue between Franciscus, the representative of the modern, world-loving, glory-loving, Laura-loving Petrarch and St. Augustine, the representative of the contrite Petrarch longing for spiritual calm. And though Franciscus bows to the superior, spiritual wisdom of St. Augustine, he never renounces the restless search for new expression and fame.

His coronation as poet laureate in Rome on April 6, 1341 was doubly symbolic: it was recognition of Rome's ancient glory as capital of the cultural world and recognition of the poet as the chief culture-bearer of his age; his ascent of Mount Ventoux was not only pioneerism in mountain climbing, it was adoration of landscape for its own sake and not for the sake of its creator. Neither Immanuel of Rome, the contemporary of Dante, nor Menahem ben Benjamin of Recanati, the contemporary of Petrarch, equal their genius. Great personalities seem to appear in Hebrew literature at the end rather than at the beginning of an era—Philo, at the end of the Hellenistic era, Saadia at the end of the gaonic era, Maimonides at the end of a long philosophical development. This is an interesting phenomenon for historians of literature. For Jewish originality consists of a genius for adaptation. And adaptation postulates predecessors: Immanuel of Rome is unthinkable without Dante and the circle of Italian poets who preceded Dante. As the ancestor and antecedent of modern Hebrew literature, he showed no less an intense interest in erotic themes than Dante. But he could not help being merely a theoretical Don Juan. For sexual morality, protected by the rigid standards of the community, showed no public lapses among the Jews of the middle ages as, for example, under William IX of Aquitaine-Poitou (1087–1127), who founded a nunnery with prostitutes as members and with a courtesan as Mother Superior. Yet Immanuel of Rome shocked the sensibilities of Jews to such an extent that the authoritative code of religious practice, the *Shulhan 'Aruk,* prohibited the reading of "profane talk and erotic discourse such as the *Book of Immanuel.*[16] It was he who introduced the sonnet into Hebrew literature when it was still unknown in France, Germany and England. Altogether European metric, paralleling Arabic metric and later superseding it, found a way into Hebrew literature through the mediacy of its Italian poets. The future will decide whether it will shackle Hebrew poetry, as did Arabic metric in medieval times, or prove to be a boon. Already some contemporary poets call for a return to biblical parallelism while ultra-moderns take refuge in blank or free verse *à la* Walt Whitman or Arno Holz.

16th and 17th Century: Poetry

In the sixteenth or seventeenth century no poet equaled Immanuel of Rome in facility of versification. Even a graceful poet like Samuel ben Moses Anau of Bologna[17] cannot compare with him. Whether his love for Miriam is a literary love or an expression of a real love is difficult to ascertain. Since Petrarch composed his poems for Laura, love poetry became an Italian fashion and an exercise in artificiality which penetrated even the fenced-in life of Jewry in Italy. At any rate, in the long poem "Hear, All Nations," four hundred and eighty-six verses in *terza rima,* all nations are summoned to listen to the poet's unhappy pleas of love. Even the virtues of the beloved are unconvincing; they are couched in conventional language: "her lips are as beautiful as jasper." And the lover, in the fashion prevalent among Jews and non-Jews alike, woos the reluctant Miriam by sending his father to talk to her relative.[18]

Occasional and liturgical verses flooded the field of Hebrew poetry in the sixteenth and seventeenth centuries. They were at best imitations or barren exercises in versecraft. In a sense the liturgical poems were also occasional poems: holidays and special days in the Jewish calendar provided the pretexts for versifying. But there were events of tragic import like the expulsion from Spain in 1492 which inspired Leone Ebreo, eldest son of Isaac Abrabanel, to write a moving elegy on the tragic event and on the enforced baptism of his son, "Complaint Against Fate."[19] The burning of the Talmud in 1554 and the burning of 24 Marranos in Ancona in 1556 were events which elicited numerous laments—especially by such poets as Jacob Fano, Mordecai ben Judah and Solomon Hazan who wrote about both of them and, in his special elegy on the Marranos of Ancona, he enumerated the martyrs by name.[20]

The seventeenth century was rich in tragic events. The instigation of riots against the Jews in Frankfurt in 1612, their expulsion from the city in 1614, the subsequent hanging of the instigator Vincent Fettmilch in 1616 and the celebration of a festival—*Purim Winz*—to commemorate that infamy as well as the Chmielnicki pogroms of 1648–9 elicited a spate of poems which are moving because of the events rather than because of their poetry.[21] But the secular occasions for occasional verse were often too trivial. A complaint against a treacherous friend elicited a poem by Jacob Frances; a gift of a silver plate and basin presented to a synagogue in Bologna by a certain Joseph ben David provided his famous brother-in-law, Joseph ha-Cohen, with an opportunity to compose some verses.[22] Some poets—in abject epigonism—wrote against physicians who were favorite targets of Immanuel of Rome, Jacob and Immanuel Frances, and Moses Zacuto. Some poets wrote misogynous tracts in monotonous verse. Though they did not achieve the limpid ease of an Immanuel of Rome—"king of poets" in the generous phrase of Frances,[23]—they penned some memorable verses on the fair sex. Abraham da Sartegno, author of "Womanhater,"[24] begins with the beginning of all evil: man's expulsion from the Garden of Eden because of Eve's misbehavior. He then proceeds to catalog evil women: Lot's daughters who intoxicated their father; Dinah who caused the destruction of Shechem; Tamar who deceived Judah; the temptation of Joseph by Potiphar's wife; the Moabite women who tempted the Israelites to whoring and idolatry; the disgraceful affairs of Cozbi and Zimri, Amnon and Tamar; the destruction of a tribe because of a concubine in ancient Gibeah; the wiles of Delilah, Bath-sheba, the cause of David's abominable behavior toward her husband Uriah; Athaliah who "destroyed all the seed royal";[25] the notorious Jezebel. From biblical women Abraham da Sartegno turns to famous women in the ancient world: Semiramis and Dido, Cleopatra and Medea.

The use of non-biblical women as paradigms of evil: that was an innovation—perhaps not unexpected of a Jewish humanist. And so was the moralizing, didactic touch which runs throughout the poem: Woman excels in arrogance and shamelessness; she cannot distinguish between right and wrong; she is oversexed; she brings grief and subjection to men of might and even more so to weaklings. In sum: Women are all alike in their destructive stance—the highborn and the lowborn.

Jacob Segre inveighed against women's love for luxury and power. Jacob Frances condemned woman in a sweeping generalization: Her kindness is a lie; her love, whoredom; her grace, deceit; her soft talk, flattery. In sum, she is total disgrace. How then did she succeed to entrap man? The answer: "with the prospect of widowerhood."[26] In another sonnet Jacob Frances commiserates with a man who has just married: His ship of joy breaks, he has no beam of hope to hold on to in the angry sea into which he has been thrown.[27] Surprisingly for an Italian Jew he even condemns education for women: The foolish, ignorant, child-bearing woman is the praiseworthy woman.[28] As against the misogynists there were the philogynists: Avigdor Fano and especially Leone da Sommo, who extolled the virtues of women in a long poem, "Defender of Women,"[29] in a mélange of Hebrew and Italian. In contradistinction to Abraham da Sartegno, Leone da Sommo mentions a few biblical women—Rachel and Leah, Esther and Abigail; from the Apocrypha, Judith; several examples of virtuous women from Roman and Greek lore and, from the renaissance, Doña Benvenida, the daughter-in-law of Don Isaac Abrabanel, her daughters, and an anonymous beauty in Bologna. It must be said, however, that the philogynists managed to write weaker poetry than the misogynists. There were also poets who took a middle course. Jacob de Fano praises women in "The Shields of the Mighty"[30] but regards them inferior to men.

Some poets like Moses ben Joab of Florence and Moses Catalano composed, in addition to liturgical poetry, verses on contemporary events. But they are hacks rather than inspired poets. Others like Samuel da Castiglione or Abraham Provenzale or Judah Moscato or Menahem Lonzano or Samuel Archevolti wrote in a traditional style on traditional themes. They had made their reputations in other fields and used poetry as a covenient vehicle for routinized emotions. Samuel da Castiglione, not to be confused with the well-known Baldassare Castiglione, author of the book on the etiquette of the nobility, *The Courtier,* and Abraham Provencale, were physicians. Judah Moscato, who is known as the commentator of Judah Halevi's *Kuzari,* was moved to write an elegy on the death of Joseph Karo; Menahem Lonzano, the lexicographer, indulged in didactic verse; Samuel Archevolti, the grammarian, wrote verse in biblical idiom. Even such scholars as Leone Ebreo or Elijah Levita, Azariah de Rossi or Leone Modena wrote poetry. The heady air of the Italian renaissance imposed poetic sentiments even on non-poetic authors.

Drama

An important contribution to the development of modern Hebrew literature was made in the domain of Hebrew drama. In the third decade of the sixteenth century Giuseppe Gallo—Joseph ben Samuel Zarfati in Hebrew—adopted *The Celestina*[31] which is attributed to Fernando de Rojas. This is the popular title of the work originally called *Tragicomedy of Calisto and Melibea* after the principal characters. The plot is really dominated by Celestina, a procuress of ready wit and many wiles who is enlisted by a nobleman to help him in the seduction of Melibea. The Hebrew adaptation was made in the beginning of the sixteenth century either from the original Spanish or from an Italian translation.[32]

But the first Hebrew comedy, written by Leone da Sommo who was also a skillful producer and author of pastoral plays and comedies in Italian, inaugurated a vast dramatic literature which was almost non-existent in previous centuries. Unlike the church in the middle ages which fostered miracle and mystery plays, the synagogue did not develop or encourage plays until the very end of the middle ages. In the period of the renaissance the Jewish playwright, like his Italian confrère, had to seek the favors of a Maecenas in order to advance his literary fortunes. It was at the court of Don Cesare Gonzaga that Leone da Sommo composed various comedies in Italian. And his *Comedy on Marriage,*[33] undoubtedly intended for production during the festival of Purim, is the first original Hebrew play. As in the Italian comedy of the sixteenth century and in the French comedy of the seventeenth century, types rather than individuals dominate the action: the disappointed lover, the loyal and disloyal servant, the *nouveau riche* who vaunts his ignorance and betrays his humble origins in speech and gesture. Love is, of course, the central theme, but complicated obstacles impede its progress to a victorious finale.

Though Leone da Sommo's comedy may have been produced in Italy, no Hebrew theatre existed there or anywhere. Acting companies were organized in the twentieth century and the first Hebrew theatre was built in former Palestine. Nevertheless, plays continued to be written and even produced before the establishment of a Hebrew theatre. At the time when Puritan England shut the doors of its theatres by order of Parliament in 1642, Moses Zacuto wrote two plays, one of which resembling a mystery play in verse and depicting punishments in hell, was sung by a musical group in Ferrara;[34] another, *Foundation of the World*[35]—a dramatic poem—centered on Abraham and his miraculous rescue by an angel from a fiery furnace. And a play was actually performed in a synagogue in Amsterdam as early as 1624.[36]

In 1668 Joseph ben Joseph Pen̦ço de la Vega (c. 1650–1692) published a small play under the title *Prisoners of Hope*.[37] It is the work of a young man of seventeen, also something of an allegorical mystery play about a king who is exposed to temptations and who fights his way back to the straight and narrow. Interestingly, some of the allegorical personages in Pen̦ço's play reappear in Moses Hayyim Luzzatto's plays. As late as the middle of the eighteenth century a biblical play was produced in the ghetto of Rome. But performances of Hebrew plays were the exception rather than the rule. Most plays, rarely intended for presentation on the stage, languished in private and public libraries. The ghetto—in Rome or in Venice—did not provide theatres for dramatic performances. Purim and Hanukkah were the only half-holidays which allowed for modified levity. And within that rigid framework it is miraculous that drama developed at all.

Histories and Chronicles

Massive contributions were made in the field of history and annalist literature, rabbinics and codes, mysticism and philosophy, lexicography and grammar during the sixteenth and seventeenth centuries. Jewish historians and annalists in that period approached the hallowed texts of the Bible and the Talmud with critical boldness. Azariah de Rossi,[38] author of the important *Light of the Eyes*[39] which appeared in 1573, broke fresh ground in Jewish historiography. In the tripartite work—"with some organic but no logical connection" in the charitable phrase of the late Cecil Roth[40]—he offers a variety of subjects: the earthquake of Ferrara in 1571 in the first part, the *Letter of Aristeas* in translation in the second part, a plethora of historical subjects in the third part, the largest in the book. From the literary point of view his lengthy description of the earthquake of Ferrara excels in thoroughness of observation, in warmth of feeling and in fine background material culled from Amos to R. Isaac Ibn Latif, from Seneca to Plutarch. Even a brief passage is apt to convey the vividness of his reaction:

> . . . Folks were peacefully asleep. Suddenly the rumbling of a very powerful and violent earthquake was heard. It lasted about three minutes. Nothing like it has happened in our time. Nor have our forefathers reported anything like it in previous centuries. Beside the terrifying detonations which resounded everywhere shingles tottered, roofs clashed with such force that anyone who heard the din—and who could have been so deaf as not to hear it—felt a tingling in his ears and a pain in his heart. Every minute brought on new horrors. It seemed that the earth would be laid waste and that the world and its inhabitants would come to an end. . .[41]

Azariah de Rossi also composed a short poem on the event and endeavored to convey the scientific causations of the earthquake—such as were known in his time. In a backward leap into the middle ages, he attributes them to the deity rather than to natural phenomena.[42] This is a nod to the conformist majority and this is the reason he called the first part of the book "The Voice of God."[43]

While the second part is mainly a translation of the *Letter of Aristeas*, the third and the largest section of the book contains sundry studies of rabbinic literature, disquisitions on sects during the Second Commonwealth and research into the philosophic system of Philo. This schematic analysis of the book does not and cannot convey Azariah de Rossi's subtle opinions on man and his universe, on the Jew and his place in the cosmic scheme. For him man is the crown of creation, Jewry the brightest jewel in that crown and the Hebrew language the most perfect of all languages. All true knowledge, in his opinion, has its source in Jewish literature, especially in the Bible. On the basis of his enormous erudition, which included expertise in Jewish sources, classical and patristic literature, Azariah de Rossi admitted somewhat cautiously—for he had "a sincere, although rather timid, love for the truth"[44]—that one may differ from the talmudic and post-talmudic sages whose personal opinions are subject to error. This was an act of boldness when one considers that two centuries later even the French Encyclopedists trod warily on religious ground.

Scientific historiography may be said to have begun with Azariah de Rossi rather than with Marcus Jost or Heinrich Graetz, who wrote their massive histories of the Jews in the nineteenth century. Salo W. Baron is undoubtedly right in saying that he was "one of the greatest, or perhaps the very greatest of Jewish historians who flourished in the seventeen centuries between Josephus and Jost."[45] It is probable that the daring author of *Light of the Eyes* would have met with the fate of Spinoza, had not Joseph Karo, the author of the authoritative code *Shulhan 'Aruk,* died before he had time to issue the ban. It was Azariah de Rossi who subjected Jewish history and literature to a critical analysis and utilized non-Jewish sources, even classical models of history writing which were consciously or unconsciously imitated by him as they had been by non-Jewish humanists. Sallust and Livy were the only models of historians worthy of imitation for Gregory of Trebizond,[46] Livy alone for Bartholomy Fontius who was rather blunt on the point: in poetry the worthiest model to be imitated was Virgil, in rhetoric Tullius [Cicero],in history Livy.[47]

This juxtaposition of poetry and history goes back to Aristotle. It was he who placed poetry above history in a famous passage of *Poetics*: "The difference between a historian and a poet. . .is this that one tells what happened and the other what might happen. Hence poetry is something more philosophic and serious than history because poetry tends to give general truths while history gives particular facts."[48] And Cicero considered truth the basic requirement for historiography. Some of these classical authors or quotations from them were not unknown to Azariah de Rossi. And though he did not produce a history which can rival Niccolo Machiavelli's *Discourses*[49] which he probably did not know or Francesco Guicciardini's *History of Italy*[50] which he knew, he was the first modern Jewish historian in the full sense of the word. So new and so audacious were his ideas and opinions that he had to publish a defense of his work against his critics and detractors. It bore the name *Refiner of Silver.*[51]

Compared with Azariah de Rossi's massive achievement, the other historians of the sixteenth and seventeenth centuries are mere chroniclers. Some have made valuable contributions on the borderline of history and geography. Such a one is Abraham Farissol, the biblical commentator and philosopher whose best work *Paths of the World*[52] mentions the discovery of America, the messianic agitation in the wake of David Reubeni and even the giraffe which Lorenzo the Magnificent received from the Sultan of Egypt and which caused a sensation in Florence.

Even epicene annalists like Solomon Ibn Verga and Joseph ha-Cohen who cannot compare with Azariah de Rossi in elegance of style and breadth of intellectual interests, have been affected by the humanist spirit. The former's chronicle, *The Scourge of Judah* which was published in Turkey in 1554 with some additions by his son Joseph and some notes by an early relative Judah Ibn Verga who lived in Spain at the end of the fifteenth century, is a selective catalogue of Jewish martyrdom from the days of the Roman empire to his own time, with particular emphasis on Spain and Portugal. The enumeration of persecutions is often interrupted by disputations between Jews and Christians on the relative worth of their religions. And the book ends with a description of the Temple in Jerusalem and the worship on Passover and the Day of Atonement in the Temple. A miscellany was added by the author—an imaginary disputation, a royal dream, a *novella* on filial behavior, a dialogue and an imaginary epistle. Religious tolerance and heretical skepticism are distinguishing marks of the book.[53] In addition to historical information, it conveys knowledge of natural phenomena such as the reason for color in vegetation[54] or the superficial array of philosophic opinions on a variety of subjects such as *creatio ex nihilo* and the eternality of the world.[55] As for religious tolerance the author—in contradistinction to one rabbinic source at least—asserts that the prayer of the Christian is as acceptable—"heard" in his style—as the prayer of the Jew. As for almost heretical skepticism, the author tends to see all religions as mere figments of the imagination.

In form *The Scourge of Judah* resembles the literary genre of the Italian *novella* which often contained history and legend in a mixed bag and a didactic moral to boot.[56] It is, in fact, a collection of sixty-four *novellae*—some short, merely a few lines, some long, numbering many pages. And it records—from *The Hundred Old Tales*[57] and from Giovanni Boccaccio's *Decameron*—an early version of the famous story of three rings which Gotthold Ephraim Lessing, the friend of Mendelssohn, used to such effect in his play *Nathan the*

Wise.[58] The author is undoubtedly influenced by the popular literature of Italy and his native Spain and perhaps even by Latin authors who were widely read in his time.[59] He mentions Sallust and Virgil, Cicero and Plato—the models of history and poetry, rhetoric and philosophy in the period of the renaissance. He does not neglect church fathers like Jerome. But there is no evidence of his knowledge of classical languages. Like so many authors in the sixteenth and seventeenth centuries, Solomon Ibn Verga was faced with a dilemma: faith in faith or faith in reason. He did not resolve it; he was rooted in the principle of faith in faith but he leaned to the fashionable principle, faith in reason.

Like Solomon Ibn Verga, Joseph ha-Cohen (1496–1576?), physician and historian, was the child of his age. A native of Avignon, though his parents were exiles from Spain, he spent most of his life in Italy. His first book *Chronicle of the Kings of France and Turkey* was published in 1554 in Sabbioneta; the third part of the book in Jerusalem in 1955 under the editorship of David A. Gross.[60] It is also a first in Hebrew literature: a general history by a Jew. Perhaps the only other preceding works on general historical themes were those by Elijah ben Elkanah Kapsali on the history of the Ottoman Empire with narratives about Jews in many countries including Spain.[61]

The book of Joseph ha-Cohen embraces nearly a thousand years, from the decline of the Roman empire up to and including the sixteenth century. Jews are considered incidentally in the book. His second book *The Valley of Tears*[62] is about Jewish martyrology. It is a Jewish book, written *sub specie Judaitatis*: the Jew is the innocent victim, the gentile praiseworthy if he is good to the Jew, execrable if he shows enmity to the Jew. The two sovereigns, Ferdinand and Isabella, suffer for their injustice to Jewry. A son and heir to the throne, Prince Juan dies in 1497, a daughter Isabel dies in 1498, another daughter, Joan (1479–1555), shows signs of madness as early as 1502. The annalist refers imprecisely to the events and concludes that God is just. The book is strongly influenced by Samuel Usque's *Consolation for the Tribulations of Israel*[63] which was written in Portuguese and published in 1553. But Samuel Usque used a poetic device: a multilog between three shepherds; Jacob representing Jewry, Nahum, the comforter, and Zechariah, the announcer of past suffering and future redemption. Joseph ha-Cohen prefers the narrative style and the biblical idiom.

Like the *Scourge of Judah* but in a more systematic sequence, *The Valley of Tears* records the ordeal of Jewry from the destruction of the

Second Commonwealth to the year 1575. And, in the last chapters, it emphasizes the plight of Italian Jewry in the sixteenth century. The author hoped that his book would be read in synagogues on the ninth day of Ab. This may have been the reason for the brilliant, biblical, simple style which touches the reader with its immediacy from the very beginning:

> Said Joseph ben Joshua ben Meir ben Judah ben Joshua ben Judah ben David ben Moses, of priestly stock, after he left Huete in Spain: Since the afflictions, suffered by us from the day of our first dispersion till the present time, are recorded in various books, I have decided to gather them together in a small tract which would contain what I found in the tracts of Hebrew and Christian writers who have written before me. I have entitled the work *The Valley of Tears* for the title fits the content.[64]

Though the book was not published until 1852, it circulated in many handwritten copies among Italian Jews. It is a minor literary misfortune that other writings of Joseph ha-Cohen are still lingering in libraries of Europe and America. They include a book of grammar,[65] poetry and epistolography. Of great importance also are letters to him and by him in the library of the *Alliance Israélite Universelle* as well as three translations—two in the field of history, one in the field of medicine. His passionate interest in the new world led to his translation of Francisco Lopez de Gomora's book *The General History of the Indies*.[66] Out of the works—in print and in manuscript—emerges a highly intelligent and erudite personality. But Joseph ha-Cohen is not a Josephus nor an Azariah de Rossi: an annalist rather than a historian, yet a man who preferred hard fact to entertaining legend. He was a humanist in the best sense of the word.

Benjamin Nehemiah ben Elnathan, author of the chronicle *From Paul IV to Pius V*,[67] wrote a concise, factual, and at times emotional evaluation of the reign of Paul IV (1555–1559), the former Cardinal Caraffa who brought back the worst medieval restrictions against Jews under his dominion in the papal bull of 1555: the ghetto and the yellow badge, heavy taxation, enforced conversion, local expulsions and massive burnings of the Talmud. The famous incineration of twenty-four Marranos in Ancona during his reign aroused Jewry in Italy and even beyond its borders. The author of the chronicle was imprisoned a whole month in Rome for an alleged attempt to convert a priest. But he used his personal knowledge and his good historical perspective to give a touching account of contemporary miseries. His style—in contradistinction to the exaggerated biblicism of Joseph ha-Cohen—leans on the Bible as well as on the Talmud and manages to preserve a popular stance.

The Chain of Tradition[68] by the prolific Gedalia Ibn Yahya (1515–1587), a work which cost its author more than forty years of labor, has been facetiously called *The Chain of Lies*[69] for a good reason. Miraculous stories have inundated the book to such an extent that the line between history and legend, between fact and fiction, has been completely blurred. The book in its tripartite scheme is a mixed bag. The first part is mainly a survey of great men from Adam to Don Isaac Abrabanel; the second embraces a variety of subjects: the spheres, the embryo, the soul, measurements and coins, heaven and hell, the seventy nations, arts and crafts, languages; the third part deals with the Second Commonwealth, medieval history and the persecutions.

The author, a linguist and a man of erudition, is neither a historian nor a *littérateur*. His immense knowledge was used in the first and salient part of the book to record the lives of scholars as Christian authors noted the lives of saints in hagiographical succession. Chronology is not the author's forte. In his book Rashi is a contemporary of Maimonides;[70] an alleged disciple of Hillel, "Jonathan ben Uzziel. . .lived so long that in his youth he received [instruction] from the prophets Haggai, Zechariah and Malachi, and in his old age he was among the friends of R. Yohanan ben Zakkai."[71] The span of time between Haggai and R. Yohanan ben Zakkai is almost six hundred years.

It is easy to confuse *The Chain of Tradition* with *The Book of Tradition*[72] by Abraham ben Solomon of Torrutiel who fled from Spain in 1492 when he was a boy of ten. He wrote his book in the form of a supplement to Abraham Ibn Daud's book by the same name. It covers more than three hundred years: from 1180 to the beginning of the sixteenth century. The author regards the expulsion as punishment for sins. He is particularly harsh in his diatribe against Jewish grandees who imitated the gentiles and forsook traditional ways. But he is not the only one whose name is linked with Abraham Ibn David. Almost all chroniclers and historians of the sixteenth and seventeenth centuries drew upon that rich source: Solomon Ibn Verga, Joseph ha-Cohen, Gedalia Ibn Yahya, Joseph Sambari, David Conforte and even Azariah de Rossi. David Gans (1541–1613), the very opposite of Gedalia Ibn Yahya, was also indebted to him but especially to his encyclopedic teacher, Moses Isserles. As a scientist of note he exercised

great care in his chief historical work *Plant of David*[73] which is both
Jewish and general history. Though he covers an immense area of
time, from the beginning to his own era, he is concise rather than
diffuse. He indicates his sources and his honest intentions. Like
Gedalia Ibn Yahya, he is interested in the great men of Jewish history,
the forgers of the links in Jewish tradition from the very inception to
R. Jacob Joshua of Cracow, the author of *Face of Joshua*.[74] He does not
forget the great philanthropist of Prague, Mordecai Meisel
(1528–1601) and pays him fitting homage at the end of the book's first
part:

> Mordecai Meisel is one of the walls and pillars of the House of
> Study, a prince of philanthropists, a father to the poor, a man who
> seeks the welfare of his people and is beloved by most of his
> brethren. He has been the leader of the merchants. Therefore, at
> the end of this book, I have thought it fit to mention some of his
> acts in order that they may be remembered in every city,
> generation, and family, so that his memory may not fade from our
> children because of all the charitable acts which he performed for
> us here with his own money in the holy community of Prague.
> He built the High Synagogue. . .He donated some Torah scrolls
> and finely wrought gold and silver ornaments to our community, to
> Poland, and to Jerusalem, the holy city. He also built the public
> bath-house, and the pool which serves as the ritual bath, the
> hospice for the needy and the afflicted. And he laid stone
> pavements for all the streets of the Jewish quarter at his own
> expense.[75]

In the second part of the book which deals with general history,
Gans uses Greek and Latin sources and he assures his readers that he
did   not   write   anything   without   supporting   and   reliable
documentation.[76] His history ends with the year of its publication in
1592—with a supplement by David Rheindorf to the year 1692. *The
Plant of David* is not a great book, but an important, factual
contribution to Jewish historiography.

Not only historians dabbled in Jewish history. Abraham Zacuto, an
astronomer who achieved fame with his nautical tables and scientific
help to Columbus, wrote his book "to make known the saintly sages of
Israel."[77] It is best characterized by its excellent editor Herschell
Filipowski as "a biographical and historical lexicon" in six sections,[78]
all of them devoted to surveys of Jewish sages, except the last which is

general history. The bulk of the book, 203 out of 250 pages in Filipowski's edition, is devoted to Jewish tradition from the creation of the world to the creation and completion of the Talmud. The author, a progressive astronomer, was a conservative historian who did not dare to question accepted notions. Thus Jesus who, according to the Talmud, was a disciple of Joshua ben Perahyah, becomes a contemporary of Alexander Yannai in Zacuto's book[79] which was written partly in Portugal and partly in Tunisia at the end of the fifteenth and the beginning of the sixteenth century. Though it brings the history down to his own time—the beginning of the sixteenth century—it was not published until 1566 in Constantinople.

The seventeenth century witnessed a decline of historiography. The incessant wars—the Thirty Years War and the Chmielnicki riots —cast a pall all over Europe. Hugo Grotius (1583–1645), the great Dutch humanist and jurist, was dismayed by the barbarization of the West and urged the rulers in vain to exercise restraint. He must have been inspired by the dictum of Erasmus that "war is sweet to the inexperienced in war."[80]

The Jews, the eternal scapegoats, suffered humiliation and near extinction in many communities of Eastern Europe. The important chronicle *Deep Mire*[81] by Nathan Note Hanover, the learned lexicographer and kabbalist, is a heart-rending account of the 1648–1649 massacres by the Cossacks under their chieftain Bogdan Chmielnicki. Their wiles and the brutal behavior of the indigenous population, the helplessness and the despairing trust of the Jews of Nemirov [Niemirów] are reflected in numerous passages. Here is one memorable instance of cruelty:

> What did those evil men, the Cossacks, do? They used Polish flags because one can't distinguish between Poles and Cossacks except through their flags. The people of the town were aware of the trick, yet they called to the Jews in the fort: Open the gate, because this is a Polish army which has come to save you from your enemies—if they come. The Jews who were guarding the wall and seeing the flags which were like Polish flags believed that the people of the town spoke the truth. Immediately they opened the gate. No sooner had the gate been opened than the Cossacks entered with drawn swords in their hands; and so did the townspeople armed with swords, spears and scythes, and some with clubs, and they killed many Jews. Women and girls they ravished at will. But some women and girls jumped into the moat

surrounding the fort so that they would not suffer defilement by gentiles. They drowned in the waters. Many of the men who were able to swim, jumped into the water and thought they would escape the slaughter. But the Ukrainians swam after them with their swords and their scythes and killed them in the water. Some Ukrainians shot with their guns into the water and killed them till the water ran red with the blood of the slain.[82]

Suicides were common—though not as many as in the days of Hitler. In Nemirov two suicides were especially tragic:

"It happened that a beautiful girl, of a renowned and wealthy family, had been captured by a certain Cossack who married her. But, before he lived with her, she told him slyly that if she used a certain magic, no weapon could harm her. She said to him: 'If you don't believe me, test me. Shoot at me with a gun; it will not harm me!' The Cossack, her husband, thought she was telling the truth. He shot at her naively with his gun and she fell and died for the Sanctification of the Name, to avoid being defiled by the gentile, may God avenge her blood.

Another beautiful girl, about to be married to a Cossack, asked that he marry her in a church across the bridge. He acceded to her request. She dressed in her wedding gown and he led her to the marriage ceremony with drums and dancing. When they came to the bridge, she jumped into the water and drowned for the Sanctification of the Name. May God avenge her blood. Many similar events occurred—too numerous to be recorded. The number of all the slain and the drowned in the holy community of Nemirov was about six thousand."[83]

N.N. Hanover related the tragedies of his people but he also chronicled the state of Jewish culture in Poland:

Throughout the lands of Jewish dispersion there was nowhere as much learning as in Poland. Each community maintained talmudic academies, and the head of each academy was given an ample salary so that he could maintain his school without worry and so that the study of the Torah might be his sole occupation. . .Each community maintained young men and provided for them a weekly allowance in order to study with the head of the academy. . .There was scarcely a house in Poland where Torah was not studied. Either the head of the family was himself a scholar or his son or his son-in-law or one of the young men eating at his table. . . .[84]

Of minor importance are the chronicles of Sabbatai Cohen, Joseph Sambari and David Conforte. Sabbatai Cohen (1621–1662), author of the *Scroll of Darkness*,[85] is better known as the commentator on Karo's *Shulhan 'Aruk*. The events of his time impressed him to such an extent that he promulgated a fast in their commemoration on the twentieth day of Sivan. Though he lacked objectivity and a sense of historical detail, he compensated his defects with an emotional commitment to his people and an extraordinary sensitivity to Jewish learning.

Joseph Sambari's work *The Words of Joseph*[86] concentrates on the life and literature of Eastern Jewry, especially Egyptian Jewry. It is chaotic, anecdotal, minute in detail. It uses such awkward literary devices as "And now let us return to the matter of our concern."[87] It mixes fact and fancy: Maimonides turns kabbalist in old age—perhaps because the author, a kabbalist, wanted to claim an important convert to the esoteric doctrines of his time. But it supplies interesting accounts of half-forgotten Jewries.

David Conforte, a talmudist who lived in Salonika, in Jerusalem and in Egypt, undertook to write a history from the completion of the Talmud to his own day. But he concentrated on the great scholars and their works. What makes his book valuable is the detailed enumeration of Jewish religious leaders in the fifteenth and sixteenth centuries. The previous centuries are based on such well-known sources as *Sherira's Letter* and Abraham Ibn David's *Book of Tradition*, on the works of Abraham Zacuto and Gedalia Ibn Yahya. Though a contemporary of Sabbatai Zevi, Conforte does not mention him.

The preoccupation with great men—mainly talmudic sages—is the distinguishing feature of Yehiel Heilprin's *Order of Generations*.[88] In the first part it deals with history from creation to his own day, in the second part it is a lexical and alphabetical arrangement of Tannaim and Amoraim. Like the *Book of Genealogies*, *The Chain of Tradition* and *The Plant of David* it concentrates on the talmudic period. Yet, in the introduction to the book, the author maintains that the *Book of Genealogies* did not mention many of the Tannaim and Amoraim. In the third part there is an important innovation: it lists and describes Hebrew books in alphabetical order.

Memoirs and Autobiographies

Memoirs and autobiographies of the period are, of course, also histories in a sense. But they reveal the individual rather than the society. The crop of Jewish autobiographies is understandably lean—even in this age of *mémoires* and *antimémoires*, merciless self-exposures and presumptuous posturings. For autobiography is a form of intellectual exhibitionism or mere narcissism. Everything in Jewish tradition militates against it: an inherent sense of modesty, a de-emphasis of one's importance and uniqueness, a pursuit of anonymity to such an extent that a Hebrew author in former ages is usually known by his book rather than by his name. In ages when Jewish tradition dominates Jewish life such geniuses of self-revelation as Pascal, Saint Simon, Kierkegaard or Freud are not likely to dot the pages of histories of Hebrew literature. And the converse is also true: autobiographies of Jewish authors tend to appear in an age when tradition begins to break down or to disappear altogether. The autobiographer—either extremely complex or extremely simplistic —reflects at such times his self-doubting personality or his staunch and simple faith. And he may be haunted like Shaw by that moral compunction which is certain that "all autobiographies are lies. . . . deliberate lies." At such times the autobiographer is either an Italian Jew of French ancestry like Leone Modena who writes his autobiography in Hebrew or a Glückel von Hameln who writes in Yiddish or Yom Tov Lippmann Heller who reminisces in Hebrew in order to teach others how to live the life of faith.

The autobiography of Leone Modena (1571–1648) is one of the most interesting accounts of the mirage of mundane and spiritual successes and failures in Hebrew literature. It is the story of a talmudist, a playwright and producer, a believer in omens, dreams and visions, an addict to alchemy, a preacher of such elegant eloquence that Christians and Jews flocked to hear his sermons, a gambler who wrote a book against gambling and squandered away his time and money in games of chance.

The gambling book—a preliminary exercise in autobiography—is really a charming little tract in dialog form. Two friends, Eldad and Medad, meet outside the city gates. Eldad loses no time to chastise his gambling friend Medad:

A gambler mixes with loose women. In anger he utters obscenities. . .When he is left destitute and penniless, all his thoughts turn to evil all day. He devises plans how to steal and how to rob and he hopes and expects to make up his loss.[89]

But Medad, the gambler, has good counter-arguments: adultery is not the monopoly of gamblers; sometimes heavy losers bear their losses with equanimity. And poor people are as likely to steal and rob as a gambler. Arguments and counterarguments fly thick and fast. Finally, the gambler promises to renounce gambling and, in typically Jewish fashion, to devote his time to learning rather than to human frailties. The dialog terminates at the end of the day: both friends hurry back to the city.

Modena was rightly called "the first of modern rabbis"[90] for he represented Judaism to Jews and Gentiles through his personal contacts, through his preachings and through his book *Historia degli Riti Hebraici* in Italian, "the first compendium of the Jewish religion for [the] general information."[91] He exercised at one time or another twenty-six professions, more than twice as many as, in another age, the versatile Jean Jacques Rousseau who was lawyer's assistant, engraver, lackey, seminary student, musician, tax-clerk, farmer, tutor, ambassador's secretary, cashier, music copyist, writer. Leone Modena enumerates his failures almost with relish. He taught Jewish students and Gentile students penmanship. He prepared his own sermons and he had ghost-written many sermons for others; he was cantor, secretary of charitable societies, rabbi; he made decisions in ritual law and officiated as judge; he taught Torah in the synagogue daily; he conferred rabbinical titles of *Rabbi* and *Haber*; he wrote letters for others; he taught music; he composed epithalamia, epitaphs and sonnets in Italian; he wrote comedies and produced them; he drew up legal documents; he translated, printed his own writings and proofread them; he taught how to write amulets and talismans and he sold books of charms; he was also a middleman in business and a matchmaker.[92] All these occupations which required many talents resulted in failure. Leone Modena was in financial difficulties most of his life and he was dogged by misfortunes. He could rightly say of himself what Jacob said to Pharaoh: "Few and evil have been the days of the years of my life."[93] As a young man he translated into Hebrew the first and the bawdy twenty-eighth canto of Ariosto's *Orlando Furioso*. With his knowledge of Latin and Italian and Hebrew at an early age this was not a difficult task. In the later years of his life he showed the typical contradictions of a Jewish humanist. For he was an opponent of Kabbalah and an admirer of the Zohar,[94] a liberal interpreter of Judaism and a man of tolerance as far as Christianity was concerned; a lover of general learning and a traditionalist, a defender of rabbinic Judaism and a potential or even real heretic. As a matter of fact, the question of Leone Modena's orthodoxy has never been satisfactorily resolved. Whatever the case may be—whether he himself wrote the heretical tract *Voice of the Fool*[95] as Isaac Samuel Reggio and Abraham Geiger and Joseph Almanzi in his encomiastic poem on Modena thought or someone else as Fritz Baer and Isaiah Sonne and especially Rivkin contend—so much is true: Leone Modena—contradictory individual that he was—could have been the author. In his many enthusiasms heresy could have played a part.

Though the autobiography of Glückel of Hameln (1646-1724) was written in Yiddish[96] "to while away the long and melancholy nights"[97] after her first husband's death, it is full of Hebraisms such as *Huppah*-bridal canopy, *Ketubah*-marriage contract, *Shammash*-verger, *Parnas*-warden or president, *Bet-Din*-rabbinic court of law, *Hekdesh*-a poor man's hospice supported by the community, *Talmid Hakam*-a sage, literally, disciple of the wise, and a host of others. Quotations from the Bible and even the Talmud as well as passages from the Hebrew prayer book punctuate the memoirs of Glückel. As a matter of fact, the opening sentence is Hebrew.[98] And her account of traditional life and traditional education, especially education of women in a small Jewish community, is significant from the historical point of view. In her own simple conformist way she is a Jewish Pied Piper of Hameln who seduces people into religious faith and trust in Divine Providence. With touching and disarming strength she pleads: "We must hold fast to the Torah."[99] Simone Weil maintains that, since the portrayal of good is boring and the portrayal of evil is interesting, immorality is inseparably tied to literature or sublimated by literature in such works as the great Greek tragedies of an Aeschylus or Sophocles. The Memoirs of Glückel are an excellent refutation of that thesis: they tell the interesting story of a good woman in a world shaken by the Thirty Years' War, the massacres of 1648-9, and the messianic fiasco of Sabbatai Zevi.

Yom Tov Lippmann Heller (1579-1654), the prolific talmudist, the author of an excellent commentary on the Mishnah,[100] the rabbi of Prague during the Thirty Years' War and the rabbi of Cracow during the Chmielnicki massacres, was a disciple of the great Maharal of Prague. The anti-pilpulistic methodology of the master was embodied in his commentary on the Mishnah. The partial story of his life is told in a touching autobiography—*Scroll of Enmity*.[101] The peculiar title is fully justified: it records the inimical acts of Jews against the rabbi and the heartaches he suffered as a result of these acts. When he was rabbi of Prague, the government had imposed heavy taxes on Jews of Bohemia because of the Thirty Years' War. The rabbi had the unpleasant task of apportioning the annual tax—40,000 thalers —among the Jews who promptly accused him and members of the commission of favoring the rich against the poor. The result was imprisonment, a sentence of death and, finally, a commutation of the sentence to an extortionist fine of 10,000 florins. The Emperor Ferdinand II agreed to the sum. Friends and relatives helped the rabbi to raise it. The matter was closed but it left memories of a scar which has been permanently enshrined in the *Scroll of Enmity*.

Lexicography

Since poetry and history were highly regarded by humanists, it was only natural that the study of language, especially grammar and lexicography, should become a matter of close scrutiny and study. Among Jewish humanists Elijah Levita (1469-1549) is the outstanding student of the Hebrew language. He was known under a variety of names: Helias as well as Elias Levita Judaeus or Helias as well as Elias Levita Germanus, Eliyyahu ben Asher ha-Levi Ashkenazi, Eliyyahu ha-Levi, Eliyyahu Bahur, Eliyyahu ha-Tishbi, Eliyyah ha-Mehabber, Eliyyahu ha-Medakdek and even, in allusion to *Job* 32:2, Elihu ben Barachel the Buzite. Some of the names point to his origins, some to his occupations, some to real or imaginery connections. All of them are replete with biographical and bibliographical details. The Latinized names which appear in the writings of Christian humanists refer to his Jewish ancestry and German origins and so do the Hebrew names Eliyyahu ben Asher ha-Levi Ashkenazi and Eliyyahu ha-Levi. Eliyyahu Bahur, in spite of Cecil Roth's confident equation Bahur–Unmarried,[102] remains a mystery: it first appears in print in the introduction to his grammar written at the suggestion of his friend Egidio da Viterbo.[103] Eliyyahu ha-Tishbi[104] refers to the biblical Elijah who came from a locality by the name of Tishbe and to the title of Elijah Levita's dictionary. Eliyyahu ha-Medakdek, the Grammarian, alludes to his role as a grammarian. And, finally, the Buzite, the despised, is interpreted as a proud adoption of an insulting adjective which Italian Jews accorded to their contemporary brethren from Germany. This internecine warfare has been going on for centuries: A Galician Jew is still referred to as the *Geshtrofter*, the punished one, by his Lithuanian confrères.[105]

Elijah Levita was a German Jew who lived most of his life in Italy—in Venice, Padua or Rome. David Kaufmann, one of the luminaries of Jewish research in the previous century, characterized him as a "a roving scholar."[105a] Elijah Levita described himself justly when he remarked: "I am neither a philosopher. . .nor a kabbalist. . .nor a talmudist; I am a grammarian, a masorete, a teacher, a poet."[106] In order to supplement his income he also became a copyist of Hebrew books. And it is an irony of fate that his Christian friends and pupils studied Kabbalah with him: a discipline for which he had neither love nor understanding. After having explained the word Kabbalah in one of his books he added: "I am not worthy to explain the subject because, regrettably, I have not studied this science and I neither know nor understand these sacred things."[107]

Though he achieved no greatness in his four chosen occupations, he ushered in a true renaissance of Hebrew lexical studies among Jews and Christians in the sixteenth century. Since every distinguished humanist aspired to become a *homo trilinguis,* a trilingual man, well-versed in Latin, Greek and Hebrew, he needed learned Jews as preceptors.[108] Elijah Levita was an ideal type of teacher: erudite, eager to impart and to learn. For he was a humanist with a scientific bent of mind, a grammarian and masorete who surpassed all contemporaries. He wrote commentaries on the grammars of the two Kimhis—Moses and his more famous brother David, the renowned grammarians of Provence in the twelfth century. He originated new theories of Hebrew grammar, especially new dates for the systems of vocalization and cantillation which were contested by Azariah de Rossi. For he contended that they were created after the final redaction of the Talmud while Azariah de Rossi adhered to the conservative view and thought that they existed even before the redaction of the Mishnah.[109] Interestingly, Zunz, Samuel David Luzzatto, Geiger and Pinsker—the great protagonists of the *Wissenschaft des Judentums*—also subscribed to the theory that vocalization originated after the redaction of the Talmud.

Elijah Levita is known to have composed more than a dozen works on lexical matters: in addition to his first grammatical work,[110] a book on "letters and vowels and other matters,"[111] a book on verbs and nouns and irregular words in the Bible,[112] a book on the *Tradition of Tradition,*[113] a monograph on *Cantillation,*[114] *The Book of Remembrance*[115] which dealt with masoretic problems and which was dedicated to his friend and patron George de Selve, the French ambassador of Francis I at Venice and later Bishop of Lavour; a lexicon in four columns, Yiddish, Hebrew, Latin and German,[116] a book of 712 biblical and post-biblical roots,[117] an Aramaic lexicon.[118]

Tradition of Tradition which was published in Venice in 1538 is undoubtedly the most important lexical work of Elijah Levita. It opened a new epoch in the study of the Masorah and the opposing schools of Ben Asher and Ben Naphtali and it is still a major point of departure for modern students.[119] It contended rightly that the vowels in the Hebrew Bible are of later date than the text and it treated problems of Masorah-accents, variants, shapes of letters—more exhaustively than any predecessor. In the famous third introduction to the book the author boasted—with some justification if boasting can be justified—that he will discuss the Masorah fully: "who authored it, one or many, who invented the vowels and the accents and when they were attached to the letters; and I shall state the opinion of ancients and moderns as well as my own. Then I shall point out. . .the method adopted by the Masorites and the work done by them, what their chief purpose was, what they said and what they failed to say."[120] He fulfilled the promise admirably and exhaustively.

Levita led a dichotomous existence; he was a Hebrew scholar and a Yiddish poet. And the scholar never alluded to his interest and absorption in poetry. Perhaps he was afraid to compromise his scholarly career. After all, there was an incongruity in the fact that a serious student of grammar and a teacher of princes indulged in "vulgar poetry" which was composed in the "language of women."[121] Whatever the case may be, he translated from the Italian a romance of chivalry which exploited the adventures of Sir Bewis of Hamtown who, in the Italian version became Buovo d'Antona. This English romance which can be traced to the twelfth century was translated into French in the thirteenth, into Italian in the fourteenth century. Like all romances of chivalry, the *Bovo Buch,* as it came to be called in Yiddish, bristles with tall tales of love and combat and intrigue. The hero, in pursuit of his lovely Druseine, spares neither time nor effort in proliferation of chivalrous deeds. Unlike Don Quixote, the most arrant of arrant knights, he is rewarded for persistence with three kingdoms.

Elijah Levita has taken great liberties with the Italian version of the romance. He has condensed some exploits which lack verisimilitude and he added Jewish touches to a Christian tale. Boys are circumcised, *Mazal Tov* (good luck) is said at the celebration of marriage, events take place in months which are designated in Hebrew. Our translator even remembers to insert the bad opinion of women which stems traditionally from Solomon:

Al' Unglik kumt fun den Frauen
Secht was Shlome hamelek's Bucher schreiben
Wie er sucht ein Frau ein Reine
Und al sein Tag wand er nie keine.[122]

Small wonder that in prose form the *Bovo Buch* became a very popular tale; it was told and retold as a *Bobe Ma'aseh* and it was understood to be not *The Tale of Bovo*, but a yarn, a figment of the imagination. For Jews, especially the less learned, had eagerly read or audially absorbed medieval romances in Yiddish translation—from the tales of King Arthur (*Kinig Artus*) to Tristan and Isolde (*Tristan un Isolda*). Indeed, one of the oldest documents of Yiddish literature stems from the Cairo Genizah and is known as *Dukus Horant* (*Kudrun* in German). Jewish troubadours or *Spielleute* sang or recited these romances and helped pass away many a winter night in delightful entertainment to the consternation and scandalization of the rabbis. Thus, one of the most famous of them, Jacob Levi Mölln known as the Maharil, forbade the chanting of religious compositions in translation.

In 1816 a Catholic priest by the name of Giuseppe Venturi brought an anonymous romance in Yiddish to the attention of the civilized world: *Paris un Vienna*. Stylistic considerations make the attribution to Elijah Levita almost certain. Like the *Bovo Buch* it is a translation or rather a paraphrase of a translation. Originally a Provencal tale, it was translated into French in the middle of the fourteenth century and then into many other European languages—Spanish, English, Swedish and Italian. From the Italian translation it was translated into Yiddish.

It is not a tale of two cities, but a love story of a beautiful girl Vienna and a young page Paris. The father of the girl, a king, would not consent to a marriage with a lowly knight. Obstacles were removed, however, after many tribulations of the princess and many peregrinations of the young lover who rose to high honors at the sultan's court. They were finally married and, upon the death of the king, Paris reigned happily ever after.

Humanists were often lampoonists and practiced the art of occasional poetry. In 1514 a fire broke out in Venice and destroyed the Rialto. Elijah Levita, an eye witness, composed his *Fire Song*[123] in Yiddish in the fashionable *ottava rima*. It was sung to the tune of a traditional chant for the Sabbath. And it gave Elijah Levita an opportunity to castigate people, who stole and robbed during the fire, to indulge in sarcastic and wry reflections on humanity. For the rich, he observed, are forgiven their trespasses, the poor pay for them with their blood.

Elijah Levita composed another Yiddish lampoon *Hamavdil*; it was directed against his poetic adversary Hillel Cohen and it took its name from the initial word in the chant at the conclusion of the Sabbath, in the so-called *Havdalah*, which means distinction (between sacred and secular). It is the author's hope that the Almighty will also distinguish between him and Hillel, the miserable boor who possesses as many vices as there are stars in the night. He did not hesitate to use libelous slander throughout the lampoon and posted it on the walls of Rome.

The Yiddish oeuvre of Elijah Levita belongs as much to Yiddish as to Hebrew literature. It is full of Hebraisms, it breathes the spirit of Hebrew literature. His Yiddish poems resemble his Hebrew poems which introduce or describe his ponderous works. On the other hand, his grammatical and lexical work does not neglect the Yiddish language.

There were deeper humanists than Elijah Levita: Azariah de Rossi with his fine insight into the history of his people, Leone Ebreo with his new philosophical perceptions, Leone Modena with his universalist acumen. None was as quintessential a humanist as Elijah Levita, the grammarian par excellence.

Though his writings did not reflect the total spectrum of human experience, they indicated that limitless thirst for knowledge which for humanists had not only redemptive but cultural value. For, in their view, it contributed to the meaning of life which they sought with the ardor of youth—in contradistinction to the humanists of our century who pursue, with the tired senescence of a Sartre or a Beckett, meaninglessness as the core of our existence.

As friend of Christian humanists—Egidio da Viterbo, Sebastian Münster, Paul Fagius—he fostered the interrelationship between Jewish and non-Jewish intellectuals. As composer of Yiddish works he became one of the important progenitors of Yiddish literature. As author of grammatical and lexical studies he became the father of modern Hebrew grammar and lexicography. From his birth at Ipsheim through his wanderings in Neustadt, Padua, Rome, Isny, Venice where he assisted the Christian bibliophile Daniel Bomberg in the publication of Hebrew classics and where he finally was laid to rest, he led a restless existence of a renaissance scholar on whom lady luck smiled at infrequent intervals.

In comparison with Elijah Levita other grammarians dwindle in

size—both those who preceded and those who succeeded him: Messer
Leon (1430–1505) also known in Hebrew as Yehudah ben Yehiel,
Saadia Ibn Danan (1450–1502), Jacob Mantino, the two Aramas,
father and son, Isaac Arama (1430–1494) and Meir Arama
(1470–1556). Solomon ben Jacob Almoli—a mediocre grammarian—is
better known by his *Interpretation of Dreams*[124] which is based on
talmudic and non-talmudic sources. Even Abraham de Balmes
(1450–1521), the translator of Averroes, the physician and talmudist,
cannot be compared with Elijah Levita. He composed but did not
complete a massive grammar[125] at the request of Daniel Bomberg.
Like Elijah Levita he criticized the Kimhis; unlike Elijah Levita, the
more skillful pedagogue and instructor, he provided cumbersome
instruction in a cumbersome treatise.

Some grammarians who were also poets on occasion devoted much
space in their books to poetics. Such a one, Samuel Archevolti, made an
impression on his generation with his widely quoted book *A Bed of
Spices*[126] which was supplemented by a grammatical treatise of no less
a scholar than Yom Tov Lippmann Heller under the title *Bunch of
Roses*.[127] What is especially piquant about it is the set of rules on
writing code letters or using vanishing script.

The book was published in the beginning of the seventeenth
century—in 1602—in that post-renaissance period which art historians and culture historians have designated as baroque and which
denotes the non-classical, ornate and even bizarre styles of architecture in particular and art including the art of writing in general. It
even designates a way of life which flourished and still flourishes in
vestigial form in Vienna, the city of the baroque par excellence. In
such an age, which lasted well into the eighteenth century, even
philosophers dabbled in grammar. In his unfinished grammar with the
ponderous title *Compendium Grammatices Linguae Hebraeae* Baruch
Spinoza, the philosopher with the "geometrical mind," intended to
apply his "geometrical literary form" to his grammar.[128] In his
assignation of priority to nouns rather than other parts of speech such
as adjectives and verbs he foreshadowed some of the advanced theories
of Hebrew grammar which were current in the twentieth century.

Jedidiah Solomon Norsa (Norzi) cultivated masoretic studies which
were so brilliantly espoused by Elijah Levita. A few authors annotated
the famous dictionary of Hebrew and Aramaic which had been
completed in 1101 by Nathan ben Yehiel, the so-called *'Aruk*, and
furnished it with addenda: Benjamin Mussafia, physician to King
Christian IV of Denmark (1605–1675) as well as Menahem Lonzano,

the Palestinian who settled in Italy. Toward the end of the eighteenth century Judah Leb Ben Zeev (1764–1811) achieved almost as great fame as a grammarian with his *Study of the Hebrew Language*[129] as Elijah Levita in his time.

Biblical Studies

Biblical studies among Jews thrived in periods of disruption: in Hellenistic times and in the age of the Karaitic schism. In the sixteenth and seventeenth centuries they were the cause and the effect of Reformation among Christians who needed the help of Jews for the understanding of the biblical text in the original Hebrew. It was no accident, then, that Jews who enjoyed maximal exposure to the Christian world should also be engaged in exegesis. Chief among them—outside Elijah Levita—was Obadiah Sforno (c.1475–1550), the talmudist, physician and preceptor of Johannes Reuchlin. He thus became, through his eminent pupil, an indirect influence on the Reformation. For Reuchlin had not only introduced Greek and Hebrew studies into Germany; he defended Jewry and its rabbinic writings against the excesses of Christians and the infamous convert Johann (Johannes) Pfefferkorn. But the enlightened voice of the humanist had no effect on the vitriolic Jew-baiting of Martin Luther, the father of protestantism who allegedly showed sympathy for Jews in his early writings and hatred for them in his later works. It is more likely that he had feigned sympathy for them in the beginning of his reformatory career in order to fan the flames of enmity between Catholics and Jews and in order to appear as a defender of justice in the eyes of Christians and Jews.[130]

Sforno's popular commentary on the Pentateuch adorns most standard editions of the Hebrew Bible. The author relies heavily on his predecessors—Rashi, Abraham Ibn Ezra, Rashbam, Nahmanides—- and he uses his own philological erudition to great advantage not only in his commentary on the Pentateuch but also in his commentaries on *Jonah, Habakkuk* and *Zechariah* as well as on *Psalms, Song of Songs* and *Ecclesiastes.* His commentary on *Ecclesiastes* and his philosophical treatise *Light of Nations*[131] were sent by him to Henry II of France. At the request of Cesare Borgia, Sforno even composed a Hebrew grammar and translated it into Latin.

The greatest exegete of the age was undoubtedly Don Isaac Abrabanel, the commentator of the Pentateuch and the Prophets. More than three hundred years after his death the scholar and poet

Joseph Almanzi finished a long poem on Abrabanel with the words, "Renowned among all nations. . .there was none like Don Isaac Abrabanel."[132] Some of his commentaries were written in Spain before the expulsion, some in Italy after the expulsion. Two facts about them are of extraordinary interest: the use of Jewish and non-Jewish sources as well as the interpretations of the political sections of the Bible in the light of his experiences as a statesman. That classical authors as well as church fathers aided him in his commentaries can be proven though the exact determination of a specific author presents difficulties.[133]

In the introduction to his commentary on *Kings* which he completed in Naples he gave vent to his feelings on the expulsion from Spain: Some fled to the adjacent Kingdom of Portugal and Navarre. . .some fled by sea. . .and were drowned. . .some were sold into slavery, some were burned to death. . .In sum. . .few out of many remained as it is written about our ancestors: Behold we die, we perish, we all perish.[134] The similarity of the first exile which is the finale of the *Book of Kings* and the expulsion from Spain was obvious. The quality of justice and retribution became a matter of urgent consideration for Don Issac Abrabanel. In a series of compendia on messianism which were written after the expulsion the last sage of Spanish Jewry endeavored to determine the relationship of expulsion to redemption. The theme reached its apogee in the messianic doctrines and movements of the sixteenth and seventeenth centuries.

Of the other biblical commentators Moses Alshek of Safed, the disciple of Karo, should be singled out. He wrote homiletical commentaries on most biblical books. The moral lesson, the didactic stance—these were of primary importance to him. Unconsciously, he followed and espoused a homiletical tradition which goes back to the Second Commonwealth. Already in the Kumran period it was an established form of literature. In the Midrash and in the Talmud, in the Gaonic period and, then, in the European centers during the middle ages, it had its powerful exponents: Rabbi Abraham bar Hiyya, Rabbi Bahya ben Asher and Judah Moscato in renaissance Italy were a few of the important representatives of the genre. But the homily in Eastern Europe went back to Safed for its inspiration, particularly to the Law of Moses[135] by Moses Alshek. Although surrounded by kabbalists, he rarely yielded to mystical blandishments in his commentaries.

There were some baroque manifestations in biblical exegesis of the period: Moses Margaliot explained biblical passages in 26 ways; Moses ben Isaiah Cohen in 50 ways, Nathan Spira in 250 ways, Elijah Ottingen, a Polish rabbi of the seventeenth century, in 345 ways. To shine with petty or absurd explanations—that was the aim of exegesis. Not till the age of enlightenment was there a serious attempt to harmonize it with the progress of humanistic studies. Modernization of biblical exegesis began with Moses Mendelssohn.

The homiletico-philosophical commentary of Isaac Arama, a friend of Abrabanel or Joseph Taitazak's kabbalistic commentary on *Ecclesiastes* and on *Daniel* together with the *Five Scrolls* which were published in Venice in 1599 and in 1608 respectively[136] or the kabbalistic and homiletical commentaries of the poet Solomon Halevi Alkabez or the kabbalistic commentaries of Abraham ben Mordecai Azulai are in a special class. The commentaries *Fort of Zion*[137] and *Fort of David*[138] which were begun by David Altschul and completed by his son Yehiel Hillel in the seventeenth century enjoyed an uninterrupted popularity since their publication in Leghorn in 1743.

Talmudic Studies

As in all major times of stress the need for conservation and conservatism found expression in the cultivation of talmudic studies which have been among the chief preoccupations of Jewry for many centuries. A noted biblical commentator like Alshek confessed in the preface to his commentary on the Pentateuch that he devoted his time to the Talmud and only on Fridays did he engage in the study of Scripture.

But rabbinic studies were not entirely immune to the spirit of the age. In 1564 David Provencale, one of the three illustrious brothers, planned to establish a Jewish school of higher studies for Jewish and secular subjects including Latin and Italian. Abraham Portaleone, the eminent physician to Duke Guglielmo and his successor Vincenzo I of Mantua, wrote a treatise on the antiquities of the Bible. To the famous commentator of the Mishnah, Obadiah of Bertinoro, we owe a statistical and sociological appraisal of Jewry in Jerusalem at the end of the fifteenth century. But the epoch-making student of oral law in the sixteenth century was Joseph Karo (1488–1575). His biography is as scanty as that of other great sages in previous centuries. As a child of four he left Spain, as a man of thirty-four he began his great commentary on the *Four Rows*[139] of Jacob ben Asher (c.1250–1346) under the title *House of Joseph*[140] in Adrianople. This is the only factual information about the most formative years of his childhood, adolescence and early manhood.[141] Probably in 1537 he settled in Safed and, before his emigration to Palestine, he was deeply impressed with the martyrdom of the Marrano courtier Solomon Molko. In 1538 he received his ordination from Jacob Berab and became the leading scholar of Safed after his ordinator's departure from the city in that year. It was Berab who planned to renew rabbinic ordination—a kind of succession of legal authority from Moses who was alleged to be ordained by God and who allegedly ordained Joshua. Through the judges, the prophets, the men of the Great Assembly, and the teachers of the talmudic periods ordination passed, it was believed, in rightful succession until it was broken in the early middle ages. Thus Jewry lived under the law without legal authority so to speak. To restore ordination as a prerequisite of eschatological fulfillment—that was the attempted task of Berab. It failed because of the opposition of Levi ben Habib, the chief rabbi of Jerusalem. But Karo dreamed of the restoration of ordination—and actually made a second attempt after Jacob Berab.[142]

He was the unmatched rabbinic scholar: author of an authoritative and voluminous code, *House of Joseph* and a shorter popular version *Shulhan 'Aruk (Set Table)* which had a normative influence for many centuries; at the same time author of a mystic diary *Teller of Truth* or *Preacher of Righteousness*.[143] The *"Doctor Synagogae"* was also a *"Doctor Mysticus."*[144] In the former capacity he became the legal guide of Jewry. The *House of Joseph* displayed enormous erudition and unmatched methodology: it traced laws to their sources over the centuries and it systematized them. The *Set Table*, the more popular and shorter code, became the handbook of legal guidance because of its conciseness, precision and practicality. Together with the glosses of R. Moses Isserles (c.1525–1572), the well-known rabbi of Cracow, it became the code par excellence. Thus Joseph Karo, one of the founders of the new center of Jewish life in Safed, became the spiritual father of Polish Jewry and the Jewries of Eastern Europe. His other works—the commentary on the code of Maimonides as well as the legal responsa—are mere *ancillae* to the two great codes.

There is an unmistakable legal *élan*—if such a thing exists—from the opening to the concluding lines of the *Set Table*. "One should gather strength like a lion to rise in the morning for the service of the Creator"; this is the opening chord of the work. And the concluding passage reads:

Our sages forbade many things because they endanger one's

life. . .One may not drink from the wells and from the pools lest one swallow a leach unseeingly. Anyone who transgresses against these or similar things and says: I endanger my life, what business of others is it? Or if anyone says: I do not strictly observe this prohibition, should suffer punishment for disobedience. But anyone who is careful in observance, a blessing of good fortune will come upon him.

The Set Table begins with the ritual obligations of man at dawn and ends with the ritual obligations of man by night. Like *Ulysses*, the novel of our century, it encompasses a day in the drama of human existence. But it is the tale of Man—rather than a particular man—in the endless set of obligations which aim at sanctification of life. Karo's work was criticized positively and negatively—positively by many scholars in succeeding generations, negatively by many contemporaries. Already his neighbor in Safed, R. Moses Trani, raised complaints against Karo's code. And so did many students of Jewish law in later centuries. But just as "one can philosophize against Kant or with him but never without him," one can codify against Karo or with Karo but never without him.

The great legalist was also a mystic who, allegedly, received instruction from a *Maggid*—an angelic mentor. Such a supernatural being seems to have associated with other famous rabbis—Joseph Taitazak, Moses Cordovero, Isaac Luria, Moses Zacuto, Moses Hayyim Luzzatto and a host of others.[145] In Karo's case the *Maggid* seems to be identical with the *Mishnah*—a personification of the code of R. Judah the Prince which, frequently and significantly, appears to him on Friday nights and admonishes him to lead an extremely ascetic life and to dedicate himself to study. Sometimes she assumes a motherly guise: "I am the mother of whom it is said: wherewith his mother corrected him."[146] Sometime Karo is commended for his diligence: God and all the members of the Heavenly Academy greet you for you are studying the law perpetually. . .[147] Through all the messages of the Heavenly Mentor Karo is strengthened in his ascetic and scholarly resolve as well as in his approximation to the ideal of a saintly man. The frequent references to Solomon present a problem: they allude to Solomon Molko according to Graetz,[148] to Solomon Alkabez almost exclusively according to Werblowsky who adduced interesting proofs —points of resemblance between the utterings of the mentor and the writings of Alkabez.[149] If Werblowsky's contention is right, then Alkabez assumes an influential role in the spiritual development of

Karo—and through him—of Jewry in the succeeding centuries.

Karo, the legalist, seemed to hold Karo the mystic in check so well that serious doubts of authenticity were entertained by scholars regarding his tract *Teller of Truth*. That a man with an addiction to the regulatory mode of life as exhibited in the *Shulhan 'Aruk* could also indulge in unchecked, almost Lurianic flights of irrational fancy—that indeed was a schizoid attitude to life, an enigma of genius which has defied elucidation.

Talmudic studies after Karo were partially independent, partially rooted in his popular work the *Set Table*. They led to a period of great efflorescence in Poland and, indeed, in the whole of Eastern Europe. The founder of the new mode of talmudic study in Poland was Jacob Polak (c.1470–c.1530). He had studied in Bavaria and refined the dissective analyses of textual components of talmudic subjects. This method of Divisions, the so-called *Hillukim*, was carried to the point of hair-splitting sophistications run amok. Though he left no writings— out of excessive modesty and fear that he will be used as an infallible authority—he made a profound impact on rabbinic studies by virtue of his erudition and brilliance. It was through him and because of him that Poland, fed by German rabbis, became the talmudic reservoir of Jewry till the middle of the twentieth century. Curiously, German in Yiddish garb remained the vehicle of teaching and translating talmudic texts as well as the day-to-day language. Disdain of Slav gentiles was probably the cause of lingual conservatism.

Jacob Polak was followed by a number of rabbinic authorities: Shalom Shahna, the renowned teacher and father-in-law of Moses Isserles; Solomon Luria, the erudite commentator of the Talmud and the restorer of precise textual readings in talmudic literature; Moses Isserles who popularized Karo's work with his glosses—the so-called Tablecloth *(Mappah)* on the *Set Table*—and who showed interest in philosophical and mystical, astronomical and even historical studies; Meir of Lublin—the famous Maharam—who excelled in the pilpulistic and halakistic method and who, in his intellectual arrogance, showed utter contempt for Karo's work and the work of his disciple, Moses Isserles; Samuel Eliezer Edels—the Maharsha—who influenced generations of talmudic scholars with the brilliance of his novellae; Yom Tov Lipmann Heller, the commentator on the Mishnah; Meir Schiff who was so precise, brief and obscure in his commentaries on the Talmud; Rabbi Mordecai Jafe, a student of Isserles who injected kabbalistic interpretation into talmudic law; Rabbi Joshua Falk, author of a popular commentary on the *Shulhan 'Aruk*; Ezekiel

Landau, the rigid opponent of Mendelssohn; Rabbi Joel Sirkes, the bitter enemy of philosophical studies, author of a commentary on Ruth and elucidator of rabbinic law as recorded in the Talmud and in later codifiers; David Halevi and Sabbatai Kohen, the well-known and popular commentators of the *Shulhan 'Aruk*.

Hundreds of eminent authorities on rabbinic studies, epitomized and culminated by R. Elijah, the great gaon of Vilna, ushered in a golden age of talmudic scholarship in Eastern Europe. They neglected the Jerusalem Talmud. Sporadically some scholars like David Frankel of Dessau produced important commentaries on that vast work. Only in our time did the study of the Jerusalem Talmud come into its own: the commentaries of Louis Ginzberg and, above all, the first-rate researches of Saul Lieberman advanced the textual and lexical knowledge of that obscure treasure-trove of Jewish literature.

The study of Talmud—through *Hilluk* and *Pilpul*—had a practical aspect: the smallest acts of daily living were rigidly circumscribed by law. But it also led to barren discussions on minutiae of Jewish law. Everyone endeavored to exercise ingenuity and brilliance in a futilitarian effort. Some great rabbis like Judah Lew ben Bezalel, the so-called Maharal of Prague (1512?–1609),[150] condemned the pilpulistic method and advocated a saner way of studying the Talmud. Some prominent authorities followed in his footsteps: his brother Hayyim, Yom Tov Lippmann Heller and Isaiah Horowitz. It was he, Maharal, who beautifully summed up the deficiency of the *Pilpul* in condemning people who "were more concerned with subtleties of their own judgment than with God's word, the Torah."[151] And the proper understanding of the Torah should be, he thought, the chief concern of Jewry. But even he fought only the "false *Pilpul*" or *Pilpul* for *Pilpul's* sake which was the prevalent method in the talmudic academies of Poland and Germany and which was a sterile exercise in mental acrobatics. As for "true *Pilpul*" which led to the theoretical elucidation of the law and to proper practice in life: Maharal approved that method unequivocally.

A talmudist and a man of erudition, he was in touch with Tycho Brahe and Johannes Kepler, the astronomers. Perhaps through their good offices he was admitted to an audience with Rudolph II, the Hapsburg emperor who believed in alchemy and magic. Legend claims many mysterious conversations in exotic places between the royal host and the princely scholar. In half a century of his distinguished rabbinate, Maharal exercised his influence far and wide. No one—except perhaps his younger contemporary, Mordecai Jafe of

Prague—wielded similar authority in rabbinic circles and among the people. "All nations go by his light; all dispersions drink out of his wells"—thus wrote a scholar of note, Yehiel Heilprin.[152]

He is not a systematic thinker but he provides his reader with remarkable insights. Commenting on *Genesis* 1:2, he mentions Resh Lakish's contention that the Spirit of God refers to the spirit of the Messiah. Thus the Redeemer of Mankind was created before man, before everything; man was created last, after everything. This remarkable juxtaposition was thus explained by Maharal:

> Man, the most complicated being, was created last of all. The spirit of the Messiah on the other hand is something entirely immaterial, and even if he possesses a body, the spirit remains separated from it. . .Therefore, his spirit was created before all else.[153]

His insight on diaspora and redemption has not lost its relevance:

> Good can truly be known through its opposite; in fact we acquire knowledge of all things by contrast. For looking at black we understand white, its opposite. . .Similarly, the matter of the final deliverance cannot be clarified unless exile is explained. Thus we will become conscious of the good and of the salvation for which we hope. . .
> Exile itself is a clear proof and confirmation of redemption. There is no doubt that exile is change and alteration of the order according to which God has assigned to each nation its proper place. He allotted the land of Israel to Israel, whose exile is a change and alteration of the prescribed order. All things which are removed from their natural place and remain outside of it cannot settle in their unnatural place and must return to their natural place. If they remained in the unnatural place, the unnatural would become natural. . .The natural place of the Jews, according to the order of things, is the Land of Israel. The diaspora is not natural.[154]

It was Maharal's contention that the world was created for the sake of the Jewish people; hence the responsibility of Jewry to mankind. It was also his contention that the world was created in the Hebrew language; hence the holiness attached to the language. Though he was a poor stylist and though his own Hebrew cannot serve as a model of correct usage, he realized the importance of grammatical and linguistic studies and commended them with certain reservations. The development of the mind through the understanding of the content of the Torah—that is of primary importance. If the study of speech, language and grammar becomes an end, then it fails to fulfill its mediative function. Interestingly, the Moravian educator John Amos Comenius almost half a century after Maharal advocated the study of languages as a means to the understanding of subject matter. Again it was Comenius, like Maharal before him, who advocated the study of natural sciences as a religious duty. But for the Moravian educator the book of nature was the divine textbook, for Maharal the natural sciences and mathematics were, at best, the dessert rather than the main meal—the study of Torah.[155]

When the Maharal writes about ethics, he follows the tradition of our medieval ethicists. His book *Paths of the World*[156] does not differ in form from Bahaya Ibn Pakuda's *Duties of the Heart*. The chapters are called *Paths* instead of *Gates*. And, characteristically for Maharal, the first chapter is the path of the Torah, the last—the path of *Derek Erez*—[157] which leads to perfection through refinement of manners and deeds. These two concepts are the covers which contain the entire book of traditional life.

The name of Maharal is connected with the creation of a *Golem*[158] who allegedly guarded the rabbi and patrolled the ghetto against inimical intruders. Since he had neither will nor reason, he obeyed his master mechanically. And he nearly caused disaster when the rabbi's wife ordered him to bring water from the well but did not indicate when to stop. The house was flooded, Maharal had to be called to the rescue like the sorcerer in "The Sorcerer's Apprentice" of Goethe. The *Golem* crumbled to dust after ten years at the command of the great Maharal.

The immense and unquestioned authority of the law was bolstered by saintly scholars like Karo and Maharal, enforced by preachers (*Darshanim*), reprovers (*Mokihim*), itinerant expounders of aggadic material (*Maggidim*). No wonder that compendia of legends became popular as sources of study, quotation and public speaking. The most famous, *Source of Jacob*[159] by Jacob and his son Levi Ibn Habib of Jerusalem, appeared in 1566, more than a year after the publication of the *Shulhan 'Aruk*. It was studied assiduously and translated into many languages.

Moral and Religious Tracts

The accolade of uninterrupted popularity was accorded to ethical literature. The *Proverbs* in biblical times, the *Sayings of the Fathers* in the talmudic period, Yedayah ha-Penini's *Examination of the World*[160] and Behaya Ibn Pakuda's *Duties of the Heart*[161] were the undoubted works of excellence which were studied as practical guides of conduct in daily life. The most favored ethical tract in the seventeenth century was the *Zenah u-Reenah*—the Yiddish translation of the Pentateuch with homiletical overtones by Jacob ben Isaac Ashkenazy of Janow. It mixed translation, paraphrase and exhortation in long-winded phrases which attracted women-folk. Thus, the first verse of *Exodus* served the translator as a pretext of a long homily:

> King Solomon, may he rest in peace, says in *Proverbs* [25:12]: 'As an earring of gold, and an ornament of fine gold, so is a wise reprover upon an obedient ear.' The verse teaches us that the best way of life is to accept the exhortations of wise men; therefore, King Solomon says here that as jewels adorn the body, so the exhortations of a wise man adorn the spirit, and this is especially true when such exhortations are addressed to children who at a tender age seek after vain pleasures. . .[162]

The most ethical tract in the seventeenth century was Isaiah Horowitz's *The Two Tablets of the Covenant*.[163] The title alludes to the written and oral law in the book which is permeated with ascetic and kabbalistic doctrines. Horowitz's rigid precepts of morality, his constant admonitions to love man and love God—these are based on the conviction that the very letters of the Bible partake of a rarefied spirituality. A later tract by Zevi Hirsch Kaidanower reached immense popularity. It was a true folk book and it enjoyed a vogue in Yiddish translation. Like many Jewish books on ethics it emphasized education:

> . . .When the time has come for the child to go to school and to study with a teacher, the father should rise early in the morning and wake the child and take him to school. Whether the father be an old man or a great man, a leader or a rabbi, he must not be ashamed to take his boy to school this first time, but rather give praise and thanks to the Holy One, blessed be He, for giving him the privilege to accord his son the privilege of placing him under the wings of the Divine Presence. . .

Very great will be the merit of childless people to rear an orphan in their home and to guide him along the straight path, as if they had borne him.[164]

Popular writers are wont to illustrate moral precepts with edifying tales. Kaidanower is no exception:

"Come and learn from the story about a pious man who lived in a small village and had no books at all except the talmudic treatise *Hagigah* [Festal-offering]. All the days of his life this pious man studied that treatise. And he lived a very long life. Finally before his death, this treatise took the form of a woman and went before him after his death and led him to Paradise. If a man transgresses even once, one prosecutor—a demon—is created. . .When he dies, his transgressions take the form of women and lead him to hell. . ."[165]

The naive author seems to have shared folk-beliefs in angels and demons with common folk. And he was influenced by popular mysticism.

Philosophy

Humanism was long on scholars and writers, short on philosophers. Like the *philosophes* of the eighteenth century in France, some philosophers of the early and late renaissance—Petrarch and Giovanni Pico della Mirandola—were philosophizing poets. None of them created an original philosophy which dominated the age. All of them were derivative Platonists or Aristotelians or harmonizers of the two ancient precursors of philosophy in the West. Petrarch who mentions the most distinguished philosophers in his *Triumph of Fame*[166] gives Plato first, Aristotle second place. Later humanists took their clue from Petrarch. Marsilio Ficino (1433–1499), who was the head of the Platonic Academy in Florence for many years, produced before 1469 the first complete translation of Plato into a Western language and, shortly afterward, his *magnum opus: Platonic Theology*.[167] Giovanni Pico della Mirandola, who was also intimately connected with the Platonic Academy, though not the first Christian to make use of the Kabbalah,[168] strove to harmonize Platonism and Aristotelianism, Kabbalah and Christian theology. No wonder that his friends, in double allusion to his harmonizing efforts in philosophy and to the town of Concordia which was a feudal possession of his family, called him Prince of Harmony.[169] And Giordano Bruno (1548–1600) who was burned to death in Rome—in the Campo di Fiori—for his heretical views, leaned heavily on Plato though he may be regarded as a precursor of modern science and philosophy. It is significant that Petrarch and Giovanni Pico della Mirandola and Giordano Bruno were poets of distinction. And this is a literary fact that has few parallels in modern philosophy. Friedrich Nietzsche, the poet-philosopher, is the exception that re-enforces the rule.

Jewish humanists—like their Italian counterparts—were also derivative philosophers. At the suggestion of Giovanni Pico della Mirandola, Yohanan ben Isaac Alemanno who was an expert in Greek and Arabic philosophies composed a philosophical commentary on the *Song of Songs* in Hebrew. Jacob Mantino, whose family stemmed from Spain, dedicated his version of Averroes's commentary on Plato's *Republic* to Pope Paul III who was also served by him as his personal physician.[170] Since a humanist like Guido Rangoni studied Hebrew with him, he also translated from the Hebrew into Latin. The influential Yehiel Nissim of Pisa, banker and bibliophile, talmudist and rabbinic authority, kabbalist and philosopher, became known as the author of the tract *Offering of Jealousy*.[171] His healthy admiration of philosophy was tempered with an even healthier admiration of religious tradition as a sole repository of metaphysical truths. It was this attitude that induced him to view students of Azariah de Rossi's historical work with suspicion unless they were given special permission by the rabbinates of their respective communities. His book was praised in prose and poetry: in prose by Yohanan ben Joseph Treves, the rabbi of Sabbioneta, in poetry by Raphael Solomon ha-Kohen of Prato and Moses ben Joab.[172]

Elijah del Medigo of Crete was one of the most prominent and eminent Jewish humanists. He did for Giovanni Pico della Mirandola what Sforno did for Reuchlin: he and the philosophical commentator of the *Song of Songs*, Yohanan ben Isaac Alemanno, instructed him in the Hebrew language and imparted to him some knowledge of Jewish disciplines, especially the Kabbalah. And Elijah del Medigo translated for him philosophical treatises and compendia of Greek philosophy in Arabic through Hebrew versions into Latin. For he was an enthusiastic translator and admirer of Averroes as his tract *Examination of Religion*[173] shows with unmistakable clarity. Like his predecessors in medieval philosophy he was exercised by the relationship of revelation to philosophy and by possibilities of reconciliation between them.[174] As a teacher of philosophy at Padua and Florence, he met many Italian humanists including the renowned head of the Platonic Academy, Marsilio Ficino.

More than a century later another scion of the Medigo family, Joseph Solomon del Medigo, better known under his Hebrew acronym Yashar of Candia (1591–1655), acquired an enviable erudition in many languages and in many disciplines. As a restless student and wanderer—he was born in Crete and he died in Prague—he came in contact, personally or epistolarily, with the most eminent Jewish and non-Jewish contemporaries: Galileo and Fabricius, Leone Modena and Simhah Luzzatto. His knowledge of medicine secured him a temporary position as physician to the illustrious family of Radziwills in Lithuania. His wanderings brought him to Italy, Turkey, Egypt, Holland, Germany, Poland, Lithuania and Bohemia.

His main book *Elim*[175] appeared under the imprimatur of Menasseh ben Israel's press in 1629 and endeavored to answer twelve questions of Karaites concerning the Jewish religion. Other books of Joseph Solomon del Medigo dealt with Kabbalah in a veiled way: they were laudatory or derogatory, according to the perception or inclination of the reader.

The interest of the Medigo family in philosophy and other humanistic disciplines was paralleled by many scholars of distinction. Calonymus ben David published a translation of a part of Averroes's chief philosophical treatise which is known under the Latin name *Destructio Destructionis*. He also translated the Arab astronomer al-Bitruji from the Hebrew version of Moses Ibn Tibbon. Another Arab astronomer Ibn Al Heitham was translated from a Hebrew version, still in manuscript, by Abraham de Balmes who also translated Aristotle's *Posterior Analytics* with Averroes's *Major Commentary*. Jacob Mantino, physician and philosopher, translated scientific works from Hebrew into Latin. Joseph ben David Yahya, scion of an ancient and famous family of Jews in Portugal and Spain, wrote a philosophical panegyric on the Jewish people. In his *Torah is Light*[176] he attacked Maimonides and extolled Halevi. And this attitude was almost repeated by Samuel David Luzzatto three hundred years later. Both Joseph Yahya and Samuel David Luzzatto defended the traditional, simplistic view of Judaism against the onslaught of critical ages: one against humanist, the other against rationalist attacks.

The most eminent of the renaissance philosophers is undoubtedly Leone Ebreo (c.1460–c.1535) who is also known under his Latin name

Leo Habraeus and under his Hebrew name Judah Abrabanel. As the son of the famous Don Isaac Abrabanel and as an eminent physician, poet and humanist in his own right, he was in touch with the best minds of his age. He not only took a lively interest in philosophy but, at the request of Giovanni Pico della Mirandola, he wrote a work on astronomy which remained unpublished. And he probably studied Plato's philosophy and especially his theory of love as it was developed by Ficino. In the light of this theory, based chiefly, though not exclusively on Plato's *Symposium* and *Phaedrus* as well as on the New Testament and later Christian traditions, human love is merely a preparation for the love of God. But in his attitude to love, Leone Ebreo was undoubtedly permeated with the concept of love for God which talmudic sages and medieval philosophers stressed again and again.[177] A true love relationship has its ultimate source in the love of the lover of God.[178]

The language in which the *Dialogues of Love* was written in 1501-2 is still a matter of conjecture: Hebrew and Ladino, Italian and Spanish have been proposed by various scholars. Its popularity is attested by the eleven editions in Italian within eighty years of its publication in 1535, two translations into French, three into Spanish, one into Latin, into Hebrew, into German and, in our own century, into English.[179] The alleged conversion of Leone Ebreo to Christianity is a calumny which was probably invented by one of his publishers in order to avoid persecution or to attract buyers for *Dialoghi d'Amore* or both. The book influenced Giordano Bruno and Baldassare Castiglione who created the image of the ideal nobleman for the renaissance in a celebrated book *The Courtier*.[180]

The three dialogues in the *Dialoghi d'Amore* between Philo and Sophia on Love and Desire, on the Universality of Love and on the Origin of Love are among the commanding pieces of philosophical literature in the sixteenth century. In the first dialogue the distinction is made between love and desire: desire is defined as "an affect of the will aimed at the coming to be or coming to be ours of a thing we judge good and have not. . .[181]love as an affect of the will to enjoy through union the thing judged good."[182] Love may or may not coincide with desire. The profitable object is never loved and desired at the same time;[183] "in respect of pleasant things love and desire are not separated";[184] as for the Good—it is the source of wisdom and virtue; and "in respect of the Good, the greatest excess of love and desire is virtuous."[185] As for human friendship and love of God, "noble friendships make of one person, two; of two persons, one. . .Love of

God not only partakes of Good, but comprises the goodness of all things and all loves."[186] "Happiness consists. . .in the conjunctive act of intimate cognitive union with God."[187]

Toward the end of the first part Philo, one of the two protagonists of the dialog, turns to Sophia, the other protagonist, with an almost poetic invocation:

> When you learn, Sophia, the important part played by Love throughout the Universe, not only among bodies, but even more among spirits; when you learn how, from the Prime Cause of all to the last created thing, there is not one but loves; you will entertain greater reverence for it, and then you may attain to greater knowledge of its origins.[188]

Thus, in the first part, like in a well-constructed first movement of a symphony, not only the main themes are announced and developed but the forward thrust of other themes and even the finale is heard in anticipatory bars. For the second part discusses the universality of love—in animals, in mankind and even in inanimate matter. And the third and longest dialogue on the origin of love deals with the birth and birthplace and the goal of all love.

The Platonic form of dialogue, the love content, the philosophical erudition and the graceful argumentation assured the book its popularity. For, though the protagonists of the dialogues are abstractions, they are endowed with the fickleness and grace of real persons. The coyness of Sophia, her unwillingness to return Philo's love, her graceful fight against the subtleties of his reasoning and the inconclusive parting of Sophia and Philo at the end of the book; these are as dramatically felt and written as a conversation of lovers. It cannot be said of the *Dialogues of Love*—as it has been said of *Bhagavad Gita*—that its meaning is that being itself is a conversation of lovers. But it can be said of them that the meaning of life is love. And this was also Dante's emotional and philosophical conclusion of his *Divine Comedy:* Love that moves the sun and the other stars.[189]

Mysticism

Expulsion from Spain affected Jewish life and letters to an unprecedented degree. The apocalyptic nightmare spread over the old and the new centers of Jewry through the influx of exiles. The entire literary output of Jewry and even the literary output of undisturbed

Jewries—and here is a parallel to Jewish literature after the holocaust during the Second World War—suffered a tangible transformation. But only mysticism in its exotic flights of imaginative daring had the power to bring alleviation of pain to stricken Jewry and explanation of its undeserved ordeal. Ironically, 1492 had been designated by some mystics as the year of redemption.[190] What happened was antithesis to redemption. A new interpretation of the event was a necessity, above all an interpretation which was satisfactory not to a small elite but to the entire people. That interpretation evolved in Safed. It was there that mysticism became a popular religion for the first time in Jewish history. Even such an esoteric doctrine as transmigration of souls became "the drama of the souls."[191] For two hundred years—roughly from the middle of the sixteenth to the middle of the eighteenth century—mysticism invaded every aspect of Jewish life. Even popular ethics became a vehicle of mystical ideas—from Moses Cordovero's *Palm of Deborah*[192] to Isaiah Horowitz's *Two Tablets of the Covenant* and Zevi Hirsch Kaidanower's *Measure of the Honest*. And from the middle of the eighteenth century mysticism gained a new lease on life in the Hasidic movement.

The entire problem of divine justice and retribution, voiced in millennial literary antecedents such as Job, had to undergo its sharpest and starkest reassessment after 1492. No single individual of genius could do justice to the problem of justice in its new guise. But entire schools of thought and new centers of learning made a cumulative assault on the problem.

It fell to the lot of a small locality in Northern Palestine, Safed, to become the avant-garde of mysticism in the sixteenth century and to affect Jewry till our own day. The mountainous town with its superb views of Galilee and with its remoteness from the great centers of new learning was predisposed to the contemplative life. It happened that in the sixteenth century it also became a center of economic activity: the wool industry created wealth and employment for the inhabitants. For a century Safed was a flowering center of Judaism: mystics and talmudists, poets and exegetes flowered in profusion. Then, as abruptly as it was born, it declined and never recovered its glory again. At the end of the sixteenth century Bedouins, Mameluks and Druse tribes ransacked the city, razed homes to the ground and even destroyed the important printing press which was established in the town in 1577 by Eliezer ben Isaac Ashkenazy of Prague.[193]

The man who changed the course of Jewish history in and out of Palestine was Rabbi Jacob Berab (c.1474–1546) who arrived in Safed before 1517 and settled there permanently, with a few years of peregrinations in Damascus, in Egypt, in Gaza, in Jerusalem. Around 1524 he was acknowledged as the Chief Rabbi and was reverently addressed by Karo: "my master."[194] With the establishment of a great talmudic academy, patterned after the great academies of Castile and the consequent aspiration to ordination in 1538, as it was practiced in tannaitic times, Safed exercised an unusual attraction to prospective immigrants. There is no doubt that ordination aimed at the re-establishment of a supreme judicial authority over Jewry. And though it ended in failure, chiefly because of the opposition of Levi Ibn Habib of Jerusalem, it was an attempt of immense daring.

By the middle of the century such luminaries gathered in Safed as Joseph Karo and R. Moses ben Joseph Trani, Moses Cordovero and Isaac Luria, Hayyim Vital and Rabbi Moses Alshek, Karo's disciple Israel Najara (1555–1625), the poet, and Solomon Halevi Alkabez, the author of numerous mystical tracts and the composer of the hymn of redemption in erotic guise, "Go Beloved,"[195] which is chanted in all orthodox synagogues on Friday nights. In addition to these luminaries R. David Ibn Abi Zimra (c.1479–c.1571), teacher of Luria, lent prestige to Safed by settling there. As an older talmudist and kabbalist he was one of the most respected refugees from Spain. A few of his responsa which have been recently published show that he was also highly regarded outside the Land of Israel.[196]

The two most important mystics of Safed—Moses Cordovero and Isaac Luria—reinterpreted the Bible of mysticism, the *Zohar* of Moses de Leon: Moses Cordovero (1522–1570) systematically, Isaac Luria (1534–1572) ecstatically. The former was a prolific writer, an enthusiastic companion of his teacher and brother-in-law, Solomon Alkabez, the latter a charismatic personality who left no literary legacy but a trail of admiration which amounted almost to apotheosis. Already David Conforte remarks in his chronicle that "Elijah used to appear to Luria Ashkenazi of blessed memory and reveal to him wondrous mysteries. . ."[197]

Cordovero insisted on talmudic learning as a prerequisite of mystic illumination. Only he who comprehended and mastered the literal interpretation of the commandments, only he who had a deep knowledge of the legal minutiae of Jewish law, could aspire to their mystical interpretation and to the higher life of the mystic. In his main work *Garden of Pomegranates*[198] as well as in his other works he developed a consistent theory of emanation on the basis of previous speculations by earlier kabbalists. The contradiction between theism and pantheism received its neatest solution—albeit paradoxical resolution—in his famous dictum: "God is total reality but total reality is not God."[199] Cordovero maintained that God can be called thought because, whatever exists, exists in his substance. The *Sefirot* are the organism in which and through which he acts. Since man is the chosen one of creation, he must lead an exemplary life. For his holiness contributes to the unity of the world:

> He is the archetype for all existing things, and all things are in Him in their purest and most perfect form; so that the perfection of the creatures consists in the support whereby they are united to the ordinary source of His existence and they sink and fall from that perfect and high position in proportion to their separation from Him.[200]

For Cordovero man was an instrument of perfectibility; God the model of perfection. Small wonder that one of his most popular books *The Palm of Deborah,* which was to guide man to a higher life, was studied with assiduity for three hundred years. Though it lacked the clarity and the order of Moses Hayyim Luzzatto's work *Path of the Upright,* which appeared in the eighteenth century and which was also intended for devotional purposes, it achieved popularity by the boldness of its imaginative discourses. It is a mystical *imitatio Dei* as the author announces in the beginning: "It is proper for man to imitate his Creator."[201] And, in a beautiful passage, Cordovero maintains the stance that even the sinner at the moment of sin is the recipient of divine affluence. Though God can punish him, he waits patiently for the sinner's return to his true self. Such patience must also become an attribute of man:

> . . .no man ever sins against God without the divine affluence pouring into him at that very moment, enabling him to exist and to move his limbs. Though man uses it for sin, that power is not withheld from him in any way. But the Holy One, blessed is He, suffers this insult and continues to empower him to move his limbs even though he uses the power in that very moment for sin and perversity offending the Holy One, blessed is He, who, nonetheless, suffers it. You must not say that he cannot withhold that good, God forbid, for it is in His power in the moment it takes to say the word "moment" to wither the sinner's hands or feet as He did to Jeroboam. And yet though it lies in His power to arrest the divine

flow—and He might have said: "If you sin against Me, do so under your own power, not with mine"—He does not, on this account, withhold His goodness from man, bearing the insult, pouring out His power and bestowing of His goodness. This is an insult borne in patience beyond words. This is why the ministering angels refer to the Holy One, Blessed is He, as the King who suffers insults. And this is the meaning of the prophet's words: "Who is a God like unto Thee?" He means: "You are a good and merciful God, with the power to avenge and claim your debt, yet you are patient and you suffer insults until man repents. This is a virtue man should make his own, namely, to be patient and allow himself to be insulted even to this extent and yet not refuse to bestow of his goodness to the recipients.[202]

Both Moses Cordovero and Moses Hayyim Luzzatto after him gathered a group of associates around them and drew up guidelines for their conduct. Cordovero's guidelines aim at an ethical life of utmost purity. There was to be no disparagement of any human being or beast; there was to be no idle talk except talk relating to study, there was to be no lying at all. Conversation among the associates was to be conducted in Hebrew at all times and, with other scholars, on the Sabbath.[203]

Cordovero and his associates would often walk in the vicinity of Safed and converse about arcane matters at the graves of ancient sages. This practice, developed by Luria and succeeding masters was called "Expulsions" or "Divorces." Cordovero even wrote a book under that title.[204] A favorite place of visit was the alleged burial place of R. Simeon Bar Yohai in Meron. But it did not necessarily take place on the thirty-third day of the counting of *Omer*.[205]

Such was Cordovero's fame that some of the most important mystics of the century were regarded as his disciples. Elijah de Vidas wrote an ethical tract *Beginning of Wisdom*[206] with the sole intention of guiding people to study Cordovero's *Garden of Pomegranates*. It utilized the master's ideas and preached an austere way of life. As its name indicated, it was intended to lead to wisdom through true God-fearing, God-loving ways. Significantly, almost paradoxically, Elijah de Vidas claimed that joy, faith and trust were the three things that lead to real love of God. The Torah can be comprehended through joy, God can be served with joy.[207] Spinoza also claimed that "pleasure is man's transition from a lesser to a higher state of perfection."[208] And the hasidic movement adopted joy even in its baser aspects as a mode of worshiping God.

There were numerous mystics who followed in Cordovero's footsteps: Eliezer Azikri who wrote the *Book of the Pious*;[209] Abraham Galante, the Italian kabbalist; Samuel Gallico, author of extracts from Cordovero's chief work;[210] Mordecai Dato, who compiled notes on Gallico's work; Menahem Azariah de Fano (1548–1620), the talmudist and kabbalist; the renowned Isaac Luria. Isaiah Horowitz, author of *The Two Tablets of the Covenant*, held *The Palm of Deborah* in high esteem and quoted from it profusely; Abraham Azulai published a summary of the book in 1685 and, as late as the nineteenth century, Israel Salanter (1810–1883), founder of the *Musar* movement in Lithuania, commended *The Palm of Deborah* for its lofty idealism. And his pupils devoted regular periods of study to the work. When Cordovero died, he was eulogized by no less a person than Karo.

Like Cordovero, Luria excelled in talmudic studies and was regarded together with the well-established authority on rabbinical matters, Bezalel Ashkenazi, as a talmudic sage in his time. But, in contradistinction to Cordovero, Luria left an insignificant legacy in writing: only a commentary on a difficult section of the *Zohar*, comments on some passages in the *Zohar* and three hymns for the three sabbath meals can be attributed to him with certainty.[211] His visionary ideas were disseminated in conversations with friends and followers. One of them, Hayyim Vital, systematized Luria's oral flashes in a massive work *The Tree of Life*;[212] another, Joseph Ibn Tabul, propagandized them; a third, Israel Sarug, transmitted them to Italian Jewry especially; a fourth, Abraham Cohen Herrera of Florence, invented an eclectical mysticism which was a combination of neoplatonism and pseudo-Lurianism.

Luria's ideas can be reduced to a simplistic triad: Contraction,[213] Breaking of Vessels,[214] Mending.[215] But they were born in ecstatic trances, in revelatory dialogues with such a superhuman individual as Elijah and, even in the schematic order, they still convey the exaltation of their original inspiration. Contraction, based on rabbinic texts from the third century, came to mean in Luria's thinking the retreat of God into himself in order "to make room for the world" or in Scholem's beautiful interpretation, the symbolic exile of God "from his totality into profound seclusion."[216] This parallel to Jewry's exile is even greater in the second idea of the triad, in the "Breaking of Vessels." For the "Breaking of Vessels" is God's exile out of himself whereas Contraction can be considered "as an exile into Himself."[217] In the beginning, which in itself is a difficult concept, the light which is

God which is infinity flowed into space. The being which emanated was primordial or ancient man,[218] the highest manifestation of God after Contraction. From the various organs of primordial man the *Sefirot* emanated. And they are "stages in the revelation of God's creative power."[219] Vessels were created to hold the light. The three highest *Sefirot* found shelter in them but the six lower *Sefirot* could not be contained in their vessels: they broke them. And to a certain extent that also happened to the last *Sefirah*. Like Contraction, the idea of the Breaking of Vessels is based on a rabbinic tract.[220] But it received an original formulation in Luria's thought. What caused the Breaking of Vessels? It was a necessity. For the Shells,[221] the forces of evil, were mixed up with the lights of the *Sefirot*. And these were cleansed by elimination of the Shells and by providing a separate identity to evil which sank to the lowest depths of primordial space. Mending or restoration or—to use a common religious term—salvation means "restitution. . .of the original whole."[222]

The Lurianic syndrome provides new configurations for the lights of the *Sefirot* which emerge from the primordial man, transformation of the *Sefirot* into Faces or Countenances.[223] For the Faces represent the entire divinity under various guises. Mending is restoration of scattered lights or sparks to their right abode.

Four worlds intervene between our world and the divinity which is the infinite: the world of Emanation,[224] the world of Creation,[225] the world of Formation[226] and the world of Making.[226] In all four worlds the Faces reveal themselves in ever deeper form, even though there is a partition between them. The process of mending or restitution can be hastened or retarded by man—especially by the Jew who is in close touch with the divinity through the Torah, the commandments, the prayers. The coming of the Messiah is the final process of Mending—*Tikkun;* the redemption of Jewry is also cosmic redemption. Hence the importance of mystical intention[228] in Lurianic doctrine. More appropriately and less literally translated as meditation, it may and may not border on magic. Man's entire life must be directed toward the restoration which was disturbed by the Breaking of Vessels.

Metempsychosis which was born perhaps in India is part of Restoration. For the exile of the soul parallels the exile of the body. The souls which fulfilled their devotional tasks are exempt from transmigration; those which have not are subject to transmigration which is a sort of hell for the soul.

On a less lofty plane Lurianism influenced Jewry's customs and practices: the fast of the first-born on the day before Passover, the nightly vigil before *Shabu'ot* and *Hoshana Rabbah,* the change of the last day before every new month into a "Miniature Day of Atonement,"[229] the study of Mishnah which has the same consonants as *Neshamah* (=Soul) in memory of the departed, the recitation of the hymn "Go Beloved" of Solomon Alkabez on Friday nights, the chanting of the three Sabbath hymns of Luria—all these practices gained a wide popularity during the succeeding centuries, first in Safed, then wherever Jews lived. The orthodox still practice them with abandon.

Lurianic mysticism was co-terminous with mystic trends in the sixteenth century. Diogo Pires (c.1500–1532), the Portuguese Marrano who reverted to Judaism under the influence of David Reubeni and assumed the name Solomon Molko, became an ardent mystic. His incendiary sermons about the approaching advent of the Messiah earned him a martyr's death at the stake in Mantua in 1532—at the instigation of the Inquisition by order of Charles V. It was the contention of a sensitive scholar[230] that the life of Molko deserved a great historical novel. This desideratum was partially fulfilled in our century by A.A. Kabak in his novel *Solomon Molko.*

David Reubeni (c.1480–1532), adventurer and charlatan, "of short stature, lean-fleshed and courageous,"[231] pretended to be an emissary of his brother Joseph, the alleged ruler of the tribe of Reuben, to the Pope and other European potentates. The object of his mission was military aid in the fight against the Turks. His appearance in Venice in 1523 and in Rome in 1524, his audience with Egidio da Viterbo, the Hebrew-loving cardinal, and with Pope Clement VII, aroused worldwide interest. His persuasive powers opened doors of kings and chests of money. In Portugal, between 1525 and 1527, he excited the Marrano community with hopes of redemption. Reubeni's fate was eventual imprisonment by Spanish authorities and probable death in prison. In his diary the exotic dreamer described with verve how he was entertained by the learned Jew, Vitale da Pisa; how his wife Diamante and other women made sweet music in the villa outside the city to while away his time and to soothe his depressed spirits. He did not spare his barbs against hostile Jews like the banker Ishmael da Rieti who declared that he loved Siena, not Jerusalem. The incident, so reminiscent of later enmity of assimilated Jews to Zionist aspirations, is worthy of full quotation:

> I said to him: What do you wish—to be in Jerusalem or to remain in your own place? He answered: I have no wish to be in Jerusalem.

I have one desire and one object of love: Siena. And I was very much surprised. . .[232]

Like so many of his contemporaries Reubeni willed salvation. He fasted and believed in his mission. But, unlike his contemporaries, he emphasized action. Hence his pose as a military commander rather than a prophet or a messiah.

Was he a Jew of the Orient or the Occident? Did he write his diary or was it a forgery by an awkward stylist? In spite of the massive researches of Eshkoli the problem of Reubeni's personality and work is a mystery wrapped in an enigma.

De-arcanization of the arcane and presentation of mysteries—Lurianic or pre-Lurianic or post-Lurianic—in a coherent and sequential system of logical ideas: this is an attempt which every serious student of mysticism makes with no success. All he can hope to do is to paraphrase. His task is not unlike that of the critic of poetry who translates a poem into prose. It cannot be done for the poetic form cannot be separated from the content. The student of mysticism and the critic of poetry can indicate, describe or conjure the frozen fire of the mystery or the poem in pedestrian prose. He should not pretend to understand every poem or every mystery. The student of Luria can use such contemporary or post-contemporary records as *The Praises of the Lion*[233] by Solomon Shlomel Dresnitz, the Moravian kabbalist who settled in Safed or *The Book of the Genealogies of the Ari* or the voluminous compendia of Hayyim Vital; he cannot explain Lurianism. For these works are hagiographic accounts of a superidealized, superhuman hero. Thus, on one occasion when Luria and his disciples discussed a passage in the Bible of the mystics, the *Zohar*, birds allegedly appeared in great numbers. "And when the master [Luria] heard their voices, he laughed and said to his associates: these birds are the souls of the righteous who came from the Heavenly Academy."[234] The hagiography of Luria reached its apogee in the story in which he was equated with Moses himself:

Two men lived in the neighborhood of the master. They were always quarreling with him. Said the master to them: You have not abandoned your evil ways. I can, if I wish, command the earth to open its mouth and swallow you up. Then the associates asked him why he said that to them. He answered that they were the incarnations of Dathan and Abiram and they are still rebellious and quarrel with him. For he was of the spark of Moses our master, peace be with him. And that accounts for his answer.²³⁵

This unselfconscious story recreates the charged air of mysticism which has enveloped the numerous disciples of Luria. What they needed at the time, what Jewry needed, was the miraculous master and guide who would bring personal fulfillment, national redemption and universal perfection. Or to put it another way: there are men of reason who make people think; there are men of emotion who make people feel. Luria made people feel.

Hayyim Vital Calabrese (1543–1620), the author of the voluminous *Tree of Life,* enshrined the kabbalistic teachings of Luria in an unsystematic medley and imposed on future scholars a superhuman task of sifting, simplification and methodization. Other votaries of Luria like Israel Sarug and Solomon Shlomel Dresnitz, his son-in-law, propagandized his teachings in their numerous peregrinations. These teachings spread to Italy first, then to Germany and Holland and Eastern Europe. What they aspired to first was equal status for mystic Judaism with rabbinic Judaism; later higher status for mysticism than rabbinism; still later to supersede rabbinism.²³⁶ The conscious devaluation of Karo and normative Judaism began with Luria's disciple, Hayyim Vital. Karo, he claimed, asked to be instructed by Luria who acceded to the request reluctantly because the great talmudist was really not in a position to achieve true wisdom. And, for Hayyim Vital, true wisdom was mystic wisdom. But neither he nor Cordovero, according to his own testimony, reached the depths and heights of Luria.

Two poets of the mystic circle in Safed—Alkabez and Najara—contributed their seductive verses to Jewish liturgy and lent a kabbalistic coloring to the observance of the Sabbath. The hymn "Go Beloved" by Alkabez became one of the most popular poems of Jewry in the last four hundred years. But the poet also wrote many devotional prayers which have been lost and many prayers which have been preserved. One such, a "Prayer for Sustenance," has recently been published. Only in the first part it is a prayer for sustenance. In the second part it is a long poem of redemption—most likely by the same author who reviews Jewish history from patriarchal times up to the expulsion from Spain and the renewed settlement of Jews in the Land of Israel.²³⁷ Both are written in poetic prose, both are pain-suffused in their attitude to life. Thus, in the prayer for sustenance: "May I not have to bother about my sustenance too much so that I may have the time to study your Torah and fulfill the commandments and the laws according to your will." And in the second part the poet does not accuse his people but the circumstances: "And if they sinned abundantly, they are not guilty. . . the king whom you set up over them strayed or led them astray. . ."

A bit less popular than the Friday night hymn "Go Beloved" was the Sabbath day chant of Israel Najara: "God, Lord of the World and Worlds"[238] which has been sung for centuries and which is still popular in orthodox circles today—though the name of the poet, an erudite talmudist, is almost forgotten. Luria seems to have regarded him as a spiritual descendant of David, "the sweet singer of Israel."

In Najara's collected poetry there are satiric and sarcastic, artful and skilful verses which are reminiscent of Immanuel of Rome and Judah Alharizi. But there are also poems of mystic longing for redemption. At their best they compare favorably with the passionate poetry of Judah Halevi. Unlike him Najara was aware of the importance of popular poetry. The people in the countries of his sojourn sang Arabic and Turkish songs; Najara was ambitious to supplant them with his own. For he believed that "songs in the holy tongue are sweet to the palate."[239] In the very first collection of his poems which was published in Safed in 1587, in the *Songs of Israel*,[240] which numbered one hundred and nine lyrical poems and which was republished with changes during his lifetime in Venice and in Salonika, he showed a mellifluous strain which was to characterize his early as well as his late poems. The tone was the same; the content changed. Toward the end of his life he leaned more to a religious attitude in his poetry. He has used the well-known metaphor of the dove which sometimes applies to the soul of man, sometimes to the Jewish people. These dove-songs are full of longing for redemption and restoration. As in the *Psalms* the poetic *I* in them is either individual or national.

Najara composed in Hebrew and in Aramaic with equal facility. He seems to have been different than the saintly and ascetic men of Safed. He loved wine and song and food; he leaned to bohemianism before bohemianism was in vogue; he improvised freely and he earned the contempt of such austere personages as Hayyim Vital.

R. Jacob Berab and R. David Ibn Abi Zimra, R. Joseph Karo and R. Moses ben Joseph Trani, Moses Cordovero and Isaac Luria, Solomon Halevi Alkabez and Israel Najara, R. Moses Alshek and Elijah de Vidas—these men and a host of lesser luminaries turned Safed into one of the most potent centers of Hebrew literature in the sixteenth century. Its influence and its way of life spread far and wide. The ethical tracts of R. Isaiah Horowitz, R. Zevi Hirsch Kaidanower, Moses Hayyim Luzzatto down to our own century owe their existence to the school of Safed. The messianic and hasidic movements stem from Safed or are influenced by Safed. There is no event of importance in succeeding centuries that cannot be traced to the tiny Galilean community. For it radiated religious sublimity—a theory and practice of holiness which bound the disparate communities of East and West in sacral brotherhood.[241]

2
The Apocalyptic Age

The Eschatological Theorists

During the ninety-four years which elapsed between the death of
Isaac Luria and the conversion of Sabbatai Zevi to Mohammedanism
in 1666, mysticism penetrated every center of Jewish life. Even
Amsterdam, the thriving metropolis of Europe and the tolerant refuge
of Jewry in the seventeenth century, was permeated with mystics who,
at the same time, were men of affairs, learned rabbis or even
philosophers. Sometimes extreme rationalism and extreme mysticism
existed side by side: Spinoza, probably a pupil of Menasseh ben Israel,
was the contemporary of the mystic Abraham Cohen Herrera. That
even he owed a minor debt to Kabbalah has been demonstrated with
finality by Harry Austryn Wolfson, the foremost Spinozist of our
time.[1]
Two Marranos, Isaac Aboab da Fonseca (1606–1693) and Menasseh
ben Israel (1604–1657), originally Manoel Dias Saeiro, who came to
Amsterdam in their childhood and who received an excellent Jewish
education from Rabbi Isaac Uziel, a former rabbi of Oran, grew up to
become well-known rabbis and preachers. Both were affected by
Brazil: Isaac Aboab actually received a rabbinical post in Pernambuco
and left it when it was conquered by the Portuguese,[2] Menasseh ben
Israel intended to emigrate to Brazil but abandoned his prospective
business ventures in the New World. Both were orators of note:
Menasseh allegedly said what he knew but Aboab knew what he said.
Aboab was a a gifted though conservative poet with a religious stance,
Menasseh was an indefatigable, almost compulsive student of
contemporary events. Both were mystics. Aboab translated the
mystical work of Abraham Cohen Herrera from the original Spanish

57

into Hebrew,[3] Menasseh's major work in Hebrew, *Breath of Life*,[4] is a compendium of mystical superstitions and esoteric doctrines. It was Menasseh ben Israel, however, who made a deep dent in Jewish history and literature. He wrote in five languages—including Hebrew. And he was well-known in Jewish and Christian intellectual circles all over the world. He came from his native Madeira to Amsterdam as a child and, through diligence and devotion, acquired a good, broad and superficial knowledge of ten languages including Latin and Greek as well as a familiarity with Christian and Jewish classics and other ancient literatures. He was admired by scholars, courted by statesmen, painted by Rembrandt. His printing press, a major achievement in his time, launched Amsterdam to the forefront of Hebrew printing. For in the eighteenth century Amsterdam became "the center of Hebrew printing for the whole world."[5] His printer's mark—By our wanderings we seek[6]—is an epitome of his life and work. For his was an indefatigable ambition—a blend of self-seeking and selflessness.

The important works of Menasseh ben Israel were written in Spanish: *Conciliador,* as the title indicates, endeavors "to reconcile" in the first part one hundred and eighty discrepancies in the Pentateuch and, in the course of the work, it quotes two hundred and twenty-one Jewish and fifty-four Gentile authors.[7] Discrepancies in other biblical books were dealt with in subsequent parts which appeared in the course of twenty years. The work made him famous as a spokesman of Jewry to the gentile world.

He was deeply affected by mystical trends of the time. As a student of the *Zohar* and the mystics of Safed, he shared the quasi-messianic excitements of his age and he regarded the alleged author of the *Zohar,* R. Simeon Bar Yohai, as the "peerless sage among Jewish sages."[8] Though he appears in the engraving by Salom Halia as theologian and Jewish philosopher—*theologus et philosophus Hebraeus*—he lacked profundity and originality. Yet so great was his erudition that eminent Jews like the philosopher Joseph del Medigo and eminent Christians like the jurist Hugo Grotius (Huig de Groot) and Rembrandt sought his acquaintance and friendship. It was Rembrandt who produced four etchings for *The Glorious Stone* or *About the Statue of Nebuchadnezzar:*[9] the image in Nebuchadnezzar's dream, Ezekiel's vision, Jacob's Dream, David and Goliath. In that book Menasseh ben Israel comments on Daniel's interpretation of Nebuchadnezzar's dream. The stone which broke the statue is the stone on which Jacob slept, with which David slew Goliath. The four monarchies represent Babylonia, Persia, Macedonia, Rome; the fifth—to come in the future—is Israel.

In his only major Hebrew work *Breath of Life* Menasseh ben Israel also shows mystical influences: the elevation of the soul through piety. In the introduction he claims to have written the book in order to provide peace of mind for his generation.[10] The four parts of the book deal with the divine soul of man, the life of the soul from birth to its demise, the imperishability of the soul, the proofs of the immortality of the soul.[11] But the tone of sober reasoning in the introduction is quickly abandoned. The extravagances of the Kabbalah—magic and magicians, incantations and amuletry, spirits and demons, exorcisms and transmigrations of souls—are presented with disturbing credulity. There is even a serious discussion of incubi, male spirits who have intercourse with women, and succubi, spirits in female form who have intercourse with men.[12] And, without a trace of irony or humor, the problem is posed: Have demons procreative organs? The question, according to Menasseh ben Israel, is unsolved: Some say yes, some say no. But even those who say yes claim that their offspring is dwarfish, "resembling apes."[13]

Menasseh ben Israel also showed familiarity with the stories which circulated about Solomon Alkabez and Isaac Luria.[14] In his Latin *The Hope of Israel*[15] which was immediately translated into English and Spanish he envisaged a peculiar redemption of his people which promised, at the same time, the practical advantage of return to England. On the strength of two biblical passages—And the Lord shall scatter you among all peoples from one end of the earth to the other"[16] and the obscure phrase "to scatter the power of the holy people"[17]—the diaspora was thought to come to an end with the settlement of the Jews all over the earth including "the end of the earth," England, before redemption would begin. Thus readmission and resettlement of Jews in England after their long absence since the expulsion by Edward I in 1290 became a compulsive drive with utilitarian overtones and a mystical necessity for Menasseh ben Israel. This combination of political opportunism and arcane fate was accentuated by the weird tales of a West Indian Marrano merchant Antonio or Aaron Levi de Montezinos about remnants of lost Jewish tribes in South America. Since practical considerations of a commercial nature swayed Cromwell, the Jews were ultimately readmitted to England—"to trade and trafficke" as his tabled motion of November 12, 1655 so quaintly expressed it; but not in Menasseh ben Israel's time who penned, besides *The Hope of Israel*, a splendid refutation of religious prejudices such as the blood libel against Jewry under the title *Vindiciae*

Judaeorum in order to influence English public opinion and parliament.

Menasseh ben Israel—like so many of his contemporaries—was saturated with an all-pervasive mysticism. The catastrophic year of expulsion from Spain resulted in a reinterpretation of Jewish destiny—a reinterpretation which reached its apogee in the cosmic musings of Luria and his fellow kabbalists and percolated to ancient and newly settled communities like Amsterdam. The times were ready for the ultimate consummation: the Messiah. Sabbatai Zevi (1626–1676), the manic-depressive individual from Smyrna,[18] kindled the flame of imminent redemption wherever Jews lived. Aided and abetted by Nathan of Gaza, his ardent amanuensis and ubiquitous prophet, he mesmerized the Jewish world as no other individual had done in recorded history. Though he had left no single sermon or saying or parable or scrap of writing, he created an upheaval by the charismatic force of his personality. Great rabbis acknowledged his superiority, poets sang his praises: he was the king, the messiah, the refuge, the crown of creation.[19] Though his brand of extravagant messianism led to the tragic apostasy in 1666, his antinomianism had an enormous influence on the course of Jewish history and literature. Enlightenment, reform, Hasidism and Frankism which resulted in apostasy of the leader Jacob Frank and his numerous followers in 1759 have their roots in the religious heresy which was theoretically buttressed by Nathan of Gaza and, later, by Abraham Miguel Cardozo, the former Marrano.

It is obvious that the tensions produced by the double standard of faith on the part of Marranos since 1391 have created a favorable atmosphere for antinomian heresies. The fasts of the tenth day of Tebet and the ninth day of Ab were to be converted into festivals of rejoicings. Special prayers in praise of the Messiah were to be said in the synagogue. Revised prayer books were printed in Amsterdam and in Constantinople: old prayers were altered, new ones composed and inserted. The apostates—the so-called *Doenmeh*—were organized in Salonika in 1683: though professing Islam, they believed in salvation à la Sabbatai Zevi. And so did the Frankists though professing Catholicism since 1759. Both called themselves *Maaminim*—believers in Sabbatai Zevi's messianism. And though some "believers"—inwardly and outwardly—professed Judaism in all its orthodox rigidity, many have become radicalized by the obvious betrayal of faith on the part of the Messiah. The most nihilistic attitude—a "religious myth of nihilism" in Scholem's happy phrase[20]—was achieved by Frank in theory and in practice. In theory the *Book of the Words of the Lord*[21] in Polish preached unbridled license; in practice a dissolute life was led by the "believers." Significantly Baruch Kunio, a leader of the *Doenmeh* in Salonika, influenced the ideas of Frank and the youthful writings of Jonathan Eibeschütz (1690/1695–1764), the crypto-Sabbatian.

In the midst of the general intoxication with the alleged Messiah there were solitary voices of dissent. Chief among them was the Morroccan Rabbi Jacob Sasportas, a descendant of Nahmanides, who was a follower of Lurianic mysticism but a determined opponent of Sabbatai Zevi. His work *The Fading Flower of Zebi*[22] is a contemporaneous account of the movement which engulfed Jewry. Since it was not published during the author's life, it could not change the fatal course of Sabbatianism.[23] But its account of the movement from 1665/6 to 1675/6 is a vibrant work. The documents of the movement and the sober interpretation of Sasportas reflected not only the contemporaneous attitudes of the Jewish community in Hamburg where the learned rabbi lived at the time, but also in Amsterdam and in Leghorn which had close ties to Hamburg and, to a lesser extent, Turkey, Palestine and Egypt. The author's knowledge of rabbinic and kabbalistic sources, his taut Hebrew style, his deep personal involvement—these qualities lend the work unusual significance. Persecuted and derided, Sasportas stood out as a staunch defender of Judaism against the adventurous destroyer and innovator, the maker of "a new Torah."[24] He wrote repeatedly letters to the leaders and rabbis of Holland, Italy, Germany, Poland, Turkey, Egypt, Syria. In a typical answer from Isaac Aboab in Amsterdam he was gently rebuked for his antagonism to the Messiah, for his attack against other leaders, including Nathan of Gaza, for his blindness to the boon of repentance on the part of masses.[25] The voice of the prophet of Gaza proved to be the stronger voice: Moses was alive—beyond the mythical river Sambation—and married and his daughter is destined to be the wife of the Messiah and "anyone who doubts this, is a heretic. . ."[26]

In his own city, in Hamburg, Sasportas suffered persecutions because he despised "the words of the prophet"[27] and he could not understand the frivolity of the masses who were so easily deluded. As he so pithily summed it up: "And sometimes I laughed and sometimes I was angry."[28] And he was forced to preach—with reservations—in praise of the Messiah,[29] though he relented immediately. It was clear to his lucid mind that the exaggerated faith in Sabbatai Zevi and in his divinity resembled the Christian tenet of belief in the divinity of Jesus

Christic.[30] After the conversion of Sabbatai Zevi, Sasportas was only strengthened in his supposition that Sabbatianism was a dangerous substitution for Christianity. For Nathan of Gaza had explained the conversion as the fulfillment of the Isianic prophecy: he was despised and forsaken of men. . .he was oppressed though he humbled himself.[31] And these verses, as Sasportas well knew, were interpreted by Christians as referring to their Messiah.[32] Sasportas was a born polemicist, supersensitive, even prickly about his personal worth: no one could be inappreciative of his authoritative knowledge with impunity.[33] He was a man of strong convictions; he was right and "the leaders of the people were leading astray."[34] And history proved him right.

The Apocalyptic Poets

On the poetical front the two brothers, Jacob Frances (1615–1667) and Immanuel Frances (1618–1710) who were married to the two orphaned Lombroso sisters, Rachel and Grazia,[35] launched vehement attacks against Sabbatai Zevi. Jacob, the more sarcastic of the two, was an anti-kabbalist who heaped scorn and derision on the alleged Messiah and especially on the believers who were smitten with the "plague of folly."[36] For folly led to arrogance and arrogance meant abandonment of tradition.[37] In savage indignation the poet cried out: "If hell has lost its fire, it will burn again with the flame of my wrath."[38] He even used daring sexual symbolism—and he had proven his competence in pornographic verse—to taunt the followers of the false Messiah.[39] But Jacob Frances, the master of the scoffing and sneering phrase, was also the compassionate spokesman of his people:

"Though my poor people hunger for redemption,
Will clods of the valley be sweet to their taste?"[40]

Sabbatianism was a personal problem with Jacob Frances; his faith was threatened by the nightmare of heresy. Dozens of poems against the false Messiah testify to his deep involvement in the movement which threatened Judaism with dangerous fragmentation. He had voiced the disappointment and despair of Portuguese Jews who were driven to the baptismal font.[41] And he was determined to use the only weapon he had in the fight against Sabbatianism: his verse—gibing and gentle in turn, denunciatory and even wrathful on occasion. It took courage to stay sober amidst the general intoxication; stones were hurled at the poet in the streets, his home was ransacked.

Immanuel Frances was an active fighter—in prose, in numerous poems and even in sonnets—against the Sabbatian movement. In prose he composed a pamphlet *Brief Story of Sabbatai Zevi and Nathan of Gaza*.[42] And in a poem he mocked the Sabbatian prophet for his aspiration to be the Ezra of his generation.[43] In one of his poems he derided the Messiah: Honor God, my son, but pour your wrath on Zevi. . .for Zevi means serfdom, not freedom, for Zevi is a fly, not a lion. . .[44] In another poem he exhorts his readers to "turn from Zevi as from one defiled"[45] and he accuses him of little knowledge in the revealed tradition—Bible and Talmud—and less in the hidden tradition—Kabbalah.[46] He is amazed at the huge following of Sabbatai Zevi: People gather around him "like flies on a corpse and on dung."[47] Since the masses did not desert him after his imprisonment and after his conversion, Immanuel Frances did not desert his anti-Sabbatian muse and sought to undermine the influence of the false Messiah. "Would God give us a Redeemer who exchanged his Law for the Koran?"[48] he cried in anguish. But he hoped in vain that the truth will be recognized. Truth is elusive.

The Luzzattos and Mendes

The death of Immanuel Frances around 1700 coincides with the birth of the best-known representative of Hebrew poets in Italy during the eighteenth century, Moses Hayyim Luzzatto (1707–1746). He is not only the last effervescence of creative strength in Hebrew literature of his native land but also the last messianic and kabbalistic poet in that country. Since he can be seen now in proper prospective against a rich background of mystic turmoil, busy playwriting and less than busy play-producing, he cannot be regarded as the father of modern Hebrew drama or the father of modern Hebrew literature. Better known and more famous than his predecessors whose reputation was localized and whose plays rarely reached the printing press, he exercised an enormous influence on Hebrew literature in Russia and Poland a century after his death. His purity of style, modeled on the Bible, dominated poetic drama, epic poetry, and even prose to the very threshold of the twentieth century. If the Hebrew language became a mosaic of biblical verses, a pseudo-classic monstrosity, a cult of a precious elite, he is partly to blame. Already in his youthful work, a poetics by the name of *The Tongue of the Taught*,[49] written at the age of seventeen, Luzzatto mastered the biblical idiom and recommended it explicitly to future writers. And in the appended play *Story of Samson*[50] he not only dramatized the biblical story but also chose allegorical figures for the plays: strength, love, deceit, bribery. In his imitation of *Psalms* he approximated the biblical style more than in any other lyrical poems.[51]

Moses Hayyim Luzzatto was also responsible for the proliferation of a genre in Hebrew literature. Popularized by Philo, allegory became a cherished vehicle of expression in the middle ages and reached its peak in the thirteenth century in the well-known *Roman de la Rose* of Guillaume de Lorris and Jean de Meun. With its didacticism and moralization, allegory was peculiarly well-suited to the medieval man, but unfortunate as a mirror to the life of modern man. Luzzatto used allegory implicitly in his *Tower of Strength*.[52] The play borrowed much from Giovanni Batista Guarini's pastoral drama *Il Pastor Fido* which was first published in 1590 and which was admired, translated and imitated all over Europe in the seventeenth and eighteenth centuries.[53] The number of characters is identical in both plays; and so is the pastoral milieu and even the prosodic framework of eleven and seven syllable lines[54] which dominated pastoral drama since Tasso's *Aminta*. Entire verses are actual translations of Guarini. Both plays were written to celebrate marriages: Guarini's play to celebrate in 1585 the marriage of Carlo Emanuele I, Duke of Savoy, to Catherine, daughter of Philip II of Spain, Luzzatto's play to celebrate the marriage of his friend Israel Benjamin Bassani. But in its moral stance, in its sublimation of sensuality and, especially, in its covert mysticism, the *Tower of Strength* is a characteristically Jewish creation.

In the third and last play of Luzzatto *Praise to the Upright*[55] the allegory is complete; such figures as Truth, Folly, Patience, Honesty dominate the play which reads like an allegorized version of *Tower of Strength*. In his choice of allegory Luzzatto must be seen as a retarding rather than a progressive force. The naive, black-and-white characterization of his dramatis personae had an equally unfortunate influence. But in his fine sensitivity to pastoral simplicity and to the call of the hill and the forest, the field and the glade, he initiated that return to nature which Rousseau made fashionable in the literatures of western Europe. With the critical minds in the period of pre-enlightenment he shared an impatience with Judaism in its petrified form. Yet, in continuation ·of the medieval tradition, he fathered many tracts on religious principles. His eminent treatise on ethics *The Path of the Righteous*[56] was studied assiduously in rabbinic academies of eastern

Europe for two hundred years—from its publication in 1740 in Amsterdam till recent times. As a devotee of esoteric doctrines Luzzatto exposed himself to attacks of Jewish authorities who, disillusioned with the dangerous adventures of Sabbatai Zevi and his followers, frowned on mystic manifestations among Jews.

As a lyrical poet Moses Hayyim Luzzatto used the traditional forms of Italian versecraft: *ottava rima, terzina, canzone.* Marriage of friends, the pretext of his plays *Tower of Strength* and *Praise to the Upright,* also served as an incentive to the lovely poem "Sea and Land":[57] Amor, the God of Love, unites the two disparate entities as he has united the two families, that of the bridegroom Marini and that of the bride Italia. Thus, the elemental union became a paradigm of the human union.

The composition of *Psalms* in verse-form had more than transitory meaning for the poet; it was part of a messianic tendency which Luzzatto cultivated since his teenage years. At fourteen he was already an adept in Lurianic mysticism. It was only natural that a supernatural personage, a *Maggid,* should guide him and reveal to him esoteric doctrines. But the rabbinic leaders of the time were determined to kill any incipient messianism in the land. The Venetian rabbis excommunicated him in 1734. The rabbis in Frankfurt where he hoped to find peace of mind forced him to renounce the study of Kabbalah. Though he found some respite from the harassing rabbis in Amsterdam where, like Spinoza, he seems to have ground lenses for a living, he decided—perhaps in a fit of messianic enthusiasm—to emigrate to the Holy Land. Like Judah Halevi six hundred years before him he reached the land of his heart's desire and died there immediately.

One of Luzzatto's admirers in Amsterdam was Hisquiau David Franco Hofshi Mendes (1713–1792) who had also an alias, Diego Franco Osorio. It had been claimed by Graetz and subsequent historians on insufficient evidence that Luzzatto was the master and the chief inspirational force of Mendes. Now it is known that three years before Luzzatto's arrival in Amsterdam, Mendes wrote his first Hebrew poems. As a matter of fact Hebrew was studied as a language and it was spoken in the higher classes of the religious school—the *Talmud Torah*—in Amsterdam. At the funeral of Abendana da Britto a Hebrew eulogy was delivered by the officiating rabbi.[58] If Mendes called Luzzatto *Mori,* my master, he may have simply alluded to the eminence of his friend from Italy.[59] It is also certain that Mendes is not a *Maskil,* a man of the enlightenment but rather one of the last poets who created new trends and new forms in tenth century Spain and who are still a potent influence in Hebrew literature.[60]

As for the dramatic *magnum opus* of Mendes—*Retribution of Athaliah*[61]—it is certain that Racine's *Athalie* and Metastasio's *Joash King of Judah*[62] contributed to Mendes's plays. But Melkman's thesis that the play is a polemic against Racine cannot be substantiated or even entertained. Racine's *Athalie* is calculated to arouse pity while Mendes's queen is a true copy of the original. His play is a drama of an ancient revolution that did away with Athaliah and imposed Joash on the throne of Judah. Hebrew poets of the eighteenth century, when writing on biblical themes, rarely deviated from the sacred text. Gentiles were more daring in their use of the Bible as a source of poetic, dramatic and narrative material. If Mendes emphasized just punishment for the dire deeds of Athaliah, he did not necessarily attack Racine: he merely followed the Bible.

The manuscript play *Eternal Love*[63]—a pastoral poem with allegorical divertissements—and the three manuscript volumes of poetry, *Lyre of David*,[64] *Tabernacle of David*[65] and an untitled volume—promise to add lovely lyrics to the treasury of modern Hebrew poetry.[66] On the strength of published and unpublished works Mendes emerges as a cultured poet, a dramatist, a scholar and linguist of no mean ability. He knew enough Dutch to translate—from Dutch into Hebrew—for the municipality of Amsterdam, and to translate Dutch poems into Hebrew; enough French to translate fragments of Voltaire's poetry; enough Spanish to translate Alkabez's "Go Beloved"; enough Portuguese to translate some Portuguese poems including Luis de Camoens's stately sonnet *"Alma minha gentil que te partiste,"* enough Italian to paraphrase Metastasio's *Betulia Liberata* under the title *Salvation of Jewry by Judith*.[67] The paraphrase of Metastasio's play deserves special attention. Mendes has intentionally chosen the work because it is based on an apocryphon and, as such, it is not included in the Bible. Already Wessely before him had translated *The Wisdom of Solomon*. Both wished to widen the scope of the reader and acquaint him with post-biblical literature; one through direct translation, the other through dramatization of a Hebrew theme by an Italian poet. But Mendes was the more inventive, the more imaginative though less influential poet. He deserves a place of honor in Hebrew literature together with the numerous Luzzattos: Moses Hayyim Luzzatto, Ephraim Luzzato (1729–1792), Isaac Luzzatto (1730–1803) and Samuel David Luzzatto (1800–1865). For they continued the tradition of significant poetry in the context of renaissance universalism. They were scions of a family which managed to provide a galaxy of scholars and poets. In the sixteenth century Jacob Luzzatto published a commentary on rabbinic legends *Calyx and Petals*.[68] In the seventeenth century Simhah Luzzatto, the Venetian rabbi, made himself famous with his treatise on economics and politics, *Discourse on the Status of the Jews*.[69] In the eighteenth century, Ephraim Luzzatto adorned Hebrew letters with graceful poetry, while his brother wrote in a more serious vein; and the granddaughter of Isaac, Rachel Morpurgo (1790–1871), was among the first modern poetesses in Hebrew literature. The massive erudition of Samuel David Luzzatto placed him among the eminent scholars of the nineteenth century.

Ephraim Luzzatto, also known by his Italian name Angelo Luzzatto, was a late descendant-in-spirit of Immanuel of Rome rather than "a Hebrew Petrarch."[70] At home in Italian and in Hebrew,[71] he represented that lighter vein in Hebrew literature which had an honorable history even in Spain: Abraham Ibn Ezra and Judah Al-Harizi wrote humorous verse with exceptional verve. He was even afflicted—or blessed—with the restlessness of his Spanish confrères. It was in London where Ephraim Luzzatto spent thirty years as physician in the hospital of the Portuguese-Jewish community that he published his collection of lyrics under the longish title *These Are the Younglings, Children of the Physician Ephraim Luzzatto When the Spirit of Poetry Rested Upon Him in His Youth in Italy, and Their Progenitor Mocked Them and Cast Them Down on Another Land Today. They Weep and Wander in London's Streets and They Have Not Prepared Any Provisons for Themselves*.[72]

Sonnets dominate the bizarre collection of poems which, in thematic variety, range from frivolous love to frivolous medicine. The Anns and the Sarahs and the Margarets are there; and Eros or rather Cupid in the Italianized form with bow and arrow and, of course, Aesculapius, the god of medicine. The book exposes the vulgar physician who unnecessarily and unprofessionally touches the unmentionable organs of the female body; the greedy physician who is interested in lucre rather than in the relief of pain; the despicable physician who spends much time in the diagnosis of young women and almost no time in the therapy of older women. No wonder that the poet concludes:

All doctors
Are evil and sinful and unrighteous.
Religion is not their heritage,

God is not their king.
Their heart goes after gain.[73]

But Ephraim Luzzatto can also be soulful: In the confessional sonnet "Who am I?"[74] he manages to give a perfect expression of modest contentedness with his lot. In its idyllic mood it seems to be a literary reminiscence of the monolog in praise of the pastoral life by his namesake Moses Hayyim Luzzatto in *Tower of Strength*.[75] In his sonnet "Against Card-Playing"[76] he echoes Leone Modena's youthful tract against gambling. And, like all Hebrew poets of the period, he pays his conventional debt to downtrodden Zion and expresses hope for its resuscitation.

Isaac Luzzatto who loved the sonnet form[77] like his brother Ephraim and who also translated a poem by Metastasio "La Liberta,"[78] differed from him radically. He stayed most of his life in his native San Daniele del Friuli and he seemed to have a serious-minded disposition. In a sonnet, written at the age of nineteen, he confesses that he does not "trespass with his pen on the boundary of a mean person."[79] While his brother Ephraim exhorts him to acquire wisdom,[80] the younger brother responds eagerly to his exhortation[81] but implicitly chides the elder brother for his light-hearted attitude to physicians.[82] But he preaches sterile didacticism; full observance of tradition means full salvation for Jewry. Was it, perhaps, the justified fear of erosion of traditional values by enlightenment? His own son David—a physician like his father—became a convert to Christianity.

In contradistinction to his brother Isaac Luzzatto wrote religious poetry which can be easily incorporated into the prayerbook. The fragment of a larger poem on "Creation"[83]—a heavyfooted panegyric of traditional values—harks back in theme and form to medieval paradigms.

The prose-satire *"Mishnayot of S. Daniele"* reads like a precursor of Gershon Rosenzweig's *Yankee Talmud*. In strict imitation of the mishnaic idiom Isaac Luzzatto castigates his fellow Jews:

> As for a visitor to the city: one provides neither a living for him nor a lodging. There are those who say: one does not even greet him. But if he owns a house, one attaches oneself to him and one joins his company. Money decides. . .[84] As for the poor who bargains: one should desert him for he may ask for a bothersome loan.[85]

This mishnaic idiom—so refreshing in a period of pseudobiblical style—could have enriched the language and content matter of Isaac Luzzatto. Unfortunately, few samples of satire have survived in print and in manuscript.

His granddaughter Rachel—her mother Berakah was a sister of Hezekiah, father of Samuel David Luzzatto—married Jacob Morpurgo. A century after her birth Vittorio Castiglioni published fifty of her lyrical poems under the title *Harp of Rachel*[86] with a brief biographical account. She studied the Bible and the Talmud and even *Zohar* privately, she was diligent and scholarly and, at the same time, an efficient manager of her household which included her husband, Jacob, three boys and a girl.

Though her poetical output is thin in quantity and in quality, she gained a solid reputation. For she was admired by contemporary scholars and poets, translated into Italian by her biographer Vittorio Castiglioni, into German by Ludwig August Frankl and also into English by Henrietta Szold and Nina Salaman. A female author in Hebrew: that was a novelty in the nineteenth century. And that fact accounts for the exaggerated accolades.

A conservatively religious outlook dominates her sonneteering and almost impersonal verse: yearning for redemption, a high and hackneyed moral tone, a demure and chaste stance. Even "Rachel's finest poem"[87] is far from satisfactory: the stilted rhyme, the prevalent hendecasyllabic metre, the high pathos, are only partially redeemed by the fine juxtaposition of the gloomy vale of trouble with the eternal hills and skies "where freedom shines forever." *Pièces d'occasion* such as the sonnet in honor of Sir Moses Montefiore, riddles and even a brief Aramaic composition round out her meagre oeuvre.

Samuel Romanelli

Other Italian sonneteers of a later period—Joseph Almanzi (1801–1860) and Hillel (Lelio) della Torre (1805–1871)—possessed meagre talents and inadequate forms of expression. And though Almanzi will be remembered as a scholar who has written the first biography of Moses Hayyim Luzzatto,[88] he is worthy of some consideration as a poet. He translated—in the anachronistic form of a sonnet—a fable of Phaedrus from the Latin,[89] a fable and epigram of Amaltheus Hieronymus,[90] a fable of Aesop, probably from the Italian, a sonnet of Torquato Tasso,[91] a sonnet and a sestina of Petrarch[92] and a few minor Italian poets.

An atypical representative of the Italian school of Hebrew poetry, Samuel Romanelli (1757–1814)[93] can be regarded as a bohemian type with a superficial knowledge of many languages,[94] a familiarity with many literatures and a fondness for women. His attraction to them is not merely physical; in his travel book[95] he relishes a phrase of Lope de Vega from the lips of a fair lady.[96] Names of foreign authors charm him in general: he mentions Shakespeare, Milton, Pope and Young, Fénelon and Fontenelle, even Hippocrates and Galen. He was a wanderer in many lands, a pauper who could not make a living either from writing or from private tutoring, a liberal in an orthodox milieu, a man with a sharp tongue who frequently earned the enmity of the fanatics,[97] the rich and the powerful. As an observer he indulged in synthetic generalizations. On the Arabs of Morocco: "Habit, sorcery and the evil eye are the three destructive factors of Morocco."[98] On the Arabs in general: "Deceit, evil, robbery, lewdness, bribery, stupidity, jealousy, lack of faith and honor—these are the ways of the Arabs."[99] As a cultured dilettante Romanelli resents the complete lack of musical and theatrical performances in Morocco.[100] And he has nothing but contempt for the dress and lodging of Moroccans: "A hut is a proper lodging, a rag a proper dress, and food, no matter how unpalatable, appropriate for consumption."[101]

Romanelli fathered many books—plays which have not been published, grammars, translations, even a translation of Pope's *Essay on Man*[102] which has disappeared. As a traveler and sojourner in Morocco for four years at the end of the eighteenth century he perpetuated a tradition of peregrinatory writers which began with the journeys of Benjamin of Tudela and which has not abated to this day. His travel book which was first published in 1792 gained immediate popularity as a mine of folklore, autobiography and even Oriental history. The vivid descriptions of Moroccan habits and prejudices earned him a large readership. Though he wrote religious and philosophical poetry—some of it still in manuscript—occasional verse and conservative content have dominated his poetic oeuvre. The best poem is, perhaps, the one recently published from the manuscript collection of the Jewish Theological Seminary in Budapest.[103] It is a soulful elegy—in the popular Italian *terzina* form—on the death of a lady of many charms who died prematurely. But, according to the testimony of the poet, it is an "amplification and transformation" (*amplificato a transformato*) of a poem by the contemporary Italian poet Lodovico Savioli.

In his plays Romanelli vaunts the allegoric stance which distinguishes the Hebrew dramatists in the seventeenth and eighteenth centuries. They resemble Italian melodramas of the period; they are texts for musical presentation or operas. Such a play—*The Thunders Shall Cease*[104]—is an allegorical skirmish between Love and Justice, Justice and Wealth, Force and Cupid.[105] At the end Peace, in the true *deus-ex-machina* tradition, puts an end to the infighting abstractions. Like Moses Hayyim Luzzatto's play *Praise to the Upright* it was written and perhaps produced for a wedding which united two wealthy Jewish families in Berlin: the Oppenheims and the Yafes.

The second allegory—*The Time of the Offering of the Evening Offering*[106]—is, like the first, a melodramatic hebraization of mythological figures and serves to enhance a Jewish wedding in Vienna. It was published bilingually—in Hebrew and in Italian. The two allegories are balanced by two translations from the Italian: the tragedy *La Merope*[107] by Marchese Francesco Scipione Maffei (1675–1755) and the melodrama *Temistocle*[108] by Pietro Metastasio (1698–1782) who was a master of the genre and generously translated by Hebrew poets.[109] While the dramatic oeuvre of Romanelli can be squarely placed in the context of Italian and Hebrew literature in the eighteenth century, his personality defies classification. In his restless quest of personal and literary adventurism he resembles the man of the renaissance; in his passion for knowledge he is identical with the Hebrew writers in the period of enlightenment.

3
Leaders of Enlightenment: Mendelssohn and Wessely

Preamble: Movement and Movers

The Age of Reason is a convenient label for the eighteenth century. Like all intellectual labels it is too generalized to be true, too comprehensive not to contain a great deal of truth. Even a superficial perusal of the dominant figures of the period discloses an astonishing variety of men and women who cannot easily be identified as individuals guided by the lofty precepts of reason: Peter the Great, the ruthless despot; John Wesley, the zealot who founded Methodism; Casanova, the sexual maniac; Jean Jacques Rousseau, the compulsive preacher and non-practitioner of idealism in social and educational enterprises; Benjamin Franklin, the not-so-moral petit-bourgeois moralist.

But Reason with a capital R was believed to be the panacea for all ills. This naive belief in the manipulation of cause and effect was not new. The so-called Age of Faith—and this label applies to the vast expanse of the middle ages—used reason as an *ancilla*, a maidservant, to prove the validity of the theological certainties about God, creation out of nothing, immortality. In the eighteenth century Reason, the servant, assumed the role of mistress: even theological certainties were subjected to her august dissections and withering annihilations. But though some intellectuals in the eighteenth century advocated atheism, Voltaire (1694–1778) maintained that "If God did not exist, he would have to be invented."[1] And he even built a church on his estate with an inscription which lends itself to ironic interpretation: *Deo erexit Voltaire.*

The new role of Reason was prepared in the previous century by the new science and the new philosophy. Both were English in origin.

Isaac Newton laid the foundations which supported the edifice of physics for over three hundred years: his *Philosophiae naturalis principia mathematica* (Mathematical Principles of Natural Philosophy), published in 1687, revolutionized the theories of light and formulated the laws of gravitation and motion. Though his voluminous correspondence, unpublished till 1959, revealed a much more complex and subtle scientist than his contemporaries suspected, his originality was appreciated and his genius revered. The presidency of the Royal Society which he held since 1703 and which he guided with austere dignity made him a virtual dictator and arbitrator of western science.[2] And, though three centuries ago, the great contributions were made in mechanics, optics and planetary astronomy, science by its very nature must have meant three things: experimental observation, cumulative collection of many kinds of knowledge and a method of investigation by objective inquiry.

Of the philosophers John Locke was the most influential. In 1690, three years after the appearance of Newton's major work, he published his *Essay Concerning Human Understanding.* It is his contention that the mind is a *tabula rasa,* a blank slate at birth with no innate ideas. Personal experiences, inscribed on the mind from birth onward, are the bases of man's reasoning faculty. With these dicta Locke established the primacy of experiential and environmental factors in man's life.

Newton was supplemented and even superseded by Einstein, Locke's seminal ideas have become curiosities in the age of Freud. And recent researches—especially from the pens of Peter Laslett and John Dunn—have considerably deflated Locke's reputation. The "new" Locke is a Calvinist thinker, not a secular but a theological liberal with theological concerns, a firm believer in God's knowledge of the world as a priori knowledge rather than a firm empiricist. Yet the scientific and epistemological theories of Locke and Newton dominated the eighteenth century and developed a new way of life. Because of their influence, institutions and ideas—especially the church and the problem of faith, the monarchy and the problem of government—were subjected to refined analyses of reason. A few brilliant Frenchmen —Voltaire and Diderot (1713–1784) among them—imported the new science and the new philosophy into the European continent. The mordant wit of Voltaire and the relaxed irony of Diderot who eventually rose to the editorship of the prestigious *Encyclopédie* popularized them to such an extent that both official Christianity and the monarchical form of government became ripe for the executioner's axe. The ideas of Montesquieu on republican government accelerated the birth of the American and French revolutions with their emphasis on a reasonable view of society, with their call for liberty and equality before the law.

Writers inside and outside the *Encyclopédie* were not philosophers in the strict sense of the word though they claimed the title *philosophe*. They were rather encyclopedists, striving to attain a balanced view of society and a synthetic view of all human knowledge through the cooperation of the best contemporary minds in the *Encyclopédie* which was published between 1751 and 1776. They appealed to the educated classes—the intellectuals and the aristocrats—and they hoped that enlightened despots like Catherine II or Frederick the Great or Joseph II would put into practice what they preached. They were naive in their addiction to rationalism but sophisticated in their social life; they indulged in a vague deism but they preached secularization which is a nonreligious explication of the universe; they created a climate of simplistic beliefs about humanity and they promoted a world view in which reason and unreason, virtue and vice, liberty and slavery, justice and injustice operated not only as convenient categories but almost as absolutes. In short, humanity got explained in predictive patterns of behavior. For the literature of enlightenment aimed at inoffensive excellence; it avoided dullness but it lacked vigor, it was equable and easy rather than exciting and absorbing.

The most important writers of the eighteenth century—Voltaire and Rousseau—are only now being fully understood. Voltaire's works in the still unfinished edition of his biographer Theodore Besterman as well as Voltaire's notebooks and correspondence in the massive edition of Theodore Besterman, are monuments of scholarship which exceed and supersede the last edition of Voltaire's works by Moland in 1877–1885. His flair for the epigrammatic and devastating phrase, his libertarian zeal and the Gallic neatness of his logic have been properly proven and securely established. Less justly and somewhat sweepingly he is accused as the father of modern antisemitism: "the man who. . .provided a new international secular anti-Jewish rhetoric in the name of European culture rather than religion, was Voltaire."[3] The multivolume edition of the complete correspondence of Jean Jacques Rousseau, under the editorship of R.A. Leigh, will probably change our basic conceptions of the Genevan sage. He may emerge as the leading intellectual in the middle of the eighteenth century. But toward the end of the period of enlightenment Kant summarized its purpose in two Latin words: *Sapere aude*—Dare to know.

It was inevitable for enlightened Christians to propagate ideas of tolerance toward Jews. Before the end of the seventeenth century John Locke published his *Letters Concerning Toleration* which not only advocated tolerance but also expressed hope for conversion of Jews. In 1714 an anonymous pamphlet appeared in London under the title *Reasons for Naturalizing the Jews in Great Britain and Ireland*. The author, John Toland, dwelled on the military and naval prowess of Jews in ancient times and accorded them—*mirabile dictu*—good qualities in medieval and modern times. He dared to assert that "the Jews. . .partake of the nature of those nations among which they live. . ."[4] Before such later spokesmen for tolerance as Christian Dohm and Abbé Grégoire he pioneered his own brand of tolerance which was strongly influenced by Simone Luzzato's *Discorso*[5] published in Venice in 1638.[6] He demonstrated the economic usefulness of the Jews to the state and endeavored to destroy the prevalent ideas of Jewish immorality. But it is an ironic fact that the great prophets of enlightenment, Diderot and Voltaire, were highly intolerant toward Jews. Diderot censured them for their fanaticism, Voltaire for their "prejudices." But the sad truth is that the heirs of the inquisition and the possessors of the only source of salvation were deeply intolerant of Jewish divergence which frightened them and Jewish culture which escaped their knowledge. With these qualifications in mind it must be said, nevertheless, that egalitarian enlightenment, in fostering a critique of nations, religions and institutions, opened up a new era for Jewry: the segregated people was faced, for the first time in centuries, with the possibility of integration.

Enlightenment in Hebrew literature bore the name *Haskalah*— from the Hebrew word *Sekel* meaning reason. The believers and the devotees of the movement were *maskilim*, reasonable men, who wished to impose standards of reason on others. They were the imitators of the German imitators of the French enlightenment. What they had in common with them was a delight in criticism of accepted values. But since they had no land of their own, they confined their criticism to rabbinic religion mainly and, to lesser extent, to social and economic conditions of Jewry. In the criticism of their religion they were often timid. Since Hasidism, the pietist movement, became a force in eastern Europe by the middle of the eighteenth century, it served as a convenient target of their literary barbs. The excesses of Hasidism—quackery, drinking, blind faith in the wonder-rabbi, superstitious beliefs in ghosts and exorcism of ghosts—all these were mercilessly attacked. The devotees of Hasidism, the *Hasidim*, persecuted the *Maskilim* for their heresies and so-called atheism. It was an internecine and complicated war that lasted well into the end of the nineteenth century and, in some remote hamlets and townlets of eastern Europe, till the First World War. The traditionally orthodox who opposed Hasidism, the *Mitnaggedim* (Oppositionists) also fought it—and not too elegantly. Thus Hasidism had to fight on two fronts. But enlightenment also suffered attacks from two fronts though it was much more timid in its assaults on traditional orthodoxy than on hasidic neo-orthodoxy. In the early decades of the nineteenth century another factor complicated the fray—Reform. And though early Reform was as extreme as early enlightenment in its opposition to orthodoxy, they never joined ranks: each movement was fighting alone, each movement contributed to that parcelation of Judaism which is still its great weakness in the current century. While both wanted a modification of orthodoxy and integration with European society through emancipation, the enlightened were not willing to give up Hebrew as a cohesive force of Jewry. Early Reform, on the other hand, led to an emasculation and eventual abandoment of Hebrew as a language of prayer.

It was, indeed, a major contribution of enlightenment to Jewry that it lavished a renewed love on the Hebrew language. In their quest for lingual elegance the enlightened went—as their predecessors in Spain and Italy for many previous centuries—to the Bible as the only pure reservoir of the language. So devoted were they to the Bible that for almost one hundred years—between the middle of the eighteenth and the middle of the nineteenth century—they rarely used extrabiblical sources for their poetry and only occasionally for their prose. The result was ludicrous: language became a goal, thought was impoverished. Circumlocution in the form of biblical snippets—half-verses or quarter-verses—was the dominant style, pseudo-biblicism reigned supreme. The Hebrew language became deified: she was the august 'Ibriyyah, Dame Hebrew; she was *Bat ha-Shamayim*, the Daughter of Heaven. Eventually, the cultic view of language was superseded by a profane attitude through the use of post-biblical sources by the seminal novelists of the nineteenth and twentieth centuries—Mendele, Agnon and Hazaz. But though the adoration of biblical Hebrew must be regarded as an aberration rather than an innovation, it served as a fence around the language and a defense of its foremost source.

Perhaps it is a curiosity, perhaps it is a phenomenon that must be studied in depth: deviationism and dissentism in Jewish life tended to base themselves on the Bible. The Sadducees who could not stomach the oral law as conormative with the written law turned to the Bible for ammunition in their fight with the Pharisees. The sectarians of Qumran had a special scriptorium for copying their favorite biblical books. The Karaites who opposed the rabbinic exponents of Judaism looked to the Bible for their inspiration. The enlightened drew their lingual strength from the Bible. The Canaanites—that extremist fringe of Israeli literature—is also Bible-oriented. Die-hard conservatives and fiery revolutionists invoked the Bible as the justificatory document for their ideas. And that is why the talmudic sages who sensed the dangerous implications of biblical teachings advocated the relative safety of normative law.[7]

But the enlightened also cherished the Bible for another reason: It was the hollowed document of an idealized, non-existent age of nature. And the cult of the rural virtues became the vogue not only in Hebrew literature—through the influence of Moses Hayyim Luzzatto—but also in Italian literature which served him as a model and, somewhat later, in French and German literature. Guarini (1537–1612) and Tasso (1544–1595) extolled the virtues of rural life, Rousseau (1712–1778) who called for a return to nature and a revival of the virtues of natural man, Chautebriand (1768–1848) with his cult of the primitive, and especially Schiller (1759–1805) with his advocacy of the pastoral also channeled European literature into rural vistas.

The enlightened had—beside their cult of the Hebrew language—a great impact on the future of Hebrew literature. They were universalists; they advocated knowledge of the sciences and the arts; and they proposed to put that advocacy into effect through a vast work of translation from German and English, French and Russian, and even Latin and Greek literatures.

Moses Mendelssohn: Intellectual Leader of Enlightenment

All major tenets of Jewish enlightenment stem from Moses Mendelssohn (1729–1786). He is the sum and substance of his period. And his influence reaches beyond his period. Almost all ages in Jewish history are dominated by men who managed to express the deepest yearnings of their contemporaries and impress their personality on succeeding ages. The hellenistic period was epitomized by Philo, the tannaitic period by Judah the Prince, the amoraic period by R. Ashi, the gaonic period by Saadia, the Golden Age of Spain by Moses Maimonides, the renaissance by Leone Ebreo, the enlightenment by Mendelssohn. He was the "philosopher" of the movement in the sense that the great writers of the French enlightenment were called *philosophes*: a writer touching in his writings on contemporary problems and illuminating them with the light of classical philosophy and original aperçus. He was the modern translator of the Bible into German—in Hebrew characters—and its modern interpreter. He was the popularizer of the sciences and current philosophies. He was the educator of his age—through his collaboration with Friedländer—on the *Reader for Jewish Children*,[8] through his interest in nascent Jewish schools and especially through his translation of the Bible which was intended, first and foremost, for his own children; second, for a better understanding of the basic classic of Judaism and third, for the education of Jewry in pure German rather than in Yiddish. And he was also the father of Hebrew journalism.

It is a paradox of Hebrew literature that one of its important figures wrote almost exclusively in German. As a lad of twenty-one, Mendelssohn published his first literary effusions in Hebrew rather than in German. Together with his friend Tobias Bock he edited a short-lived weekly in Hebrew *Kohelet Musar* which lasted a fortnight. It was an imitation of the popular periodicals in England, the *Tatler* and the *Spectator*. And it reflected Mendelssohn's deep concern with the Hebrew language:

> Like slaves we have learned the language of our masters and we have forgotten our own . . . Have not our ancestors been sold as bondsmen and bondswomen to Egypt? Yet they have not forgotten their language. . .Let us learn from other nations. They neither rested nor were they at ease till they have widened the boundaries of their language. Why. . .not do like them to our own language which is first in rank and first in time?[9]

Excessive love of Hebrew characterized Mendelssohn and his successors. Even a poet of genuine merit like Joseph Efrati could write in the introduction to his play *The Reign of Saul* that his sole aim was "to widen the range of our own language." Lebensohn *père* and Judah Leb Gordon wrote ecstatic panegyrics in praise of the Hebrew language. And a contemporary poet like Abraham Regelson composed an ecstatic poem on the greatness and suppleness of Hebrew. This peculiar adoration was never shared by the orthodox majority which regarded Hebrew as a holy language and which suspected the incipient secularization of the language in Mendelssohn's time.

The demise of *Kohelet Musar* may have been due to the opposition of orthodoxy and to a lack of financial support through patrons and subscribers. But the experience had a profound effect on Mendelssohn: He gradually abandoned Hebrew as a vehicle of expression for his thoughts. Hence the paucity of his Hebrew writings: a few semipublic Hebrew letters to such well known contemporaries as N.H. Wessely, Avigdor Levi and Mendel Lefin of Satanov,[10] a Hebrew commentary on a minor treatise of logic by Maimonides, collaboration on the famous Hebrew commentary on the Pentateuch, possibly a treatise on the soul, a fragment of a Hebrew translation of his own *Phaedo*.[11]

Though Mendelssohn wrote his major works in German, he was a polemicist and an intercessor on behalf of his people, a defender of Judaism against its challenger, Christianity. In this sense he was continuing the medieval pattern of Jewish apologeticism. When the Swiss theologian Johann Caspar Lavater and later the convert Joseph Sonnenfels drew him, against his will, into controversial polemics on the merits of Christianity and even urged him to become a Christian, he proudly asserted his commitment to Judaism.[12] And he earned the respect of his Christian friends for his steadfast faith and influenced his friend Lessing to compose the famous drama of tolerance *Nathan the Wise*.[13] His treatise on the *Rites of the Jews*[14] was also a defensive tract on Jewish customs and ceremonies. And toward the end of his life, in 1783, he published his *magnum opus Jerusalem or About Religious Power and Judaism*[15] which had a seminal influence on the entire period of enlightenment and was, in a sense, a personal as well as an ethnic defense of Judaism.[16]

State and Religion—*Staat und Religion*: these are the opening words of *Jerusalem*. And the entire book seeks to determine the relationship between these two concepts and set precise boundaries to the sources of their authority. The State regulates relationships between man and man, religion—through the church—concerns itself with relationships between man and God. The State orders and compels, religion teaches and persuades. The State uses physical might, the power of religion rests on love and good deeds. The State can punish for certain deeds or rather misdeeds, but it must not punish for beliefs and opinions. The State cannot curb any individual's rights because his faith differs from others. The State, to put it tersely, concerns itself with man's acts, religion with man's being. Like some spokesmen of enlightenment in France and Germany, Mendelssohn sought to separate the authority of the State from the sphere of religion. Church and State were henceforth uncomfortable bedfellows when they were forced to dwell together. A divorce between the two entities seemed to be their predestined path of development in the coming century and, in America, in the same century.

The critics of Mendelssohn detected Christian influences in his emphasis on faith. But Mendelssohn asserted that Christianity was based on Judaism. The divine legislator, Moses, gave the Jews practical commandments which led to the fulfillment of ethical precepts. Ancient Judaism was a religious society; government and religion were one. When the Jewish state was destroyed, the power of punishment ceased to exist. The laws and traditions have still full relevance and binding power as moral obligations, but Jews cannot be punished for their transgressions. Excommunication should not be the business of religion: Those who were damned by church, synagogue or mosque were often more religious than their damners. With the passing of the Jewish state only the practical commandments—a divine gift—remained to the Jew. Even the founder of Christianity fulfilled the mosaic and the rabbinic precepts. The late disciples of Christ who wished to liberate Jews from the practical commandments, did so without authorization and without understanding. Mendelssohn would probably have deplored Spinoza's contention that Jewish laws had become obsolete with the disappearance of the Jewish State. In his opinion those who believe in the final victory of one faith are only deluding themselves: such a victory would entail religious compromises or hypocrisies. It was apparently not God's predestined plan to gather all sheep in one fold. One faith is not tolerance; it is the antithesis of tolerance. The varieties of thoughts and thinkers cannot lead to one eternal truth which also becomes the political truth. If citizenship or human rights for Jews depend on abandonment of Judaism, then it is better to forego citizenship and such rights. Mendelssohn sought to convince his readers that the tenets of Judaism were not antithethical to reason. Indeed, Judaism was for him the most perfect expression of the truth of rationalism.

Though one of his great French contemporaries, Mirabeau, thought that *Jerusalem* deserved to be translated into all European languages, Hebrew literature ignored it for more than eight decades. Many Hebrew writers, friends of Mendelssohn, read the book or heard about its contents from the author. It was translated twice in 1867 by Abraham Ber Gottlober and again, in 1876, by I.C. Grünberg who assumed the name of Wladimir Fedorow after his conversion to Christianity. And at that time it created a belated furor, for nationalist trends were beginning to replace the dominant ideas of enlightenment. And Hebrew writers accused Mendelssohn—unjustly—of reducing Judaism to a religious entity, of denying it nationhood or peoplehood, to use a more popular and modern phrase, of destroying the hope of ultimate redemption and of paving the way to assimilation or conversion. There was a basis for this accusation: Of the six surviving children out of the ten that were born to Mendelssohn all embraced Christianity, with the sole exception of the eldest son, Joseph.[17]

The only good Mendelssohn was alleged to have accomplished was an amelioration of the civil status of Jews. Unconsciously and unwittingly he created the philosophy of assimilation. *Jerusalem* served as justification of ways that led away from Judaism. For in his naiveté Mendelssohn regarded equality of rights and citizenship without restrictions as a solution to the Jewish problem. But it is also well and just to remember that his philosophical interpretation of Judaism inaugurated a line of German-Jewish philosophers in succeeding centuries: Hermann Cohen, Franz Rosenzweig and Martin Buber.

The chief detractor of Mendelssohn, Perez Smolenskin, was in turn attacked by admirers of the philosopher of Dessau, especially by his Hebrew translator, Abraham Ber Gottlober (1811-1899), Samuel Joseph Fünn (1818-1890) and Moses Leb Lilienblum (1843-1910). There were also middle-of-the-roaders like Simon Bernfeld who tried to present him as a characteristic representative of his period rather than its creator. And this, essentially, was also the position of Ahad Haam (1856-1927) who endeavored to reduce his stature to even smaller dimensions: Mendelssohn, in another time and another place, could have been an author of scholarly works like Joseph Solomon del Medigo of Candia or Menasseh ben Israel. He had neither the ambition nor the talent for greatness; he was a weakling but undeniably a gentle, erudite scholar and a man of taste.[18] But Mendelssohn was more than a scholar. He grew out of his time and impressed the seal of his personality on his time. His undue emphasis on practical observances was, of course, dangerous at a time when religion was losing its hold on the people. The non-observant drew their not-wholly-unwarranted conclusions from the writings of Mendelssohn and abandoned Judaism altogether.

The acerbated polemic for and against Mendelssohn toward the end of the seventies died down—though not altogether—in the next decade. The pogroms in Russia and the rise of nationalism dominated the minds of Jewish intellectuals at the time. But while the polemic lasted it was conducted with the relentless zeal that characterized the internecine strife around the philosophical works of Maimonides in the thirteenth century.

As a true leader in the age of enlightenment Mendelssohn transmitted classics of Hebrew literature to a wider readership. In his youth he translated the Zionide[19] of Judah Halevi and part of the *Examination of the World* of Yedayah ha-Penini. His translation of the *Pentateuch*, the *Song of Songs, Ecclesiastes* and the metric translation of *Psalms* was an educational work of primary importance. The *Interpretation*[20] was condemned by orthodoxy as a heretical work and it was the chief target of its attacks.

Translation was one of Mendelssohn's major literary activities. In addition to Pope's poetry he also rendered into German the famous monolog of Hamlet in the first scene of the third act. One of the later translators of Shakespeare into German, August Wilhelm Schlegel, retained words and phrases of his predecessor in his own classic translation.

Mendelssohn's love for the Bible was one of the factors that contributed to the new pseudo-biblical style which dominated Hebrew literature for one hundred years. Modern scholars have shown that the language of enlightenment was not as homogeneously biblical as it was previously assumed. Rabbinic and Tibbonic elements were freely used from Mendelssohn till Bialik. But *belles lettres* were overwhelmingly biblical in lingual inspiration. And so was the first important periodical in Hebrew literature, *The Gatherer (ha-Meassef)*. Mendelssohn collaborated with his friends and disciples who were the editors of the new periodical, but he contributed insignificant poetry and insignificant correspondence with Rabbi Jacob Emden, some old articles which had been published in *Kohelet Musar* and, possibly, two fables for juvenile minds.

The name of Mendelssohn on the entrance door of enlightenment is Jewish but his writings are German. And he had no contact with his great Jewish contemporaries, the Baal Shem Tov who fathered Hasidism and the Gaon of Vilna who inaugurated a renaissance of rabbinic learning and teaching. Not only are his works German but he is the first German writer of Jewish extraction who figures prominently and permanently in German literature as the philosopher of German enlightenment. The Jewish physician Aaron Emmerich Gumpertz had introduced him to Gotthold Ephraim Lessing (1729-1781) in 1754. And the friendship with the German writer became a seminal event in German literature.

Mendelssohn's *Philosophical Conversations*[21]—his first published

German work—owed its publication to Lessing. His tract *Metaphysician Pope*[22] was written jointly with Lessing. Numerous other disquisitions were either products of collaboration or owed their inspiration to Lessing. And the last essay of Mendelssohn—another major defense of Judaism after the polemic with Lavater—bore the title *To Lessing's Friends*.[23] His relationship with Lessing was a case of mutual admiration and influence. Lessing's theory of art in *Laokoon* owes Mendelssohn more than is generally conceded. And Lessing's famous play and plea for tolerance *Nathan the Wise* is probably a tribute to Mendelssohn. The chief character bears a family resemblance to the Jewish philosopher. The German writer, it should be pointed out, had written as a young man a play by the name of *The Jews*.[24] And he was chided at the time by his contemporaries for creating a noble Jew in German drama. Johann David Michaelis, the orientalist at the University of Göttingen, thought that such a Jew was perhaps not an impossible but surely an improbable individual.

Mendelssohn, who developed his fine sensitivity to style through his contact with Lessing, became one of the great molders of the German language. It was also Lessing who interested him in Rousseau's ideas. But Mendelssohn had only words of condemnation for the sentimental novel of Rousseau, *La Nouvelle Héloise*, which charmed the literary circles of Europe. Yet, rationalist that he was, he still possessed an emotional admixture, a warmth which was, perhaps, the secret of his popular success. In a letter to his wife-to-be, Fromet Gugenheim, he praised her delicacy of expression, her true, natural emotionalism.[25] And it was no accident that he wrote about the emotions[26] and sought to determine the nature of pleasure. The contemplation of beauty, he thought, was not only the most characteristic trait of man; it was his mode of cognition, *Erkentniss*. Finally, through Lessing, Mendelssohn met Friedrich Nicolai who edited an important German periodical and induced him to become its distinguished contributor.

Mendelssohn was not an original philospher. He made it abundantly clear that he was not ambitious to create a new system of philosophy but rather enhance the philosophies of Leibnitz, Wolff and, to a certain extent, Spinoza.[27] Yet he made an enormous impression on his times. Princes of the spirit and princes of the blood sought the company of this unprepossessing, hunchbacked man. Lessing, Nicolai, Wieland, Herder, Kant and even the great Goethe were among his admirers. And so were the hereditary prince Wilhelm von Braunschweig and his mother Philippine Charlotte who was a sister of Frederick the Great, Count Wilhelm von Schaumburg-Lippe and the Duchess of Kurland,

Elise von der Recke. For Mendelssohn was not only an exotic curiosity; he was learned and witty and brilliant, and he possessed the gift of self-mockery. Thus, in a few verses, he commended himself to his contemporaries: they admired the stuttering orator, Demosthenes, the hunchbacked creator of fables, Aesop; since he united both characteristics in his person, the hunchback and the stutterer, he claimed to be doubly great and wise.

Only the "enlightened" monarch of Prussia, Frederick the Great, gave him grudging recognition. The Marquis d'Argens, the court philosopher, pleaded with him to accord Mendelssohn the right of residence in Berlin. The recommendation of the marquis is worth quoting:

> A philosopher who is a bad Catholic implores a philosopher who is a bad Protestant to accord the privilege of residence to a philosopher who is a bad Jew. There is too much philosophy in all this; reason cannot but support the petition.[28]

It was this witty commendation of Mendelssohn's petition which gained him personally—and not his descendants—the right of residence as a protected Jew.[29] On another occasion Frederick the Great denied him the privilege of membership in the Berlin Academy of Sciences. And he was chided for importing sophists from France and neglecting an indigenous Plato or rather "the German Socrates"—a sobriquet which became associated with Mendelssohn after the publication of his *Phaedo*.[30] In his philosophical work on the immortality of the soul Socrates speaks, in Mendelssohn's own characterization, "like a sage from the seventeenth or eighteenth century," like an exponent of "rational psychology" which was established by Christian Wolff. This is as clear in his youthful tract on metaphysics "About Proof in Metaphysical Sciences"[31] which earned him the first prize—a sum of fifty ducats—from the Berlin Academy of Sciences as in his last work *Morning Hours* or *Lectures About the Existence of God*.[32] Kant also competed for the prize of the Berlin Academy of Sciences. It was a challenging theme: "Are metaphysical truths capable of such proof as mathematical truths?" And though his treatise was more original and more thorough, he received the second prize. Mendelssohn was the traditionalist and he won the applause of his fellow traditionalists in the Berlin Academy of Sciences; the groves of Academe are not hospitable to the winds of change.

Schooled in the theories of Descartes and Spinoza, Leibnitz and

Christian Wolff and Baumgarten, Locke and Shaftesbury, Voltaire and d'Alembert, Mendelssohn wrote out of the fullness of contemporary thought and out of a frantic commitment to the ideals of enlightenment rather than out of saturation with classical thought. But he was also nurtured—perhaps chiefly and above all—by Jewish classics and by the ethical universalism which characterizes so much of Jewish thought. And in strict adherence to the minutiae of Jewish observances he hardly differed from R. Moses Isserles, the illustrious popularizer of the *Shulhan 'Aruk* from whom he claimed descent.

When Mendelssohn died he was hailed by no less a man than Herder as "the philosopher of the German nation and language." Among Jews he came to be revered as the third Moses[33]—after Moses the law-giver and Moses Maimonides. This was a high compliment, indeed, for the enlightened regarded Moses Maimonides with awe.[34] But Mendelssohn lacked the mystic fervor of the makers of religion and the original insights into the eternal problems of mankind which mark the true philosopher. His ideas on Judaism, on philosophy, on literary criticism, on esthetics are superannuated.

It is, perhaps, not too much to claim him as a forerunner of the *Jüdische Wissenschaft* which sought to interpret Judaism objectively and scientifically.[35] With his translation of the *Pentateuch* and other portions of the Bible he paved the way for the various refinements of German biblical translations by Bernfeld, Tur-Sinai and Rosenzweig-Buber in our time. He will live as the liberator of Jewry from the physical and spiritual ghetto.

N.H. Wessely: The Poetic Herald of Enlightenment

Naphtali Hartwig (Herz) Wessely (1725–1805), the poet and friend and disciple of Mendelssohn, was a more potent figure in Hebrew literature than his master. Though he lacked philosophical insight and poetical acumen, though his intellectual interests were narrow, almost parochial, he played, paradoxically, a predominant role in the development of Jewish enlightenment. His voluminous epic on Moses, with its plagiaristic echoes of Klopstock's leaden and boring *Messias*, was regarded as a model of purist poetry. Its rhythms, its rhymes, its metre, its vocabularly, were imitated by countless poetasters for over a hundred years. Today it is a neglected classic: its poverty of imagery, imagination and invention, and its slavish adherence to the biblical account of Moses have made Wessely's epic one of the most perishable products of the Hebrew muse. Unabashed didacticism motivated the poet. The purpose of his epic was "not to show off sweetness of poetry or purity of diction but...to guide people...to a deeper understanding of the Pentateuchal stories..."[36] And in the general introduction he adumbrated his full intent in an unmistakable phrase: "to interpret the words of our God by way of poetry."

A naïve characterization must be added to the faults of Wessely's epic: the Jews are "seed of truth," "a beautiful vine"; the Egyptians lack wisdom. Similarly, the leader of the Jews, Moses, is characterized in numerous passages of the epic as a paragon of wisdom, Pharaoh as a hardhearted fool. This simplistic attitude to people was to plague the novel, the play, the epic poetry during the nineteenth century: Abraham Mapu's protagonists were either black or white, and so were the dramatis personae in the elder Lebensohn's play *Truth and Faith*[37] or in Judah Leb Gordon's narrative poems. In its time Wessely's epic was considered an event of primary importance in Hebrew literature; it was even translated into German by two Christian scholars, J.J. Spalding and G.F. Hufnagel.[38] Literary fashions and literary tastes change with the rapidity of sartorial fashions and tastes.

Wessely's tract in prose, *Words of Peace and Truth*,[39] was of much greater importance for the immediate future—especially for the subsequent education of young Jews—than his epic. Historically, it was an instant and enthusiastic reaction to the famous Patent of Toleration which was promulgated by Joseph II in 1781. Since Wessely realized that a major intellectual opportunity would open for Jews, he endeavored to destroy prejudices against secular education. He argued in *Words of Peace and Truth* as well as in his *Wine of Lebanon*,[40] a commentary on the *Sayings of Fathers*—and he adduced a generous amount of quotations from rabbinic literature—that there is a distinction between human learning and divine laws. The written and the oral law, enshrined in the Bible and in the rabbinic sources, belong to the divine category; general disciplines like history and geography, mathematics and languges, natural sciences, behavioral and moral knowledge were in the human category. But Wessely stressed an important point: human learning precedes divine laws. Therefore, general knowledge antedates religious knowledge. Persecution and poverty caused neglect of secular study among Jews. With the prospective relaxation and liberalization of Western society, Jews will wish to take their rightful place in their native countries. They will, therefore, do well to study languages again since they are not conversant either with their native language or with Hebrew. The study of the Bible—and this is another point of importance—without knowledge of history is an exercise in futility. And the study of the Talmud without the knowledge of natural sciences leads to an inadequate understanding of Jewish law. Wessely dared to insist that the Talmud was not a suitable subject of study for all Jewish children. He recommended that those who have no special talents for that difficult subject should study the Bible, the Mishnah which is the easier, the more comprehensible part of the Talmud, ethics and some general subjects.

Orthodoxy reacted strongly. The Gaon of Vilna approved the public burning of the book. Another contemporary rabbi, Ezekiel Landau, called Wessely "an evil man." Others heaped upon him such denunciatory epithets as despicable, hypocritical, boorish, foolish. Few rabbis or lay leaders of Jewry dared to say a good word about him.

Wessely answered his critics in subsequent tracts which were amplifications of *Words of Peace and Truth*. But he was depressed and dejected. Outside of a few elementary schools in Berlin and in Trieste which adopted some of his recommendations, Jewish education remained what it was: an unrelieved, centuries-old preoccupation with the Talmud. Ultimately Wessely won: The need for secular education became an overwhelming necessity. The leaders of the enlightenment —with Wessely in the vanguard—paved the way for the modernization of Jewish education in this century.

4
The Pioneering Generations of the Enlightened: 1783–1832

Three graceful poets: Efrati, Löwisohn, Letteris

1783 is an *annus mirabilis* in Jewish history and it may be said to herald the nineteenth century for three reasons. First, it marks the publication of the first influential periodical—*ha-Meassef*—in Hebrew literature. Second, Moses Mendelssohn's *Jerusalem,* as well as his translation of the *Pentateuch* and *Psalms,* appeared in that year. Third, it is the date of the emergence of the United States as a separate political entity at the end of the American Revolution.

The periodical *ha-Meassef* disseminated the new ideas of enlightenment by reason rather than by faith; Mendelssohn's *Jerusalem* proclaimed the right of the Jew to unrestricted freedom of conscience and equality with others before the law, while his translations introduced his coreligionists into the arcana of a Western language; the United States gave political sanction to the ideas of liberty and equality of all men.

In 1832, the periodical *Bikkure ha-'Ittim* (First Fruits of the Times), the successor to *ha-Meassef,* expired.[1] The succeeding periodicals—*Kerem Hemed, Kokebe Yizhak, Ozar Nehmad, ha-Maggid* and *ha-Meliz*—were repetitive in tone and frequently redundant in content. Thus the early thirties can be regarded as the end of the pioneering generations in the period of enlightenment.

If the early eighteenth century has been called a period of "general barbarization of Jewry" by no less an authority than Graetz,[2] the early nineteenth century may be designated as a period of general

88

barbarization of Hebrew literature. With the sole exception of three graceful poets, Joseph Efrati (1770?-1804), Solomon Löwisohn (1789-1821) and Meir Halevi Letteris (1800?-1871)[3] who wrote some deathless poetry, no creative spark illumined the myriads of verses which marred the books and periodicals of that time. And Efrati made his reputation with one play *The Reign of Saul*.[4] It suffers from diversionary monologs on the pursuit of happiness à la Rousseau and a complicated, unfocused plot; it suffers from flowery language; it suffers from close reliance on the biblical texts of *Samuel* I and II. And alert critics have detected other influences: Shakespeare and Racine, Goethe and Schiller, a minor Swiss poet Albrecht von Haller, Moses Hyyim Luzzatto and Naphtali Herz Wessely.[5] Yet, in spite of these strictures, the play unrolls the main conflict between Saul, the royal figure and David, the pastoral and poetic figure. From its inception—the harsh aftermath of the victory over Amalek—to Saul's death on the mountains of Gilboa, the play moves with tragic predestination. Certain biblical personages like David are idealized. Others like Ahinoam, Saul's wife who is mentioned in *Samuel* I, 14:50, is created almost *ex nihilo*. She is the personification of loyalty; her mission in life is the happiness of her husband. She worries about him even when she bewails her own fate:

Is this my doleful lot, the king's wife's lot,
To go from grief to grief, from woe to woe? . . .
I know Saul's war-webbed heart:
He will not stop to face the archers of the foe.
Who knows what will befall him in the clash of arms?[6]

In spite of Efrati's emphasis on Saul's envious character and paranoid persecution mania, the play exudes a general atmosphere of optimism: this world is the best of all possible worlds; the just get their just rewards; the instinctual drives succumb to rationalist judgments. Or to put it in Efrati's own words in the introduction to the play: "This book is suffused with moral intent..." Like so many poets before and after him Efrati was fascinated by the tragic king who was a popular figure in the literatures of the world from the days of the renaissance to our own time. Hans Sachs, immortalized in Wagner's opera *Die Meistersinger von Nürnberg* consecrated one of his two hundred and eight plays to Saul. Ten years before the publication of *The Reign of Saul*, Vittorio Alfieri published his neo-classical play *Saul*. And although no connection can be established between the two plays, their mere contemporaneity arouses curiosity and interest. In our own time Karl Wolfskehl, André Gide, Howard Nemerov and, in Hebrew literature, Saul Tschernichowsky devoted their literary energies to the fissured soul of Saul.

Solomon Löwisohn also began his literary career with a dramatic piece, *A Dialog in the Soul-Realm*.[7] This was a quaint discussion between David Kimhi, the medieval grammarian and commentator and Joel Bril, Löwisohn's contemporary, on the merits of the Hebrew verb. Though Löwisohn continued with grammatical and, later, with geographical and historical researches, he found his poetic vocation and fulfilment in his most important book, *The Poetry of Israel*.[8]

This critical evaluation of biblical poetry—with comparatist examples from classic and modern poetry— was a unique contribution to the esthetics and poetics of the period. For Löwisohn judged the Bible as a human document of literary dimensions rather than a divine document with unquestioned literary and moral authority. *The Poetry of Israel* also presented, for first time in Hebrew literature, the translation of a Shakespearean passage: the monolog or rather the ode to sleep from the first scene of the third act in the Second Part of King Henry IV. Löwisohn made good use of Herder's book *Of The Spirit of Hebrew Poetry*.[9] But the drift of his sensitivity is as original as it is startling for his times. The famous introduction—the Monolog of poetry in verse-form—is a sublime monument to Löwisohn's lyric strength. It presents Beauty as one of the earliest creations of God. And Poetry, the daughter of Beauty, is commended by God in the beginning of time to be the constant companion of man:

> Descend to earth, and be a plaything
> to man. Be also queen of all
> his thoughts. I made him ruler
> of all the earth's creatures. I made you
> ruler over him and all his generations.[10]

This regal might and moving power of poetry is described by Löwisohn with uncommon vigor; it is poetry that inspires great deeds; it is poetry that changes cruelty to pity; it is poetry that strengthens the weak in battle, that dissolves hatred, that consoles the bitter heart. For poetry dwells everywhere—from one end of the world to the other.

In the graceful Italianate metre of alternating decasyllabics and hexasyllabics Löwisohn has created a double ode to beauty and poetry which is one of the glories of Hebrew literature.

Meir (Max) Halevi Letteris was one of the few nineteenth century Hebrew writers who had an academic education and earned a Ph. D. at the University of Prague. He wrote and edited periodicals in German; he translated from the works of Racine, Schiller and Byron. His paraphrase of the first part of Goethe's *Faust*[11] is a literary curiosity that has been superseded by Hebrew versions of J.L. Baruch and Jacob Cahan. Moreover, it is neither a good translation nor a good paraphrase. And, already in the lifetime of Letteris, it was bitterly attacked by Solomon Mandelkern, the poet and the author of the biblical concordance, as well as by Perez Smolenskin, the novelist and essayist. The real claim of Letteris to fame rests on a few lyrics which have not lost their freshness. Poems like "Moaning Dove"[12] or "Waves"[13] have a scintillating, dancing movement. The latter is a parable: Life's pleasures are as fleeting as the waves of the sea. The former is an allegory: Jewry is like a weak dove wandering from land to land, wondering about God her lover who has abandoned her for her treacheries.[14] The poet fascinated Hebrew readers with the grace and simplicty of his verse. After the leaden periods of a Wessely or a Shalom Cohen or Lebensohn *père* the verses of Letteris had the effect of a spring breeze in Hebrew poetry.

Scholars as Poets

Not only poets but scholars who still enjoy enviable reputations, Solomon Judah Rapoport (1790-1867) and Samuel David Luzzatto (1800-1865), produced large quantities of undistinguished verse.[15] A monotony of form and content was the inevitable result. The six-line stanza, used by Naphtali Herz Wessely in lyrical sections of his epic *Songs of Glory,* by Joseph Efrati in some sections of his play *The Reign of Saul* and by Abraham Dov Ber Lebensohn (1789-1878) in his most ambitious poem "Pity"[16] with depressing regularity of rhyme and syllable count, dominated most narrative poetry for a hundred years up to and including Bialik's time. Not only solemn and sublime themes but trivial subjects, mere *pièces d'occasion,* were cast in six-line stanzas. Shalom Cohen, for instance, celebrated the appointment of Solomon Judah Rapoport to the rabbinate of Tarnopol in eastern Galicia with a poem of ten six-line stanzas.[17] Abraham Goldberg published two satirical poems of considerable length in stanzas of six lines: one in seventy-six stanzas, the other in forty-one stanzas.[18] And as late as 1868 a series of elegies was composed in six-line stanzas by

Moses Danzig.[19] Even a treatise on chess, reminiscent of the famous poem of Abraham Ibn Ezra on the subject, was tortured into that unhappy mold.[20] The four-line stanza, with slight variations, dominated most lyric effusions beyond Bialik's time. Content was usually didactic, though a variety of themes compensated for the poverty of rhythm and rhyme. To put it bluntly: the poems were not poems. When Leopold Zunz (1794–1886) wrote in his very first scholarly article that "in our time the Jews . . . are witnessing the funeral of the neo-Hebraic literature,"[21] he may have not only had the rabbinic but also the poetic output in mind.[22]

On the other hand, all attempts to exonerate the pedestrian pedantry of Hebrew poets in the early years of the nineteenth century must end in failure. It is because of the perseverance of naive critics of literature that such attempts have been made at the end of the eighteenth century by the liberal French cleric, Abbé Grégoire, in the early decades of the nineteenth century by Franz Delitzsch, in mid-century by Heinrich Graetz, and in our own time by Joseph Klausner. The authority of Delitzsch contributed to the favorable reception of poets who first concentrated their efforts in ha-Meassef.[23] They formed, in his opinion, a small republic of brilliant scholars and poets who raised the Jews to an equal level of culture with Germans "at the very least."[24] Abbé Grégoire thought that they would help to bring about the regeneration of their people and that they announced "the dawn of a beautiful day."[25] If one remembers that Schiller died in 1805, that Goethe was still an active force in German literature in the first two decades of the previous century, that Heine had published his first book of poems in 1821, one can only wonder at an enthusiasm run amuck. Delitzsch and Abbé Grégoire were the gentile dealers in hyperboles. Graetz valued a poet of limited abilities like Eliyahu Halfon Halevi (1760-1826) above Gabirol and Judah Halevi and Moses Hayyim Luzzatto.[26] Even Zinberg, a more cautious critic than Graetz, thought highly of E.H. Halevi's poem "Peace"[27] which, in forty-nine five-line stanzas, extolled the greatness of Napoleon.[28] Klausner, although he would not rate Halevi as highly as Graetz did, accorded him high praise.[29] For he pleaded the cause of early Hebrew versifiers and he even waxed enthusiastic over lines and stanzas of Wessely in praise of Mendelssohn which no critical sensitivity could excuse or tolerate; the poem "In Praise of a Friend"[30] was in his estimation the creation of an inspired poet.

Bilingual Authors

Exaggerated evaluations were also accorded to Shalom ben Jacob Cohen (1772?-1845), one of the editors of *ha-Meassef* and *Bikkure ha-'Ittim*,[31] the arbiter of literary taste and the central figure in Hebrew poetry after Wessely. He began his writing career with didactic *Proverbs of Agur*[32] in Hebrew and German; he continued with a collection of poems *Plants of the Orient on Northern Soil*,[33] again in Hebrew and German; he then published his allegory *Amal and Tirzah*,[34] "the first social drama in Hebrew"[35] and a slavish imitation of Luzzatto's *Praise to the Upright.* This poetic output was crowned with the voluminous epic on David,[36] an acknowledged derivative of a derivative: an imitation of Wessely's epic which in turn stems from Klopstock's *Messias.*[37] In the subtitle, the poet characterized the epic as "Songs of Glory[38] . . .to David son of Jesse." Incidentally, the first poem in *Plants of the Orient on Northern Soil* is also called "Song of Glory."[39] Shalom Cohen lived all his life in the shadow of a shadow. And yet Isaac Erter, who had the gift of mockery, called him "sweet singer of our generation," as he himself was later called "sweet satirist of Israel." And Letteris sang his praises in an uninspired epitaph.[40] Lesser luminaries like Gabriel Berger consciously imitated him. *Sweet Plants from the Land of the East, Planted in the Soil of the West*[41]—this is the title of his volume of verses that retell in measured lines biblical episodes: the story of Creation, Paradise, Adam and Eve, Cain and Abel, Noah, Abraham and Isaac on Mount Moriah, Jacob and Joseph, Moses on Mount Horeb.

Like their numerous predecessors, Shalom Cohen and his leading contemporaries were bilingual writers. This is not a remarkable fact. Bilingualism has a long tradition in Hebrew literature: it begins with biblical writers and continues to our own day, but usually the bilingual writer wrote poetry in Hebrew and prose in another language. Thus the medieval Jewish poet-philosophers of Spain reserved philosophy for Arabic and poetry for Hebrew. Shalom Cohen wrote the self-same things in two languages. Not only did *Proverbs of Agur* and *Plants of the Orient on Northern Soil* appear in both Hebrew and German but the very title page of the first *Bikkure ha'Ittim* was printed in Hebrew and German (in Hebrew letters).[42] And the German text delineated the functions of the periodical with greater precision. Shalom Cohen as well as his contemporaries had little faith in the Hebrew language as a vehicle of communication. Though his introductory poem to *Bikkure ha-Ittim* expresses hope for the eventual flowering of "the garden of

Hebrew," it is pessimistic in tone: "nettles cover its face."[43] David Samość who published an anthology of translations and his own poetry under the title *Drops of Poetry*[44] in a bilingual edition, expressed the hope in his introduction that "days will come when the Hebrew language will be loved. . . .and not abandoned." This alternation of despair and hope became the dominant attitude toward the Hebrew language in the nineteenth century.

Lack of faith in Hebrew was one reason for the bilingualism of Hebrew poets in the beginning of the nineteenth century. Another was their childish belief in knowledge as a redemptive tool and in knowledge of German as a guarantee of intelligence and intellectuality. One who could write German was already a superior being. But neither bilingualism nor naive rationalism was conducive to the production of poetry. With few notable exceptions Hebrew poetry *qua* poetry ceased to exist in the early years of the nineteenth century.

That the public also tired of the verses of poetasters is evident from the simple fact that the annual *Bikkure ha'Ittim* published less verse than had its precursor, *ha-Meassef*. And the successor to the former, *Kerem Hemed* (1833-1856), published almost no verse. That did not discourage the versifiers who assembled their products in many volumes at their own expense or at the expense of solicited "friends." Graetz is wrong in thinking that the contributors to *Kerem Hemed* felt that this was no time "to dilly-dally (*tändeln*) in verse, to write Hebrew plays or dialogs in rhyme, to offer Racine or Schiller, Petrarch or even Anacreon in Hebrew form. . ."[45] They continued to produce poetry, but they published only their scholarly research in *Kerem Hemed.*

Though the Hebrew poems of the early nineteenth century were no poems or non-poems, they had parapoetic value, which must be sought alongside the poems.[46] They occupy a zone beside poetry in all ages and in all civilized countries. Just as medieval philosophy, which was theology to a large extent, projected preconceived ideas about the universe in massive structures of logic, so the poetry of enlightenment succeeded in fixing certain ideas of the age in the minds of people. In this century we need no proof to show that jingles, verses, lyrics, incantatory phrases, and proverbial sentences have served indiscriminately to advertise the products of industry and the products of intellect. Sociologists and psychologists and cyberneticists have combined to use new techniques for processes of information, influence, and even indoctrination. And they have often succeeded in producing planned emotional results.

Biblical Idiom

The entire body of early nineteenth century Hebrew poetry served four main purposes and succeeded in popularizing them to a far greater extent than prose: It bent the Hebrew language to biblical idiom in the mistaken notion that only the Bible was a source of linguistic purity; it encouraged secular education as a means of intellectual, social, and economic assimilation; it indulged in translation from European languages, and it regarded them as an effective vehicle of enlightenment; it fought against Hasidism, though it did not join ranks with its opponents, the *Mitnaggedim.*

It is not mere coincidence that the first four editors of *ha-Meassef* —Isaac (Isak) Euchel, Mendel Breslau, Simon and Sanwil (Seinwel) Friedländer—stood at the helm of a cultural organization in Königsberg which called itself "Society for the Exploration of Hebrew."[47] But they were conscious that Hebrew was an exotic importation. In contradistinction to contemporary Hebrew poets who have deliberately occidentalized their imagery and even their syntax, the Hebrew poets of the last century hewed closely to biblical idiom and biblical grammar. The Bible was their exclusive source of inspiration during most of the nineteenth century. Foreign classics were imitated, but they were throughly adapted to biblical prototypes. Even translations adopted biblical idiom and biblical form. Marcus Rothberg, for instance, rendered the hexameters of Goethe's *Hermann und Dorothea* into biblical vocabulary and biblical parallelism.[48]

Subject matter was also biblical in inspiration: Moses was the subject of Wessely's epic. Abraham, David, Nabot of Jezreel—these were the subjects of Cohen's poetry. The language, except for grammatical mistakes, was thoroughly biblical. That is why "post-biblical poetry" is more than a chronological term; it is a value-laden term. The *Hymns of Thanksgiving* in the Dead Sea Scrolls, the poems of Kalir, the entire body of Hebrew poetry in the Spanish, the French, and the Italian middle ages is biblical in style. It is a continuum almost deadening in its uniformity. For more than two thousand years biblical poetry was normative and authoritative in language and in style, a fountain of beauty and a source of religion. And post-biblical poetry was merely a poetical commentary on a poetical appendix to biblical poetry. This was especially true of Hebrew poetry in the nineteenth century. When the Hebrew language was mentioned or singled out for praise in that period, biblical idiom was meant and biblical idiom was used. And since the Bible was regarded as a divine rather than a human document, the language of the Bible was not only a holy language but "a sweet and beautiful language" in the words of Samuel David Luzzatto,[49] an ancient sapphire in the words of Cohen,[50] "our life and length of days" in the words of Letteris.[51] In time it came to mean the alpha and omega of Hebrew literature, language for language's sake, phrase-mongering of the worst kind. *How* beautifully and closely to the biblical idiom something was expressed—that was of prime importance; *what* was expressed—that was essentially of subsidiary value. Hence the many praises of an author's language in the various introductions or in the commendations[52] and hence the numerous odes to the Hebrew language in works which had no relation to linguistics except the fact that they were written in Hebrew. The cult of biblical figures of speech, especially homonyms, was carried to ridiculous lengths by Solomon Pappenheim (1740-1814) in his lengthy poem *Legend of Four Cups*—a threnody à la Young.

This ecstatic attitude to biblical idiom was taken for granted by the poets and even by a critic like Delitzsch, who thought that Hebrew lost vitality when it abandoned its biblical word-structures and imagery. It is this criterion which impelled him to accord greatness to poetasters like Rafael Fürstenthal (1781-1855) and Aaron Wolfsohn (1754-1835). An earlier poet, David Franco Mendes, was regarded by him as the greatest of modern Hebrew poets because he based his work on Jewish tradition, not on Olympian gods or superficial deism.[53]

The roots of the unsophisticated poets in the early decades of Hebrew enlightenment were biblical, their pattern of thought was Hebraic. Even Wessely, an innovator in educational theory, insisted on a better knowledge of German only because reading a German translation of the Bible would lead to a deeper knowledge of its language and contents.

Successive generations of Hebrew poets did not abandon his theories. But they sometimes carried their zeal for non-Hebrew languages and secular education to points of no return: to complete assimilation or even conversion. Since most of them were teachers, they were ideally suited to influence their charges. Shalom Cohen proudly announced his occupation on the title-page of one of his books: "Teacher of Ethics and Hebrew at the Jewish Free School in Berlin."[54] He also tried, unsuccessfully, to establish a modern school in London. Joseph Perl was the founder and director of an exemplary Jewish school in his native Tarnopol in eastern Galicia.[55] Samość, who was a teacher—he even wrote an elegy on the death of one of his pupils—produced a biting sestet on idiotic students who would be better off as shepherds: they should listen to the song of birds rather than frequent the homes of teachers in vain.[56] He also described the pupils' ordeal on the day when educational inspectors or supervisors came to visit and discharge their official functions.[57] Bernhard Schlesinger, author of a drama *The Hasmoneans*[58] and translator of fragments from Klopstock's *Messias*, taught in the Bohemian town of Kolin. All these poet-teachers accomplished a revolution in educational practice; they contributed to the gradual deterioration of the *Heder* and the *Yeshivah*. And they were in no small measure responsible for the emergence of a new type of Jew: nontraditional, domiciled in the culture of his environment rather than in the ancestral culture.

Secular Education

Education, of course, was based on the rationalist attitude to *Hokmah* which connoted more than wisdom in the nineteenth century. It was regarded as a divine instrument which was placed by a benevolent deity at the disposal of human beings, a powerful force, a devouring fire.[59] The poems in *ha-Meassef*, as announced in the programmatic proclamation,[60] were to disseminate *Hokmah*, morality, and friendship.[61] And before the end of the century Joseph Efrati had King David address *Hokmah* as "the oar of the world" in the beautiful monolog in the play *The Reign of Saul*; the movements of *Hokmah* direct all life in animate nature; the movements of *Hokmah* direct man's life after death and his wanderings from world to world.[62] In later times Abraham Ber Gottlober prayed for the union of religion and *Hokmah*.[63] The absorbing drama of the middle ages—the clash and fusion of philosophy and faith—was being played again on a different stage of history, with different characters and different arguments.

In the first canto of *The Songs of Glory* Wessely turns to God in order to draw pearls from the sea of God's *Hokmah*.[64] Abraham is full of *Hokmah*.[65] The heart of Moses is like a flowing fountain of wisdom.[66] All men should search for *Hokmah*; the lovers of wisdom are loved by God, and those who are loved by Him shall not lack the good things of this earth. Though this is a naive belief in divine reward at its crassest, a certain nobility of concept accompanies this belief; all men are created in order to become wise and do good.[67] In the poetical introduction to his lexicographical work *Lebanon* Wessely calls *Hokmah* his sister, the very image of God's goodness, the balance in the hands of God.[68] The entire book is devoted to the tedious elucidation of the root *Hakam* in the Bible. And whatever light the talmudic sages and medieval philosophers shed on that fateful vocable is adduced with merciless thoroughness.

Succeeding poets often began their book with odes to *Hokmah:* Isaac Ber Levinsohn (1788-1860) published an ecstatic apotheosis of *Hokmah* as a preamble to *Instruction in Israel.*[69] David Samość, in an unpaginated introduction to his *Drops of Poetry* made the epigrammatic statement: "He who despises *Hokmah* will not prosper." He also wrote a bilingual poem in praise of wisdom: He who acquires wisdom finds happiness, joy, success, and comfort.[70] In short, he attains superhuman status.

Hebrew rationalists—in prose and poetry—were mild and conservative counterparts of their German and French confrères. There was among then no Voltaire with mordant wit, no radical Baron d'Holbach who spurned religion and denied the need of theology. Their brand of enlightenment and common sense was propagated by such philosophers of the eighteenth century as Jean le Rond d'Alembert, who consistently considered his age as *l'age des lumières.* Forthem reason meant progress, development of science, restratification of society. It meant tolerance as conceived in Pierre Bayle's *Dictionnaire historique et critique* and in John Locke's *Letters on Toleration.* It meant democracy and the right of the people to govern themselves as propounded in Jean Jacques Rousseau's *Contrat social.* But it was not an unmixed and undiluted rationalism: Rousseau was not only the father of the French Revolution but also the begetter of romanticism. The irrationality of many spokesmen for rationalism can be convincingly argued and easily demonstrated.[71] In poetry there were few romantic excesses a hundred and fifty years ago. Nature was celebrated in its usual aspects. The seasons of the year, day and night, seascapes and landscapes, were given banal encomia. In the prose play of David Samość one of the characters waxes poetic and addresses nature as his "sweet sister who bestows upon us the very gift of love."[72] Jacob Samuel Byk, in a poem entitled "Loneliness," based on Alexander Pope's "Ode on Solitude," declares that the enlightened man chooses to live in rural rather than urban surroundings and to spend his time in amiable pursuits.[73]

Translation as Vehicle of Enlightenment

Translations, which served to widen the horizons of Hebraic readers, also had a share in stimulating appreciation for rural environments and idyllic modes of life. They practically inundated the field of Hebrew literature in the nineteenth century. Periodicals, annuals, volumes of poetry—they all carried their ponderous weight of translations. Though the translations were, in the main, made from other languages into Hebrew, there were also translations from the Hebrew. Mendelssohn's translation of the Bible was of prime importance as an instrument of national enlightenment. The famous "Zionide" of Judah Halevi in Mendelssohn's translation[74] was published bilingually and evoked Goethe's admiration. These and other translations—such as a fragment of *Examination of the World*[75] by Yedayah ha-Penini—may have been intended to show the beauty and wisdom of Jews to other nations.

Translations into Hebrew were far more numerous. But they lacked precision. And what Saint Jerome said about translations of the Bible which preceded his own may be said with equal justice about Hebrew translations of the nineteenth century. They were not "versions but evasions."[76] And they were made by scholars and poets, in fact by anyone who wielded a Hebrew pen. In bad verse Rapoport urged translations from all languages and all peoples.[77] The enormous fertilization of Hebrew literature by European literatures has been more than matched in our times by numerous translators who were encouraged first by the well-known publisher Abraham Joseph Stybel and then by many publishing houses in Israel. But it is a gross exaggeration to say that Hebrew literature between the fifties and the eighties of the previous century was mainly "a literature of translations" (*Übersetzungliteratur*) because the writers, who were great Hebraists but authors of small talent, had to limit their literary activities to translations from other languages.[78]

Though the translators of the previous century had no princely Maecenases to subsidize their efforts, they ranged over a wide lingual area. They were conscious of the fact that they were imitating and paraphrasing rather than translating.

Letteris frankly confessed on the French-Hebrew bilingual title-page of one of his translations: *Esther . . . an Imitation after Jean Racine*.[79] Similarly, the bilingual German-Hebrew title-page of his most famous translation bears these unabashed words: *Goethe's Faust—a Tragedy in Hebrew Paraphrase*.[80] The readers, like the translators, set low standards of precision. Few, if any, of the hundreds of translations of the nineteenth century, can really be called translations. But, then, great translators are extremely rare in the literatures of the world. For they must effect in themselves a union or rather fusion of extraordinary qualities: familiarity with the original language, mastery of the language into which they translate and, above all, empathy with the alien work and humility before its brilliance.

Books with Jewish themes, like Racine's *Athalie* and *Esther* or Ludwig August Frankl's cycle of poems, *Rachel*,[81] had priority. Non-Jewish themes were usually judaized in title and content. Though translations from German predominated, there was no lack of translations from the French and English and Italian, the Russian and Greek and Latin. But Greek and sometimes even Latin works were translated from translations. Of the German poets, Schiller was the most popular among Jews in the period of enlightenment. His moral tone, his didactic stance, his serious and unsophisticated manner appealed to the Hebrew poets. In the course of the nineteenth century many of his plays and poems had been translated. Goethe, on the other hand, had few translators before the twentieth century. But he had many admirers. It is said that Rabbi Zebi Hirsch Chajes of Żółkiew was so distressed at the death of Goethe that the members of his congregation noted his mournful mood at the Sabbath morning prayer. At their insistent inquiry the rabbi told them that Goethe had passed away. The congregation knew nothing about Goethe, of course, but took it for granted that a great one in Israel had been gathered unto his fathers. And so the news spread all over town that Rabbi Goethe had died, and everybody said the proper benediction.[82]

Heine, who was neither moralist nor philosopher, was thoroughly neglected in the first half of the nineteenth century. The first translation of Heine appeared in 1853.[83] Herder and Kleist, Klopstock and Lessing, and a host of minor poets also found their way into Hebrew literature in the early decades of the nineteenth century. French poets, with the exception of Racine, were not cultivated by Hebrew translators. Only a few poems of Jean Pierre de Béranger, Alphonse de Lamartine, Arnaud Berquin, and Antoinette Deshoulières were laboriously rendered into Hebrew by various translators in the early decades of the nineteenth century.

Though the twentieth century has seen the greatest growth of interest in English and American writers—largely through the pioneering efforts of Hebrew poets in America—they had occasionally been translated in the previous century. Benjamin Franklin's extremely popular aphorisms in praise of prudence and honesty in *Poor Richard's Almanack* found a translator-imitator in Mendel Lefin of Satanow (1749–1826).[84] But, while translations from American literature were still very rare, translations from the English trickled steadily into the Hebrew language. It is interesting to note that a fable, "The Shepherd and the Philosopher" by John Gay, the famous author of *The Beggar's Opera,* found an early translator.[85] And so did Addison's "Ode on Gratitude"[86] which appeared in the very first issue of the Hebrew annual *Bikkure ha-'Ittim.* That was poetic justice. After all, *Bikkure ha-'Ittim,* like its predecessor *ha-Meassef,* owed its form and format to the *Tatler,* which had been jointly edited by Addison and Steele and which inspired a spate of journalistic effusions all over Europe. Very popular throughout the nineteenth century were poets like Edward Young (1683–1765). His voluminous poem *Night Thoughts* was eagerly translated even though Goldsmith in his "Essay on English Poetry" had warned that the poet seemed "fonder of dazzling than of pleasing." The elevated language, the numerous maxims on morality and religion, in spite of their ponderous rapidity and relentless mediocrity, were irresistible to Hebrew writers in the previous century. Young's paraphrase of the imperious call to self-knowledge—"Man, know thyself; all wisdom centres there"—must have been more palatable to them than the terse summons of the Delphic oracle to Socrates. His stress on the primacy of reason—"reason the root, fair faith is but the flower"—must have pleased the enlightened writers in Hebrew. And the flowery apostrophes to "night, sable goddess" who "in rayless majesty'" stretched forth "her leaden sceptre o'er a slumb'ring world" must have sounded like sublimest poetry to their uncritical sensibilities. Today Young is almost totally and justly forgotten.

Translations from the Russian were still very rare at that early period; a poem of Mikhail Matveevich Kheraskov (1733–1807) in a translation by Baruch Czaczkes is a good example.[87] Translations from the classics were also rare. Samuel David Luzzatto, who translated poems of Petrarch, Giambattista Marini (1569–1625), and Pietro Antonio Metastasio (1698–1782), made his translations of Anacreon from Italian renderings by Silvio de Rogati. In later life, Luzzatto translated fragments of the Latin of Boethius's *De consolatione philosphiae* and parts of Ovid's *Remedia amoris.*[88] Joseph Almanzi (1801–1860) translated but did not complete Horace's longest epistle on poetry, *De arte poetica.* M.J. Lebensohn translated from Schiller parts of Virgil's *Aeneid* under the title *Destruction of Troy*[89] and

Bernhard Schlesinger dabbled in the work of Lucian.[90] But the measure of Schlesinger's knowledge of Greek can be gauged from one of his verses in Hebrew: He mentions Sophocles and Aeschines, who sang (!) within the walls of Athens, and he misspells the name of the disciple of Socrates.[91]

Enlightenment versus Hasidism

There was a fatal and inevitable misunderstanding between two movements which aimed at the regeneration of Judaism: Haskalah and Hasidism. Haskalah strove to impose regeneration from without, Hasidism from within; Haskalah had its roots in foreign languages and literatures; Hasidism relied on mystical antecedents within Judaism; Haskalah was Hebrew, Hasidism was overwhelmingly Yiddish.[92] Finally, Haskalah was rationalist and its representative was the intellectual or *philosophe* as he was popularly known in French; Hasidism was intuitive and its central character was the charismatic leader.[93] As a result, Haskalah had little or no understanding for Hasidism.[94] It vaunted a mood of tolerance, but it acted out extreme intolerance against Hasidism. Even the opponents of Hasidism from the orthodox ranks of Jewry rarely exceeded the envenomed barbs of "enlightened" men like Perl or Erter.[95] Rare "converts" from enlightenment to Hasidism like Jacob Samuel Byk complained about lack of brotherhood or toleration on the part of the enlightened. And it is unfortunate that the enmity took nonliterary forms: memoranda to the Austrian or Russian government which incited and encouraged persecution of Hasidim. It is also unfortunate that the memoranda were successful and resulted in harassment and imprisonment of Jews. They were penned as early as 1791 by Mendel Lefin in French and later by Perl and by Isaac Ber Levinsohn. Perl went so far as to call Hasidism "a damaging cancer spreading by the hour. . ."[96]

The enlightened vied with each other in denunciations and defamations. It was only more than a hundred years after the rise of Hasidism that its positive contributions were more justly evaluated.

Philosophical and Scholarly Prose

Philosophical and critical prose reached maturity of thought in the early decades of the nineteenth century. Three men were chiefly responsible for the intellectual flowering: Nachman Krochmal (1785–1840), Solomon Judah Rapoport (1790–1867) and Samuel David Luzzatto (1800–1865). They were all influenced and they influenced in turn the so-called *Wissenschaft des Judentums* which had its origin in Germany and which was fathered by Leopold Zunz.[97]

Krochmal was one of the most original Jewish thinkers of the previous century. He had a vast command of Jewish literature and a good knowledge of philosophy. As a self-taught student he reflected deeply on the unique destiny of his people. And, toward the end of his days, he left a manuscript which was published posthumously by Zunz and called *The Guide of the Perplexed of Our Time*.[98] The title—a choice of the editor—indicated the considerable debt of Krochmal to Maimonides. But Krochmal was equally indebted to Giambattista Vico (1668–1774) and his cyclic theory of history, to Hegel who asserted the primacy of the spirit in world history, to the writings of Fichte and Schelling and Kant. What interested him, above all, was the unique destiny of the Jewish people as it was mirrored in Jewish history. It was his hope that, with a massive marshalling and illuminating of the facts of Jewish history, he could, perhaps, become the guide of his generation as Maimonides sought to become the guide of Jewry in the twelfth century. But he was not confronted with the Maimonidean need of synthesizing Judaism with Aristotelian philosophy. He had to find a new meaning and a new appreciation of Judaism for Jews who faced other options after the first emancipatory attempts on the part of Western states.

Judaism was, in Krochmal's estimation, absolute spirituality synonymous with absolute truth; philosophy of religion was only a higher rung on the ladder of faith. Krochmal believed that the essence of a people was its spiritual essence and that the progressive deterioration of spirituality spelled the death of a people. These were the general premises of his book. But its core—Jewish history—was interpreted as a chain of cyclical events. All nations, in Krochmal's view, had a tripartite history. The first part or period was the time of growth, the second the time of strength, the third the time of destruction. That cycle applied to Jewish history as well. With this qualification: When the Jewish people reached its final period in the cycle, it began to show regenerative powers and it developed a new cycle. The entire Jewish history was divided by Krochmal into three cycles which ended with the death of Gedalia, Bar Kohba and the expulsion of Jews from Spain respectively. The modern cycle was merely indicated but not interpreted.

The philosophy of Jewish history is sandwiched in between the opening chapters on religion in general and the closing chapters which represent a miscellany of subjects: post-biblical literature, the development of oral law and of Jewish philosophy and, finally, a concluding chapter on Abraham Ibn Ezra. The opening chapters—with their allusions to contemporary religious trends and with their dissection of the psychology of religious types—arrive at an interesting conclusion: Faith and reason draw their sustenance from one source, from the spiritual source of man. Even the most primitive faith is based on a spiritual foundation.

In the discussion and illumination of the varieties of religious experience, Krochmal anticipated the classic work of James. In the closing chapters he subjected Jewish tradition to a deep historical analysis. His unparalleled knowledge of the legal and non-legal aspects of Jewish tradition and his new insights into their development paved the way for generations of Jewish scholars who, consciously or unconsciously, borrowed from him and modified his ideas. The massive researches of Bacher and Ginzberg into the rabbinic heritage of Jewry owe Krochmal a greater debt than has been acknowledged by them and their critics.

There is an inescapable impression that the book is really a three-volume book; that it was hastily compiled and edited; that, had Krochmal lived, the book would have had a different character. Yet, in spite of its uncompleted form, it is a massive monument of Jewish learning and original insights into Judaism. In contradistinction to Mendelssohn who had no interest in Jewish history, Krochmal inaugurated a new and neglected discipline: Jewish historiosophy or philosophy of history. Though writers on Judaism in Western languages have not paid sufficient attention to him, Hebrew writers cherished his memory and his ideas. For Ahad Haam, the strict critic of Hebrew literature, Krochmal and Eisik Hirsch Weiss (1815–1905), author of the massive history of rabbinic literature, were the only Hebrew writers in the nineteenth century who merited serious consideration.[99]

Solomon Judah Rapoport, a close friend of Krochmal, was neither a philosopher nor a critic. His main interest—apart from miscellaneous translations and poetic effusions of no merit—lay in research into Jewish biography and lexicography. In the field of Jewish biography he produced studies of importance which shed new light on the post-talmudic period and served future scholars well: a biography of

Saadia, the author of *Beliefs and Opinions,* a biography of Nathan of Rome, the author of the encyclopedic dictionary, a biography of Hai, one of the last gaons, a biography of Kalir, the liturgical poet who inaugurated a new era in the development of medieval poetry, a biography of the great talmudists R. Hananel and R. Nissim of Kairuwan, a biography of Hefez ben Yazliah. All these biographies centered around personalities who appeared immediately after the redaction of the Talmud and—with the exception of Saadia—steered Jewish life into an exclusive rabbinism. Even the poet Kalir glorified Jewish holidays with allusions to rabbinic sources. The lexical work of Rapoport remained a rump: it never went beyond the first letter of the Hebrew alphabet.[100]

Samuel David Luzzatto was more emotional in his attitude to Judaism than Krochmal or Rapoport. His deep knowledge of Jewish sources was not only a matter of erudition to him; it transformed his life and it bolstered a naive and innocent faith. Though he read and wrote Italian and French with great ease, he was peculiarly unaffected by their literatures. His knowledge of classical literatures aroused his antagonism to what he regarded as Atticism.

He wrote voluminously and unsystematically. Nothing Jewish was alien to him. His works include a study on the Aramaic translation of the Pentateuch, the so-called Onkelos, biblical dissertations, notes on Hebrew grammar, researches on the poetry of Judah Halevi. He also had his philosophical predilections. Judaism, to him, was the apotheosis of mercy as deed not as doctrine. He prized emotion above reason and showed himself to be a true romantic. Spinoza was his pet aversion and so were medieval Jewish rationalists. Rashi, the popular commentator, symbolized for Luzzatto the ideal Jew for he followed in the footsteps of his people's sages while Abraham Ibn Ezra was attracted to Moslem and Greek sages. This negative attitude to Abraham Ibn Ezra (1092–1167), the great commentator and poet, traveler and grammarian, aroused the ire of Rapoport who chided his friend in no mistaken terms: "Who am I and who are you in the face of this great mountain. . .We are like grasshoppers before this great giant. . ."[101] And though Luzzatto seemed to regret his negative attitude, he did so to please a friend. For he was an unregenerate opponent of Abraham Ibn Ezra. Krochmal also joined issue with Luzzatto: "Both [Maimonides and Abraham Ibn Ezra] are guides to understanding and shapers of untold generations after them. . ."[102] Perhaps the last chapter of *The Guide of the Perplexed of Our Time* owes its inspiration to the epistolary controversy which raged in the pages of *Kerem Hemed* in the thirties of the nineteenth century.

Krochmal was a true rationalist, Luzzatto a true emotionalist. Yet, in spite of his emotionalism, he objected to mysticism. It was too esoteric a doctrine, too dangerous a way of life. In his own days he was considered a poet because he wrote many verses on many occasions.

Hebraism and Hellenism

The cleavage between Hebraism and Hellenism was one of Luzzatto's chief preoccupations. It exercised the best minds of the previous century. All men are either Jews or Greeks, said Heine,[103] who derived the antithesis from Ludwig Börne. And Moses Hess (1812–1875), one of the early ideologists of Jewish nationalism, devoted much thought to the differences between Greeks and Jews.[104] But in Hebrew literature Samuel David Luzzatto was one of the chief exponents of that cultural cleavage, though he gave it other names: Atticism and Abrahamism. Similarly, in English literature Matthew Arnold was deeply concerned with Hellenism and Hebraism. For the sake of simplification it may be said that Luzzatto insisted on the superiority of the Hebrew genius, while Matthew Arnold preached the superiority of Hellenism for modern England. Both forces, according to Arnold, move and influence our world—the Hebraic force of practical morality and the Hellenic force of intellect, the ideal of perfect conduct and the ideal of precise thought; the ethical man is the ultimate aspiration of the Hebrew, the intellectual man the ultimate aspiration of the Greek.

Samuel David Luzzatto who wrote on the subject in prose and poetry, in Italian, French and Hebrew, echoes mid-nineteenth century concepts about the two ancient cultures: Athens gave us philosophy, arts, sciences, order, esthetics, rational ethics; Judaism is mainly responsible for religion, for emotional ethics, for the love of the good.[105] In a letter to Joshua Heschel Schorr (1818–1895),[106] published in 1863 but written twenty-five years earlier, he writes:

> For twenty-four years I have studied the writings of philoso-
> phers . . . and I found that all of them, more or less, are lost in a
> pathless wilderness . . . and the worst of it is that Greek
> philosophy—especially in this generation—not only does not make
> its students wiser and better than they were before, but it also does
> not make them happy. . . . On the contrary: it changes their

natural happiness to sorrow . . . but our ancient sages of blessed
memory succeeded with their traditional Jewish wisdom to fortify
Jews like a pillar of iron and a wall of brass . . . and they made
them happy.[107]

In another letter Luzzatto chides the young poet Micah Joseph
Lebensohn for mentioning Minerva and Medusa in one of his poems
"Solomon and Ecclesiastes:" "It is strange that a Jewish youth of
Lithuania who was brought up on prophets and rabbinic sages, should
expostulate on the useless pagan gods of antiquity. . ."[108]

Simplicity rather than sophistication attracted Samuel David
Luzzatto; hence his championship of a Rashi and his deprecatory
attitude to an Abraham Ibn Ezra: "This one [Rashi] believed his
peoples' sages, and that one [Abraham Ibn Ezra] believed the Greek
and Moslem sages. . ."[109] Even minor figures in the dawn of
enlightenment felt moved to confront or juxtapose Judaism and
Hellenism. Gabriel Berger, with his meager knowledge of history,
contended that biblical poetry is the oldest known poetry in the world
and that Homer lived in the days of King Solomon.[110] And Avigdor
Levi of Glogau, the grammarian, wrote a didactic poem with fifty-six
notes[111] to show that Socrates and Plato and Aristotle, though they
succeeded in opening the eye of man's intellect ('En Siklo), they were
immediately contradicted by other philosophers until Moses came and
brought truth and salvation to mankind.

Today this ever-fascinating subject of Hellenism and Hebraism is
still very much alive with us though not in the adulterated form of the
enlightenment era. On the scientific plane surprising interrelations in
mythology, in custom, in alphabet, in ritual, and in belief have been
uncovered. On the philosophical plane the dichotomy has recently
again been subjected to searching analysis. Biblical patterns of
thought and Platonic patterns of thought have been compared and
fruitful analogies have been established. The audile Hebrew, in the
opinion of Thorleif Boman, the Norwegian scholar, developed a keen
understanding of the dynamic aspects of life: movement, passion,
power; the visual Greek strove for the static aspect of life: repose,
discipline, harmony. Space was the thought-form for the Greek, time
for the history-minded Hebrew. Finally, the Greek cherished things,
the Hebrew, words. Both peoples made a lofty contribution to culture
because of their one-sided physiological and psychological
endowments.[112]

While the Norwegian scholar attacked the problem of Hellenism and

Hebraism from a philological, philosophical, and theological point of vantage, the American scholar, William Barrett, studied the problem in the context of existential philosophy. He reached conclusions which, though not startlingly original, are in the tradition of Western philosophy. "The ideal man of Hebraism is the man of faith; for Hellenism. . .the ideal man is the man of reason. . .there follows for the Greek the ideal of *detachment* as the path of wisdom. Hebraic emphasis is on *commitment*."[113] In short, the Hebraic man is existentialist, involved in existence; the Greek man is non-existentialist, involved in eternity through his contemplative intellect. The fact remains, the modern West rests firmly on Hebraic and Hellenic bases;[114] on the dynamic, history-conscious concept of Hebraism and on the static, philosophy-conscious concept of Hellenism. That they have not been thoroughly fused may account for many a malaise in our present era.

5
Flowering of Enlightenment in Eastern Europe

Early Protagonists of Enlightenment in Eastern Europe

Till the Russian Revolution in 1917 Hebrew literature had its most important home and center in Russia and Galicia. In Western Europe few men played a role comparable to the poetic spokesmen of enlightenment—Abraham Dov Ber Lebensohn, his son Micah Joseph Lebensohn and Judah Leb Gordon. And no Hebrew writer in Western Europe developed the dominant genre of all great literatures in the nineteenth century, the novel. But in eastern Europe Mapu and Brandstädter, Braudes and Smolenskin and especially Mendele Moker Sefarim, laid the foundations for the Hebrew novel of the twentieth century.

In eastern Europe enlightenment was not only a matter of philosophical and theological concern. It aimed at transformation of the cultural as well as the religious and economic life of Jewry. Thus, the first rural settlements were established in the south of Russia thanks to the zealous propaganda of the "enlightened" writers. And these were the ancestral types of the rural settlements in former Palestine. As in Germany, Hebrew periodicals were the rallying points for the enlightened. With a difference: there were more of them and they had a wider and more knowledgeable readership. Of the most important and the most durable—and they all had their suspensions—the following deserve to be singled out: the Austrian *Kerem Hemed* (1833–1842), a successor of *Bikkure ha-'Ittim* and a research-oriented journal; the first Hebrew periodical in Russia, *Pirhe Zafon* (1841–1844); *Kokebe Yizhak* (1845–1873), also a successor of *Bikkure ha-'Ittim* with an emphasis on literary productivity; *he-Haluz*

(1852–1889), also in Austria, attracted such writers as Isaac Erter and such scholars as Abraham Geiger; *ha-Maggid* (1856–1890); *ha-Karmel* (1860–1880); *ha-Meliz* (1860–1904); *ha-Zefirah* (1862–1931); *ha-Shahar* (1869–1884). While Austrian Jewry was proud of its *Kerem Hemed, Kokebe Yizhak, he-Haluz* and *ha-Shahar*, Russian Jewry exulted in *ha-Karmel, ha-Maggid, ha-Meliz*. Samuel Joseph Fünn (1818–1891), one of the two editors of *ha-Karmel* and the founder and editor of the first Hebrew periodical in Russia, was widely known for his popular histories of Jews and for his many translations from the German. And he was esteemed as an editor and educator though he lacked daring. *Ha-Maggid*, under the editorship of Eliezer Silberman and *ha-Meliz* under the editorship of Alexander Zederbaum, became synonyms for flowery Hebrew.

The fight between enlightenment and traditional orthodoxy, between enlightenment and Hasidism, was long and bitter in eastern Europe. The relaxation of orthodox ways, however, came about as a result of environmental factors rather than internecine strifes. The dissolution of orthodoxy everywhere, the secularization of life, the political surrogates of religion played havoc with orthodoxy.

The eastern European counterpart of the western European Mendelssohn was Isaac Ber Levinsohn who was known under the Hebrew acronym Ribal. Though he had a sound and traditional Jewish education and though he acquired a knowledge of many languages at an early age, he had neither the philosophical interests nor the polished linguistic talents of a Mendelssohn. His cumbersome tracts like *Instruction in Israel*[1] and the *House of Judah*[2] dealt with ponderous theses: modern civilization and Judaism, history of Jewish faith, Judaism within the context of Christianity. But, above all, they pursued practical objectives: they preached the desirability of secular and Jewish learning, the necessity of knowing another language beside Yiddish and Hebrew, preferably the language of one's native land; they proposed reforms in education, in communal leadership, in the economic stratification of Jewry; and they buttressed their arguments with quotations from biblical and rabbinic sources. Their ultimate purpose was de-ghettoization or normalization of Jewish life—especially diversification in earning a livelihood by manual or agricultural labor. In the wake of Levinsohn's proposals Jewish farms were established in Bessarabia between 1838 and 1839.

Other works of the father of enlightenment in Russia defended the Talmud in the form of tired tirades which continued the trend of medieval apologetics. But, unlike his enlightened friends in Galicia,

Perl and Erter, he attacked not only Hasidism but also Karaism. And he bitterly denounced blood libels[3] which were rampant in Christian theory and practice. Thus he fought on two fronts—inside and outside the Jewish camp—largely from a sickbed to which he was confined in his native Kremenetz in Volhynia for four decades.

The tone, set by the father of enlightenment in Russia, was followed, imitated, plagiarized for more than half a century. Hardly a new idea was added to the stock-in-trade of Ribal's ideas. Thus, Mordecai Aaron Günzburg [Remag] (1795–1846), a prolific translator and compiler of texts in mathematics, optics and astronomy in the best tradition of enlightenment, preached endlessly that Jews must devote themselves to secular knowledge and that religion did not oppose but rather required that kind of knowledge. In his autobiography *Abi'ezer* he epitomized in himself the model of an enlightened man and an ardent admirer of Mendelssohn. But some of the traditional customs he depicted with a cherishing heart: his own wedding at fourteen, "the end of his youth" [sic], he described in amusing detail, his life in the home of his wife's parents with chagrin and regret.[4] All in all, it is a charming autobiography of a young man, a forerunner of a better and more tragic autobiography—*Sins of Youth*[5] by Moses Leb Lilienblum (1843–1910). It appeared more than fifty years after Günzburg's autobiography and it reflected the tenor of enlightenment at its decline. Günzburg's autobiography is a document of maturation; Lilienblum's autobiography is a document of maturity veined with despair: disillusionment with the ultra-orthodox environment and the panaceas of enlightenment color the contents of the book. Both autobiographies demonstrated an incontestable fact: The old religion was breaking down, the new forms of Judaism struggled for recognition.

Simultaneously with the writers and propagandists of enlightenment, Jews of influence endeavored to organize the intellectual life of their people. In Germany, Friedländer and Jacobson, Ben-David and Itzig were active as promoters of reform in synagogue service, education and general relaxation of orthodoxy. In Russia the Society for the Promotion of Enlightenment counted among its original officers the baronial Günzburgs, father and son, the Brodskis, Rabbi A. Neuman and Leon Rosenthal. It endeavored to spread the knowledge of the native language, the pursuit of general knowledge and the sciences, to publish and assist others in publishing, in Russian and in Hebrew, useful works and journals. The first periodical, devoted to Jewish affairs, the *Razswet* (Dawn), saw the light of day because of their efforts.[6]

But disunity among Jews hampered the efforts of the Society. Petty quarrels almost disrupted its work. The death of Günzburg in Vilna in 1846 was marked by factional strife; the slighting euology of the official preacher of the community aroused the ire of the poet who was considered, after the death of Günzburg, as the chief representative of enlightenment: Abraham Dov Ber Lebensohn. It led to the publication of a proper eulogy by him and to the establishment of a special synagogue where the poet became the preacher.

At that time two rabbinical seminaries were established by the Russian government: one in Vilna, one in Zhitomir. Lebensohn was appointed to the faculty of the seminary in Vilna as teacher of Hebrew and Aramaic. For twenty years—from 1847 to 1867—he held the post which suited his talents perfectly for he was in love with the Hebrew language and with Hebrew grammar to such an extent that he had an almost cultic attitude to their importance. That attitude prevailed among the enlightened for a long time after his death.

As a poet Lebensohn showed neither originality nor imaginative inventiveness. His forms and genres and meters were the hackneyed forms and genres and meters of Hebrew poets in the early decades of the century. The inordinate length and the stanzaic monotony of his best-known poem "Pity" is matched by a catalog of weak creatures who are victimized and brutalized by stronger creatures. As for playwriting, he was devoid of dramatic talent. In his allegorical verse-play *Truth and Faith* he simply imitated Moses Hayyim Luzzatto. And he inaugurated an imitational trend. The poet A.B. Gottlober also wrote an allegorical play *Glory to Men of Understanding*,[7] in which Yair, the protagonist of enlightenment, conquers the powers of darkness. The occasion of the play: the wedding of a friend. Shades of Luzzatto! Klausner admired Lebensohn's strong emotionalism and penetrating gifts of observation. But he had to concede that his abstractionism was a debt to "his generation and his time."[8] Yet for many of his contemporaries he was the greatest Hebrew poet.[9] Such are the perversions of literary tastes.

The greatest gift of Lebensohn to Hebrew literature was his son, Micah Joseph Lebensohn, the young, consumptive poet who lived less than twenty-four years—from 1828 to 1852—and who is still an important force in Hebrew poetry. As a son of a Hebrew poet he had the unusual advantage of a good Hebrew and general education. He studied many languages—German and French and Italian, Polish and Russian. He translated from German, French and Polish. But he had no knowledge of classical languages: his partial translation of the second book of Virgil's *Aeneid* was done from Schiller's German translation *The Destruction of Troy*[10] and not from the original. And it is still a moot question whether he translated Vittorio Alfieri's play *Saul* from the original or from the German. On the basis of the extant fragment—it was never published in its entirety—it is impossible to make a decision. Micah Joseph Lebensohn also paraphrased beautifully a French poem "La Feuille" of Antoine Vincent Arnault under the title "A Driven Leaf" and allegorized its meaning: The driven leaf is the wandering Jew. The poet's literary and scholarly connections played a role in his development. Such figures as Samuel David Luzzatto and Meir Halevi Letteris, Isaac Samuel Reggio and Senior Sachs were among his correspondents. Kalman Schulman, the translator of Eugène Sue, and Judah Leb Gordon, the poet, were his close friends. They served him well—some as admirers, some as advisers. In the introduction to a volume of his poetry *Songs of Zion*[11] Micah Joseph Lebensohn tells us that the great scholar, Leopold Zunz, persuaded him to abandon foreign themes and devote himself to Hebraic motifs. And so did Senior Sachs and Samuel David Luzzatto. It was good advice: In his biblical poems from the period of the *Judges*, in "The Revenge of Samson"[12] and in "Yael and Sisera"[13] Lebensohn showed a fine sensitivity to the inner struggles of Samson and especially Yael. Moses in "Moses on Mount Abarim"[14] is given an opportunity to bare his grief of unfinished leadership. While Wessely wrote an epic on Moses, Lebensohn chose a moment in his life; the aging leader, on the threshold of his heart's desire, died of a broken heart. In "Yehudah Halevi" Lebensohn depicted a tragic moment in the life of the medieval poet who allegedly reached the object of his life's longing and died under the hoof of an Arab horseman. In Lebensohn's time legend and truth about Halevi were subjected to the intense researches of Senior Sachs and Samuel David Luzzatto. And two poets—Lebensohn and Heine—utilized them each for his own purpose, each with his own lingual and poetic devices.

Unlike his father Lebensohn had a happy gift of words, imagery and poetic technique. It was especially prominent in his lithe, lyrical poems and in the philosophical ode "To The Stars."[15] The latter poem is, as Klausner rightly remarked, suffused with the prevalent romantic notions of pantheism.[16]

Today, no less than in his own time, his place is secure in Hebrew literature. The early poems of Bialik and Tschernichowsky owe him debts in thematic and metric and stylistic innovations. And the most powerful poet of the enlightenment, Judah Leb Gordon, repeatedly acknowledged his debt to Micah Joseph Lebensohn as poet and friend.[17]

Apogee of Enlightenment in Eastern Europe

With Judah Leb Gordon the poetry of enlightenment reached its apogee. His native talents for narrative poetry were strengthened by his absorptive reading of the great classics in epic poetry: Homer and Virgil as well as Tasso and Ariosto, the Italian poets of the Renaissance. In three narrative poems he managed to present a new, revolutionary evaluation of Judaism. Each one of them recreated a historical phase: "Zedekiah in Prison"[18]—the end of the First Commonwealth in 586 B.C.E., "Between Lions' Teeth"[19]—the end of the Second Commonwealth in 70 C.E., "In the Depths of the Sea"[20]—the expulsion of Jews from Spain in 1492. "Zedekiah in Prison" is a long monolog of the last king of quasi-independent Judea. It is also a bitter denunciation of the prophets, especially the contemporary prophet Jeremiah, for leading the people into an impasse of spirituality with concomitant political and economic strangulation. The king speaks for the institution of kingship and against prophecy. He is convinced that political leadership can be destroyed by the interfering prophet with devastating consequences for the state.

That problem of spiritual versus material leadership of the people exercised the Jewish intellectual in the nineteenth century. It was Gordon's contention that excessive spirituality led to annihilation of the people. That contention was later developed by Micah Joseph Berdyczewski who, under the added stimulation of Friedrich Nietzsche, preached a transvaluation of values in Jewish life with heavy emphasis on non-spiritual values. It was also cherished by Saul Tschernichowsky who called for a return to the mythical, half-pagan, pre-Canaanite past. And, finally, it became the philosophical underpinning of the so-called "Young Hebrews" or "Canaanites" in the fifties of this century when, after the establishment of the State of Israel, they advocated separation between Jew and Israeli as well as total amnesia of the long diaspora after the demise of Bar Kohba in 135 C.E.[21]

"Between Lions' Teeth" depicts in a series of vivid vignettes the immediate period before and after the fall of Jerusalem in 70 C.E. The pair of lovers—Simon and Martha—are only incidental to the blasphemous message of the poem: God is indifferent to the fate of Jewry; only Jewish strength can prevail against non-Jewish strength. In bitter irony the poet denounces God's smugness and Rome's exuberance after the victory over a small people in a small land. He regards the tragedy of Jewry as an act of abdication on the part of a debilitated deity. However, in the poem "In the Depths of the Sea" Gordon's voice seems to soften. Since a young woman is the heroine, the tone is admirably suited to the content. Gordon does not castigate a class or a people or the deity itself; he seems to fight on behalf of Jewish womanhood. And he deplores again the weakness of a people which depends on acts of feminine martyrdom. For in his poem an entire ship of Jewish exiles from Spain is saved by the sacrifice of a young woman.

Gordon was one of the first Hebrew poets to plead the cause of Jewish womanhood. In a series of poems and stories he endowed women with kindness and goodness and depicted their husbands or suitors as unpleasant characters or downright rascals. In four famous poems "The Stroke on the Letter Yod,"[22] "Waiting for a Brother-in-Law,"[23] "Wagon's Shaft,"[24] and "Rejoice in Your Festival"[25] the Jewish woman is victimized by the rigidity of Jewish law as interpreted by reactionary rabbis. In his biblical poems she is often idealized; in his stories she is described with empathy. It is no surprise that in his correspondence with women Gordon encouraged their self-educational efforts and praised their knowledge of the Hebrew language. In his autobiography he painted the portrait of his mother, the third wife of his father, with infinite sympathy. It is not a far-fetched claim—even without recourse to psychoanalytic insights—that respect for his mother seems to have influenced his attitude to all women.

Pessimism colored Gordon's poetry. The ideals of Jewish enlightenment—the acquisition of secular knowledge and emancipation—were not implemented. The fight against secularism grew more bitter, the pogroms of the eighties buried forever the mirage of emancipation as a solution to the Jewish problem. Even knowledge of classical Hebrew became more and more of a rarity as the tides of assimilation threatened to engulf what was unique in Jewish life. No wonder that Gordon wrote an unforgettable lyric of desperation: "For Whom Do I Toil."[26] No wonder that he asked himself whether he was the last Hebrew poet though he felt like a "slave to Hebrew forever."[27]

The pogroms—after the accession of Alexander III to the throne of Russia—had a profound effect on Gordon. He had castigated his people in a well-known poem and called it a herd rather than a nation.[28] But he also became the singer of infinite pity especially after the pogroms. Suddenly he felt the elusive unity of the people, the strong chain of suffering which bound the people together forever. He even evinced a hesitant nationalist tone in his last poems which were sung and known by heart throughout eastern Europe. While, a generation later, Bialik turned a finger of accusation toward his own people after the pogrom of Kishenev, Gordon threw the entire blame on the perpetrators of the criminal acts. The Jew was the eternal Abel, the gentile the eternal Cain with Abel's blood on his forehead.

Publicly, Gordon seemed to favor immigration to America as a temporary solution to the Jewish problem and immigration to Palestine as the ultimate goal. But he wavered and vacillated and exposed himself to the attacks of fellow-writers who embraced nationalism with fervor. Though he postulated spiritual redemption as a necessary condition for geographical redemption and anticipated the main tenets of Ahad Haam's creed, he was regarded to the very end of his life as a man for whom religious reform and Europeanization of Jewry was far more important than the acquisition of Jewish statehood. "The language of Jerusalem is on our lips and the thoughts of Europe in our hearts"[29]—this terse declaration in a letter to a younger poet, M.M. Dolitzky, at the end of 1881, sums up the poet's ideological stance. As for nationalism: he simply did not believe that the nations of the world would consent to a Jewish state and that the Jews would abandon their passive messianism for an active effort toward the establishment of a state. And even if the nations did not prevent the Jews from returning to their land, the Jews would destroy each other. Hence his reiterated need for the re-education of Jewry and the reclamation of the land of Israel.[30] It is not without interest and significance that a thesis on Gordon for the rabbinical degree was accepted by the Hebrew Union College of Cincinnati in the year 1902 when early reform was at the peak of its militant attitude to the Hebrew language.[31] Correctly, it viewed that language and literature as a medium of Zion-oriented expression. Years later, the Russian revolution incorrectly branded it as an anti-revolutionary and reactionary tool in the service of theocracy and imperialism.

Gordon practiced what he preached. He was a lifelong student, a voracious reader, a consumer and distributor of knowledge. His didactic stance found its ripest expression in the hundred odd *Fables*[32] which were imitations or paraphrases of Aesop and Phaedrus, Lafontaine and Krilov. Only one-fifth of the fables was original work.

Though naive in conception and simple in metric structure, the fables were studied by Jewish youngsters in India and even by Karaites in the Caucasus and Crimea. Gordon was a true teacher of his people. As a poet he changed the orientation of Jewry to its past. As editor of the influential *ha-Meliz* for five years (1880-1883 and 1885-1887), he molded Jewish attitudes to emergent nationalism in the crucial period of pogroms. Unfortunately Gordon, the prose writer, has been overshadowed by Gordon the poet. Yet his essays, stories and, especially, his autobiography deserve a place in the history of Hebrew literature. The stories resemble the feuilleton—the fashionable genre which counted Theodor Herzl among its brilliant practitioners. They anticipated some ideas of Ahad Haam and provoked heated debates in their time. Problems of emanacipation, emigration and incipient nationalism were often aired in them for the first time. They vaunted a realistic vision of Jewish life and, linguistically, pioneered a greater use of post-biblical language.

Most of the stories are vignettes of the *Shtetl* which was the chief theme of Hebrew novelists and story-tellers from the middle of the nineteenth century to the end of the First World War. Eccentric types and ordinary types, the humble and the rich, the excitement and the boredom: They are portrayed with a leaden hand and an unsympathetic heart. The best that can be said of them is this: The grosser types of waggoners anticipate the world of the vulgar man which dominated more than half a century later Shneour's novel *Noah Pandre*. And their scorn of Hasidism has been excelled by Gordon's predecessors: Perl, Erter and Isaac Ber Lebensohn. His fragmentary autobiography, especially the section entitled *On the River Kebar*,[33] reveals early biographical details and environmental factors which have shaped the life of the poet. The visit to Leopold Zunz in Berlin is described with a mixture of humor and chagrin. The scholar was unaware of the existence of the poet, the poet scorned his ignorance with biting comment: "Had I been a contemporary of Kalir, Zunz would have been expert in my poetry."[34] The poet's remark illustrates the age-old complaint of the maker of poetry who often works in obscurity against the scholar who often gains renown by research into the minutiae of form or content of obscure makers of poetry in a remote past.

Sections of the diary afford glimpses into the final year of Gordon's life. Almost every page breathes dejection, despondency, despair; cancer is slowly sapping his strength. Some nostalgic reminiscences on the tenth anniversary of the banquet in his honor in 1881 are penned with embarrassing detail and not without sarcasm and vanity; of the fifty-six dignitaries at the festive occasion "who gathered and came on that day to honor the Hebrew poet (!) there were many people who could not read Hebrew properly . . ."[35] In the last entry, three weeks before his death, he noted—with disgust and anger—an unidiomatic Hebrew phrase in *ha-Meliz*. The eternal servant of Hebrew remained loyal to his vocation till the end.

6
Interpretations and Reinterpretations of Hasidism

Preamble

Hasidism is a paradox: popular in appeal and esoteric in doctrine, communal in its emphasis on religious experience en masse and elitist in its cult of the chosen individual, the *Zaddik*.[1] As a regenerative force in modern theology it has become an object of discussion among scholars and thinkers. Popular writers like Isaac Bashevis Singer forced literary critics to confrontations with a movement which has its roots in a millennial milieu of mystic visionarism and visionaries and which aimed at an inner transformation of man and an ultimate leap into the spiritual stratosphere—beyond the concerns of the merely human world. Small wonder that serious students of literature fall into error of characterizing Hasidism as a "puritanic sect."[2] Others, aided and abetted by Martin Buber, the master-interpreter of Hasidism, draw far-fetched analogies between Zen and Hasidism, the Sufis and Hasidism.

Biography of the Word

The movement derives its name from the biblical word *Hasid* which means pious or loyal. It denotes a person who practices *Hesed*—piety or loyalty.[3] While the noun and the adjective are common in the Bible, the verb appears only three times there.[4] The scarcity of the verbal root seems to imply: Hasidism involves the entire human being, not a sporadic action.

In hellenistic times—especially in the period of the Maccabean

119

revolt—a pious group of Hasidim seems to have existed.[5] They opposed idolatry and resented immorality which they associated with Hellenism or Hellenization. They participated in the Maccabean revolt and in the conquest of Jerusalem by Judas Maccabeus in 165 B.C.E. But they eschewed political goals; they considered preservation of pristine piety as their objective.

In talmudic times, roughly between the second century B.C.E. and the end of the fifth century C.E., the term Hasid was applied to some sages.[6] Hillel who died at the dawn of our era was eulogized as a humble man, and a Hasid.[7] And he himself used the word in a famous saying: ". . . and an ignorant man cannot be a Hasid . . ."[8] The term was even extended to gentiles: Thus the pious gentiles, in a characteristic gesture of generosity, were admitted to "a portion in the world to come."[9]

Hasid was given a new connotation in talmudic times. It seemed to imply a good, law-abiding man who fulfilled his moral obligations. For he was often mentioned in one breath with "men of deeds"[10]— a loosely knit group of people who were held together by the intensity of their ethical beliefs, by extreme devotion and by impeccable ways of life. There was also an early group of Hasidim[11] who were especially addicted to prayer.

In talmudic times the abstract noun Hasidism[12] appeared with increased frequency as a desirable virtue or in connection with some sage; "the fear of sin leads to Hasidism and Hasidism leads to holiness of spirit."[13] It seems that in biblical times the Hasid was a pious or loyal person, in hellenistic times a member of a conservative group who opposed Hellenism, in Talmudic times the keeper of a privileged type of piety. In medieval times a movement of piety was initiated by Samuel the Pious and his son Judah of Ratisbon. That movement found its maturest expression in the *Book of Hasidim*[14] which was written in Germany in the thirteenth century and which was authored by Samuel the Pious, his son Judah who was regarded as the author of the book, his pupils, and R. Elazar Rokeah. The fifty years between the end of the twelfth century and the middle of the thirteenth century are, of course, a time of cultural growth among the Jews of Spain, Provence and Germany. It is the golden age of Tosafists, Jewish philosophy and Jewish mysticism. It is also the great age of German Hasidism with its mystic overtones.[15]

The *Book of Hasidim* was held in high esteem as a manual of popular ethics in the form of parables, tales, epigrams. It was unabashedly edifying; it was written for "God-fearing men . . . so that they will learn how to fear God."[16] And it was undoubtedly influenced by monasticism: mysticism, asceticism, saintliness, scholarliness—these were the virtues extolled by the book.

Around 1700, Judah Hasid Levi of Podolia preached the proximate advent of the Messiah in Poland. He represented a type of Hasidism in an era which was receptive to new visionary overtures. In 1666 Sabbatai Zevi was converted to Mohammedanism and the most popular messianic movement among Jews ended in a fiasco. Judah Hasid Levi, perhaps a crypto-Sabbatian, founded a movement of Hasidim which advocated repentance, ecstatic prayer and emigration to the Holy Land. In 1699 and in 1700 he organized about 1000 or 1500 followers who settled under his leadership in Jerusalem. When the Messiah failed to arrive in 1706—the date of Sabbatai Zevi's reincarnation exactly forty years after his conversion—many Hasidim became discouraged and returned to their previous domiciles. Some fell under the spell of Christian missionaries and became Christians in the Holy Land. Yet the failure associated with R. Judah Hasid Levi's venture is such a redemptive failure that a serious historian, Professor Ben Zion Dinur, begins modern Jewish history with this immigration to Palestine rather than with the French Revolution.[17]

Despair and disappointment and spiritual emptiness characterized the masses of Jewry in the beginning of the eighteenth century. The times were ripe again for a redemptive drive under charismatic leadership.

Hasidism: Origins and Characteristics

The seminal work of Gershom G. Scholem on *Major Trends in Jewish Mystisicm* concludes with a chapter on Hasidism, "the latest phase" in his own phrase. It is undeniably the last efflorescence of esoterism in an uninterrupted tradition of growth for more than two thousand years. In the first millennium it is cultivated by individuals and small coteries. By the beginning of the second millennium it gains ever wider acceptance till, as a mystic movement of national redemption, as Sabbatianism, it engulfs all Jewry during the second half of the seventeenth century. A hundred years later Hasidism dominated the religious experiences of Jewry in Eastern Europe—and in Eastern Europe only. Even in our own times, after two hundred years, it is still a *force majeure* in New York City and in many communities of Israel. And, through the transpositions of Martin Buber, it has vitalized contemporary Christian theology. It seems, therefore, just and fair to regard Hasidism not only as a latter day development of Jewish mysticism–though some scholars have denied its mystic qualities—but also as a fresh phase of non-rational theology in Judaism and, to a certain extent, in Christianity.

Within the context of theocratic and aristocratic nomism, Hasidism would not and could not flourish as an antinomian reaction against rabbinic learning. But, to a large extent, it was a rebellion of starved emotionalism against hyperintellectualism, folk wisdom against philosophical wisdom, intuitivism against rationalism, lighthearted-ness and joyfulness against seriousness and joylessness, inwardness instead of adherence to outer forms of religion. It continued to mythicize Judaism in the spirit of kabbalist antecedents. It became —to borrow a metaphor from physics—a new field of meaningful significance. The Jew rather than Judaism dominated the center which emanated and absorbed holiness of living. It had been written: "You shall be holy, for I the Lord your God, am holy."[18] The Hasidim converted the future tense of the biblical verse into the present tense.

On the sociological plane Hasidism was an uprising of the masses against the dominance of the supercilious scholar, the emergence of the 'Am ha-Arez[19] against the Talmid Hakam.[20] Ultimately the Talmid Hakam was exchanged for the Zaddik; the intellectual snob gave way to the charismatic leader. But the charismatic leader leads by virtue of mysticism and emotionalism rather than by logic and knowledge of the law. He is one of God's intimates whose prayer, enthusiasm and superhuman power reshape and restore spirituality to this world. He is not a recluse but a missionary to the masses and an intermediary between the deity and the people. He is even dragged down to depths of evil by the sinfulness of the masses. For they are the men of matter while he is the man of form. And his descent is a condition of his ascent. The hasidic rabbi is addressed by a Hebrew acronym which means: our lord, our teacher, our master. This is not merely a change in nomenclature; it is a shift in emphasis. But it is wrong to regard the new title as an authoritarian sobriquet. It is more likely a bending of the divine to the human, a deization of the human rather than a humanization of the divine. There is here, perhaps, an approximation to Christianity and the reason for the fascination of Christianity with Hasidism via Buber's interpretation. The Zaddik who is lord, teacher and master, can be easily translated into a Christian figure.

That there were hasidic individuals, perhaps even hasidic groupings before Hasidism, is an established fact.[21] That they had connections with or that they were inheritors of Sabbatianism has been proven by Scholem.[22] Yet the man who is regarded as the founder of Hasidism reshaped Jewry. Meek, not excessively learned, optimistic: These were his outstanding qualities.[23] A simple faith, a sunny temperament, a love for the common people—these traits led him to popular leadership. His brand of Judaism was traditional Judaism with slight modifications and ample changes in emphasis. Popularly he was known as Baal Shem Tov (1700-1760). And in Jewish mysticism Baal Shem or Baal Shem Tov is a man who possesses knowledge of the name or names of God and uses magical formulas, apotropaic terminology[24] or natural therapy for the cure of the sick. Both he and his followers, however, employed folk cures in such a way that "after the usual method of the conjurer they sought to turn the attention of the spectator from these, and direct it to their kabbalistic hocus-pocus."[25] For the environment —except for the scholarly elite—was permeated with superstition. In his *Autobiography* Solomon Maimon tells the story about a cook who was cutting up a carp and preparing the fish for the Sabbath. It seemed to him that the dead carp uttered a sound. This threw everybody into a panic. The rabbi was asked what should be done with this dumb fish that had ventured to speak. Under the superstitious idea that the carp was possessed of a spirit, the rabbi enjoined that it should be wrapped in a linen cloth and buried with pomp.[26] Later leaders of Hasidism exploited the simplistic faith of the masses for their own benefit.

In primary hasidic sources Baal Shem Tov appears as a man of many successive occupations till he finds his vocation as charismatic leader: teacher's assistant, ritual slaughterer, cantor. Seven years of solitude in the Carpathian mountains strengthen his resolve for leadership. His gregariousness—in the streets, in the market places—brings him recognition. Pipe in mouth, he converses with men and even women—against the explicit warning of the sages:. . ."and talk not much with Woman."[27] He settles in the Podolian town of Mezbizh and becomes the sage and saint of Mezbizh.

From the first important author of hasidic lore, Jacob Joseph ha-Cohen of Polnoye, we learn about the founder's habits. Prayer looms large in the life of the Baal Shem Tov and his successors. For prayer with intensity and enthusiasm leads to a divestiture of corporeality.[28] It was R. Nahman of Bratzlav who maintained that "the main vitality comes from prayer."[29] And it was said of Shneur Zalman of Liady that "privately he would pray in silence but in his public prayers he would shout for all the world to hear."[30] Other traits cultivated by the founder of Hasidism were adhesion to God,[31] intensity of mystical intention[32] or revival of the ossified rites[33] in the beautiful phrase of Martin Buber. These virtues—prayer, adhesion to God, intensity of intention—led to true self-realization. An acute observer of early Hasidism, Solomon Maimon, noted that the "new sect" maintained these new principles: elevation of the body through the intensity of prayer; devotion with exertion of all our powers, and annihilation of self before God; satisfaction rather than restriction on suppression of bodily needs; cheerfulness which is a function of a genuine piety rather than fasts and vigils and constant study of the Talmud;[34] mass visits to the leaders in order to enjoy community of spirit and be inspired by their holiness.

Since much has been made of the gaiety of Hasidism, a caveat is in order. It was not a gaiety which celebrated the sensual outlook on life. It was not a gaiety which advocated insouciance. It was a gaiety which led to spiritual resuscitation. Already Maimon maintained that the new sect spread because it advocated vitality and cheer instead of ascetic study;[35] it tended to be fanatical and it propagated the love of the marvelous.[36]

The cardinal virtues of Hasidism center around the relation of the individual to God. They are based on naive yet original interpretations of Scripture. Yehudah Steinberg, who experienced Hasidism in his native Russia, makes one of the Hasidim interpret the verse in *Deuteronomy* 34:10 thus: "Never again did there arise in Israel a prophet like Moses"—People think that this is praise; in reality this is accusation. Woe to the *Zaddik* who was not able to raise a man like him in his generation. As a matter of fact, this is not a *Zaddik* at all; this is a eunuch.[37]

Baal Shem's grandson, Rabbi Baruch, told a story about his grandfather who was asked about the essence of service and replied in a characteristic way: "I have come into this world to point another way"—away from asceticism and mortification of the body. And he continued: "Man should try to attain to three loves: the love of God, the love of Jewry, the love of Torah. This is the new emphasis on an old triad which has its root in the *Zohar*, the holy classic of the mystics.[38] The search for the three loves must be an individual concern: We say God of Abraham, God of Isaac and God of Jacob; we do not say God of Abraham, Isaac and Jacob, so that you may be told: Isaac and Jacob did not rely on Abraham's tradition, but they themselves searched for the Divine.[39] But search alone is not sufficient: "Genuine religiosity is *doing*."[40] Searching and doing by individuals who share common beliefs create a true community of holiness.

What is novel in the hasidic movement is its revivalist enthusiasm, its de-emphasis of learning, its cult of personality. Its revivalist enthusiasm expressed itself in prayer which involved the body in dancing, in clapping of hands, in communal singing.[41] The de-emphasis of learning produced popular learning and literature: the folktale and the epigram, the parable and the legend. Hasidism relied on edifying tracts and commentaries of the middle ages, on mystical disquisitions, on Sabbatian sources and, possibly, on the illuminations of the Paduan scholar and poet, Moses Hayyim Luzzatto.[42] The cult of personality was the early strength and the later undoing of the movement. In the heyday of Hasidism, between the middle of the eighteenth century and the middle of the second decade in the nineteenth century, a procession of saintly personages appeared in eastern Europe: Dov Ber of Mezritch (1710-1772), Jacob Joseph ha-Kohen of Polnoye (?–1782), Levi Isaac of Berditchev (1740-1809), Jacob Isaac, the Seer of Lublin (1745-1815), Nahman of Bratzlav (1772-1810), Shneur Zalman of Liady (1747-1813). Some of these personages became the unwitting founders of hasidic dynasties which deteriorated as they grew in power. Their princely ostentation, a costly trait, encouraged the worst obscurantism among the people.

Already the founder was believed to be on terms of intimacy with God. The special relationship to the Supreme Being granted him the power of miraculous therapy and special "rabbinic sight," *dem Rebben's Kuk* as it was expressed in the vernacular Yiddish. As a matter of fact, the famous Jacob Isaac the Seer, the main protagonist of Buber's only novel *For the Sake of Heaven,* is so called because, "when he was born, he had been able to see from world's end to world's end."[43] Moreover, he had the gift of seeing whether a man was good or evil. "He saw each soul's ultimate descent and root, whether it had once proceeded from the side of Cain or Abel . . ."[44]

There are differences of attitude and emphasis among the groupings of Hasidism. Baal Shem Tov, Dov Ber of Mezritch and his pupils Shneur Zalman of Liady, the founder of the Habad movement, Rabbi Nahman of Bratzlav and his disciples—they differ in their mystic fervor and in their messianic de-emphasis. Most of them stress redemption of the individual rather than redemption of Israel. It is true: Menahem Mendel of Vitebsk and his followers settled in Israel in 1777 and Rabbi Nahman of Bratzlav spent almost a year (1798-1799) in the Holy Land. But they are the exceptions which confirm the rule.

The best known splinter movement of Hasidism developed in Lithuania. It derives its name *Habad* from an acronym of three intellectual concepts: *Hokmah*–wisdom, *Binah*–understanding, *Da'at* –knowledge. Yet it is best described as emotionalism tinged with intellect rather than intellect tinged with emotion. For the founder of the movement, Shneur Zalman of Liady, the triad is a ladder of contemplation. The first rung, wisdom, gives birth to the idea that "all is in God." Understanding, the second rung, is meditation on the idea that "all is in God." Knowledge, the third rung, is adhesion of the heart to its source in God.

Habadism presents an ethical and mystical stance. To change from evil to good, that is the ethical obligation; from good to divine, that is the mystical endeavor. It was the mixture of the exoteric and esoteric doctrine and practice which gained for the Habad movement hundreds of thousands of adherents. Even their present headquarters in Brooklyn attract endless processions of visitors and disciples to their leader. They call themselves Lubavicher Hasidim because Duber (Dov Ber), the son of Shneur Zalman of Liady, settled in the town of Lubavich in White Russia. His son-in-law, Menahem Mendel, adopted the name Schneorsohn which is, to this day, the distinguished family name of Habad leaders. The adherents of the movement are also scattered in many communities of Israel. There is even an agricultural settlement, *Kefar Habad*, which carries on a long-standing tradition of buttressing moral stance with economic solidity. For it was the son of Rabbi Shneur Zalman of Liady who envisaged Jewish agricultural settlements in Crimea.

Other hasidic enclaves did not fare as well as Habadism. They deteriorated after the first flush of Hasidism in the first five or six decades after the birth of the movement. Mystical intention was vulgarized by magic letter-manipulation (*Gammatria* and *Notarikon*),[45] Zaddikism was corrupted by political manipulation. Leaders of Hasidism were often bribed by the state to drive their adherents into submission to political authority. They became easy targets of scorn for enlightened Jews and Christians.

Sources of Hasidism

The two hundred thirty years of Hasidism can be divided into two periods: a short period of growth (c.1750–c.1815) and a long period of decline (1815–).

Almost from its inception Hasidism had to fight on two fronts: defensively against entrenched Judaism and offensively against reformist enlightenment. The fight against entrenched Judaism reached its apogee in 1772 when a ban was pronounced upon Hasidim under the influence of Elijah of Vilna, the chief representative of rabbinical Judaism. Ironically the great Gaon was called a Hasid but his Hasidism was not identical with that of Baal Shem Tov; his piety consisted of strict adherence to rabbinic precepts, almost perpetual study which included the totality of traditional lore—even Kabbalah.

The fierce opposition against Hasidism by rabbinic Judaism continued into the nineteenth century but the ban and the persecutions and the burnings of hasidic books fanned the zeal of the adherents. They emerged victorious in entire sections of eastern Europe: in Galicia, in the Ukraine, in Volhynia, in Podolia and even in Lithuania, the bastion of rabbinism. The Oppositionists[46] did not concede defeat. But they were quite powerless against the attractive suasions of the new movement.[47]

The first writers who transmitted stories about the Baal Shem Tov were his disciples or members of his family. Such a disciple was Jacob Joseph of Polnoye, the author of several works including the first printed work of Hasidism.[48] The grandson of the Baal Shem Tov, Moshe Hayyim Ephraim, was the author of the work *Camp-Flag of Ephraim*.[49] The homilies of Dov Ber of Mezritch were published after his death by his disciple Solomon of Lutzk[50] and by another famous disciple, Levi Isaac of Berditchev.[51] The literary form of these books was the homiletic commentary on the Pentateuch, the *Haftarot*,[52] the Five Scrolls, the talmudic sayings. The chief books of Jacob Joseph of Polnoye used that form. They present sometimes sermons which combine knowledge, folklore, meditation and original interpretation. A beautiful homily on the folly of sin is given in Jacob Joseph's commentary on "And this is the story. . . (*Genesis* 25:19 ff). First, the biblical connection between folly and sin is established: We have done foolishly and we have sinned (*Numbers* 12:11). Then, with less justification, another biblical verse is adduced to buttress the contention (*Isaiah* 5:20). Then a talmudic passage is brought to bear on the subject: A man does not transgress unless a spirit of folly enters into him (*Sotah* 3a). Then the author reverts to the original application of Scripture and Talmud and makes his point. There are three types of man: the straightforward, honest man who acts according to his intellect; the bestial man who is guided only by his will; the median man who sees both good and evil, who is guided by intellect and/or will and who makes decisions after inner struggles.[53].

The books of Dov Ber of Mezritch, Rabbi Elimelech of Lizensk, and Rabbi Levi Isaac of Berditchev are essentially homiletic tracts. Their comments on the Bible or the Talmud were oral; later they were committed to writing. Most hasidic books imitated medieval genres: edifying tracts, mystic and homiletic commentaries, anthologies of epigrams by famous rabbis. Even the so-called new genre of hasidic literature—the moral story—is hardly innovative: it is designed to preserve the sense of the miraculous, the intuitive wisdom of the Zaddik, the moral stance. The hasidic stories derive from the founder who loved the brief, incisive tale–almost a parable. And they reach their apogee in Rabbi Nahman of Bratzlav, the best and the profoundest of hasidic story-tellers. In spite of the seductive paraphrases of Buber and the fine English translation of Buber by Maurice Friedman, the immediacy and the simplicity of the original[54] suffer serious losses in their impacts on both the sophisticated and unsophisticated readers. A creative rephrasing of hasidic stories has been attempted by numerous anthologists. None was done with greater ardor than by Jiri Langer (1894-1943). A native of Prague he decided to experience Hasidism at its source. In 1913 he visited Belz in eastern Galicia which had been thoroughly hasidified and which nourished the most sensitive interpreters of Hasidism: Agnon and Buber.[55] There he not only observed Hasidism; he lived it. And he penned a moving account of life in Belz—perhaps the best modern account of Hasidism in its native habitat.[56] In nine chapters—or gates in medieval terminology—he has retold oral and written stories about the saints of Hasidism in their spiritualized world. But unlike Buber, the sophisticated and metaphysical spokesman of Hasidism, Langer moves his listener with uncommon simplicity which flows from the source—from the contact with the saint of Belz and his followers.

Opponents of Hasidism

Not only orthodoxy but also secularized scholars and writers opposed Hasidism and Hasidim. One of their earliest observers and critics, Solomon Maimon, has castigated them from an "enlightened" point of view: Their emotionalism leads them into excess; their vanity accounts for their belief that they are "organs of the Godhead"; they are apt to regard an impulse as a divine call. In short, they are ruled by passion instead of reason and knowledge.[57] Graetz, the historian, and Krochmal, the thinker, were also implacable foes of Hasidism. Graetz went far in his animosity: He called Hasidism "this odious excrescence of Judaism.[58] Krochmal, the gentle philosopher, called the Hasidim "the hypocritical sect. . . . Fumes from hard liquor confuse their brain and obfuscate their intellect. . . ."[59] Mapu intended his abortive novel *The Visionaries* as a critique of the period of Sabbatai Zevi the source of Hasidism in his view.[60] Joseph Perl, Isaac Erter, Isaac Ber Levinsohn, A.B. Gottlober, Abraham Mapu, Judah Leb Mieses, Perez Smolenskin and Mendele Moker Sefarim attacked Hasidism in word and deed. Judah Leb Mieses—and he was not the only one—played the role of an informer. He denounced the Hasidim to the Austrian authorities as near-heretics, "religious fanatics."[61] Even Ahad Haam remembered Hasidism with bitterness in his autobiography: "I was born. . .in the town of Skvira, in one of the darkest corners of hasidic regions of Russia."[62] But already Isaac Ber Levinsohn, father of Hebrew enlightenment in eastern Europe, poked fun at Hasidim: these "men of God" are everywhere but mere men can nowhere be found.[63] They despise general education; they are manipulators of Hebrew letters for purposes of general obfuscation; they love "the bitter drop" and their religious enthusiasm is generated by alcohol; they are prone to lewdness; they are full of superstitions; they interpret Scripture willfully and foolishly; they are ultra-conservative; they fear the corrupting ways of large cities. And their leaders are venal liars and deceivers.[64]

The favorite weapon of enlightenment against Hasidism was ridicule. And the inventor of that weapon was Joseph Perl (1773-1839). Already in 1791 Mendel Lefin of Satanov (1749-1826) had indicated in his French brochure that satire was the most effective way to fight the new piety, the stupidity and the depravity of its leaders and its adherents. Yet he composed a rational critique of the movement—significantly, in epistolary form.[65] Perl, Lefin's admirer and friend and neighbor, was guided by his older contemporary in his communal, pedagogical and literary work.[66]

As the only son of a rich father he received a thorough traditional education in Tarnopol, the Galician town of his birth which was to become a center of enlightenment under his leadership. Married at fourteen and induced into the extensive and diversified family business interests—wine, lumber, manufactured goods—young Perl met hasidic rabbis on his voyages and was attracted to them. Since Rabbi Nahman of Bratzlav, the Seer of Lublin, and Levi Isaac of Berditchev were his contemporaries, he could have known any or all of them personally. But we do not know whom he knew and why he cultivated the ones he knew—much to the displeasure of his father who was an opponent of Hasidism.

As an eager young man Perl also met the leading luminaries of enlightenment and sought to improve his mind with general knowledge. For three years he was tutored by Bernard [Ber] Günzburg (1776-1811), a scholar and poet from Brody who was invited to Tarnopol and taught him German, French and Latin, history, mathematics and natural sciences.

The family fortunes grew in the years of Napoleonic turmoil; armies had to be fed, barracks had to be built. Hundreds of people were employed by the enterprising Perl who became head of the Jewish community and head of an exemplary educational institution.[67] Though it did not replace the *Heder*—as Perl fondly hoped—it combined general studies which were taught in the forenoon and Judaic studies which were taught in the afternoon. An eight year curriculum for youngsters from seven to fourteen was carefully worked out and refined from time to time under Perl's supervision of the school for thirty years. It was a combination of an elementary school and a junior high school. And it served as a model for similar institutions in eastern Europe.[68]

While Lefin was Perl's active guide in pedagogical affairs, he also advised him in his frequent intercessions with the Russian and Austrian governments on behalf of fellow-Jews. And, like Lefin, Perl began his literary career with a rationalist critique of Hasidism. The pro-hasidic man of affairs changed, slowly and imperceptibly, into an anti-hasidic author; the ideas of enlightenment won a complete victory. The chapter on Hasidism in Peter Beer's work on Jewish sects was largely written on the basis of a manuscript by Perl in German: a cold denunciation of Hasidism as a lecherous, fanatic, retrogressive movement.[69] But Perl's most important work against Hasidism—*The Revealer of Secrets*[70] in epistolary form—was partly inspired by Lefin and partly by the literary polemic between Reuchlin and the Dominicans of Cologne in *Epistolae obscurorum virorum* of 1515. It mounted an attack which was to become a classic of Hebrew literature, a masterpiece of invective and the first Hebrew novel.[71] The one hundred and fifty one letters with an epilogue, written by twenty-six individuals, revolve around a central theme: consternation in hasidic circles by the appearance of an anti-hasidic tract in German.[72] The two chief correspondents—Zelig and Zanvil—are not only in hot pursuit of the elusive tract which must be consigned to oblivion; they experience an ever-growing tension which communicates itself to the reader; they even suffer bodily harm from the tract *par distance*. Zelig dies from an overdose of spirits but his death is attributed to the mysterious effect of the tract. The same natural cause—alcohol—and the mysterious cause—the tract—cause the death of a wonder-rabbi.

The foibles of Hasidim dot every page of Perl's book. The journey to the Zaddik is a farce: "it is known that the whole of Judaism depends on the journey to the Zaddik."[73] The fusion of eroticism and mysticism—so typical of so many religions—elicits the remark that "prayer is like intercourse."[74] Elegance of style is sin: "when someone writes pure Hebrew he is regarded as a heretic . . ."[75] Erudition is the preserve of the Zaddik: "Sages are not erudite; the true Zaddikim are."[76] They are also rulers of the world: "the Zaddikim can force God, blessed be His name, to do what they will; they perform miracles with their holy words."[77] The adoration of the Zaddik replaces, in a certain sense, homage to God; hence a semblance of relic worship which is foreign to Judaism. Thus the pipe of the Baal Shem Tov is endowed with special powers: it can put to sleep evil men and render them harmless.[78] In a sweeping hyperbole the wonder-rabbi is endowed with greater powers than the Almighty: "and the Zaddikim in our generation are more important than the Holy One, blessed be He and the patriarchs and Moses our master. . ."[79] It goes without saying that the Zaddik can see and not be seen.

Special attention is given to hasidic hagiography in Perl's book. The collection of legends about the founder of Hasidism, *In Praise of the Baal Shem Tov*,[80] is castigated mercilessly:

> I don't know who the author is and what the word Besht signifies: is it the name of a man or an angel? Sometimes it seems he is a man among men, eating and drinking and sleeping with his wife in one bed like a rustic... sometimes it seems to me that he is an angel conversing with angels, with the Messiah, with Elijah, with the dead.[81]

Such verisimilitude was there in the language of Perl that the Viennese censor who had to approve publication denied it under an old Austrian law which forbade the dissemination of absurd practices and exorcisms. For more than a hundred years anyone using poor Hebrew was referred to as "a writer in the style of *The Revealer of Secrets*."[82] The parody was intentional, conscious, devastating: Humanists in the *Epistolae obscurorum virorum* imitated the corrupt Latin of the monks, Perl parodied the corrupt Hebrew of the Hasidim.[83]

The book was Perl's favorite; he had translated it into Yiddish.[84] The sequel, *The Examiner of the Zaddik*,[85] is a less vigorous satire against the same target: Hasidism. And the didactic end of the book carries no conviction: The Hasidim are blamed for the pollution of faith and the abandonment of the simple arts of the artisan as a means of economic survival.

The three letters which were appended to the anti-hasidic brochure of Isaac Ber Levinsohn discuss Perl's *The Revealer of Secrets* as if it were a hasidic work. The correspondents are trying to fathom "the great secrets which are hidden in the book."[86] As for the anti-hasidic story in Yiddish "The Greatness of R. Wolf of Cherny Ostrov,"[87] it has been proven that the author was not Perl but Hayyim Malaga, a friend of Mendel Lefin.

As a master of sarcasm Perl has few equals in modern Hebrew literature. Contemporaries and successive writers have borrowed his techniques and his themes: Isaac Ber Levinsohn, Jacob Samuel Byk, Isaac Erter. They refined them sometimes and sometimes they coarsened them. But they never appoximated his stature as a satirist.

Isaac Erter (1791–1851) scorned Hasidism with subtle vigor. As a physician he was sensitive to the droll and crude therapy of the hasidic rabbis; it consisted of an unholy mixture of incantations and folk-remedies. And it was a very profitable business. Unlike Perl, Erter used self-mockery to drive home his disgust with the new sect. Like the rabbis, he maintained, he was in the business of healing. But they assumed superior airs and spoke about everything under the sun and understood nothing. Yet he, Erter, practiced medicine as successfully as they did; his dead were as dead as the individuals who had been in the healing custody of the rabbis. But there is a difference between him and them: "I go on foot, they rush in the street with horse and carriage."[88] Interestingly, Mendele Moker Sefarim also exposed the medical fakeries of the Hasidim in the novel *The Fathers and the Sons*: Vile concoctions and magical incantations—these were the remedies given to the sick by the wonder-rabbis.

Metempsychosis and medicine are strange bedfellows; they lie side by side in hasidic lore. Erter deprecates this union and exposes the failure of therapy and the mystic fraud as they were practiced by unscrupulous Hasidim. Unlike Perl again he combined allegory which was popular in the age of enlightenment with an imaginative stance which was rare among the addicts to reason. In a chapter of his book *A Watchman Unto the House of Israel* he describes a vision: Hasidism and Wisdom appear to him in the guise of two ladies. The former seeks to convince him how easy it is to become her devotee and guide the people in her name: with a bit of cunning and folly "it is not difficult for a man to lead astray a straying people who seek miracles."[89] He is promised greatness and urged to imitate Israel Baal Shem Tov. But he is drawn to wisdom which is a quest for truth and a satisfaction of intellectual curiosity.

Somewhat later Gottlober disparaged the lechery of Hasidim in fiction. In a story "Voice of Joy and Salvation in the Tents of Zaddikim" he ridicules a certain Hayyim Michal who serves God in fear and love, studies hasidic lore all the days of his life, prays with enthusiasm, refrains from seeing man and woman—except one young woman who visits him daily and asks him to intercede with a wonder-rabbi and crave his blessing for the curse of her childlessness. She is successful; she bears a son with a strange resemblance to Hayyim Michal.[90]

The most prolific writer in the age of enlightenment, Perez Smolenskin, mounted a relentless attack on Hasidism. The foe was the incarnation of multifaceted vice. Ignorance, lack of decorum, mystical obfuscation, miraculous fakery and false exaltation, thievery and bribery, lying and lewdness—this is the incomplete list of hasidic transgressions. At best the Hasid is a carefree rascal:

> He will revel and sing, and whenever there is a celebration or a glass of wine, he is sure to be there. . .but you will not find him leading the life of a sensible man but rather that of a madman, without rhyme or reason.[91]

Smolenskin hurls his most venomous shafts at the Zaddik and his holy machinations:

> . . .every eye was riveted on the door which the Zaddik was about to enter. . .young and old they regarded him with awe, scarcely daring to look at him before he took his seat like the lord in judgment—ready to pardon penitents who had come to confess their sins and bare their sorrows before him. . .[92]

In other passages of his novels Smolenskin ridicules the wonder-making powers of the Zaddikim, their ostentation and their pseudo-erudition. The awesome respect of men and women for these individuals is a ludicruous farce in his view, an homage of innocently ignorant to the consciously ignorant.

In Smolenskin the caricature of Hasidism reached its peak; only fifty years later the idealization of Hasidism found its greatest master in Agnon.

7
Heyday of Enlightenment

Novelists of Enlightenment

Though only historians of Hebrew literature and the innocent victims of antiquated curricula in Hebrew high schools and colleges read the Hebrew novels of the last century, they still reflect—better than the histories and the sociological tracts—the life of Jewry as it was lived in the Pale of Settlement. The paintings of Marc Chagall are a belated and nostalgic commentary on that period: the Jews of his native Vitebsk—fiddling on the roofs, dancing on the clouds, praying in the empyrean—are all the Jews of Russia and Poland, Rumania and Galicia. They were driven by a religious fervor which reached ecstatic proportions on the High Holy Days, beginning with Rosh Hashanah and ending with Simhat Torah. Their faith was a matter of course; their communion with a superhuman realm of being a daily ritual. They were the spiritual Don Quixotes of the world.

The Hebrew novelists of the nineteenth century preserved the flavor of that Jewry in their novels—for their own generation and for future generations. Even when they wrote on historical themes, they managed to infuse long-forgotten Jewries with their own zeal. They were, except in their historical novels, the negative assessors of Judaism.

While Hasidism was a favorite target of Hebrew novelists in the nineteenth century, romantic and sensational novels of France exercised an unholy fascination on them. A great popularizer of the ideals of enlightenment, Kalman Schulman (1819–1899), introduced one of the worst samples of the European novel into Hebrew literature. His translation of Eugène Sue's *The Mysteries of Paris*[1] into Hebrew

135

created a faulty model for future Hebrew novelists. Braudes, Brandstädter and Smolenskin wrote bulky novels with plots à la Sue. Even Mapu who deprecated Schulman's translation learned much from Sue and Dumas. But he is no more the first Hebrew novelist than Samuel Richardson (1689–1761) is the first modern English novelist. Both have antecedents and ancestors in earlier times: Richardson harks back to John Bunyan, Mapu to such medieval story-tellers as Joseph ben Meir Zabara.[2] Both have affinities with the ancient Greek romances which are indebted to Egyptian prototypes.[3] Thus both have their roots in the past though both are conscious of contributing a new element to narrative tradition.

Mapu—the romantic and the realist—lived simultaneously in two worlds: in Judea and Samaria of the eighth century B.C.E., and in nineteenth-century Russia. He romanticized the period of Isaiah and Hosea in two novels: *The Love of Zion*[4] and *The Guilt of Samaria.*[5] And in them he created an unsophisticated world of idyllic characters. These models of innocence he confronted with unregenerate malefactors in his novels. He attempted neither psychological dissection *a la* Proust nor naturalistic detail *à la* Zola. Such techniques were beyond his capabilities. But he managed to breathe excitement and wistfulness into the top-heavy plots which mar the architecture of his novels.

Mapu created a peculiar language for his historical novels—an unadulterated mosaic of fragmentary passages from the Bible. Yet he managed to adapt it—not unsuccessfully—to the delineation of a landscape he had never seen:

> Bethlehem, the cradle of Judah's kings, lies south of Jerusalem, built upon a pleasant hump-backed hill and served by numerous wells and fountains whose crystal waters are sweet to the taste. In this delightful setting the olive trees grow fresh and the vintage vines turn purple beneath the ripening clusters. The hills are girded with delight, and the valleys adorned with a rich embroidery of flowers. The young lambs gambol, the herds of cattle pasture and the land flows with milk and honey. . .The silvery waters are flanked about with pleasing willows, while the turtle-doves and fledgeling pigeons frolic lovingly among the branches.[6]

This idyllic and idealized environment is matched by nostalgic evocations of biblical characters who speak a flawless Hebrew. Even in his violent denunciation of contemporary leadership Mapu uses the biblical idiom with anachronistic abandon. In *The Hypocrite*[7] one of the characters castigates modern writers with ancient words:

> Even from the depths of hell they would still cry out in elegant phrases! . . .Nor will they be there alone, for those who honour them will accompany them down. But why should I joke about things which are so serious? All who look for righteousness in them are deluded; for their fine words are like deadly flies that hover boldly about the flowers of paradise, daring even to penetrate the sanctuary and pollute the fragrant oil. They are saturated with lies, they shoot out their lips against both God and man, and tear out holy ideas root and branch leaving not a shred, and rejecting them utterly.[8]

Mapu was not only an incurable addict to an impossible idiom but an incorrigible dreamer who toyed with messianic delusions. His fragmentary novel about Sabbatai Zevi, *The Visionaries*,[9] might have told us more about the innermost Mapu than about the deluding and deluded visionary of Smyrna. For he regarded the book as an apogee of sublimity where the reader would find "wonderful visions in the days of the false Messiah, Sabbatai Zevi."[10] It was a broadly conceived canvass which claimed the full enthusiasm of Mapu. But only seven meagre chapters remained;[11] the rest disappeared.[12]

It is not sufficiently realized that Mapu played an important role in the history of Jewish education. He taught most of his mature life and loved both teaching and writing. If talent for writing was his God-given gift, teaching was almost an inherited profession. His father Yekutiel was a teacher of Talmud—a rung above the ordinary *Melammed.* And he tutored his own son to such an extent that he became a proficient talmudist when he was barely twelve. At fifteen Mapu studied the mysteries of Kabbalah under the tutelage of his father. Languages—Russian, German, French and Latin—he acquired without aid of teachers. For many years he was a private tutor of Hebrew; then teacher of Hebrew in a boys' school in Kovno. Though he loved Hebrew more than any other language in the world, he did not fire his charges with zeal for his subject. He was too much of an introvert, too much of a shy and retiring personality to be an effective teacher in the classroom. On the other hand, he had an immense store of Hebraic knowledge, an uncommon sensitivity to the Hebrew language, a genuine sympathy with the child and the adolescent not to be a good tutor and guide to the individual student.

It is safe to assume that Mapu represents a paradox not uncommon among Hebrew writers: a good theorist and not so good a practitioner of the art of education. That is why he suffered indignities from contemptuous students and brutal parents. A father of one of his pupils and a man of wealth, Judah Opatov, hit him once with a leather strap on his face, on his head, on his shoulders. Mapu never forgot the traumatic experience. And historians of Hebrew literature recognized Opatov as a prototype of one of the despicable characters in Mapu's fictional work: Gaal in *The Hypocrite* or Nahbi in *The House of Hanan*.[13]

An episode of a different hue made a profound impression on Mapu. On a visit to Kovno the Minister of Education in the days of Alexander II (1855–1881), Norov, met Mapu and praised his novels. The gracious attitude of a minister of the Tsar and, subsequently, the governor of Kovno, aroused a great deal of interest and jealousy among his fellow-teachers. Mapu probably added fuel to their inimical attitude. In his preface to *The Visionaries*, he boasted inordinately that Norov had told him: "I read your books, I examined them. They are written in a language as resplendent as the language of Holy Writ."[14]

It seemed inevitable that as a teacher Mapu would wish to utilize his experience and publish textbooks. In *Amon Pedagog*,[15] he effected an excellent synthesis of pedagogy and story-telling. It was Joseph Klausner who discovered a continuous thread of narrative in the lingual exercises of *Amon Pedagog* and published them as a short story under the title *The House of Hanan*.[16] He was able to do this by a few excisions and very slight editorial work. And he earned the gratitude of lovers of Hebrew literature by adding a story to the three extant novels of Mapu: *The Love of Zion, The Guilt of Samaria* and *The Hypocrite*.

Amon Pedagog was one of the most popular textbooks in Hebrew in the nineteenth century. It appealed to Jews because it stressed moral values. As a grammar and a book of exercises it endeavored to interest the adolescent and to speak to rather than above his mental capacity. Mapu used the translation method. New vocabulary and new rules of grammar were translated into transliterated German–German in Hebrew characters. For German rather than Russian was the language of the Jewish student a hundred years ago.

Amon Pedagog was designed for Jewish youth. It was the last book Mapu wrote—the swan song in his writing career. And he read the proofs in bed, during the last illness which was to put an abrupt end to his unhappy life. But *Teach the Lad*[17] is designed for Jewish children "aged seven to eight years"; it is a primer of Hebrew. The textbook claims to impart the rudiments of the language in a concise and untried "natural method" in progression from the easy to the difficult—according to the absorptive capacity of children.

Another principle guided Mapu in the composition of his textbook and in his teaching: "One should always teach his pupils in concise terms."[18] The rabbinic injunction, with its aura of respectability and validity, fortified Mapu in his own educational thinking. The child, he felt, should not be overburdened or underburdened; he should just absorb what he can absorb concisely and playfully.

According to Mapu, the foundation of knowledge, faith and religion is Hebrew. And Hebrew is also the foundation of other languages or "mother of all languages"[19] as it was widely asserted by Jews and gentiles for centuries before his birth. Quick acquisition of Hebrew through a good method—such as Mapu claimed to offer—would leave the child ample time for learning Russian, the language of the land and German, the language of the intellectual. These languages, he believed, will provide the child with tools for his chosen profession.

In his introduction to *Teach the Lad* Mapu promised two more educational books, "small in quantity and in price and very great in value..." Did he refer to *Amon Pedagog* which appeared in 1867 and *Der Hausfranzose* which appeared in 1859? Or to books designed to teach other languages like *Basic Russian* which is mentioned in the preface to *Der Hausfranzose* and, possibly, a textbook of German? *Der Hausfranzose* was intended to teach basic French quickly and almost effortlessly. But Mapu was well aware that he was doing something out of the ordinary; he used French with and without Hebrew transliteration. He also endeavored to approximate the right pronunciation through German transliteration of French words in Hebrew script—an impossible feat. And, like other leaders of the enlightenment, he assumed that the golden fruits of emancipation were to be plucked from the tree of knowledge. Moreover, Mapu loved French: Dumas *père*, author of *The Three Musketeers*[20] and Victor Hugo, author of *Les miserables,* were his favorite writers. And Eugène Sue, author of *The Wandering Jew*[21] which appeared in a Hebrew translation in 1866–1873 and *The Mysteries of Paris* which was published in a Hebrew translation in the years 1857–1860, delighted Hebrew readers. Mapu liked to think that even his name was a derivative of René Nicolas de Maupeou (1714–1792), the famous chancellor of France under Louis XV.

Der Hausfranzose was, choronologically, his first educational textbook. He hoped it would earn money and pay for still unpublished sequels of his novel *The Hypocrite*. But he was impractical in his practicality; a textbook in French was not the way to affluence. His brother Mathatias knew him well: In a letter of discommendation, published before the preface of *Amon Pedagog*, he chided him, in ungentle terms, for giving vision to a people that had no vision to provide him with a living. And he counseled him to disconcern himself with the improvement of his fellow-Jews and to concern himself with the improvement of his own lot.[22]

The idiosyncrasies and the literary predilections of Mapu vein his three textbooks and his three novels. The pedagog is merely an extension of the writer. Judah Leb Gordon, in his epitaphic sonnet on Mapu,[23] mourned the loss of the novelist and pedagog with the sure instinct of a poet. Both functions were merely dual aspects of one creative personality.

The novels of Mapu's contemporaries and followers are distinguished by unreadability; their obvious didacticism, pointing to the joys of enlightenment and the sorrows of traditionalism, starves them of verisimiltude to life. Their character delineation is a study in black and white. Their style is stilted, archaic, arty. And, since it is not fed by the spoken idiom, it courts lingual perversions: a cigarette is rendered by Smolenskin as "bitter leaves in a paper shroud";[24] a newspaper as "leaves which make new things known."[25] Weisbrem, a minor figure in the period of enlightenment, called a post office "the stage of the house of runners."[26] This is language gone astray: *Melizah*–ornate expression—for common objects. Even ordinary dialog or description of banal events degenerates into rhetoric. Disharmony of form and content is the most pronounced characteristic of the novel in the period of enlightenment. The artificiality of language is matched by melodramatic plots of violence borrowed from Eugène Sue and Alexandre Dumas.

Yet the historical value of the Hebrew novels in the second half of the nineteenth century is incontrovertible. For the protagonists of these novels are the living embodiments of contemporary problems. The slow dissolution of traditional values, the deviations from orthodoxy, which were regarded as major revolutionary acts, the fight for enlightened secularism and economic viability—these are the major themes and tensions that agitate the characters and their makers.

Braudes

Reuben Asher Braudes (1851–1902) ridiculed strict adherence to nomistic Judaism in his novel *Religion and Life*[27] which purported to reflect Jewish life in Lithuania in the years 1869–1871. And he showed how the harsh interpretation of Jewish law by the rabbi led to an ever-increasing rift in the Jewish community. Life demanded reform, but religion resisted change in the Pale of Settlement. The resultant impasse was frequently accompanied by financial hardship or starvation. In a later novel *The Two Extremes*[28] Braudes struck a new note: Neither condemnation of the traditional life nor glorification of enlightenment were the answers to the Jewish dilemma. Perhaps the will to conservatism, as represented by one protagonist of the novel, Solomon Ahitob, is stronger than the will to reform as represented by the other protagonist, Jacob Hezron, who even accepts such aspects of Hasidism as individual and communal singing with whole-hearted approval. Enlightenment has come full circle, from revolt against tradition to idealization of tradition. The dignity and the peace associated with idyllic family life is contrasted with the shoddiness and turmoil associated with the urban life. Rousseau wins on all counts; the natural man and the rural man—these are celebrated in the novel *The Two Extremes.*

Like Gordon, Braudes was sensitive to the plight of women who suffered most from rabbinic intransigence. The law of 'Agunah—the woman who cannot remarry if her husband has abandoned her or if her husband's whereabouts are unknown—and the law of Yibum—the man who must marry his brother's widow if his brother dies childless: Both were applied with merciless rigor in life, in the novel *Religion and Life* and in Gordon's poems "The Stroke on the letter Yod" and "Waiting for the Brother-in-law."

Brandstädter

A somewhat gentler attitude prevails in the stories of M.D. Brandstädter. Love is an all-pervasive theme; since young men dedicated themselves to the service of Minerva, Goddess of Reason, they were also exposed to the arrows of Amor, God of Love. This original linkage of love and enlightenment permeates the short stories of M.D. Brandstädter and accounts, to some extent, for the gentler satire against Hasidism. Still the "miracles" and the greed and the lust of the *Zaddikim* and even their silly and novel interpretations of the traditional verses and stories of the Bible are castigated with unrestrained glee. And in the narrative poem or rather story-in-verse "A Terrible Story"[29] Brandstädter creates a Jewish oedipal myth. A children's epidemic breaks out in town. The guilt is traced to the tycoon's wife who let her hair grow a bit instead of wearing a wig. The rabbi threatens her with excommunication. But she counterthreatens to grow her hair to such length that all will die. The counterthreat is effective; the rabbi capitulates. Gordon and Braudes and Brandstädter knew that the inferior status of women in the home and in society could not but lead to ignorance and to mental inferiority:

> In the towns of Lithuania most men held the common fallacy that a woman's opinion was to be despised, that woman was simply not endowed with intellect.
>
> For that reason whatever a woman said was regarded by her husband as stupid, inane or innocuous.
>
> Not infrequently one would hear women making such statements as "I'm only a dumb brute," or "What can I say? I'm only a stupid, foolish woman" or "What can a silly woman like me do?". . .They learn that they are mere animals in human guise. . .Many a woman has struggled to show her husband that she isn't a dumb brute but, on the contrary, a rational being.
>
> Finally, however, they yield, and admit that they are only ignorant women after all. In many towns the term "woman" is used to denote stupidity and ignorance; and when a man wants to dub his neighbor ignorant and stupid, he will say: "You're talking like a woman. . ."[30]

This is a quotation from the prolific Yiddish writer Nahum Meir Sheikewitz (1847–1905) who describes in his Hebrew work *The Female Outcast*[31] the misery of a girl whose father attempts to marry her off against her will. A similar plot, belabored and boring, mars Manus M. Manassewitz's (1858–1928) *The Sin of Parents*.[32] And in *Esther* Israel Joseph Sirkis (1860–1928) submits his heroine to a series of humiliations before she decides to emigrate to the United States.

Many novelists depicted the life of the Jewish woman as it was: early marriage or coveted marriage to a talmudic scholar of a respected family without regard to the age or economic standing of the groom. The bride's father was expected to provide a living for the young couple till the wife could run a store or an inn while the husband pursued his rabbinic studies in leisure. Since marriage was a matter of arrangement, romantic love was an anomaly. But the "enlightened" novelists introduced the theme of compatibility or ideal marriage either in an artificial setting or in the context of learned discussions. And they also depicted the lot of miserable women who did not marry and who worked for a mere pittance as seamstresses or servants.

Even men had few opportunities for economic advancement. Jobs were neither lucrative nor varied. The artisans, the *shusters* (cobblers) and *shneiders* (tailors), were at the bottom of the list, working long hours, eking out a meagre living. The *Melammed* (teacher) commanded a miserable income and enjoyed little respect. He frequently engaged in his profession after he proved a failure in another calling. But the teacher in the government school, with his fixed salary and official status, commanded respect.

The *Shadkan* (marriage-broker) and the *Badhan* (the jester at wedding ceremonies) lived on their wits; the former employed all tricks of persuasion, the latter all the arts of doggerel or didactic discourse. Since marriages were arranged without consultation of bride and bridegroom, the marriage-broker performed a vital service.

There were men in some lucrative professions: pawnbrokers and money-lenders, middlemen and tax-farmers, bookkeepers and inn-keepers, and even quack doctors. But wealth was enjoyed by the fewest of the few. Poverty was the hallmark of the ghetto, bribery of officialdom a way of life. Frequently men engaged in several occupations without making ends meet. The *luftmensch* was ominipresent.

Liberalization of religion, acquisition of secular knowledge and westernization of Jewish life: This is the triple ideal of education in the literature of enlightenment. Small wonder that the relentless fight against the monotonous and meagre fare of the *Heder* and the *Yeshivah* characterizes all Hebrew novelists of the nineteenth century. But not all of them display the same vehemence or subtlety. Some recognize the immense value of Jewish academies of learning. In *The Joy of the Godless*[33] Smolenskin apostrophizes the *Yeshivot* with lyric longing:

> O sacred institutions, the retreat and refuge of the remnant of Israel! It is from your gates that the chosen few still continue to emerge, those who are destined to serve as a torch for their people and infuse the spirit of life into dry bones.

Who knows but that the spirit of Israel might not have vanished completely from the face of the earth like a cloud; who knows but that the springs of truth might have been stopped up with the silt of nonsense and deceit brought by false teachers in such abundance and presented as jewels to all who would behold; who knows but that such falsehoods might have been implanted in the minds of the younger generation in the name of the Lord and His prophets?[34]

This is culture-oriented Judaism; it adumbrates, crudely and naively, the spiritual centrism of Ahad Haam, the hesitant idealization of the House of Study by Bialik.

8
Transition to Nationalism

Smolenskin as Novelist and Essayist

Between the total collapse of the emancipatory ideology and the emergence of nationalist trends there was an extremely fruitful period which may be characterized in the biblical phrase of Elijah: leaping "between two opinions."[1] Some spokesmen of the enlightenment like Judah Leb Gordon had been shaken to the core by the pogroms of 1881–1882. But they were too old to restructure their lives and, especially, their creative stance. Other leaders of the enlightenment reversed themselves completely. They were caught by the minor holocaust of the eighties when they were in their prime and they evolved a new ideology or, more importantly, a new art.

Four men played a crucial role in the period of transition: Smolenskin (1842–1885), Lilienblum (1843–1910), David Frischmann (1865–1922) and Mendele Moker Sefarim (1835–1917).

Smolenskin achieved, in his short life, an enviable literary reputation with his realistic novels, the periodical *ha-Shahar*[2] which he edited in Vienna, the nationalistic articles and books like *Eternal People*[3] and *A Time to Plant*[4] and the nationalistic novella *Vengeance for the Covenant*[5] which was the swan song of his literary career.

His life was the life of a wanderer—in Russia, in Germany, in Bohemia—before he finally settled in Vienna, the capital of the Austro-Hungarian empire. The peregrinations enabled him to observe Jewish life in its traditional and untraditional molds and acquire at the same time a thorough knowledge of Judaism and an adequate knowledge of Russian and German. His years in Shklov, the enclave of orthodoxy, in Odessa, the then emergent center of modern Hebrew literature, in Prague where he met the dying Rapoport and in Vienna,

145

the light-hearted city of graceful musicians and nimble litterateurs gave him a rare insight into many facets of nineteenth century life.

Most of his stories and novels appeared in the monthly *ha-Shahar* which he founded, published and edited from 1868 to his dying day. They were vacuous and wordy; they were weighted with discussions and criticisms of Shakespeare and Lessing and Goethe; they were tortuous in style and in content. But they managed to convey the plight of Jewry under the unfriendly regime of Russian bureaucracy and the internal pressures of fanatic leadership. For almost all his stories and novels present the present—the contemporaneous moment in history. Unlike Mapu with his penchant for the past, Smolenskin had an eye for Christian-Jewish relationships; more than Mapu he developed a realistic disdain for the seamy side of human nature and communicated it to his readers: treachery, unsavory gambling on the stock exchange, fanatic excesses. The most characteristic of his novels *The Wanderer On The Roads of Life*[6] which made its debut in the first issue of *ha-Shahar* is a quatrepartite tale of a wandering orphan. In the first part he is exposed to the gentle and not so gentle care of relatives and strangers and even a miracle man; he lands in the City of Darkness or Darkville[7] where intrigues poison the daily lives of the inhabitants. In the second part he is in the City of Bereavement[8] where he studies in a traditional academy and imbibes the first draughts of enlightenment. In the third part he wanders to the City of Hypocrisy[9] where he observes the unsavory ways of hasidic life, the wonder-rabbi and the blinded disciples and admirers; he moves to St. Petersburg and also manages to amass a fortune in Hamburg and lose it; he decides to join a singer-actor group and to get as far as London. In the fourth part the protagonist resides in Paris, Brussels and Berlin and returns, by way of Rumania, to his native Russia.

The Wanderer On the Roads of Life is a complicated novel with autobiographical and adventuresome admixtures. It depicts hypocrisy with more sarcastic contempt than Mapu's novel *The Hypocrite* which influenced Smolenskin; it is bitter in its denunciation of the foes of enlightenment; it is unforgiving to Hasidism and its excesses; it castigates the fanatics and their cruel denunciations of heresy—imagined or real—which frequently led to abduction into military service for life. Smolenskin never forgot the tragedy in his own family: His brother was kidnapped for a lifetime of military service.

Slowly and imperceptibly Smolenskin shifted from denationalization of Jewry to nationalism in the two books which appeared serially in *ha-Shahar: Eternal People* and *Time to Plant.* Just as the pogroms a decade later destroyed the viability of enlightenment, the pogroms of Greeks against the Jews in Odessa in 1871 may well have had the effect of an initial breakdown of enlightenment. Smolenskin had lived in Odessa and he was deeply touched by the events of the unhappy city. And when he criticized the critics of religious reform in his book *Eternal People,* he made a declaration which lost nothing of its lustre after 100 years:

> "Since Jewish religion is the one bond that binds and unites Jews wherever they live, we have to regard it not only as a faith but as a land and a state and a language. . ."[10]

Smolenskin extended the meaning of religion to include the nationalist triad—land, language, state—and defended it as an asset which must be studied in the original Hebrew and which must not be shortchanged by well-meaning or ill-meaning reformers.

But he is still a man of the enlightenment in the early seventies of the previous century; he is deeply committed to the economic and intellectual advancement of Jewry. In his estimation this objective can best be accomplished by a vast organizational and administrative set-up like the *Alliance Israélite Universelle.*[11] The time is ripe: it is "a time to speak and a time to act."[12]

Nationalist stirrings in Europe during the better part of the nineteenth century, Smolenskin's involvement in quasi-political work and the work of his predecessors—Alkalay, Kalischer and Hess—had a profound effect on his ideological outlook. Greece, ancestress of the arts of living and thinking, achieved independence in 1831, Belgium in the same year, Italy in 1861, and the German Empire was proclaimed in 1871. In the seventies Rumania, Serbia, Bulgaria became independent. There were revolutions—some abortive, some partially successful—which demonstrated unquenched desires for national liberation. Hungary became semi-independent in 1867 in a compromise arrangement with Austria; the Czechs and the Poles, unable to achieve liberty in the nineteenth century, became independent states after the First World War. Even more than the national liberation movements the lingual and literary renaissances which preceded and precipitated the birth of many states in Europe, affected Smolenskin and all his contemporaries. Adamantios Korais fostered the development of modern Greek and clamored for independence from the Turks; Mazzini's writings, especially his letters, advocated a noble nationalism for Italy; Josef Jungmann who composed a Czech grammar, a

Czech-German dictionary and a history of Czech literature, regarded language as *the* criterion of nationality; Vuk Stefanović Karadžić [Vuk Stefanovich Karajich] who published a Serbian grammar, a Serbian dictionary and a collection of Serbian folk-songs contributed to the rise of nationalism in southeastern Europe. Eliezer ben Yehudah was well aware of the nationalizing and unifying power of language when he began working on his monumental dictionary of the Hebrew language; for him as for Korais, Karadžić and Jungmann, philology was not merely the leisurely occupation of a scholar but the most revolutionary tool for the acquisition of independence.[13]

Smolenskin's contact with Rumanian Jewry in 1874 as an emissary of the *Alliance Israélite Universelle* fortified him in his nationalist tendencies. For a while the *Alliance* was so highly regarded by him that he called it a "Holy Society." When it advocated and supported emigration to America in the eighties, he was so disappointed that he thought of establishing a rival organization.[14] But his organizational talents were meagre and would-be allies like Sir Lawrence Oliphant were uncongenial.

Nationalist tendencies of Smolenskin were fed by such antecedents as the Serbian Yehudah Alkalay (1798–1878), Rabbi Zevi Hirsch Kalischer of Posen (1795–1874) and Moses Hess. It was Alkalay who believed in evolutionary redemption,[15] in Hebrew as a unifying language of Jewry and in an international Jewish organization which would negotiate with Turkey for the return of Palestine to the Jews.[16]

In a similar pragmatic stance Kalischer preached redemption with a complementary idea which was in vogue among his enlightened contemporaries: "Jewish farming would be a spur to the ultimate messianic redemption."[17] The influence of Hess on Smolenskin was so blatant that Frischmann bluntly accused Smolenskin as a plagiator: the *Eternal People* was, in his estimate, a copy of *Rome and Jerusalem*.[18] It was an unjustified and gross exaggeration. The book of Hess drew an historical analogy: Rome revived, Jerusalem will also rise from its ruins; the ideals of the French Revolution which gave new life to Italy will eventually liberate Judea. But Smolenskin preached educational reform and emphasis on the Hebrew language prior to eventual redemption. While Hess stressed the social aspects of future liberation, Smolenskin endeavored to reclaim the past cultural heritage as a condition of redemption.

Time to Plant is a declaration of war against the pioneer of enlightenment, Moses Mendelssohn, and his alleged thesis that Jewry is simply a religious entity.[19] Smolenskin wrote it at the height of the "cultural struggle" (Kulturkampf) in Germany in 1873–1876.[20] That struggle was to determine the dominant priority of either religion or the state and, thanks to Bismarck, the Iron Chancellor, it ended with victory for the secular rather than the sacred state.

Smolenskin contended in Time to Plant[21] that the specificity of Jewry was its unique immortal spirituality[22] "for the spirit does not die—ever";[23] that the content of spirituality was "national feeling.[24] Others have stressed the spirituality of Judaism: Krochmal in the Guide of the Perplexed of Our Time, Geiger who called Judaism a religion of the spirit and, after Smolenskin, Ahad Haam who postulated a spiritual center for Jewry in former Palestine. For them the aspirations of Jewry were the embodiment of spirituality. But Smolenskin maintained that "only the national feeling and our living Torah, not the laws, will revive our people."

The conquest of Palestine by agricultural labor was not Smolenskin's goal in Time to Plant. The establishment of rabbinical seminaries and teachers' colleges—that was the main objective. In propagandistic terms Smolenskin asserted: "The great and important thing is. . .colonization of the Land of Israel."[25] But the practical means leading to the establishment of a state were not spelled out. Vague allusions to the national will and national consensus which are fed by hopes of redemption which, in turn, are fed by eternal hatred for the eternal people—these were evaluative statements rather than programs for action. But they hastened the demise of enlightenment with its emphasis on integration into the gentile environment and absorption of gentile culture. That the end of enlightenment was achieved by Smolenskin, the novelist of enlightenment par excellence—that was one of the ironies of literary history.

It was not only Smolenskin the editor and essayist who embraced nationalism in his mature years. It was also the novelist who adopted a new stance. In a word: the total man changed totally. His last novella Vengeance for the Covenant is a nationalist story. Two points of view, represented by Ben Hagri, the youthful assimilationist, and Ben Jacob, the youthful nationalist, are tested against a background of pogroms. The former's sister is the victim of theft; her necklace, stolen by his aristocratic Christian friend during anti-Jewish riots, appears on the neck of his beloved, a gift of the noble thief. To add insult to injury, the lady retains the stolen property even after she realizes what circumstances brought it into her possession. Ben Hagri's rival manages to injure him in a scuffle in the aftermath of the scene which divulges to her the secret of the gift. Finally, confronted with a group of his own people on the ninth day of Ab, the day of mourning for fallen Zion, Ben Hagri is converted to nationalism—against the wishes of his mother and with the blessing of his father and grandfather.

Smolenskin maintained that redemption of Israel was possible only in the Land of Israel.[26] The individual redemption of Ben Hagri—like that of his people—was the result of his personal defeat. Unfortunately, longueurs marred even his short story "Vengeance for the Covenant." If his major fault was longwindedness, his major virtue was complete dedication to his people. As a writer he succeeded to transmit that dedication to his readers.

Lilienblum: Propagandist of Nationalism

Moses Leb Lilienblum an architect of the center of Hebrew literature in Odessa, was a Lithuanian Jew who had experienced small-town fanaticism and reacted against it mildly or angrily in turn. Like other leaders of the enlightenment he preached the doctrine of economic sanation: useful occupations must form the basis of a useful life. Unlike other leaders of the enlightenment he regarded rabbinic Judaism as a technique of adaptation; our sages were "men and not angels"; they marched with the times. The need for constant change according to changing circumstances—that is the supreme desideratum. Adaptibility against rigidity: that is the message of Lilienblum toward the end of the sixties and the beginning of the seventies in his autobiography, in his articles on the Talmud, in his satire on traditional Judaism.

The pogroms of 1881–1882 effected a radical change: Lilienblum became one of the founders of modern nationalism in Hebrew literature. Or to use his terminology: he found "The Way to Return"[27] and to national resurrection. Henceforth he regards emancipation as an illusion because antisemitism is the reality and the mystique of the diaspora: "You have forgotten that we are strangers here [in Europe]. . .The peoples of Europe are Aryans; we are Semites. . .The Land of Israel is given to us in perpetuity."[28] This was the new manifesto in black and white: either the return to the Land of Israel or assimilation, disappearance, death of the people.

More effective in practical leadership than Smolenskin, Lilienblum took an active part in the pre-Zionist and Zionist organizations. As secretary of a committee for the colonization of Palestine he became an energetic and distinguished activist. For his practical work as a Zionist was a corollary of his theoretical tracts on Jewish nationalism. In the period of transition from enlightenment to nationalism he was a major journalist and propagandist of a Palestine-oriented direction for Jewry.

Frischmann: Arbiter of Literary Taste

It was a paradoxical twist of literary history that David Frischmann, the enemy of enlightenment, was guided by an idolatrous love for the Bible. His best stories are based on pre-Canaanite wanderings of the Jews in the desert. His poetry—including the declamable "Messiah" —deserves the scathing evaluation of Jacob Fichmann: "It was perhaps more of a will to poetry than poetry itself."[29] But his critical essays were envenomed shafts which hit leading writers and second-raters indiscriminately. They bore a strange resemblance to those articles of Anatole France which were originally written for *Le Temps* and later collected in his *Vie littéraire*. The pessimistic tone, the fine irony and, above all, the highly impressionistic approach to literature, were common to both of them. Frischmann's dictum that "criticism is the most personal manifestation of feeling in the world as art itself"[30] might have been written by France.

Frischmann was admired and feared as an arbiter of taste. He made and unmade reputations with his potent pen. One of his earliest essays, *"Tohu wa-Bohu,"* established his immediate fame. At an early age and throughout his life he was quick to notice pompous verbosity and confused thinking. His literary taste and tact which showed to great advantage in his short-lived periodical *ha-Dor* were not infallible. He had a blind admiration for European literature, not because he was an "occidental writer"[31] but because his outlook on life was dominated by the obsession that the world outside the ghetto was a miracle of beauty. Hence his adulation of European writers, his insolence to Hebrew writers.

Frischmann was not only a short story writer and a critic but also a prolific translator. Byron's *Cain*, Wilde's *De Profundis*, Tagore's *The Gardener*, *Fruit-Gathering* and *The Crescent Moon*, Nietzsche's *Also sprach Zarathustra*, Pushkin's lyrics and Andersen's tales owe him their Hebrew versions which are charming though not literal. His crowning achievement was the vast work of translation which he directed as editor of the quarterly *ha-Tekufah* and adviser to its publisher Abraham Joseph Stybel. That periodical which commenced its career in Russia during the First World War and expired in America after the termination of the Second World War raised the level of Hebrew literature. And hundreds of translations which appeared in its pages and under the imprimatur of its publisher infused new blood into the life stream of Hebrew belles lettres.

Frischmann was the first man of letters in modern Hebrew literature. He lived by his pen and he had no interests outside literature. An esthete and interpreter of contemporary trends in European poetry, not unlike Arthur Symons in England on the threshold of the new century, he imposed his literary taste on an entire generation till the end of the First World War. Ahad Haam dominated Jewish thought, Frischmann had a hold on the imagination of his contemporaries. And no critic of Hebrew literature ever matched his authority. For he managed to mold his readers without recourse to mystic flirtations and decadent perversions which were popular in the first two decades of the twentieth century.

Mendele as Master Novelist

S.J. Abramowitsch, better known by his pseudonym Mendele Moker Sefarim[32] became the leading Hebrew novelist in the course of his long writing career. His youthful penchant for natural sciences resulted in the translation of a popular German book on natural science. Already at that early age he showed originality; numerous terms of his coinage served as the nucleus and model of the modern scientific vocabulary in Hebrew. His preoccupation with nature was not an accidental whim of youth. Hardly any other writer had that tender attachment to the grass of the field, to the bird on the wing, to the tree of the forest. Berdyczewski urged Jews to establish a new covenant with nature but Mendele made nature live in his work in spite of the squalor and dirt which are the inevitable corollaries of ghetto-life.

Like Shalom Aleyhem and Isaac Leibush Peretz, Mendele was primarily a Yiddish writer but, unlike them, he translated his most important works into Hebrew.[33] It is, indeed, the point of coalescence between Hebrew and Yiddish literature that is most clearly observable in the works of these three writers. Nevertheless, to claim—as Isaac Bashevis Singer is reported to claim—that "modern Hebrew literature is a product of Yiddish literature" is unadulterated nonsense.[34] Both literatures grew in different dimensions. While modern Hebrew literature cultivated many genres in many centuries, modern Yiddish literature may be said to have had a single period of bloom: from the end of the nineteenth century to the thirties of this century—some fifty years all told. That brief period was also a period of cross-fertilization. Often writers wrote in both languages or were cognizant of both literatures. Mendele who translated his works into Hebrew, yiddished the Book of Psalms. The manuscript—now lost—was never published but some passages and even entire psalms in his translation are extant.[35]

Mendele's translations or free adaptations mark an epoch in Hebrew literature because they definitely abandon the biblical style or rather the quaint mosaics of biblical half-verses and quarter-verses which, since the eighteenth century, reigned supreme in prose and poetry and gave them a pseudoclassical and pseudopoetical flavor. Mendele delved into rabbinic writings, found in them untapped sources of conversational language and utilized them on a large scale. There were already in the period of enlightenment men like Menahem Mendel Lefin and Judah Leb Gordon who occasionally drew upon the resources of mishnaic and midrashic Hebrew, but Mendele created out of them a prose style which was, and still is, one of the dominant influences in modern Hebrew literature. There was a danger, of course, that the talmudic phrase would be used *ad nauseam* as the biblical phrase had been used in the eighteenth and even in the nineteenth century. And though Mendele did not avoid it completely, his younger contemporaries—Berkowitz and Barasch, Agnon and Hazaz, Kabak and Steinman—overcame it successfully. This new style is evident from his first novel *Fathers and Sons,* published in 1868, till his last work. Even the earlier version of the novel,[36] *Learn Well,* published in 1862, and republished in a facsimile editon by *Yivo* in 1969, indicates the new style, the new approach to nature, the new sense of realism. The story is full of villainous intrigue and sentimentalized love. As such it belongs to the period that produced Mapu's *Love of Zion* and Schulman's translation of Eugène Sue's *Mysteries of Paris*—novels of extreme plot complication and naive characterization. But Mendele knew the social ills of his period and he castigated them mercilessly—whether he found them in upper or lower segments of Jewry. He also knew the secret of novelistic relief. In skillfull vignettes he caught the multiform moods of nature and blended its rhythms with the thoughts of characters. As for his own personality, he painted his self-portrait in the fictionalized autobiography *In Those Days*[37] which reads like a minature *Dichtung und Wahrheit.* Unfortunately it covers only his early days—from childhood to the period of adolescence when he rose to the beggarly status of a Yeshivah student. An *odor iudaicus*, in the good sense of the word, permeates this and all his other works.

> Writing is a madness, a sort of weakness and folly like the desire of certain people to perform cantorially in the synagogue and astonish the congregation with their voice.[38]

With a self-knowledge, rare in a *littérateur*, he confesses frankly:

> "This world of mine, alas and alack, is a very small world and its people are simple Jews with beards and earlocks and long *kapotas*, emaciated, withered and poor, bent and sickly and depressed, anxious and fearful. . .We have not been dukes and governors, generals and warriors; we have not made love to pretty girls, we have not gored each other like goats; we have not been seconds when blood was shed in duels; we have not known how to dance with brides and women at drinking parties; we did not hunt animals in field and forest; we did not travel to the ends of the earth and we did not sail the far seas and we did not discover new islands."[39]

There is pity for the ghetto Jew in these words and an envious disdain of the great, wide world which charmed and repelled Mendele and his generation. But they also convey the outline of a literary program which was elaborated by him in such detail that no historian can afford to write about Russian Jewry in the nineteenth century without having recourse to his writing. With an insight into people and a descriptive ability which were suffused with lyrical warmth he depicted the Jews in their abject poverty; in their tattered dress, in their unprofitable occupations and in their miserable recreations. Their defects, bred by an unwholesome and unhygienic environment, were subjected to microscopic observation and to scathingly ironical or mildly merciful evaluation. One gets the incorrect impression from his works that the Jews are a people of beggars. Even the fictitious places in which he makes them live are symbolical projections of their shortcomings: Fooltown, Idletown, Poortown. In a typical passage, laced with irony, Mendele paints the ghetto with a few bold strokes of his brush:

> Fooltown is a perfect Jewish town in all details. It is comtemptuous of the art of the architect and does not obey its laws.

The houses do not stand upright and arrogant against the sky. They are small, some even bent, with roofs sloping to the very ground; no paint, no adornment outside. For grace is deceitful and beauty is vain and not worth the loss of a penny.[40]

Only Dostoevsky showed such sympathy with poverty. And only the contrapuntal effects of fields and forests relieve the monotony of misery. Whether Mendele writes an allegorical novel where he compares an entire people to a moribund mare as in *My Mare*[41] or a travesty on an adventurous expedition to a fabulous country as in the *Journeys of Benjamin the Third* he makes his plots incidental to milieu and character. But these he handles with consummate skill.

> When you ask an inhabitant of Idletown: 'What do you do for a living and how do you maintain yourself?' He looks confused and does not know what to answer but, having regained his composure, he stammers, "What do I do? Vanity of vanities. There is a God in heaven, I tell you, who feeds all creatures in his great goodness. . ." "Tell me, nevertheless, what do you do? What trade or business are you engaged in?" "Praised be the name of the Lord. As I am standing here before you life-size, I have a great gift from the Lord, praised be His name. I have a good reputation and a pleasant voice, so I am a cantor in the synagogue and I pray during the high holidays in one of the neighboring towns. I am also skilled in the art of circumcision and in the perforation of unleavened bread. Indeed, in these things I have no equal in the world. Sometimes I dabble in matchmaking. I also have my permanent seat in the synagogue and, by the way, but let this remain a secret between us, I have some liquor in the house for sale which brings in some profit; also a milking goat with resourceful udders—may the evil eye have no power over her. And in this neighborhood I have a relative, a man of wealth and influence; and, he too, pities and gives willy-nilly, and gives again and again in time of need. And besides all that, I tell you, God, blessed be His name, is a merciful father and the Jews are merciful men, sons of merciful men. Why, then, should a man complain?"[42]

No writer has succeeded as well as Mendele to enclose the economic misery of an entire people in a few sentences charged with sarcasm and satire.[43] Appropriately, he entitled one of his novels *The Book of Beggars*[44] and another *In the Valley of Tears.*[45] But Mendele also knew the valley of enchantment:

> When I came into the depth of the forest, I chanced upon a valley full of bushes and thorns. . .The forest slumbers. The tree-tops form a dark veil over its head. Peace and silence. You only hear the whisper of two tall and tender trees which stretch their branches toward each other, embrace and kiss. This is the voice of leaves which tremble and shake on one of the trees as if frightened in their repose by an evil spirit. This is the language of the forest talking in its sleep and this is its dream—a vision of yesterday and yesterday's mishaps. There is a rustle there like the rustle of dry branches—that's the murmur of poor trees which come before the forest in a dream and complain that they were felled before their time. There is the voice of falling from above there; it is the falling of a bird-nest with its tender and innocent chicks destroyed by the cruel hawk suddenly. And that is why the leaves stir now; they mourn with the mother the young that were killed and appear to the forest in a dream.[46]

Such a feeling for the poetry of the forest was afterwards reached again in Hebrew literature by Mendele's admiring disciple, the poet Saul Tschernichowsky. But before Mendele no one had such a gift of landscape painting in words. Dostoevsky had a deeper knowledge of people. But it was knowledge unrelieved by the soothing ministrations of nature to humanity. The sufferings, conveyed by Mendele, are bearable; they are the sufferings of man in a green environment.

Assessment of Enlightenment

Some writers of the enlightenment deplored the onesidedness in traditional education, others resented the smug superficiality in secular education. Some defended ancient ways, others advocated radical breaks with the past. Some fought the excesses of Hasidism, others rejected the rabbinical seminaries which were established by the czarist government in Vilna and Zhitomir as tools of assimilation. All aspired to western culture either through autodidacticism or through a university education. All believed that European dress and manners and professional diversification were the best means of integration into the majority culture. And all were rudely awakened from the comfort of their futile beliefs and opinions by the pogroms of

1881 and 1882, and all of them were compelled to change their aspirations. The new ideal was nationalism in its multiple shadings—from orthodox to liberal, from socialist to chauvinist. What remained from the legacy of enlightenment was pursuit of secular learning—a counterpart or complement of the age-old passion for learning which characterized Jewry from biblical times. This passion can still be sensed in a writer of Jewish origin, Ilya Ehrenburg (1891-1967) who became the pillar of Soviet literature and who wrote immediately before his death:

> I am old in years, but now I know with certainty that I know little. One must go on learning as long as there is breath in one's body, and a student's bench becomes even an old man. . .[47]

9
Ideologues of Nationalism

Varieties of Nationalism

Literature anticipates life; it sets up models of political and social structures in intuitive shocks of wisdom. In a book, published in 1912, *A Very Wakeful Sleep*, the translator of Shakespeare into Turkish, Abdullah Cevdet, outlined a utopia which envisioned the entire reform program of Kemal Ataturk, the founder of modern Turkey. As for Jews, more than any other ethnic group they relied on the wisdom of their sages for the conduct of their lives. And most if not all the creative aspects of contemporary Jewry stem from Hebrew literature. Even the nationalist movement which culminated in the establishment of the Jewish State is its unacknowledged creation. A vague form of political Zionism was advocated by Smolenskin before Herzl, orthodox Zionism (*Mizrahi*) was originated by Pines and Jawitz, spiritual Zionism was molded by Ahad Haam, labor Zionism was formed and fostered by Aaron David Gordon and Joseph Hayyim Brenner, Revisionism was partly inspired by Jacob Cahan and Micah Joseph Berdyczewski, the little-known though important branch of Jewish nationalism which might be called ultra-nationalist Zionism was launched by Jacob Klatzkin and Ezekiel Kaufmann, Canaanism could be traced, ideologically, to the poetry of Judah Leb Gordon and, partially, to Tschernichowsky.

Contemporary Hebrew literature has its immediate antecedents in Russia on the eve of the last decade of the nineteenth century. Enlightenment, the movement which regarded emancipation and relaxation of orthodoxy as a panacea for all Jewish ills, ended in the impasse of assimilation or conversion, and died with its most forceful exponent, Judah Leb Gordon. Zionism and socialism, in combined or isolated form, replaced the ideals of enlightenment. Sensitivity to political events in Europe also molded the rise of nationalist feelings among Jews. It was right sensitivity. For in the twentieth century nationalism was the *force majeure* in politics; it made and unmade empires, it created new states and demolished old ones; it brought independence to the dependent and, in some cases, it subjugated peoples in tyrannical vises; it became the great molder of the third world in Africa, and it reshaped Asia. Nationalism was a force of destruction and liberation which had few ideological analogues in durability.

Ahad Haam and Ahad Haamism

It was Asher Ginzberg, better known as Ahad Haam[1] (1856–1927) who gave a new direction to Hebrew literature and dominated its ideological outlook for a generation: from the publication of his first article "This is Not the Way"[2] in 1889 till the First World War.[3] He won immediate recognition as a man of spiritual authority in Odessa where he settled in 1886. And Odessa was *tonangebend*: it set the tone and pace of Hebrew literature for half a century—from the seventies of the nineteenth century to the early twenties of the twentieth century. Before Ahad Haam, Lilienblum and Pinsker, the precursors of Zionism as well as Mendele, the father of modern Hebrew prose, lived there and created there. A decade after Ahad Haam had settled in Odessa, scholars like Joseph Klausner and Hayyim Tchernowitz [*Rav Zair*], poets like Bialik and Tschernichowsky sojourned there for briefer or longer periods of time. Like a magnet it drew younger Jews from their idyllic retreats in small towns and villages—in spite of dire warnings of conservative parents that the fires of hell burn around the city and that "the air of Odessa leads to heresy."[4] It was the Southern Belle, the atypical Russian city of sun and fun, sea and light: "In Odessa there are sweet and relaxing spring evenings, the strong scent of acacias, and, over the dark sea, a moon which radiates a steady, irresistible light."[5] The author of this lyrical aperçu, a native Odessan and martyred Russian writer of Jewish descent, attributed Odessa's easygoing, straightforward charm to Jews.[6] But it was not only a city of scholars and scribblers; it also hosted Jewish thieves and thugs in the slum-suburb of Moldavanka.[7] In an ironic *tour de force* Isaac Babel prophesied that "the literary Messiah. . .will come from there—from the sunny steppes washed by the sea."[8] The literary Messiah failed to come from Odessa but his precursors filled the streets with premessianic excitement.

Even when Ahad Haam moved to London in 1908 and ceased writing frequently, he was the acknowledged master of Jewish thought in Odessa, in all Russia, in the entire Jewish world. In 1922 he moved to Tel Aviv and spent there his last five years. There he edited a selection of his letters—close to 1700—with some deletions. Though in his own opinion he was only a guest in literature, he impregnated it with his ideas to a greater extent than the official hosts. For a guest is a creature of tension. And his condition can be creative and inventive. Steeped in the Talmud and the medieval codices and considered a rabbinical authority before his twentieth year, he managed, nevertheless, to preserve a refreshing originality of thought and a lucid style. So scrupulously did he avoid the worn phrases and the profuse quotations which most of his contemporaries used for padding their writings that he achieved an almost occidental rhythm in his prose. That is why Ahad Haam lost little or nothing in translation.

Throughout his creative period which terminated in the second decade of this century, he never swerved from the ideas which he propounded at the outset of his literary career. And he never deviated from the form of the essay which proved to be his only mode of expression. He wished to systematize his ideas in a book which was to capture "the essence of Judaism."[9] He even had a name for it: *Ethics of Judaism*.[10] But the book was never written, and the ideas, sometimes embryonic or half-developed, were scattered in pint-size and king-size essays which are known by the collective title *At the Crossroads*.[11]

It was a small circle of ideas. But Romain Rolland justly remarked that art always moved in a narrow circle of ideas. The force of personality which the artist succeeds to impose upon the world remains active beyond his lifetime.[12] Ahad Haam had that force. He drew it from the *Guide of the Perplexed* of Maimonides, from the ethical distillates of biblical and post-biblical sources and, to a considerable extent, from the great Victorians—Thomas Carlyle, John Stuart Mill, Charles Darwin and Herbert Spencer.[13] Their involvement in the science versus religion controversy, their high-minded, low-humored personalities appealed to Ahad Haam, who was "an eminent Victorian" by inclination rather than by birth.

Unlike many of his older and younger contemporaries—Pinsker, Lilienblum, A.D. Gordon—he is not dated. His sensitivity to the dangers of assimilation and his search for a new nationalism, his belief in spiritual redemption in the form of a spiritual center for Jewry in the Land of Israel—these are valuable guides for contemporary Jewry. For assimilation which leads to severance of all ties with Judaism is a constant danger for the comtemporary Jew. And the lack of a viable ideal—such as Ahad Haam postulated and proclaimed—led to nihilistic emasculation. What he did not foresee was the sudden ascendancy of Oriental Jewry as a redemptive force in Israel—both demographically and religiously.

Ahad Haam was one of the most harmonious personalities in modern Hebrew literature, at peace with himself though often, being uncompromising and unyielding, at war with the world. His theoretical abilities were so well blended with practical acumen that his activities appeared to him and to others as corollaries of his writings. Thus, five days before the publication of his first article, he founded an organization called *Bene Moshe* (The Sons of Moses).[14] It was expected to live up to the lofty ideals of Moses who, according to a talmudic legend, was born and died on the seventh day of the month of Adar.[15] It was also meant to incorporate the principal ideas of his first article, especially those ideas which aimed at the moral regeneration of Jews. Though small in size—it numbered more than 200 members—it had a far-reaching influence in eastern Europe and even in America. For its zealous adherents were fed up with the pre-Zionist movement known as Love of Zion[16] and devoted themselves to the colonization of Palestine. They founded the first colonies with great enthusiasm but without adequate preparation. After a few years the colonies were on the verge of bankruptcy and, far worse, the idea of a national revival in Palestime was destined to become a delusion. Edmond de Rothschild's financial assistance saved the colonies from doom. But Ahad Haam and his band of zealots saved the idea with his very first essay.

> Every belief or opinion which leads to action must necessarily be founded on the following three judgments: First, that the attainment of a certain object is felt by us to be needed; secondly, that certain actions are the means of the attainment of the object; and thirdly, that those actions are not beyond our power, and the effort which they require is not so great as to outweigh the value of the object in our estimation.[17]

Ahad Haam maintained that the mosaic code had one purpose only: the welfare of the nation in a land of its own. Consciously or unconsciouly, he repeated Hess's assertion: Judaism is a national religion; not the individual but the nation is its chief interest, not individual salvation or immortality but social justice is its aim. That, incidentally, was a view diametrically opposed to Karl Marx who regarded Judaism as the source of egocentrism. Moses Hess, first a disciple of Marx and later an opponent of his former master, posed the thesis that Judaism is the embodiment of solidarity. This point of view prefigured the main theories of Ahad Haam. Unsystematically and somewhat sketchily he traced the development of Judaism after the fall of Jerusalem in 586 B. C. E. With the first destruction of the Temple and with the loss of political independence the philosophy of individual welfare prevailed in Jewish life. Since it was well suited to the exigencies of a scattered people, it contributed to the disintegration of national feeling and, consequently, of national responsibility. The first task, therefore, that devolved upon the modern Jew was the education of the heart.

With this plea for emotional re-education Ahad Haam finished his first essay which is characteristic of all his writings: a practical problem serves as a stimulus and justification for criticism, usually negative, of a prevailing state of affairs. Allusions to Jewish history, philosophical ideas and examples from the natural sciences are adduced to buttress the criticism. Sometimes the process is reversed; an abstract problem serves as a stimulus and the practical application is the real aim of the essay. Ahad Haam is rarely interested in the mere elucidation of an abstract problem. His emphasis on the education of the heart has often been overlooked by critics who depicted him as a cool and detached writer.[18] Yet his belief in the potency of national feeling amounted to a mystical creed. He even asserted that western Jews who have become assimilated with an amazing rapidity remained Jews only because a spark of national feeling was still alive in them.

> Every true Jew, be he orthodox or liberal, feels in the depths of his heart that there is something apart in the spirit of our people. . .He who still has that feeling will remain within [the fold of Judaism.] This national feeling permeates even such men as Maimonides to an extent that it conquers their logic.[19]

That he harped on the revival of the heart was more than a need of his heart; it was mature wisdom not unlike that of Montesquieu who maintained that certain truths must be felt. Ahad Haam aimed at a national movement, and national movements live on the heart rather than on the brain. Even in his essay "Truth From Palestine"[20] he endeavored to show that the colonization of Palestine, in spite of the massive support of Baron Edmond de Rothschild, became a gigantic failure in the nineties of the last century because of insufficient idealism on the part of the Jews

Political Zionism incurred the enmity of Ahad Haam. He was too much of a realist to relish Herzl's diplomatic activities which were to lead to the acquisition of former Palestine from the Turkish government. This, to him, was a strange fantasy conceived in the brain of a Jew whose nationalist fervor grew out of an assimilationist background. That is why Ahad Haam acted as a constant corrective to Herzl. With a knowledge of Jewish affairs which has lost nothing of its timeliness and without a trace of bitterness he complained:

> Almost all of our great men. . .are spiritually removed from Judaism, and they have no true conception of its nature and its value.[21]

This oblique allusion to Herzl and other leaders was fully justified. The father of political Zionism wrote *The Jewish State*[22] in a period of two months in Paris. But he sought and found relief from creative tension at the Paris Opera in Wagner's *Tannhäuser*.[23] In a curious irony of history, the creator of Zionism acknowledged his debt to one of the most virulent antisemites of the previous century. His very notion of Jewish nationalism is, in his own opinion, the effect of antisemitism: the Jews are a nation because the nations of the world refuse to accept them as their equals.

In Vienna Herzl had ample opportunity to observe and feel the venomous antisemitism in the press, in literature, in society. Rohling's *Talmudjude,* published in 1871, became a source-book of antisemitic diatribe like the *Protocols of the Elders of Zion* in the twentieth century. Student fraternities at the University of Vienna such as *Libertas* shut its doors to the Jews. Schönerer and Lueger developed a virulent political antisemitism. Yet Austria, at the end of the century and during the first decades of the twentieth century, played an important role in world literature and culture because of the achievements of its Jews: Freud, Hofmannsthal, Schnitzler, Werfel, Zweig, Kafka, Musil, Broch, Reinhardt.

But, in justice to Herzl, it should be said that he was driven by an élan and an exaltation which were capable to inspire large masses of people. Thus, after the adjournment of the First Zionist Congress in Basle, he wrote in his diary: "In Basle I laid the foundation for the Jewish State. Perhaps in five years, and certainly in fifty, everyone will know it."[24] In 1947 the United Nations voted the establishment of the Jewish State.

A month after the First Zionist Congress in Basle in August 1897, the proletarian organization of Jewish workers in Russia and Poland, the so-called *Bund* was founded in Vilna. Both endeavored to create a new life for the Jew: Zionism for all Jews in Palestine, *Bund* for Jewish masses in all the lands of the world. Zionism with its "narrower," nationalistic base prevailed; the *Bund* with its socialist bias was an adventure in political futility. It can be said in its favor that it encouraged the development of Yiddish literature. Zionism inspired and was inspired by Hebrew literature. Herzl had little understanding for either literature; he advocated a panacea for the ills of the Jews. Ahad Haam emphasized the urgency of the ills of Judaism. This divergence of ideas was conditioned by temperamental differences. Ahad Haam was slow and careful in his judgments; Herzl impatient and flashy in his actions. Perhaps the former had, to use a mystical notion of Thomas Mann, a physiological foreboding of a long life.[25] At any rate, he did not see the immediate necessity for an independent state. Even a good-sized settlement of Jews in their ancestral home could

> become in the course of time the center of the nation wherein its spirit would find pure expression and develop in all its aspects up to the highest degree of perfection of which it is capable. Then, from this center, the spirit of Judaism will go forth to the great circumference, to all the communities of the diaspora, and will breathe a new life into them and preserve their unity.[26]

This idea of a spiritual center which is attributed to Ahad Haam has been given embryonic expression by Eliezer ben Yehudah in his famous article "An Important Problem:"[27]

> We have to create something like a center for an entire people, like a heart in the body from which blood will flow into the veins of the body of the nation and give it life.[28]

It is one of the ironies of history that the house in Tel Aviv where the chief protagonist of the spiritual center resided was demolished and in its stead was erected the building *Migdal Shalom*—an embodiment of the material center.

Ahad Haam elaborated the idea of a spiritual center in his essay on Leo Pinsker and colored most of his writings with its essence. He had, incidentally, such a high regard for the author of *Autoemancipation* that he translated the classic tract of early Zionism from German into Hebrew. And that was his only translation from any language. Curiously neither Herzl nor Ahad Haam invented the nomenclature for their special brands of Zionism. It was probably Nathan Birnbaum who coined the term Zionism in 1893 and Joseph Klausner who coined the term spiritual Zionism at the turn of the century.

Spiritual Zionism, that was the central idea of Ahad Haam. He felt that Jews and Judaism in the post-emancipatory era will not be isolated from the influences of the surrounding world. And, since he foresaw the growth of nationalism in Europe, he realized that two possibilities remained for the Jew: either to lose his essence or to renounce his unity. Judaism

> is in danger of being split up into as many kinds of Judaism as there are countries of the Jewish dispersion.[29]

That is why "the spirit of our nation" strives for a return to its historical center where it can perfect its cultural heritage; the small center in the Land of Israel will influence the large circumference, the diaspora; the prophets who have advocated the supremacy of spiritual power over material might will be vindicated.[30] Ahad Haam did not intend to build a spiritual center in an economic void. It was to be "a place like other places where men...needed food and clothing."[31] It was to be, above all, a place where men applied themselves to problems of their material well-being with skill and efficiency.

The wide-spread notion of Ahad Haam's alleged indifference to the economic problems of the Jew rests on a superficial knowledge of his writings. He pleaded for a restratification of the Jew in the diaspora and stressed the importance of agriculture in Palestine. It is true that he was somewhat skeptical about the metamorphosis of the Jew into a simple farmer for

> the Jew is too clever, too civilized to bound his life and his ambitions by a small plot of land and to be content with deriving a poor living from it by the sweat of his brow. He has lost the primitive simplicity of the real farmer...whose work is his all and

who never looks beyond his narrow acres.[32]

Ahad Haam did not believe that the system of rural cooperatives would spread, as it did, and effect a radical change in the economic and social life of Palestine because he tended to minimize the importance of labor. Spirit, spirit before all—this, to paraphrase Verlaine, was the principal thesis of the father of spiritual Zionism. He acknowledged the indubitable fact that in the past only those were considered Jews who adhered to the tenets of the Jewish religion. But, as a result of the emancipatory trends, there emerged a new type of Jew: unobservant yet national. Ahad Haam gave him a *raison d'être* because he postulated a nationalism limited to ethical duties only. In his essay "National Ethics"[33] he endeavored to secularize ethics and divest it of religious accretions.[34] This was no easy task for the orthodox segment of Judaism still maintains that there is no Jewish nationality outside Jewish religion. Ahad Haam tends to separate two seemingly inseparable entities, ethics and religion. And he also distinguishes between ethical principles which are common to all civilized nations and form an international code, and ethical principles which are typical of a single nation and may be termed national ethics. The latter is the national asset par excellence and mirrors the peculiar spirit of the nation. It is difficult, of course, to distinguish between cause and effect: Did national ethics mold the Jews or did the genius of the Jews create its ethical structure? It was Moses Hess who maintained that the genius of the Jews created the Jewish religion. And, in his opinion, the two most important religions in ancient times—Hellenism and Judaism—were national religions: Hellenism a natural religion, Judaism a historical religion based on historical facts like the exodus.

Ahad Haam wished to perpetuate the essential feature of historical Judaism: national ethics. But he advocated ineffective ways and means for its preservation—rigid gapping between the ethic of Judaism, based on justice, and the ethic of Christianity, based on love; establishing societies for the study of national ethics which would be coordinated into a popular movement. Ahad Haam was impressed by the Society for Ethical Culture which was founded by Felix Adler, an American, in 1876 and which aimed "to assert the supreme importance of the ethical factor in all relations of life—personal, social, national, and international, apart from any theological or metaphysical considerations."[35] The emphasis on ethics by the Society could not but please Ahad Haam. But the dissociation of ethics from religion led to cavalier attitudes toward religion. Though the Society held religious services, the members were free to choose any religious affiliations they pleased. In short, it was a way-station for Jews to Christianity even though Christians were not the dominant element in the Society.

It is difficult to define the precise nature of national ethics as it is difficult to say what constitutes the national element in language. Ahad Haam attached importance to the dissemination of Hebrew among the Jews and argued for its preservation on historical, psychological and demographical grounds. Yiddish, the language of the Jewish masses in eastern Europe, was doomed to oblivion in his estimation.

> Even in its native countries—Russia, Galicia and Rumania—the jargon is being driven to the wall by the language of the country in proportion to the dissemination of education among the Jews. . . Before long Yiddish will cease to be a living and spoken language. The process of its decay is an inevitable outcome of the conditions of life; and all the efforts of its supporters to raise it in the popular estimation through an attractive literature will not avail to stem this process, any more than Hebrew literature. . . availed to preserve Hebrew as a spoken language when the conditions of life demanded its abandonment in favor of other forms of speech.[36]

Love for Hebrew did not blind Ahad Haam to the poverty of its literature. He was undoubtedly too severe a critic when he contended that only one original book was produced in the last century: *The Guide of the Perplexed of our Time* by Nachman Krochmal. But even this book, he argued, belonged in form and content to medieval philosophy. He also acknowledged the importance of Eisik Hirsch Weiss's book on the development of oral tradition. All other Hebrew books of the nineteenth century he discarded; they were, in his opinion, imitative and second-rate products of inferior talents.

This harsh and unjust critique is more valuable as a measure of Ahad Haam's limitations than as an estimate of modern Hebrew literature. Though admired by Bialik, the nationalist poet par excellence, he was peculiarly insensitive to poetry which was, after all, the most valuable product of the Hebrew genius from biblical times to our own day.

> Mere poetry, the outpourings of the soul on the beauty of nature and the joys of love et cetera—all these can be gotten in other

literatures.[37]

In all the six volumes of his letters there is rarely a reference to a landscape. Like Socrates he learned nothing from the trees. But his disciple did: Aaron David Gordon (1856–1922) who shared the date of birth with his master was a practical thinker and an idealist. The idea of rural labor appealed to him to such an extent that he settled in former Palestine and became a farmer when he was almost fifty. The remainder of his life was a legend and an inspiration to the labor movement in his adopted country. For many years his essays were regarded as the bible of labor, and they managed to transform the vague spirituality of Ahad Haam into the determined spirituality of work. Although not as lucid as Ahad Haam, he impressed his philosophy of labor on his contemporaries. Reduced to its simplest terms, it consecrates labor as man's marriage with nature. Through labor—and not through mere residence in a setting of rural beauty—man establishes contact with the earth. Apart from sensing or knowing nature, man must also *live* it and appreciate its forces and moods. The more civilized the man, the more profitable, materially and spiritually, will be his contact with nature. Unfortunately, the very opposite takes place in modern life. Man "withdraws into his walled cities like a turtle within its shell until he has accustomed himself to find this a first principle: life apart and nature apart."[38] Science and art reveal nature to man but they cram it into laboratories and museums.

At most...they invite man to take an occasional and temporary excursion into nature.[39]

The result is an impoverishment of the spirit and a corruption of taste in literature. This can be remedied: To *live* nature, one must work in nature. The Jew, living his new natural life, will redeem his land, dunam by dunam, with hard work. To the megalopolitan civilization of our day A.D. Gordon opposed a rural civilization of the future. Like the Irish poet A. E. he combined mystical nationalism with practical economics. And, like him, he managed to disseminate his ideas with a missionary fervor.

Ahad Haam's Antagonists: Micah Joseph Berdyczewski; Jacob Klatzkin

Aaron David Gordon was a disciple of Ahad Haam, Micah Joseph

Berdyczewski (1865–1921)[40] an antagonist. He had read Nietzsche too assiduously and Ahad Haam too critically. And he strove to effect a break with the past and transform the people of the spirit into the people of the sword. He pleaded for a wider scope in Hebrew literature while Ahad Haam endeavored to limit it to subjects of Jewish interest. And he advocated contempt for the book because it had stood between the Jew and nature. For two thousand years Jews had over-intellectualized their minds with study; they had sacrificed everything to the Moloch of the book. That was a mistake which needed immediate correction; the book which stood between the Jew and nature had to be set aside. The well-known adage in the *Sayings of the Fathers* epitomizes, in Berdyczewski's opinion, the false relationship between the Jew and the non-bookish world:

> He who walks by the way and studies and breaks off his study and says "How beautiful is this tree" or "How beautiful is this fallow" Scripture counts it to him as if he were guilty against himself.[41]

Berdyczewski comments with passionate zeal:

> I think that only then will the Jews be saved when a new Mishnah will be given to us saying: "If a man walks by the way and, seeing a beautiful tree, a beautiful fallow, he turns from them to some other thought, he is guilty against himself." Bring back to us the beautiful trees and the beautiful fallows, bring back the world to us.[42]

In his attempt at the revaluation of the spiritual history of his people, Berdyczewski hoped to demonstrate that Judaism in the diaspora was dominated by the two well-known schools of thought, the House of Hillel and the House of Shammai. The ascendancy of the former, symbolizing gentleness and submissiveness, over the latter, epitomizing strength and bravery, was a misfortune in his view. Louis Ginzberg showed in an illuminating lecture at the Hebrew University in Jerusalem that the difference between the two Houses was largely determined by social and economic factors.[43] Berdyczewski made the psychological distinction for his generation.

Not only the content but the form of his thought was diametrically opposed to Ahad Haam. Berdyczewski eschewed weighty sentences and composed lyrical utterances in an aphoristic style which was reminiscent of Nietzsche. For he was a poet in prose, a recipient of truth from sources inaccessible to the scholar. To put it briefly and bluntly, he clamored for the universalization of Hebrew literature while Ahad Haam aimed at its nationalization.[44] And he had a poet's feeling for poetry; he devoted a number of critical essays to problems of poetic style.

He was also a writer of fiction which was camouflaged autobiography: "My words are isolated chapters of my memoirs."[45] His simple plots are burdened with philosophizing heroes and heroines. His first stories like "Two Camps"[46] as well as the novel *Miriam* which was written toward the end of his life suffer from long discourses. This defect he shares with the writers of the enlightenment. But, unlike them, he was attracted to Hasidism, to its rich folk-tales and folk-traditions.[47] And, together with Peretz and Ansky, he effected a revaluation of that movement in Hebrew literature.

While Berdyczewski attacked the excesses of spirituality in the essays of Ahad Haam, Jacob Klatzkin (1882–1948) rejected the idea of a spiritual center in Israel. In his opinion, it would only hasten the process of assimilation.[48] In the course of a few generations there will develop two Jewish nations: Israelis and non-Israelis.[49] That is why those who, according to Klatzkin, "postulate the necessity of two ways, the way of the diaspora and the way of Palestine, divide our national will into two wills and weaken its force."[50] Klatzkin's fanatic, almost fantastic nationalism, enhanced by an immaculate prose, not unlike Santayana's in American literature, rises in square contrast to the father of spiritual Zionism. His objections to Ahad Haam's spiritual center rest on religious grounds. For he regards Judaism as a way of life rather than a way of thought, a religion of deeds rather than a theoretical entity. And he makes a brilliant point that, though the spirit of Judaism might prevail in Christianity or in Socialism, the Jewish people could disappear at the same time.[51]

Against Herzl, Klatzkin argued that the assimilation of the Jews was a distinct possibility.[52] The only barrier that halted the process of disintegration of Jewry in the past, religion, has crumbled before the onslaught of the emancipatory era. This demise of religion amounted to a national calamity in the history of the Jews:

> The destruction of our religion is the destruction of our state in the diaspora, the destruction of our Third Temple, our Temple on foreign soil.[53]

With passionate conviction Klatzkin asserted that, since the diaspora became wide open to the corroding forces of assimilation, it must be discarded as a stronghold of Jewry. At best, it could serve as a temporary evil and a reservoir of recruits for Israel.

Reinterpretation of Judaism by Kaufmann

Klatzkin gave a new meaning to Zionism: on the negative side he regarded it as a total denial of the diaspora, on the positive side as a new, secular interpretation of Judaism with the twin articles of faith: the redemption of the land of Israel and the revival of the Hebrew language. This interpretation of Judaism and nationalism which originated after the First World War found eager exponents in and out of former Palestine. It was advocated by Ezekiel Kaufmann (1889–1963) who, in a very comprehensive and thorough estimate of the destiny of the Jews, made short shrift of the continuation of the diaspora by linking together exile and alienism. As a historian and sociologist, he traced the development of the Jewish minority in the lands of dispersion and showed that, in its initial stages, it followed the beaten road of assimilation. That it maintained its nationhood was not due to antisemitism as popular orators were wont to declare. For antisemitism was the effect rather than the cause of Jewish separatism. Like Klatzkin, Kaufmann attributed the survival of the Jews to religion. But unlike Klatzkin he delved into the history of heathen and Jewish beliefs, and showed that the Jews, because of the universalist character of prophetic and pharisaic teachings, could not and would not accept any other religion. For the past hundred and fifty years, however, religion ceased to guarantee the national survival of the Jews. Hence, in order to remain Jews, they have to be inspired by a holy hate of the diaspora and its chief defect, alienism, and re-establish a normal state in their own land. That does not mean a socialist state which is the fond dream of Labor Zionism. Since, according to Kaufmann, there cannot be socialism in one country, Zionism will have to adopt the realities of a capitalist regime; Hebrew labor will establish Hebrew villages and cities and blot out the curse of alienism.

Kaufmann was not only an original sociologist; he was undoubtedly one of the most important biblical scholars in this century and the most seminal thinker in Hebrew literature to have emerged between the two world wars. This gentle recluse made an indelible imprint on

biblical scholarship and on contemporary thought with two monumental works: an eight-volume *History of Jewish Faith*[54] and a
four-volume study of the destiny of the Jewish people—*Diaspora and
Alienism.*[55] In a letter, written to a friend in 1946, Kaufmann disclosed
the dual nature of his intellectual interests:

> I work. . .and try to write the last volume of my book [*History of
> the Jewish Faith*]. . .But I also read the paper every day and
> swallow the. . .poison. . .This poison paralyzes my work. This is
> my hellish torment day by day.[56]

Kaufmann lived a deeply committed life. His study of the past and
his study of the present were the twin compulsions of his life. To the
study of the past he added a new dimension; to the study of the present
he added an immense erudition and a passionate interest.

Aaron David Gordon and Berdyczewski, Klatzkin and Kaufmann
—each one, in his own individual way, created a new framework for
the new Judaism which emerged at the turn of the century and in the
first decades of the twentieth century. They were, in a sense, disciples
of Ahad Haam or reactors to his ideas. And so were numerous essayists
and scholars of note: Rav Zair and Zevi Woislavsky, Mordecai
Ehrenpreis and Simon Rawidowicz, Moses Kleinmann and Shemaryahu
Levin.

The search for a definition of Judaism, for a re-interpretation of
Judaism, for an harmonious adjustment of Judaism to a secularized
world began with the disintegration of religious values in the period of
the renaissance. It assumed urgent proportions toward the end of the
nineteenth century when nationalism was the predominant theme of
Hebrew literature. And it became a compulsion with the establishment of the State of Israel. David Ben Gurion, when he was Prime
Minister, addressed himself in a letter dated October 27, 1958 to a
selected number of Jewish scholars all over the world and asked for an
answer to the age-old question: Who is a Jew? The answers—some in
their original English, some translated from their original languages
—have been collected in a volume under the title *Jewish Identity* and
under the editorship of Sidney B. Hoenig.[57] But the question is still
with us.

Other Nationalist Thinkers in the Twentieth Century

At the end of the nineteenth century Ahad Haam and Berdyczewski struggled with an answer. In the beginning of the twentieth century Klausner and Bernfeld, Neumark and Shaul Yisrael (Shai Ish) Hurwitz, Sokolow and Brainin, struggled with the problem. Klausner was the most articulate among them. As a teacher and guide of Jewry since the nineties of the nineteenth century to the end of the first decade after the establishment of the State of Israel he interpreted Jewish history and Jewish literature to Jews first and, in later years, when his book on Christianity had been translated into European languages, to non-Jews as well. He pioneered recognition for Bialik and Tschernichowsky and, as editor of the prominent periodical *ha-Shiloah* after Ahad Haam, he published some of the classics of Hebrew literature in the first two decades of the twentieth century. As the author of *Hebrew Language—Living Language*[58] he fathered the dissemination of spoken Hebrew in Europe, as first president of the Academy of the Hebrew Language he widened the scope of the language and as the first Professor of Hebrew Literature at the Hebrew University of Jerusalem he encouraged scientific research and publications in his field which to him, at least, was "a continuation of the Bible."[59] Already in Odessa, at the Hebrew Academy under the direction of Rav Zair, he taught the young Ezekiel Kaufmann, Zevi Woislavsky and Joshua Gutman who were to make important contributions to the interpretation of Jewish history and sociology. In Jerusalem hundreds of students owe him their inspiration and their initial erudition.

Klausner did not resolve the dichotomous difficulty which bedeviled the thinkers and poets in the age of enlightenment. Judah Leb Gordon had advocated one approach: Be a Jew in your home, be a man outside your home. Klausner strove for the synthesis of particularism and universalism and over the entrance of his home in *Talpiot,* a suburb of Jerusalem, he engraved his philosophy of life: *Yahadut we-Eno-shiyyut,* Jewishness and Humanity. In his book under the same title which was first published in 1905 he argued that Judaism is neither mere religion nor mere nationality. It is "a nationalist world view on a religio-ethical base." It is a way of life rather than a philosophical theory, a continuum rather than a sum of unrelated eras. All the chapters of its long history are merely links in a chain, some stronger, some weaker, some more, some less important than others. Klausner felt rightly that the Second Commonwealth was one of the most seminal periods of Jewish history. Hence his massive five-volume *History of the Second Commonwealth.*[60] But even before he worked on his *History,* he explored the idea of messianism and subjected it to a thorough investigation and evaluation. He was equally enamored of the nineteenth century. Hence his other monumental work in six volumes: *The History of Modern Hebrew Literature.*[61] Yet his prolific output remained a torso. For he intended to write four books on the five great religions: Judaism, Hellenism, Christianity, Islam and Buddhism. Within that context he proposed to isolate the real essence of Judaism. But the plan was only partially fulfilled; he managed to write massively on Judaism and less massively on Christianity. His books on *Jesus of Nazareth* and *From Jesus to Paul* have been translated into many languages. But he treated Hellenism in his *History* incidentally and he wrote little on Islam and Buddhism.

Simon Bernfeld (1860–1940) was the popularizer of Jewish research *par excellence.* Since he studied and lived for many years in Germany, he was strongly influenced by German culture and, especially, by the protagonists of the *Wissenschaft des Judentums.* Not unlike them he regarded Judaism as a monotheistic force, prophecy as an ethical phenomenon and the mission of Jewry as a drive for social justice in the world. His books and essays summarized the latest advances of knowledge in the numerous fields of Judaism. Since he was interested in vast systems of thought, he wrote multivolumed tracts on the history of Jewish philosophy under the title *Knowledge of God,*[62] a three-volume source book on Jewish martyrology,[63] a book on the reform movement,[64] a book on Jewish savants of the nineteenth century,[65] essays on historical personages from the eleventh to the eighteenth century, from Rashi to Moses Hayyim Luzzatto,[66] monographs on Solomon Judah Rapoport[67] and Gabriel Riesser.[68] There was scarcely an epoch in Jewish history which his facile pen did not touch. These elegant and easy-to-read books delighted the Hebrew reader for two generations and gave him a vast amount of information. Though they have become largely obsolete, they are interesting as products of a bygone age.

David Neumark (1866–1924) who taught Jewish philosophy at the Hebrew Union College in Cincinnati, contributed to the Hebrew periodicals of his day—*ha-Shiloah, ha-Doar, ha-Maggid*—and wrote most of his books in Hebrew. His *History of Jewish Philosophy*[69]—in German and in Hebrew—and his articles on Jewish philosophers were not startling in their originality.[70] For him—as for many others—religion in its purified, rarefied monotheism was the essence of Judaism; the entire history of the Jewish people was merely a long road to one God—the embodiment of ethical perfection. Unlike other ethnic groups, Judaism in Neumark's estimation was the eternal people in possession of eternal verities. This is almost a neo-orthodox stance, not as rigid as that of his contemporary, Yizhak Isaac Halevi Rabinowitz (1847–1914), but remarkably similar in essence. The former, however, represented pure orthodoxy and became one of the founders of the ultraconservative movement *Agudat Yisrael.* While he bent his intellectual energies to battle in his massive book *First Generations*[71] with such well-established authorities on Jewish law and Jewish history as Zechariah Frankel, Abraham Geiger, Heinrich Graetz, Eisik Hirsch Weiss, Neumark maintained that "Faith is. . .a psychological sense like the logical sense, the esthetic sense, the ethical sense."[72] That sense, in Neumark's opinion, is peculiar to Judaism. "If you ask for the meaning of our existence in history: is it national or religious? The answer will be: national. Our religiosity is our nationality."[73] This was a conscious bow in the direction of Ahad Haam; this was the credo of an entire generation.

But there was a lonely voice of doubt. Shaul Yisrael Hurwitz (1861–1922) or Shai Ish Hurwitz—as he was known by the Hebrew-reading public—enveloped the problem of Judaism with tragic overtones. It was for him both a personal and national experience of pressing urgency. In numerous essays, in a periodical *he-'Atid* which he founded in 1908 and to which he attracted the foremost popularizers of Jewish thought—Bernfeld and Brainin, Horodetzky and Simhoni, Berdyczewski and Klausner—he struggled with answers to his anxieties. Like the great poet in the era of enlightenment, Judah Leb Gordon, he was obsessed with the fatal possibility that he was "the last ring. . .in the great chain of fathers and sons."[74] And like Shakespeare he posed his dilemma in the stark phrase: to be or not to be. In an article which provoked a sharp polemic in the press of the time, "On the problem of Jewish Continuity," he summarized under four headings the modern answers to the query: Why preserve Judaism? The first answer was desperately theological: Moses Mendelssohn and Solomon Maimon refused to embrace Christianity —the one because denial of Judaism would have meant for him denial of Christianity which grew out of Judaism; the other because affirmation of Christianity was inconsistent with his atheistic premises. The second answer was ethical: it was best expressed by Geiger who advised a would-be convert that it was better to remain "a conscientious unbeliever than an unconscientious one." And he maintained that it was unethical to flee from the oppressor to the oppressed.[75] Moreover, it ceased to be a problem of good or evil; it degenerated into personal attitudes which depended on personal endowment, education, evaluation.[76] The third answer was metaphysical: Judaism was only briefly a political entity. Its mission is spiritual, non-national or universal: to be a light for the nations,[77] to establish justice on a monotheistic base. The fourth answer was the anthropopsychological answer: "We are Jews because we are Jews, because we can't be different from what we are."[78] And this is also the answer of nationalists like Ahad Haam.

All these answers to the problem of continuity are inadequate answers, abstract chimeras spun by the head and not by the heart, totally impotent in preventing assimilation or conversion. Even the so-called anthropological answer, unanchored in the strong faith of our forefathers, collapses in the first confrontation with the prevalent culture. As a matter of fact, the two great movements of Judaism in the last two hundred years—enlightenment with its rationalist criticism of traditionalism, Ahad-Haamist nationalism with its cultural centrism in the Holy Land—were experiments of salvation which failed to succeed.[79]

Hurwitz—like Shakespeare's *Hamlet*—did not answer his query. But by his apostasy of doubt he quickened the processes of re-evaluation which have not ceased to engage the attentions of Jews all over the world.

Sokolow (1860–1936), an incorrigible optimist in contradistinction to Hurwitz, saw himself as a transitional figure.[80] And, chronologically, he was right: All writers who reached their maturity in the eighties of the previous century—alumni of talmudic academies—were imbued with the spirit of enlightenment. To acquire and impart learning—that was their aspiration. With Sokolow it was a passion which spent itself in pursuit of multilingual acquisitions and a kaleidoscopic fund of knowledge. His output was enormous. Articles on miscellaneous and disparate subjects flowed in fertile profusion from his ready pen. History, geography, politics, sociology, all branches of Judaism—these were some of the disciplines cultivated by Sokolow.

His editorial work also derived from his single-hearted passion. As co-editor of *ha-Zefirah* with Slonimsky and as its sole editor for many years, as founder and editor of *ha-Asif* he made an unforgettable impact on eastern European Jews. In a sense he became their teacher and mentor. His column "*A Watchman unto the House of Israel*"[81] in *ha-Zefirah* was eagerly read by thousands, by myriads of people. It should be remembered that in the period of enlightenment even popular periodicals had small circulations. *Ha-Maggid* in its heyday had eighteen hundred subscribers, *ha-Meliz*—two to five thousand, *ha-Shahar*—approximately seven hundred. But Sokolow's first annual *ha-Asif*, published in 1884, sold ten thousand copies immediately after publication[82] because it offered a varied fare: history, criticism, politics and enlightening editorials. Moreover, the financial success of the annual and his interest in intense journalism paved the way for the first daily *ha-Yom* which appeared on February 1, 1886 under the editorship of Judah Leb Kantor, the talmudist, the physician and the exquisite journalist who wrote under many pseudonyms—"more than Jethro's names."[83] The assistance of another scholarly physician, Dr. Judah Leb Katzenelsohn[84] and David Frischmann assured the daily's intellectual success.[85] Thus Sokolow should be regarded as the father of modern Hebrew journalism.[86]

Literary portraiture was the real mark of Sokolow's excellence. His essays on contemporaries will probably rank as the more enduring monuments of his journalistic career. Longueurs flaw—but not fatally—his lively reminiscences and his penchants for characterization. The portraits of the self-taught heroes of erudition—those equivalencies of ponderous pedants in German universities or brilliant savants in French schools of higher learning—sparkle with wit and wisdom. And what a gallery of portraits: Bornstein who acquired an immense expertise in the fields of mathematics and astronomy and translated Hamlet to boot; Slonimsky who educated a generation in the sciences through the mediacy of *ha-Zefirah* which he founded in 1862; Solomon Buber, grandfather of Martin Buber who, in spite of a rich career as businessman and communal leader, managed to publish excellent editions of midrashic literature. With a few bold strokes Sokolow impressed personalities on the memories of his readers. In characterizing Bornstein he emphasized his "refined erudition, probing, sharp, crystal-clear mind, breadth of perception, a critical spirit, an immense memory, a sense of style developed to the level of artistic perfection, an extraordinary amount of mathematical knowledge. These were joined to extraordinary capability of work, diligence and perseverance."[87]

A very apt characterization Sokolow reserved for Slonimsky:

Hayyim Zelig Slonimsky was a talmudic mathematician. . . . Laymen don't understand this; those Karaites of ours who don't know what our sages have said stand before a phenomenon they can't comprehend at all. . .they lack a whole spectrum of ideas, images and symbols. They think sometimes that this talmudism is

an artificial thing, an archeological prop for the old generation . . .

But this talmudism is a certain way of life that developed during
many centuries and penetrated our hearts.[88]

As for Buber:

Who didn't know Solomon Buber? Who didn't know the tourist
among the treasures of our ancient literature, the searcher after
cached writings, the critic of *variae lectiones*. . . the great exegete,
the diligent student, the keeper of the keys to our national
archives, the manager of the libraries in the entire world as far as
they impinged on our ancient scrolls?[89]

Ideally suited for leadership in the Zionist movement—with his tact,
with his kindness, with his considerable knowledge of languages and,
above all, with his rootedness in the culture of his people—Sokolow
played a prominent role in the first three decades of the twentieth
century. A wanderer all over the globe in pursuit of the Zionist mission
he became a veritable Benjamin the Fourth,[90] a roving teacher who
never held a teaching position, a general of an elusive army, a builder
of Zion with the force of his convictions and with the might of his
actions.

Sokolow was the classical intercessor on behalf of Jewry—in the
tradition of a long line of intercessors from the renaissance to his day:
from Josel of Rosheim to Baron Edmond de Rothschild. He pleaded
with the powerful Jews in Russia and France and England—the
Poliakoffs and the Günzburgs and the Rothschilds. But, unlike the
intercessors of previous ages, he also used his diplomatic skills on
democratic governments. For he was totally committed to his people.
His was not a shallow nationalism, a yearning for a state in a remote
corner of Asia; it drew sustenance from a millennial source of religious
strength and zeal. Zionism—he maintained—"has nothing to do with
nationalistic tendencies and currents among the gentiles in modern
times."[91] That exaggerated notion of no-indebtedness protected the
spiritual roots of Jewish nationalism. And, in the spirit of no-indebtedness, Sokolow regarded the resuscitation of the Hebrew language as
the high achievement of Zionism, not, as Toynbee falsely maintained,
"the temper of a nouveau riche who furnishes himself with portraits of
appropriate ancestors."[92]

In the annals of Hebrew literature Sokolow will maintain his place as an architect of nationalism alongside of Herzl and Ahad Haam, Klatzkin and Kaufmann. What he lacked in depth, he compensated with breadth of vision which captured tantalizing vistas of Jew-lit landscapes all over the world.

Brainin the Anomalous

In spite of his numerous contacts with the West, Sokolow remained essentially a Jew of eastern Europe. But Reuben Brainin (1862–1939), who was born in White Russia, made a determined effort to confront Hebrew literature with the contemporary literatures of the world. As a young man of thirty he settled in Vienna and published an influential periodical *From East and West.*[93] True to its title it featured articles on such seminal figures as Tolstoy, Nietzsche, Ibsen and—the Gaon of Vilna.

Hebrew literature in the context of world literature—that was the major theme and preoccupation of Reuben Brainin. His flair for biography—one of his many talents—came to the fore in two books on two central figures of the period: Perez Smolenskin and Abraham Mapu. His unfinished *Life of Herzl,*[94] the translation into Hebrew of Herzl's play *The New Ghetto*[95] and Nordau's *Paradoxes* must be singled out as labors of love.

There was a freshness of tone and approach in Brainin's critical oeuvre: his championship of the young and unknown Saul Tscherni-chowsky, who became one of the great Hebrew poets of the twentieth century, was an act of daring and discovery.[96] In *ha-Dor,* under the editorship of David Frischmann, Brainin published articles on contemporary Hebrew writers and artists. There was hardly a Hebrew periodical of the time to which he did not contribute. He also wrote in Yiddish extensively and participated in the Russo-Jewish press.

In America, where he settled in 1909, he edited *ha-Deror* before and *ha-Toren* after the First World War. But neither his writings nor his activities in the New World enhanced his reputation. At the end of his life he wrote Yiddish almost exclusively. And his championship of the ill-fated Communist attempt at an autonomous Jewish province in the Far East, Biro-Bijan, alienated him from Hebrew readers and Hebrew literature.

The three volumes of the uncompleted edition of his works[97] afford an insight into his multifarious activities as critic, publicist, author of sketches and impressionistic stories. A style, unencumbered by flowery turns of phrase, and an erudition, carried with an easy grace, gained him a wide readership and influence in his heyday. But his later years shamed the early years of his youth.

10
The Three Stars of the Modern Hebrew Renaissance: Bialik, Tschernichowsky, Shneour

Bialik—Poet of Nationalism

Hayyim Nahman Bialik (1873–1934) was the singer of the spirit of Judaism and the uncrowned king of Hebrew letters in the first three decades of the twentieth century. His phenomenal reputation in modern Hebrew poetry, paralleled in contemporary British and American poetry only by that of T.S. Eliot, is perhaps to be attributed to the felicitous blend of personal and national elements which has characterized poetry since the days of the Psalms. Not only did he mirror the misfortunes of Jews in alternately gentle and irate verse, but he sought to strengthen their inner resolve and resources.

His nationalistic poems—often second-rate—encouraged the rising nationalism of the Jewish masses in Eastern Europe. His glorification of a dying institution, the *Yeshivah,* which had been the alpha and omega of Jewish education for most of his contemporaries, also contributed to his extraordinary fame. His first printed poem, the sentimental ode "To the Bird"[1] which, on its return from the warm lands, is harangued by a series of dull questions about the fate of Jewish pioneers in former Palestine and by an equally dull recitation of the sorrows of the poet and the Jewish people in Russia, established him as the national poet.[2] Even today it is studied and analyzed and learned by heart in Hebrew schools. His valuable poems are either neglected or given perfunctory praise. *Habent sua fata poemata.*

The ode "To the Bird" was succeeded by other second-rate poems such as "A Short Epistle"[3] and "Surely the People is Grass".[4] But in

"The Blessing of the People"[5] which was published in 1894 Bialik rose to psalmodic heights: Not only the poet but, with him, entire Jewry expressed its fateful association with the heroic pioneers in former Palestine. In the poem "In the Field,"[6] written in the same year, Bialik achieved a truly national song in a minor key. In a few stanzas he created a melancholy mood: His miserable lot has driven him to a field full of sheaves which his hands have not sown and his hands will not reap; yet the field is dear to him because it reminds him of the tillers of the ancestral soil in Palestine who, in a happier mood, may be shouting from hill-tops and mountain-tops an answer to his silent greetings.

The gentle Bialik rose to heights of prophetic ire after the pogrom of Kishenev in 1903.[7] His savage lyric "About the Slaughter"[8] is a helpless *cri de coeur* in the face of overwhelming brutality. His long poem "In the City of Slaughter"[9] is not merely a subtle indictment of the gentiles who attack an innocent people; it is primarily an indictment of Jewish weakness, a revulsive disgust with impotence. The effect of the eternal cruelty of men to men is heightened in the poem by the contrapuntal effect of indifferent spring. And the poet's ineffectuality in the face of national tragedy is converted into a memorable outburst of wrath and despair:

> . . .Arise and flee to the desert
> And take with you the cup of sorrows there.
> Tear your soul to shreds,
> Consume your heart with impotent ire,
> Shed your heavy tear on the cold heads of the rocks
> And send forth your bitter cry to vanish in the storm.[10]

This poem, with its sombre charm and spontaneous form, with its studied incursions into dactylic hexameter, may be regarded as Bialik's most finished product in the realm of national poetry. Some of his critics prefer "The Scroll of Fire."[11] This lyrical fantasy, based on the legends of the destruction of the First Temple in 586 B.C.E., is an incoherent, highly symbolical and allegorical jumble, a riddle wrapped in a mystery inside an enigma, to use a Churchillian phrase. It lacks spontaneity, it is brimful of labored obscurities. Yet Klausner regarded it as the acme of Bialik's achievement. This honor, on internal evidence, should be reserved, perhaps, for "The Dead of the Wilderness"[12] which neither the poet nor his younger contemporaries have equaled in technical perfection and visionary grandeur. "The Dead of the Wilderness," the six hundred thousand Jews who are not dead according to a talmudic legend, slumber and wait in some sort of suspended animation. The eagle, the serpent, the lion, the Arab rider—all magnificently described—recoil in fear from this weird army. For it is dead and alive, frozen in a centuries-old sleep and rising at times with the ancient vigor and rebellious *élan*:

We are the last generation in slavery, the first in freedom.[13]

This line became the slogan of the pioneer, the favorite quotation of Zionist oratory. The biting irony of the poet toward the end of the poem was not heeded—the half-line which expressed the poet's critique of contemporary Judaism:

These are the ancestors of the people of the book.

This appraisal did not fit the mock heroics of self-appointed leaders of the people.

As a disciple of Ahad Haam, Bialik glorified the House of Study, that perennial fount of the people's ethical rejuvenation. But the roads that led to its spiritual treasures were overgrown with grass; the ill-omened raven croaked on its torn roof. And the poet, faced with the inevitable decay, reacted with sensitive alarm:

Shall I weep for your ruin or weep for my wrack?[14]

Yet in a sudden access of self-confidence he asserts that he will rebuild and revise that age-old institution. And in a magnificent poem, "If You Would Know,"[15] the House of Study is depicted as the source of Jewish strength, the house of life and the treasure of the soul.[16] Emphasis on the spirit of Judaism pervades these poems. For Bialik was infected with the ideas of Ahad Haam and called him "teacher, paladin of truth and champion of the spirit"[17] in one of his poems. The most famous of the "spiritual" poems, *ha-Matmid*,[18] is a loving critique of institutionalized study and students. With an accuracy of observation and an intimacy of knowledge Bialik portrayed the transmutation of a normal boy into a dim-eyed, pale-faced scholar whose world has shrunk to a number of folios and whose life has become a series of agonizing triumphs over such distractions as the sight of a tree or an innocent conversation. His soul had become an arrow aimed at an exact mark: the rabbinate, the spiritual leadership of the people. Doubts which arise in his mind are drowned in the talmudic chant. And though hope fashions the crown of victory on the head of the student, there is no happy end to the poem. The poet feels that the healthy seeds in the House of Study need wind and light to make them grow. Perhaps he alludes to secular culture. In an autobiographical account which he submitted to Klausner at the latter's request he wrote ruefully that neither sciences nor languages were taught in the well-known Yeshivah in Volozhin.[19] And the presiding rabbi, Naphtali Zevi Yehudah Berlin (1816–1893), encouraged thorough study of rabbinic literature *ex fontibus* and literal interpretation of rabbinic texts. As author of a brilliant commentary on R. Aha's work[20] he showed the immense erudition which was expected of the Berlins of Volozhin. And he undoubtedly inspired Bialik with a lifelong respect for scholarship.

More than his contemporaries the poet knew that his praises of total scholarship were also the swan songs of an era. The exclusive study of the three T's—Talmud, Talmud, and Talmud—was doomed, and every individual had to make a search for his own citadel of strength. Bialik found it—and it is a fact not fully appreciated by his critics—in the world of his childhood. The first six years which he spent in the Volhynian village of Radi inspired his soft landscapes. They shimmer with an array of pastel colors in his long poems "Brightness"[21] and "The Lake,"[22] in his lovely lyric "Dwarfs of the Night"[23] and even, by implication, in "Let My Portion Be with You"[24] which could not have been written had not childhood landscapes inspired the poet with an ideal of purity and humility. At the end of his life he reverted to childhood in a series of poems which were to form an autobiography in verse.

Nature in Bialik's poetry wears a holiday garb. And so does love—a phantom decked out in finery rather than a real experience. But both nature and love share the poet's vision of innocence. There are touches of sensuality in "The Scroll of Fire." But Bialik's desire for woman is a tepid thing. In one of his best-known love lyrics "Shelter Me Beneath Your Pinion"[25] the poet implores his sweetheart to be mother and sister to him. And he makes a disarming confession in the form of a question: "What is love?"

Not only his poems but some of his stories may be characterized as *la recherche du temps d'enfance*. And it was the fondness for his own childhood which prompted him to adapt old Jewish legends and figments of his own imagination to the exigencies of the infantile mind in a wonderful volume of stories *And it Came to Pass* and in the rhymed tale *Knight of Onions and Knight of Garlic*.[26]

The poet was also an inspired educator. With his friend J.H. Rawnitzki he edited the impressive anthology of rabbinic legends and

planned the critical ingathering of Jewish classics from the Mishnah
to modern times. His anthology of rabbinic legends accomplished for
young men and women more than his books for children. It introduced
them to talmudic lore, it opened for them the resources of talmudic
language in Hebrew paraphrase and it enriched the style of the
younger Hebrew writers.

Like most Hebrew poets, Bialik was a scholar of no mean abilities.
His critical edition of Gabirol's poems is a creditable piece of work. For
the first time in nine hundred years the loving care of a modern
Hebrew poet brought together hundreds of poems of a great—if not the
greatest—medieval poet which had been scattered in accessible and
inaccessible books and manuscripts. This edition was only part of
Bialik's plan of *Kinnus*—the ingathering of Jewish classics, medieval
and modern, in critical, yet popular editions. His unfinished collection
of Moses Ibn Ezra's poetry, his unfinished commentary on the
Mishnah, perhaps even the folksongs paraphrased by him from the
Yiddish, were part of the plan.[27] It is still carried on by the publishing
house *Devir* which he founded and by the Bialik Institute.

The *Kinnus* also aimed to enrich the Hebrew language. In a sense it
was a continuation of the work done by the scholars in the period of
enlightenment. Samuel David Luzzatto and Senior Sachs and, later,
their inheritors Harkavy and Brody and Bialik, Kahana, Simhoni and
Davidson, Yellin, Sassoon and Schirmann, Habermann and Yarden,
Mirsky and Pagis and a host of others ingathered most of the important
and not so important works of medieval poets. Thus, Sassoon published
Samuel the Prince, Brody—Halevi and Moses Ibn Ezra, Yellin—To-
dros Abulafia, Yarden—Immanuel of Rome, Kahana and Aloni—Du-
nash Ibn Labrat, Mirsky—Yitzhak ben Halfon, Pagis—Levi · Ibn
Altaban. Yet Bialik's original works as well as his translation of
Schiller's *Wilhelm Tell* and his paraphrase of Cervantes's *Don Quixote*
are comparatively free from neologisms which flood the works of
medieval poets. But his conservatism in language did not prevent him
from evolving original phrases and phrase-combinations in his
writings and, especially, in his conversations.[28] Had he had an
Eckermann or a Boswell, he would have delighted the world with his
lingual improvisations and philosophical aperçus. For besides being a
poet, he was a master of soliloquy.

The Bialik cult continues with undiminished vigor—in spite of the
fact that his poems are neither read properly nor evaluated with rigor.
Since he wrote only three poems in Israeli pronunciation, only three of
his poems are read as he wanted them to be read. All the rest of his

poetry in the so-called Ashkenazic pronunciation is read improperly in the Israeli pronunciation. The result is cacophony instead of euphony. The sycophantic evaluation of his poetry during his lifetime and the panegyric evaluation after his death have also barred effectively a proper understanding of the poet. More has been written on Bialik than on any Hebrew poet of the last one hundred years. A Bialik Year Book, *Keneset,* was published annually from 1936 to 1946.[28a] It contained, besides contributions from scholars and writers, a section devoted to unpublished manuscripts of Bialik and essays on the poet. Scholars like Lachower, Avrunin and Sadan have mined his philological contributions to the Hebrew language from his poetry, his fiction, his essays on language and literature, his contributions to the Academy of the Hebrew Language, his speeches, his letters and his conversation. But he is not likely to impress the poetry of the seventies and the succeeding decades. With his fine scholarly equipment, with his nostalgic songs of the past and his lyrical longing for a nationalist future, Bialik marks the end of a literary road.

Tschernichowsky: Poet of Revolt

A new note in Hebrew poetry was sounded by Saul Tschernichowsky (1875-1943)[29] who suffered from contemporaneity with Bialik. His name was fatefully coupled with the name of Bialik though he had little in common with the elder poet. Both were born in the country: Bialik in a Volhynian village, Tschernichowsky in a Crimean village. Both were brilliant poets. But Bialik, son of a scholarly father, was subjected to traditional Jewish schooling; Tschernichowsky, scion of simple, able-bodied ancestors, acquired Hebrew as a foreign language from a well-trained pedagogue and a doctoral degree from the University of Lausanne. And his life was an interplay of two callings: the poet intruded into his scientific interests, the scientist impinged on his poetic calling.

In contradistinction to Bialik's sorrowful stance Tschernichowsky vaunted an exuberant joy and strength. And rash critics dubbed him "the Greek." Poems with hellenic overtones like "Outlines,"[30] with mythological content like "Deianira" and "Before the Statue of Apollo,"[31] rhythmic and metric variety modeled on Greek prosody perpetuated the ill-chosen epithet. But even in the poem "Before the Statue of Apollo" Tschernichowsky pays dubious homage to the divinity of youth and light and beauty. Though mindful of the gulf that separates the Jew from the Greek he hints at the similarity between Apollo and the God of the Hebrew conquerors of Canaan who was also a God of life and strength before the Jews bound him with straps of phylacteries.

The poet felt that the Jews were sufficiently removed from the hellenic world to borrow safely some of its saner qualities. Till the very end of his life he courted Greek symbols, images and meters. In one of his last poems "I've Nothing of My Own"[32] Tschernichowsky expresses the sincere desire that, since he is destined to be poor and destitute, a private pantheon adorn his bare room: statues of Moses, Isaiah, Astarte, Shakespeare, Goethe, Plato and Homer, "that seer of a world of beauty."[33] Thus Tschernichowsky again paid tribute—as he had done in the youthful "Outlines"—to the genius of Greece which reached its perfect expression in the epics of Homer and the dialogues of Plato.

Among the hellenizing poems of Tschernichowsky "The Statue"[34] holds a unique place. Though the theme is Greek, the sentiment is Hebrew. In measured, unrhymed lines—as befits a classical subject— the poem evokes the dedication of a statue of Zeus in the presence of its sculptor and emissaries of the entire Greek world. The awe of the people, suddenly confronted by the statue, the ecstatic genuflections and the roars "*Kalos, Kalos, Kalos*" (beautiful, beautiful, beautiful), so reminiscent of the Hebrew *Kadosh, Kadosh, Kadosh* (holy, holy, holy), are described with proper unrestraint as the occasion warrants. But the attitude of the sculptor is Hebrew rather than Greek. For he alone stands upright amid the prostrate crowd, unmoved by the statue which he has fashioned but awed by the deity, more beautiful than the statue, "more pure, more divine."[35] It was God who hovered before his eyes in visionary splendor while he worked and it was God who remained, even after his act of creation, an unreached, unreachable ideal. God as an abstraction is Hebrew rather than Greek in concept.

Even in his stories which do not add to his literary stature Tschernichowsky has wrestled with the problem of Hellenism. He never really resolved the conflict and the confrontation with the alien culture. King Agrippa I (41-44) speaks with the poet's accents when, in the story "In Agrippa's Vineyards,"[36] he confesses to the chief justice of the highest court in the land:

. . .We, the hellenizing Jews, are the best Greeks there are, disciples of Plato and Socrates. . .Greek philosophers were my teachers, Roman centurions my guides, and precisely because they wished to make me a citizen of Athens or a Roman knight, I became a Jew. I am with the Jew in his sorrow, I feel his pain, I cherish his festivals, I am offended when he is hurt.[37]

Jew and Greek: that ever-present dichotomy overwhelmed Tschernichowsky. He drew upon the resources of Greek philosophy and withdrew into his Hebrew shell. He drew upon the resources of Greek poetry and enriched his own with its boundless variety. Homer was a constant presence. In the story "In the Palace of Herodium"[38] the disillusioned and disappointed Berenice quotes verses from Homer (Iliad XIV: 321-325) in the original Greek. It was partly due to the influence of Homer that Tschernichowsky shifted his attention from the lyric to the epic and effected a literary revolution.

For it is generally conceded that the genius of Hebrew poetry is predominantly lyrical. The utterances of the prophets, the hymnal raptures of the psalms and, in medieval times, the poems of Gabirol and Halevi, are mostly curt translations of ethical passion into verse. And since the very word "lyrical" is associated with a musical instrument, lyrical verse tends to rely on musical devices: alliteration, repetition, rhyme and assonance. These devices are not missing from Tschernichowsky's poetry which is predominantly epic[39] but they are not as prominent as in the work of his contemporaries. Plasticity rather than musicality, clear images rather than a melody of feelings—these were the dominant characteristics of his poetry. ·

Homer, the acknowledged master of epic poetry, had an indisputable share in the vivid poetical narratives of Tschernichowsky. Both poets dwell on the daily routines of life with an effortless love. They show craftsmen at work and they describe people at table out of sheer joy in physical existence. The episodes embellish the narrative and frequently heighten an emotional effect or a dramatic suspense. Yet both poets—Homer in his epics, Tschernichowsky in such idylls as "Circumcision"[40] and "Elka's Wedding"[41]—have achieved that ineffable harmony in composition which Aristotle called "the unity of incidents."[42]

Another trait of Tschernichowsky was strenghtened, perhaps, by his contact with the Greeks. The general tenor of his poetry, even where it is sad or funereal, scintillates with a vaunted exuberance of spirits. Towards the end of the nineteenth century it was fashionable to popularize Greek civilization as a fount of perpetual gaiety.[43] Tschernichowsky was a victim of this fallacy. But while an erroneous assumption may be fatal to a philosopher or a scientist, it has often proved to be a boon to the poet. In fact, the best poets flourished at times when sets of stable ideas, true or false, were shared by poet and public.

Tschernichowsky who accepted the assumption that Hellenism signifies joy and affirmation of life became the conscious singer of spring, strength and love. With his departure from the lyric and his translation of Homer,[44] cherished by Greeks as myth-maker, educator and pre-eminent poet,[45] he ushered in a new era in the development of Hebrew literature. The great Hebrew epic, so clumsily cultivated by such second-raters as Wessely and Shalom Cohen, at last had a chance to become a reality.

The translation of the Greek epics by Tschernichowsky marks a milestone in the development of Hebrew literature. For next to the Bible, the *Iliad* and the *Odyssey* have been the most potent influences in world literature. Together they form a triad of literary excellence and eminence. With that ancient magic which primitive poetry possessed in a larger degree than modern poetry, they have quickened our perceptions and enlarged the range of our spiritual life.

There is no doubt that Tschernichowsky grasped intuitively what scholars confirmed at a later date: that the pagan Greeks and the early Hebrews had wide areas of culture in common. He did not hesitate to identify with the worshippers of Tammuz-Adonis, Bel and Astarte. He was even moved to compose a sequence of liturgical sonnets "To the Sun"[46] which, in perfection of form and ardent homage to the forces of nature, have no equal in Hebrew literature. The austere lines seem to be carved by a master-sculptor who, overwhelmed by the beauty and brilliance of light, translates religious awe into religious art.

Tschernichowsky was the Hebrew sonneteer *par excellence*. The masters of the genre before him—from Immanuel of Rome[47] in the late thirteenth and early fourteenth century to Judah Leb Gordon in the nineteenth century—rarely rose above the trivial and light-hearted flirtations with the love-theme. Tschernichowsky gave that genre a tenseness, a terseness, a compactness from his earliest to his maturest years. All his major themes reverberated in the sonnets: revolt against accepted norm, admiration for the fiercer aspects of nature, disgust with diaspora-bred weakness, passion for freedom. In the sequences "To the Sun" and "On the Blood"[48] he achieved poetic statements of credal significance. In the fifteen sonnets "To the Sun" the poet enunciates a paradox and an anachronism. The paradox stems from the fact that, as a Jew, he worships what pagans worshipped: an element of nature. The anachronism lies in the fact that such a personal cult is an impossibility after centuries of scientific evolution. "On the Blood" manages to transmit the romantic notion of imagination as a source of individual renewal and the notion of the poet as the superior priest of beauty. These are Shelleyan notions which have their source and origin in Plato's *Phaedrus* and *Symposium*. But they are announced and developed with unmatched vigor in the sonnets. And they gain validity through an adroit manipulation of contrast with the so-called reformers who promise reform when they woo power and who drown their promise in rivers of blood when they achieve power.

Past and present are not only categories of time for the poet; they are blocks of marble to be hewed into poetic shapes of sequence and simultaneity. Tschernichowsky may have overworked his romantic attachment to the remote past. If he did, it was with the enthusiam of a lover who has found his world in the object of his affection and tapped, almost inadvertently, a forgotten source of poetry and emotion. For him it was only a step from Semitic mythology to the young mythological world of other peoples. His vast work of translation which included beside the Greek epics, the Babylonian epic *Gilgamesh*, the Finnish epic *Kalevala* and parts of the Icelandic *Edda*, was neither an accident nor the result of economic exigency; it was a basic necessity of his poetic personality. Almost accidentally he became the most prolific mediator of culture in modern Hebrew literature. Plato's *Symposium* and *Phaedrus*, Anacreon's poems, Sophocles's *Oedipus Rex*, Shakespeare's *Macbeth* and *Twelfth Night*, Goethe's *Reineke Fuchs*, Longfellow's *Hiawatha* and *Evangeline*—not to mention smaller poems from many ancient and modern literatures —owe their Hebrew versions to him.

On themes of medieval life and literature he brought to bear an ancestral vigor. His "Baruch of Mayence"[49] resembles Bialik's "In the City of Slaughter": Both poems presuppose a national disaster. Bialik's poem reacts to a contemporary pogrom; Tschernichowsky's poem, to a medieval slaughter in the period of the Crusades. But Bialik's center of attention is the people; Tschernichowsky's, an individual. Baruch, crazed by the death of his wife at the hands of hooligans and converted against his will, slaughtered his two daughters in order to save them from disgrace. And he heaped curses of deuteronomic vigor on the heads of the Crusaders and set a vengeful fire to the town. Yet in his tragic soliloquy all of Jewry cried out with him:

And if I weep two thousand years
With treble tears,
Will I wipe out that which appalls
The eyes before they turn at last
To crystal balls?[50]

The poem, with its fierce resentment of senseless persecutions and with its gentle reminiscences of connubial contentment against a lurid background of blood and fire, bursts with explosive strength. The lovely vignette of domestic bliss in "Baruch of Mayence" first appeared as an independent idyll in *Visions and Melodies*.[51] In its later setting, in the lurid plot of "Baruch of Mayence," it gained color and depth. The togetherness of the Jewish family, the unmarred love of husband and wife, were accentuated by the total annihilation of the individual and the community in the crusading zest of misguided Christianity. And the whole poem gained structural strength by the inclusion of the idyllic fragment.

Again and again Tschernichowsky returned to the crusading period and the unfathomable attitude of Christian to Jew, of man to man. And he lavished all his poetic tenderness on the suffering individual. Worms, the seat of medieval Jewish scholars, famous for its ancient synagogue which the Nazis destroyed, and for its ancient cemetery which they desecrated, had an almost symbolical significance for the poet. It was the first city on the Rhine to suffer the impact of crusading slaughter. And to that city Tschernichowsky turned his poetic skill in "The Wonderwall of Worms"[52]—the story of a pitying wall that receded and hid a pregnant woman from the unpitying hands of Crusaders—and in the seven awesome "Ballads of Worms"[53] which were written immediately before his death. For the Jews of Worms suffered during the Crusades and during the Black Death in 1349 and during the days of the Second World War. But Worms or Dortmund, Germany of the Crusades and the Black Death and the Nazis, Poland and the Ukraine in the seventeenth century or Russia in the nineteenth and twentieth centuries—all such cities and countries had only one meaning for the Jew: suffering relieved by merciful death. Tschernichowsky gave a new interpretation to Jewish martyrdom. Dying is not senseless but rather the prelude to a life of dignity which is being built with the blood of meek and rebellious and even blasphemous martyrs—as in "Baruch of Mayence" and "The Dead of Dortmund."[54] These two poems are, incidentally, violent indictments of medieval Christianity. Although the first was finished at the very beginning of the century, in 1902, and the second after an interval of thirty-five years, they read like two chapters of a bloody story-in-verse. The past received garish illuminations from atavistic factors in "Baruch of Mayence" and from sadistic realities of Nazism in "The Dead of Dortmund."

Tschernichowsky's favorite genre was the idyll. He was as much the father of the Hebrew idyll as Theocritus was the father of the Greek idyll. There is, indeed, a close relationship between these two poets, separated though they are by more than two millennia. Both modeled themselves on Homer. Both borrowed from him the dactylic hexameter and both observed and depicted the details of everyday life as he did. But Homer dealt with gods and heroes. Theocritus and Tscherni-chowsky preferred simple folk and simple talk, the joys and sorrows of rural life, the influences of the seasons on man and nature.

The translation of Jewry's existence in rural, southern Russia into poetry was Tschernichowsky's gift to Hebrew literature. Before him Hebrew writers confined themselves to the traditional urbanism of their people. When they explored rural themes they turned to history. Tschernichowsky was the first modern Hebrew poet to celebrate his native district. And he had the power to lift segments of life from regional obscurity to the status of literature. In his idylls Tscherni-chowsky achieved mature serenity. No overt fight against accepted norms, no iconoclastic stance mars the inner repose of his long hexametric lines. The Jew is at peace with nature; he is the good neighbor of the gentile. Gitl in "Boiled Dumplings,"[55] Eliakim in "Circumcision," Velvele in "In the Heat of the Day,"[56] Berele in "Sick Berele,"[57] Mordecai and his only daughter Elka in "Elka's Wedding," Eli in "Eli," Simhah in "Not Exactly Simhah"[58]—these are unsophis-ticated characters who seem to have been born before the Fall. Young Berele and young Velvele are not like the boys of former generations; study is not their forte. On the contrary, exultation in physical strength is their real concern. As if to underlie the contrast with Bialik's portrayal of the ever-diligent student, Tschernichowsky uses, almost at the beginning of the idyll "Eli," a half-line which is almost identical with the opening of Bialik's "Ha-Matmid."[59]

Men like Eli are not only well-built, but almost heroic in daily feats of valor. As for religious observances: Men like Eli are apt to treat them perfunctorily. Even the older folk are not rigid in their observances: They have felt the impact of Zionism and the rise of socialism. Yet Tschernichowsky is able to describe traditional ceremonies and observances—all the abundant Jewish life in the villages of southern Russia—with homeric abandon, with the skill of an accomplished craftsman. The Russians—the coachman, the servant-girl, the peasant—live in intimate association with their Jewish neighbors. Antisemitism, the blight of Czarist Russia, is a distant, faint echo in the idylls. The world is a world of pleasant days and nights. Russian and Jew share a sensitivity to the gloomy, gentle sadness of the great plains in the Crimea and in the Ukraine.

All idylls of Tschernichowsky reflect an enviable tranquillity. Even the single exception—"The Broken Spoon"[60]—begins its attack on civilization gently. For, after all, it is natural for prisoners, the *idyllii personae* of "The Broken Spoon," to view the world as a prison, the inhabitants as prisoners to traditions and historical facts, wisdom subject to senses, psychology fettered by meteorological and environmental factors, free will chained to cause and effect. But even this breathless indictment of cosmic dimensions, this harsh tirade is preceded by the good-natured, detailed account of the mending of a spoon and succeeded by the melancholy chant of a socialist song.

About twenty years elapsed between the composition of the longer idylls: "Circumcision" and "Elka's Wedding"; yet both exhibit a startling similarity in ideas and imagery, milieu and meter. In "Elka's Wedding" the art of the Hebrew idyll reached perhaps its greatest flowering of form and content. As folklore alone, it presents a subject of unusual interest to the sociologist and cultural historian. Here is a traditional Jewish wedding with all the trimmings: the ceremonious preparations, the ritual dances, the foods, the meals, the gifts. And in the earlier idyll, "Circumcision," Tschernichowsky captured the melancholy mood of the Russian *steppes*, their grasses and flowers, beasts and birds, all unknown to the ghetto Jew and to the ghetto literature before him.

Only the novelist Mendele Moker Sefarim had as unsophisticated an attitude toward nature as Tschernichowsky. And there was indeed a bond of friendship between the novelist and the poet. One of the latter's finest nature poems, "Charms of the Forest,"[61] was dedicated to Mendele in gratitude—and perhaps in payment of a debt. For Tschernichowsky owed Mendele his lingual posture. He did for Hebrew poetry what Mendele had done for Hebrew prose: He enriched it with talmudic idiom. Thus Tschernichowsky became the personification of a living paradox: for though he was the most biblical personality in modern Hebrew literature, he used post-biblical language to depict the lives of rural characters in southern Russia.

Toward the end of his life, he produced a poem unique in its blend of scientific material and poetic imagination, "The Golden People."[62] It was a bold effort to interpret life in non-mythical terms. It probes the origins of prehuman existence, but dwells with special fondness on the golden people—the bees—who are merely exemplars of human behavior; the cruel laws of the beehive and the mating flights of the queen-bee are duplicated in the wars of nations and the flights of love and imagination. Against the background of the highly organized, almost totalitarian society of the bees, the poet focuses on the friendship of Father Anthony, a bee-lover, and a young Jewish pioneer. The Russian and the Palestinian landscape contribute their share of charm to this poem. Thus a triple motif, richly orchestrated, runs through it; and in spite of its tedious scientific nomenclature and monotonous enumeration of mineral and plant varieties, "The Golden People" attests to the sublime maturity of an aging poet. It was an attempt, perhaps, to embark on a new poetic course.

Tschernichowsky was not only the father of the Hebrew idyll; he may be regarded as the innovator of the Hebrew ballad. There is evidence that he admired Scottish ballads: He paraphrased "The Two Corbies"[63] in 1896. Although he preserved the frame of the ballad—the worrisome concern of the two ravens with their next meal—he changed the picture. It is no longer the slain knight, abandoned by "his hawk, his hound and his lady fair" who will serve as dinner for the ravens, but the dying poet on a Judean mountain. The metamorphosis of knight into poet is Tschernichowsky's invention. Absence of knighthood among Jews necessitated a shift of emphasis. Yet the emotional core remains the same in the Scottish ballad and in the Hebrew paraphrase—the desolate abandonment of knight and poet alike.

About a year later, in 1897, Tschernichowsky translated "John Barleycorn"[64] and "My Heart's in the Highlands"[65] by Robert Burns. Though the latter poem is not a ballad, it attracted him because of the sheer simplicity of its nostalgic theme.

Original ballads are numerous in Tschernichowsky's work. Some center around the personality of king Saul and date back to 1893 when he was a lad of eighteen, others were composed at the very end of his life. Of the earlier ballads "The Last of the Koraita"[66] is a sample of Tschernichowsky's heroic pose. In the battle with Mohammed's hordes in the Arabian peninsula, the Jewish tribe of Koraita had been annihilated. The last of the survivors preferred death and immortalization in poetry to escape engineered by a magnanimous friend in the enemy camp. The near-ballad "Mohammed" from the same period is a study in veneration. The prophet sits among his admirers in the wilderness; the immense silence is interrupted by the roar of a young lion; the prophet, unperturbed, fixes his sandal, rises and bids his admirers go in peace. But the calm, ordinary action and the calm, ordinary phrase in a threatened environment raise him to extraordinary dimensions in the eyes of the admirers: He was like Moses descending from Sinai, like the angel Azriel who will come on the day of judgment, like the sun emerging from primeval chaos, like Allah himself when he created heaven and earth.

In his early years Tschernichowsky cherished a certain exoticism. But he also utilized familiar themes in his ballads; traditional legends in a near-ballad "Sabbath Night"[67] and in real ballads "On the Eve of Sabbath,"[68] "The Negro Boy,"[69] "Three Crowns"[70] and "How to Dance."[71] Of special significance are the pain-laden ballads of martyrdom.[72] That polarity—heroism and helplessness—fascinated Tschernichowsky and dominated his conscious and unconscious faith. Twice in his life he felt the urge to enunciate a credo, a confession of faith. When he was nineteen, he wrote the immature poem "I Believe."[73] It achieved a greater popularity than many more deserving poems by Tschernichowsky and it was sung by students of Hebrew all over the world. The boyish confessional is a disarming plea to a girl not to laugh at his belief in man, in liberty, in social justice, in friendship, in co-existence of nations, in the resuscitation of Jewry. In the final stanza Tschernichowsky expresses the hope that in the era of fulfillment of his ideals a new type of poet, alert to the beautiful and the sublime, will arise in the world. And this young poet will be crowned with flowers from Tschernichowsky's grave.

The confessional of an idealist at the turn of the century is an adumbration of the other confessional written twenty-two years later, "I Have a Melody."[74] The poet has found himself at last. He no longer indulges in generalities but vaunts his specific aspirations, his conceptions of liberty, his brand of personality. The road from "I Believe" to "I Have a Melody" is the road from immaturity to maturity, from adolescent expression to manful art.

That art was not flawless: it included second-rate translations such as *Macbeth* and *Twelfth Night;* it included stories which, had they not been written by a famed poet, would have passed unnoticed; it included a conventional play *Bar Kohba.*[75] But these shortcomings do not detract from his unique position in Hebrew literature. For all his greatness Bialik, the only other Hebrew poet with whom Tschernichowsky can be compared, marks the end of a road with his attachment to a dying past and a lyrical longing for a nationalist future.[76] But Tschernichowsky wafted a brilliance of sonnets, ballads and idylls over the shattered youth of his contemporaries in the disintegrating talmudic academies and over their burning hopes for a resuscitated Land of Israel. It was he who marked out a new road by his attachment to a vigorous past and by his epic insight into the healthy elements of diaspora Jewry. And, unlike any figure in the history of Hebrew literature he created, to use a phrase of Edwin Arlington Robinson, a "poetry of the commonplace." Bialik caught the imagination of his contemporaries and overshadowed the immense importance of Tschernichowsky. But the historian of Hebrew literature must say, after all due evaluation of the respective merits and flaws of the two poets, that the Jews produced one major poet toward the end of the nineteenth century. And his name was Tschernichowsky. Marvell's marvelous lines on Milton apply to Tschernichowsky no less:

> Thou singst with so much gravity and ease;
> And above human flight dost soar aloft
> With plume so strong, so equal and so soft.[77]

Urban Poet: Shneour

Zalman Zalkind Shneour (1887–1959) was a self-taught poet; not only town-born but also Shklov-born. And Shklov in the gubernatorial district of Mohilev was a town with a difference: an enclave of hasidic extravagance, a Hebrew publishing center of renown, a business place on the river Dnepr. In the beginning of his novel *Men Of Shklov*[78] there is an amiable description of Shneour's hometown with its numerous superstitions:

> Walls of tall pines surround the town . . . beside the Dnepr there is a lovely, calm lake in Shklov: its beginning—a narrow strip of water in the dense forest, its end wide as the sea . . . On the other side of the lake which glistens between grey houses and a green field cows come back from pasture. A reddish cow running before the flock—that means one thing without a doubt: Tomorrow will be a sunny day. A black cow in front of the flock is a certain indication of a rainy day tomorrow. That's for sure. A bruised finger is bandaged with cobwebs. The more dust on the cobwebs, the better

they are. Sometimes the finger heals, sometimes it swells. But to scorn that sublime remedy which costs nothing: no Shklovian would ever dare. . .[79]

This rural setting in an urban community was to haunt the poet throughout his life. At the time of his birth it presented a picture of immutability: the centuries-old way of life was good enough for the ancestral stock; it was good enough for the young shoots.

As a scion of the Schneurson family, the founding dynasty of a hasidic sect which sought to combine ancestral learning with emotive enthusiasm, Shneour was exposed to a traditional education. The great event in his life happened at the beginning of the century: a trip to Odessa in the company of an elder brother. There he met the sages of the city: the novelist Mendele Moker Sefarim, the historian Simon Dubnow, the literary team Bialik and Rawnitzki, the last of the enlightened and the first of the nationalists Moses Leb Lilienblum. Bialik immediately recognized young Shneour's ability. In a famous essay,[80] published in 1906, he hailed him as a youthful Samson of unquestionable literary merit. And Shneour loved Bialik and devoted more than half of his book on *Bialik and his Contemporaries*[81]—two hundred and sixty-one pages—to the most formative relationship in his life, a father-son relationship with Oedipal overtones.

It was in Odessa that Shneour wrote the poem "Had It Not Been for My Hopes"[82] which was published in 1902 and launched him on his literary career. In the best romantic tradition it portrayed a youngster on the verge of suicide; illusory hopes for a better future prevented him from extreme action. The belated Wertherian streak exercised the imagination of the poet; his youthful story on "Suicide"[83]—jottings of a one-month diary—was published before the First World War.

Odessa not only developed the literary sensibilities of Shneour; it also encouraged his lifelong love affair with big cities. Warsaw and Vilna, Geneva and Paris, Tel Aviv and New York—these were to become the great stations of Shneour's passionate life. But he was especially fascinated by the capital of Europe and the capital of America: Paris and New York. From 1907 to 1941 he resided in Paris, from 1941 to his death in 1959 in New York—with the exception of six years which he spent in Israel.

Shneour claimed to have written sixty books—each of approximately four hundred pages. Since most of them remained in manuscript, it was impossible to ascertain the reliability of such a sensational statement which he may have made out of sheer bravado or exaggerated exhilaration. Like Tschernichowsky he was interested in a reinterpretation of Judaism. Under his influence he wrote, slightly before the discovery of the Dead Sea Scrolls, a sequence of poems on Jewry before the first destruction of Jerusalem.[84] Again, like his older contemporary in the fifteen sonnets "To the Sun" and in "Before the Statue of Apollo," he emphasized the pagan excesses of Jewry three thousand years ago. What mars his poems is a mist of gushing rhetoric.

Only in short lyrics has he been able to avoid the flourish and the fanfare. And they are the more striking in their calm because so many of his poems are polluted by excessive noise. For a youthful romantic it was right though banal to choose the title *At Sunset*[85] for his first book of poems and to give to individual poems—throughout his life—such names as *"There Was Night,"*[86] *"The Sunset"*[87] and *"Under the Sun."*[88] His future weaknesses strike the eye from every faded page of the thin volume: his shouts of defiance, his aggressive boldness—a Hebrew version of the Baudelairean *épater le bourgeois*—and his unbridled rhetoric. But his strengths are also apparent: the sensual image, the almost animalistic savoring of all things which increase life and which give it variety and vitality.

"Urban poet":[89] this is how Klausner who pioneered studies of Shneour—as well as studies of Bialik and Tschernichowsky—characterized our poet. It is a just characterization. And it illumines Shneour's entire poetical output—its rootlessness, its loudness, its disgust and its despair. But, at the same time, it presents a positive face: confrontation with civilization in urban settings, escape from the narrowing and stifling provincialism of rural or small-town life. Alone of the three major poets he produced three portraits in verse of three cities: Paris and Vilna and Tel Aviv. The poem "On the Banks of the Seine"[90] was a youthful attempt to paint in verbal images a city of decadence on the eve of the First World War. Like Baudelaire, the poet of Paris *par excellence,* Shneour suffered from erosion of faith and recalled in verse the thousand hands of the artists who built a symphony of mortar and stone and spirit, Notre Dame, under the dark looks of bishops and cardinals. In the contemporary world the cathedral has become a forgotten queen with a musty dream about a splendid past.

"Vilna," published in the first issue of *ha-Miklat* under the editorship of I.D. Berkowitz in New York in 1919, then again in a sumptuous edition with ten illustrations of Herman Struck in Berlin in 1923 and, a year later, in his book *Visions*,[91] is a nostalgic portrait in verse of a layered city, "layer upon layer of dead eras." Many Hebrew writers extolled the intense traditions of learning which had characterized the city. But Shneour trapped its past and present with a Dantesque simplicity: the intellectuals, the Strashun library, the publishing house of Baruch Romm's widow, the moving throng, the beautiful girls, the architecture, the streets, the Pushkin Park, the landmarks in the city and the Karaite town of Troki beyond the city. Love for the city and pity for the poor Jews is spiced—as so often in Shneour's poetry—with sarcasm. For the poet is aware that his brethren "bask in the mud of their heritage, pray with their mouth for the redeemer and fear his coming in their heart . . ." This dichotomic hypocrisy fills him with disgust and with a desire to escape. Or perhaps—"Vilna" was written before the poet's marriage—marry one of its girls with eyes as deep as mother's and take root "in the soft and coddling ancestral rot."

The desire to remain and the desire to escape: these twin drives are symbolic of the entire generation at the turn of the century. The poet moved away physically but remained spiritually in Lithuanian Jerusalem. Hence the paean of solace to the city in the finale of the poem with its echoes of Bialik on the significance of the House of Study. Unlike Bialik, Shneour visualizes the return of the orthodox and the unorthodox to the ancient center of worship where all would chant their morning prayer redolent with new hopes for the city and its inhabitants.

After half a century the poet revisited Vilna in search of his lost youth and wrote a brief epilog to his lengthy poem. What he found was the pungent realization that his youth had come to an end. But the epilog was not his final payment on a debt to Vilna.[92] In his novel *The Gaon and the Rabbi*[93] he again returned to his beloved city and its internecine wars more than a hundred years before his time. But the narrative art forced human protagonists on the poet: a double portrait à la Plutarch of two significant personages in the eighteenth century, the Gaon of Vilna and the hasidic rabbi Shneour Zalman of Liady. The city, the protagonist of living stone and mortar, receded into the background.

Homage to Tel Aviv elicited less memorable poetry from the pen of Shneour. In a light vein he praised the city where "girls and bananas bloom." In a somewhat more serious vein he drew comparisons between past arrivals in the port of Jaffa when Arabs heaped—with yells and curses—human and non-human cargo on uncertain launches and orderly arrivals in the port of Tel Aviv where Jews were greeted by Jewish officials who served them like priests in an independent commonwealth.[94]

Shneour found the proper tone for his hymns to the three cities. Nostalgia dominates the poem on Vilna, regrettable decadence prevails in the poem on Paris, confidence marks the poems on Tel Aviv. These are sentiments of reminiscence recollected in uneasy tranquillity. A more characteristic effort of his muse is the celebrated poem "Poppies."[95] The themes and motifs in the seven sections of the poem play a cumulative role; they strengthen the central symbol or image. Thus, in the first section, the poet stands in the field of poppies, the "frozen shouts of desire," the "fires of summer joy" surrounded by waves of flame; he is the gold which is being refined in the kiln of white heat. In the second section he bids the wind to blow and whirl the poppies in a flaming dance; then the opium scents will mingle with the boiling blood of the field and magic incense will rise heavenward; blue flies, drunk with poison and blood, will fall to the ground; birds with weakened wings—like withering leaves of narcissi, like grains of living snow—will droop to the accompaniment of killing laughter in the warm-hearted field. In the third section the slow tempo accelerates: the poet among the dozing poppies—a black flower among bloody flowers—is witness to a mythical experience: the earth calls the sun, her lover, voicelessly; she is enflamed flamelessly; she is drawn to the object of her desire but her arms don't reach; and the sun laughs in brightness and arrogance, the poppies shout their madness, Zuleika flits among the poppies, Joseph flees and leaves his coat in her hands. The fourth section—an interlude—celebrates a cornflower among poppies, a blue incongruity in a red field. The poppies shout defiance at heaven: Long live evil; down with purity and holiness and all fettered feelings; the cornflower listens in fright; a tear glistens on her eyelid, a drop of innocence in a sea of sins; she can only survive by a miracle in blue loneliness; a cherub can save her, perhaps, from incineration. In the fifth section the poet is confronted by a woman in a white dress among the poppies; he warns her that her dress will be consumed by the fire of the red flowers; she laughs and walks on and succumbs; the poet and the woman embrace among the poppies. The sixth section presents another antinomy: not man and woman, but the blue sky and the red field of poppies; and the contrast in nature evokes another contrast: the poet, the man of the east, cannot identify with the faded colors; his blood is like wild poppies; and the poppies are the poet's passions which have become red flowers. In the seventh and final section the poppies wither, the desires die. Do they remember the summer? They seem to have forgotten; they are full of the fruit of the future; the poet is cheated: the poppies strove for the fruit; he aspired to the flowering and burned his youth in their flaming cups; they are full of the seed of hope; he is poor and alone.

The poem reveals Shneour's weaknesses in profusion: his rhetorical élan, his repetitious stance, his defiant posture. But it also carries the reader on a surging wave of imagery, on a lustful journey in a summer field, on a consistent vision in red. An epitome of full-blooded youth, it is also a denial of youth. Flowering is an illusion; fruit is the finale of flowering: That seems to be the poetical message of the "Poppies." Eight hundred years before Shneour, Judah Halevi warned his readers not to yield to the Greek way of life—to flowers which bear no fruit. Shneour embraced the illusion of flowering and he paid the price.

In the same period—immediately before the First World War— Shneour composed his "Daisies"[96] in Yiddish and in Hebrew. In contrast to "Poppies" it is a poem in white. A girl walks among the daisies which bloom like miniature suns with miniature beams. She has searched for a daisy, the young man has found one. The inevitable union of simplicity and strength—her simplicity and his strength—is consummated before the sun sets. The poem was immensely popular in the first decades of the century; it was sung wherever Hebrew was taught and Yiddish was spoken.

For a major contrast to "Poppies" one must turn to the lyrical poem "In the Mountains."[97] In five chapters it evokes the natural beauties of the Alpine landscapes in Switzerland. But the poet never loses sight of the fact that he is a stranger who is desperately determined to fill his eyes and ears with sights and sounds which have been withheld from him for centuries. As for the Swiss, they know the cheeses and the wines of their country but not the soul of the mountains.

This is the overture. In the first chapter—"The Legend of Spring"—the poet contrasts the winter in the plain with the winter in the mountains. In the plain the birth of winter is invisible; in the mountains the winter—the white royal grandfather—begins to flex his muscles at the height of summer and to shake his white beard and "head crowned with a wreath of ice." When the plain dons a mantle of green, the moutains wear their shrouds. With consummate artistry Shneour describes the slow, hesitant descent of the white royal grandfather to the valleys. His legions come with a clashing of ice-swords, with a rain of cold arrows and with a whistling of the "flutes of wind"; they trample on the last flowers of fall and they leave a white trail behind them. The white king establishes his secure rule and looks with pride from the heights.

Shneour also paints the birth of spring with a master's brush. The verse quickens, the heavy hexameters yield to prancing dactylic tetrameters. The white king flees in confusion; mists rise and cover the shame of vanquished winter. Then the wind comes, scatters the mists and "a confused, weak chick of spring" emits a sound of a pale green laugh in the valley. This is one myth of spring. Shneour creates another: spring imprisoned in a cave which is closed by seven doors of snow. Outside the Lord of Winter himself hovers over the entrance to the cave with a spear of ice. When snowstorms dance, the Lord of Winter whistles: Queen of Spring, you shall never leave the cave. Months go by; the sun of April shoots golden arrows into the heart of the Lord of Winter. This is the death of one season, the birth of another. Sun and Queen are united in a wedding procession; swallows sing, waterfalls shout, insects buzz. And the two walk and send "kisses of light, kisses of air" to beast and tree. Thus ends the first and best chapter of the poem "In the Mountains." The others trace the changing seasons and provide new mythologies in grand logorheas.

One cannot but admire—in spite of the rhetorical unrestraint—Shneour's capacity to produce poetry in bulk, often uninspired but mostly honest in its descriptive flair. Swinburne's longueurs minus Swinburne's tiresome musicality—these are Shneour's nearest of kin in English poetry.

But Shneour's passions—in spite of their rhetoricity—are more genuine, certainly more sensuous. The poet plays Casanova, boasts of conquests, pretends to be a young Samson imprisoned in the tresses of blond and black Delilahs.[98] The fair sex is a mere object of desire with cosmic dimensions: Woman is the keeper of the world's grain of truth—the call of blood to blood:[99]

> Woman is a deep wound,
> A rib torn out of the body,
> Red and living flesh
> Which God took stealthily
> From man in sleep
> When, in the treasure-trove of creation,
> There was no stuff to finish the primal job.
> Wounded man is wandering all his days
> And searching for his stolen flesh.[100]

This is a modern version of the Jewish myth mixed with an

Aristophanic ingredient which Plato has preserved in the *Symposium*. The Jewish lover—unlike Casanova—reflects on love more than he indulges in love. Hence the numerous pseudophilosophical disquisitions, the strange addresses to the beloved in the midst of lovemaking in poetry, in prose and in poetic prose:

> Know then that there is no great love in the world and no perfect love . . . How can it be great when many strong men stand before you? And how can it be perfect when many beautiful women surround me? . . .[101]

Shneour seems to be a bit contemptuous of woman:

> I have always despised the well-known enigma
> Clothed in arcane and rustling silk.[102]

Even in the famous poem "With the Strains of the Mandoline"[103] Shneour uses his love for an Italian girl as a pretext for multiple dissertations: the glory of the pagan world, the Nietzschean sin of religion against unrestrained instinctuality and, above all, the fate of Jewry from the confrontation with Rome to the imposition of a Jewish God on reluctant humanity, the long Jewish exile and the long Jewish hope. All these themes seem to break the frail framework: the meeting of a poet, scion of ancient Judea, with an Italian girl, daughter of ancient Rome. But the grand poem and thematic multiplicity are characteristic endowments of Shneour. His descriptive powers reach their zenith in the trilogy "Songs of Fate."[104] The lengthy poem is not only a hymn to stiff-necked perseverance but, in a sense, a Jewish poem though the word Jew does not occur in its numerous verses. The three representatives of assiduous toil—the gold-digger, the pearl-diver, the man of spirit—are committed to a monomaniacal pursuit. The rock must yield up its vein of precious metal to the gold-digger, the oyster must secret the pearl for the pearl-diver, the flesh must release and free the imprisoned spirit for the man of the spirit. They all have this in common: They are the misunderstood and misjudged workers in darkness who are fated to be the purveyors of pleasure. But they are essentially too lonely and too remote to enjoy the simple life of ordinary humanity.

The poet has shown concern for the Jew and the fate of the Jew throughout his creative life. In a poem which gave him a certain notoriety before the First World War, in "The Middle Ages Are

Drawing Nigh,"[105] he indulged in an inspired prophecy of what was to take place with the advent of fascism: an inflated nationalism instead of the black clericalism of the middle ages with the hatred of the Jew as an international bond.

Like Bialik the poet often assumed a recklessly sarcastic pose toward his people:

> Houses of clay they build in their land
> And pioneers' tents—rows upon rows.
> But the towers of real and imaginary strength
> They build in the lands of their foes.[106]

The eternal people scattered its prophets and sanctuaries in all the lands; it helped each tribe to achieve liberty, each slave-nation to inherit the land of its masters.[107] That the poet dedicated his poem on Spartacus,[108] the would-be liberator of slaves in ancient Rome, to Zev Jabotinsky and his "Poems of the Land of Israel"[109] to Menahem Ussishkin is no mere coincidence. Both represent expansionist views on the rebirth of Israel. And extremism suits his exuberance. For, over and above his temperamental excesses, he had a strong and abiding faith—in spite of many despairing utterances—in the eternality of his people, in the ultimate victory of its high ethical stance; a people which has survived the dark ages will be saved from the promised salvations of the present.[110] In a fine couplet he pointed to the Jewish source of religious strength:

> Awesome, orphaned mourns the Wailing Wall.
> Three more walls there are—in my heart they are all.[111]

In Israel, Shneour was aware of the new historical role of Jewry; in America, he caught the peculiar rhythm of the general milieu: the generosity, the technology, the laissez faire, the nervous pull toward uncharted goals. But he was also aware of the Jewish impact on America and of the Americanized Jew on Jewries everywhere. The poorest of the poor and the most ignorant emigrated from Europe and earned contempt or pity of the wise, the respected, the well-to-do. But the future denizens of the sweat-shops were fated to repeat the miracle of Joseph: They made good and settled in the Bronx and Brooklyn. And they were the supporters of the wise, the respected and the fallen well-to-do.

For all the thematic wealth Shneour made no innovations in form or in genre. The prominent characteristic of his style is the question mark—an indicator of rhetorical verve. Yet he cannot be accused of a serious interrogation of reality. He faces the world not in humility but in arrogance. A colossal hubris marks his personality from the beginning of his poetical career. And hubris is tragic in Greek drama and in Shneour's life-drama, it is—to use his own phrase—a self-destructive poison.

As an intense instinctualist, sensualist and colorist Shneour made his impact on Hebrew poetry. But he rarely rose above mediocrity as a novelist. Realism as it was practiced by Balzac or Zola, Tourgenev or Andreev, was his hallmark. Novels from his pen filled the issues of Yiddish newspapers all over the world and satisfied the humble reading needs of his unsophisticated public. Contemporary life and Jewish history of the last two hundred years in eastern Europe were the narrative grist of his mills. The beloved locale of *Men of Shklov* and its continuation, *Uncle Zhame,*[112] *Noah Pandre,*[113] and *The Gaon and the Rabbi* was his native town.

The theme of decadence—so prominent in Shneour's poetry—also dominated some of his prose. *Downfall,*[114] for instance, not only depicts the decline of a rich Jewish family in Warsaw during the German occupation in the First World War; it also describes the dissolution of Jewish values in a deteriorating milieu. Perhaps it was disgust with decadence that turned Shneour to an appreciation of physical strength, exuberance and exhilaration in *Men of Shklov* where he reached his maturity as a novelist. The subject was congenial, the talent was equal to the subject: an ideal circumstance. Published first in Yiddish—and much later, in 1944, in a Hebrew version—the novel attracted immediate attention. For a hundred years—from Mapu to Shneour—Hebrew novels had been so overburdened with philosophical and historical disquisitions that they often became inflated essays. Shneour created at last a straightforward story of small-town characters in unidealized splendor. And he reproduced a total milieu: not only the separatism of the Jew from his gentile neighbor but also the togetherness of the Jew with his gentile neighbor. Since the child is least conscious of his specificity, Shneour often exposes him to the non-Jewish environment, to the Christian holidays, to the "unclean" animals. In the description of Jewish food Shneour is a first-rate master. As for olfactory and gustatory sensibilities, he has no match in Hebrew literature.

In *Noah Pandre* Shneour achieved extreme expression of physical strength. Published first in Yiddish then in English translation by J.

Leftwich in 1936, it appeared in a Hebrew version in 1946. Instead of a preface Shneour launched a defiant panegyric into Jewish space:

> . . .Coachmen, butchers, water-carriers, plasterers, hewers of wood. . .redolent of forests, cart grease, corn-flour, fresh hides. . . They called you ignoramuses. . .If a fire broke out in town, you were the first to rush half-naked to the rescue. If there was an epidemic in town, you came stamping along in your heavy jack boots to help the victims. . .If drunken peasants started a fight on a market day, you ran to help the poor, weak shopkeepers. . .You were the reservoir of the healthy blood and the earthy passions of the people of Israel.[115]

The others were weaklings, goody-goodies, neurasthenics, contemptible parasites living off the fat of the strong and the ignorant. Hence the apotheosis of a butcher-boy turned coachman: Noah Pandre. This modern Samson "wielded a butcher's axe like a delicate instrument," pinched every servant girl in the shop, got properly drunk on the holiday of the Rejoicing of the Law and was always ready to help Jew or gentile in distress. A clumsy but tender lover he showed natural refinement in his relationship to his wife. He was even perceptive in his understanding of animals—cows and goats and horses who were the familiar members of the household in the little towns of eastern Europe. A Chagallesque tenderness was lavished on them: they worked for the family and the family depended on them. But economic necessity created—as so often in life—a bond of love between man and animal.

Noah is not only the idealization of the boor; he is the epitome of the forgotten Jew, a monochrome study of the righteous who suffers indignities and injustice because of his righteousness. Serialization in newspapers damaged all of Shneour's novels including *Noah Pandre* as it played havoc with the greater novels of Dickens and Dostoevsky. Sensationalism was one of its casualties; another—a number of chapters which were often self-contained units. The episodes in *Noah Pandre* seem to be strung as so many independent pearls on a thin thread. Yet, in spite of the many faults of composition, the book succeeds in presenting a portrait of a small town from a new point of vantage. The protagonist—as actor and observer—is not an emasculated scholar but a man of flesh and blood. An expanded version of the novel was translated in 1945 under the title *Song of the Dnepr.* Fourteen chapters were added, some excisions in the earlier chapters were made, some chapters were re-arranged. More than half of the novel comprises new vicissitudes in Noah's life which engage him and his family in a trip to the land of promise: America.

Out of his love for the little towns and townlets of eastern Europe Shneour also created his historical novel *The Gaon and the Rabbi*. The gaon emerges in traditional stance: an ascetic and a recluse with an insatiable thirst for learning. But such a person is obviously not the stuff of a novel. And so, for plot and drama, Shneour concentrates on the gaon's relentless fight against Hasidism which leads to the ban of the sect and to the burning of the books. The internecine fight is fed by unholy flames; frustrated ambitions, fierce vendettas. For the gaon it is a personal fight: if pursuit of learning is less than prayer with holy intent or joyous worship or perfect faith, then he labored in vain:

> They contend that the best way in the world to serve the Lord, blessed be He, is through one's eyes–what they term gazing–and through one's heart–what they term intent. In this connection, what could be more pertinent than the *Shema*' which we recite three times daily: in the morning prayer, in the evening prayer and before going to bed at night? And what is written in the *Shema*'. . .and that you go not about after your own heart and your own eyes?[116]

This is a devastating answer of a scholar who has been wounded in his innermost convictions. But Shneour is unhappy with fanaticism: In the past it has led to inquisitions and expulsions and bans.

The second part of *The Gaon and the Rabbi* is loosely connected with the first. It concentrates on Rabbi Shneour Zalman of Liady who strives for unity and peace, an amalgam of intellectual aspiration and emotional satisfaction. Yet he himself serves as a point of polarization rather than a magnet of unity. Since the Gaon died in 1797 and Rabbi Shneour Zalman of Liady was first imprisoned in 1798, he only suffered from a posthumous gaon. Shneour has drawn the saintly character with sympathy, with empathy, with wisdom. One feels that he loves his namesake, but he only admires the gaon.

Since Shneour produced a considerable quantity of prose, he must be judged both as poet and as novelist. The poet is, of course, the more important figure. But the prose writer has brought a new theme and a new value into Jewish prose: physical in lieu of spiritual valor. In the establishment of the State of Israel and in the furtherance of the destiny of the Jewish people valor played a significant role. It was a non-literary dividend of Shneour's literary labors.

11

The Nimble-Winged Poets: Cahan; Isaac Katzenelson

Cahan: Singer of Insouciance

The three stars of the modern Hebrew renaissance were matched by luminaries of lesser brightness: poets of an ingratiating grace like Cahan and Katzenelson. And they, in turn, continued a tradition of blitheness and fickleness which originated in the biblical Song of Songs, in the frivolous verses of the medieval Abraham Ibn Ezra, in the verbal laceries of Moses Hayyim Luzzatto and Micah Joseph Lebensohn. The link between Luzzatto and Lebensohn on the one hand, Cahan and Katzenelson on the other hand is Mordecai Zevi Mane (1859—1886). In his popular poem "My Ideal,"[1] written shortly before his death, he succeeded in mingling personal and national concerns after the manner of ancient psalmists. And he inspired contemporaries and successors with a realistic rather than platonic love of the Holy Land, with a desire to live rather than to die on its sacred soil. His unsophisticated simplicity reverberated in the poetry of Jacob Cahan. While the former prayed for eternal childhood, the latter identified with boyhood as the innocent expression of insouciance. And Mane's predilection for awakening nature in spring inspired Katzenelson's early poetry.[2] Alone among his contemporaries Mane studied painting, engaged in the art actively and wrote articles on the plastic propensities of mankind in order to revive the dormant sense of esthetics among Jews. But no one learned more from him—consciously or unconsciously—than Cahan and Katzenelson.

Jacob Cahan is the lyrical singer of insouciance. Bialik compares him to a lark, his poetry to a girl who looks at herself in the mirror and delights in her own image.[3] There is coquetry and self-admiration and youthfulness in his work. Jacob Cahan, who resided many years in Switzerland, developed an unusual sensitivity to mountainous scenery. Like Shneour, he delighted to invent Alpine myths. But they only succeeded to add such still-born deities as *Alpiel*, God of the Alps, to the dormant pantheons of the Jews. In a long poem, "Switzerland,"[4] he evoked the world of clouds on steep mountain sides and the world above the clouds, the city of wolves, Bern, and its indescribable *Oberland* and, above all, his own zest of life. Yet his forte remained the brief lyrical poem. More than the interminable pages of "The Vision of the Man of Tisbe,"[5] "Legends of God"[6] and "My Harp,"[7] the simple verses of the lyrical sequence "From the Songs of a Bright-eyed Youth"[8] disclose the true nature of the poet:

> I would like to play
> Like a little boy
> But now and then
> Evil men
> Give me advice and say:
> "Work and toil, work and toil."
> And I recoil
> In dismay.
>
> I would like to fly
> Like the light-winged fowl
> But now and then
> Evil men
> Impede my flight
> And my feather's might
> And I grow weary
> And weak and shy.

Cahan's musical grace is matched by his light-hearted philosophy. Against the defeatism of Ecclesiastes he teaches a modified Epicureanism, a lovelier *carpe diem* than Horace dared to preach in his hyperdidactic poetry. Sorrow was an unwelcome intruder, death "a restful sleep after a festival of laughter and life."

There is something ironical in the fact that this poet has become the spokesman of an intense and militant nationalism, the darling of the Revisionists. Two lines of his poems "Terrorists"[9] became their slogan:

> In blood and fire Judah fell,
> In blood and fire Judah will rise.

The First World War accentuated Cahan's painful awareness of the peculiar situation of the Jews who were fighting for all nations on all fronts. Though he welcomed the Balfour Declaration, he feared the enemies from within and from without. His fears were more than justified; in 1920 and in 1921 the first Arab outbreaks against the Jews occurred in Palestine. The victims who included the well-known writer Joseph Hayyim Brenner were eulogized by him in defiant verses:

> We want peace but you want war,
> We are few but you are more
> Than we. Barbarian brutes! As long
> As we have strength to right our wrong
> With arms, our right will be our might
> For ever.[10]

His long sojourn in Switzerland, with its lingering memories of Herzl and the first Zionist congresses, strengthened his extreme nationalism. He regarded diaspora as a capital offense, not as a punishment for past transgressions. After the First World War when he edited a monthly in Poland he justified the literary venture as a temporary measure; his real aim was to transfer it as soon as possible to Palestine.

Though Cahan's specific strength lies in the realm of lyrical poetry, his considerable talents as playwright and translator have matured with the passage of years. Neither comedy nor tragedy but rather the play in verse and prose which combines the ridiculous with the passionate, serves as the best vehicle of his dramatic abilities. When he attempts to create a mystery-play like "The Giants"[11] or a dramatic legend like "David King of Israel,"[12] he fails in an effort which is incompatible with his powers. His "Ezra and Nehemiah,"[13] a thinly veiled verse-play of modern times, endeavors to portray the two aspects of the Zionist movement which complement each other: the practical and political Zionism of Herzl on the one hand, the spiritual and prophetic Zionism of Ahad Haam on the other hand. But since the chief characters are the slaves of their views, they lack dramatic vitality. Nehemiah-Herzl consumes his energies in the building of the wall of Jerusalem, Ezra-Ahad Haam worries about the spirit of the people. They don't even clash in a dramatic exchange of verbal blows. Convinced by the success of Nehemiah's undertaking, Ezra asks his aid in the building of "the wall of God." In subservience to the man of affairs who completes his task in spite of traitors Ezra appears as the weakling. On the other hand, Nehemiah, who knows how to conquer spiritual hesitancy and arrogant inefficiency, overshadows all the characters.

In the one-act play in prose, "The Great Shame,"[14] Cahan introduces his readers and hopefully, spectators, into the milieu of Parisian painters. But the speeches of the characters resolve themselves into a prolegomenon of an essay on economics and art rather than into dramatic situations. "The Last Testament"[15] also tends to degenerate into a metaphysical disquisition. The theme—the extermination of human beings by contraception—is promoted by a doctor who is anxious to create a new religion, a new and last testament which is to supersede the Old Testament of Judaism and the New Testament of Christianity. Only in the one-act play, "The Cup of Elijah,"[16] Cahan succeeded in producing a work of dramatic intensity. In an earlier play he toyed with the symbolism of the cup: In "The Last Testament" the wife of the doctor drops the cup when the guests raise a toast to the last testament. But in "The Cup of Elijah" the cup assumes a major role.

It is Cahan's most graceful play, both in choice of characters and in construction of plot. Dafner, the unsuccessful composer, acquires a fortune in America by prostituting his talents and writing cheap music. After an absence of fifteen years he returns to Europe and to his youthful sweetheart, Maya, who has become a director of an orphan asylum in Geneva. His yearning for real work which gave him no peace in America and his meeting with the former sweetheart create an arc of intensity where late passion and mature wisdom vie for supremacy. So much for the purely human aspect of the play. The Jewishness of the characters comes to the fore in subtle symbolism. In Maya's room Dafner notices a big cup which brings back to him memories of the *Seder* nights: "We all drank from our little cups while the big cup, full to the brim, stood apart and no one touched it. At the end of the *Seder* the big cup was emptied into the bottle." The simple remark acquires momentum by Maya's wistful reaction: "It is strange, indeed, that there is a big and beautiful drinking cup which stands in readiness all the time, and no one drinks from it." The cup of life is overflowing but everyone drinks from his own little cup. Dafner had gone to America because he was afraid of love. He came back in order to drink from the cup of life. The wine sparkles, the mouth waters. But the voice of Maya warns: "Perhaps the big cup was created in order to stand and sparkle. Perhaps its wine was not to be imbibed?" But the cup is more than life. It is also a symbol;

a beautiful symbol and hint of that other and higher world

which we dream of and aspire to, consciously and unconsciously, all the days of our lives. The wine is consecrated to the prophet Elijah, the bearer of the good tidings of redemption and the sublime future; one ought not to drink from the cup and spoil the symbol.

The woman, Maya, who has learned the art of renunciation prevails upon Dafner to renounce his passion for the superior passion of creative endeavor. The tension of the chief characters resolves itself into mutual sacrifice. The little play ends, like a lyrical poem, on a note of exaltation.

As a translator Cahan devoted his energies to Goethe. In the last thirty years Hebrew literature has been flooded with translations from world literature. Shoddiness was their chief characteristic. Amidst an avalanche of inferior products Cahan preserved the high ideals of artistic translation. Poetic affinity as well as sound judgment guided him into translating *Iphigenia in Tauris, Torquato Tasso* and *Faust* of Goethe.[17] Among the important translations of this generation—the Hebrew versions of the *Iliad* and the *Odyssey* which were done by Tschernichowsky and *Ethica* of Spinoza which was done by Klatz-kin—Cahan's translation of Faust will be remembered as an important contribution to the ever-widening scope of Hebrew literature.

In one of his lyrics Cahan aspired to the life of "the simple spring that descends from the mountains."[18] Like the simple mountain spring his limpidity sparkled in his poetry and translations, and sometimes even in his essays and plays. Alone among the poets of his generation he abandoned the penultimate accentuation of Hebrew words and passed unequivocally to the so-called Sephardic pronunciation which prevailed in Palestine. Though the poems lost their freshness here and there, they gained in harmony and modernity. What they could never lose was the overflow of song which seemed to gush from them in imperishable strains.

Katzenelson: Poet of Innocence

Isaac Katzenelson (1885–1944) was a poet of good cheer till the holocaust. The poems, the stories and the plays—in Hebrew and in Yiddish—which emerged from his pen were created out of naive experiences and childlike dreams.

His first work which made a name for him in Hebrew literature *Within the Boundaries of Lithuania*,[19] was written in the form of a travel-diary. Like Heinrich Heine, whose lyrical poetry Katzenelson translated into Hebrew and whom he resembled in impishness though not in depth of feeling and breadth of satire, he loved to poke fun at people and countries. Poor Lithuania was his chief target:

> She has no prince, she has no king,
> She has no castle in the dell.
> In little tents, in little huts
> Her menfolk dwell.
> Her women milk the sturdy cows.
> The husbands drink.
> The girls are all barren there:
> The boys don't think.[20]

He was one of the few modern Hebrew poets who dared to use humor in verse. Bialik produced one witty poem, "Badger and Drum."[21] But Katzenelson, without harboring malice against the bourgeois or capitalist, loved to play pranks as consistently as Immanuel of Rome in the middle ages. There is, indeed, more than a superficial resemblance between the two poets. While Katzenelson did not compose commentaries on the Bible, he shared with the medieval bard an almost Italian lightness of touch and an almost Italian grace of expression. Both of them invented Hebrew verses as volatile as a dance of elves. It is not surprising, therefore, that he, alone among modern Hebrew poets, composed songs for children free of adult condescension, full of "that sweetness of childhood that neither knows its own strength nor its own weakness."[22]

The poetical play *The Prophet*[23] may be regarded as Katzenelson's highest poetic achievement. It is a series of loosely connected scenes and situations. It features laborers in fields of Shunem, love-dialogues at the foot of Mount Carmel, Elisha lording it over the living and the dead. The scenes are a mere pretext for the lithe verses of the poet which reach in *The Prophet* a rare virtuosity: a word or two form a line, the lines dance like the human body in passionate movement:

> I dance
> And dance.
> Like fire I wheel
> Around, askance.

I move to the left.
I move to the right.
My heart
Is light.

My body is stubble,
My flesh is grass
And all my bones—
An inflammable mass.

If I imprison
My dance within,
I'll sear my heart,
I'll burn my skin.[24]

Almost all the two hundred and twenty pages of the play are composed of light four-verse stanzas. Such a variety and elasticity of grace has not been achieved even by Cahan and Tschernichowsky. These poets can be light, Katzenelson cannot be anything else. Even when he presents some melancholy verses on the fleeting life to a nonagenarian, he belies his gravity by the lightness of form. No one in Hebrew poetry came nearer than Katzenelson to the ideal song.

The Prophet was not his only dramatic effort. The Circle[25] a comedy in prose, aims at a gullible, undiscriminating public, not at literary excellence. Linguistically and structurally it is one of the poorest works of Katzenelson. Jargonisms jar upon Hebrew sensibilities, sensationalism mars the plot. All the characters, except the old Nahum, are sexually infected and travel to a foreign country in order to be cured by Ehrlich's 606.[26] This, in brief, is the theme of the comedy. While the similar play Les Avariés[27] by Eugène Brieux has dignity, The Circle lacks even that redeeming quality.

Shortly before his death the poet returned to biblical verse-drama. In Amnon he projected the incestuous character of the Bible and his unfortunate passion for his sister Tamar:

This woman. . .
This leech
Which sucks the tremor of my limbs. . .
And does not know. . .
She robs; she gains no loot.[28]

The poet also managed to create a delicate portrait of Amnon's mistress Hoglah and endow a host of biblical characters—David, Ahinoam, Nathan the prophet, Yonadav—with that lightness of touch which was his chief characteristic.[29] A year before his death he centered a verse-play around Hannibal, the military genius of Semitic provenance. And an unfinished prose-play *At Military Headquarters*,[30] written in the year of his death, probed the characters and authors of the final solution: Hitler, Göring and Göbbels.

The end of Katzenelson's life was as tragic as the end of Jewry in eastern Europe during the Second World War. In the ghettos of Warsaw and Vittel he composed—in Yiddish[31]—the most mournful poem he ever wrote, "The Song of the Slaughtered Jewish People."

Then his voice died—with myriads of others.

12
Poets of the Monochord: Vogel; Baruch Katzenelson

Vogel as Avantgardist

There is a biographical link between Isaac Katzenelson and David Vogel: Both were born in Lithuania, both died in concentration camps. The poetical link between them is forged out of their respective styles rather than their thematic concerns. Both are addicted to the short line, both are apostles of brevity. And here the similarity ends. The poetry of Vogel which enjoys posthumous popularity in Israel is nascent poetry. His typical poem is a budding thought, an inchoate image, the first faint stirring of emotion. The content relies on allusion; the form lacks polish.

Subconscious life invests Vogel's poems with strength. Lack of logical order between lines and stanzas, complete absence of poetic music: these are Vogel's weaknesses. Like the works of Gruenberg and Shlonsky, his poems cannot be isolated from world literature. But the former depend on the futuristic and expressionistic schools of the West; the latter derives from a trend which has come to be known as the "stream of consciousness." The seminal poem of T. S. Eliot "The Waste Land" which is its outstanding product in the realm of poetry heaps image upon image and stanza upon stanza with no logical transitions and no logical connections. Yet, when it appeared in 1922, it immediately affected modern English and American poets: Auden, Lewis and Spender, Williams, Stevens, Hart Crane and MacLeish. Vogel has created no poem of similar weight. But his volume of poetry *Before the Dark Gate*[1] impressed Hebrew poets, especially Baruch Katzenelson, with its delicate, almost fragile texture. For the poet seems to be standing before the dark gate of the soul and listening to

217

the echoes which well up from its deepest recesses. The dark gate is the dark gate of death itself.

> The black flags wave
> In the wind
> Like the wings of captive birds.
>
> In the days, in the nights
> We walk with bent backs
> And muffled steps
> Until we come
> To the great, dark gate.
>
> Like silly children
> We stand there in awe
> And expectation
> Until the gate opens—
> The great, dark gate.[2]

Even when Vogel joins image to image in logical sequence and not in unpredictable caprice, he succeeds in creating a poem which has little in common with the poetry of the past. An ineffable silence hovers over his lyrical output; what is said is merely an infinitesimal portion of what is left unsaid. The lines are short and shy like the speech of a weak-voiced, weak-bodied individual. The poems never exceed the length of an ordinary page and never lack mysterious allusions. The sunset that touched the heart of the poet, the passing shadow on the trembling wheat in the field, the longing girl at the window, the call of desire, the remembrance of the chant that accompanied talmudic studies, the waiting-rooms of physicians who have treated the tubercular poet—these are the themes of his poems. They are easily absorbable in small quantities; twenty or thirty of them produce a monotonous effect; they require little or no effort on the part of the reader. Even the mysterious allusions want no unraveling; they are like the humble objects of daily life which surround us with their familiarity and escape us in their symbolism. It is no accident that Vogel has written few poems; he knew his limits and limitations.

The conservatism of his prose is unaffected by the originality of his poetry. Both in his translation of *The Heretic of Soana*[3] by Gerhard Hauptmann and in his original story *In the Sanitarium*[4] he uses ordinary language. The novelty of his story lies in the plot rather than in the form. The vicissitudes of the tubercular Jews in an Austrian sanitarium before the advent of Hitler win the sympathies of the reader. On the brink of death they indulge in pathetic love experiences with hungry avidity. Even their constant consciousness of impaired health which causes them an infinite amount of worry does not prevent them from struggling for an intense and passionate mode of existence.

In the novel *Marriage*[5] Vogel also preserves an austere conservatism in language and content. The young Jews and Jewesses in the gay turmoil of pre-Hitlerian Vienna—the heroes of the novel—live their drab lives on the periphery of metropolitan life and die a melancholy death. Their sketchy characters leave sketchy impressions and their insignificant lives evaporate from memory. Yet, in justice to Vogel, it must be said that an unsuspected trait of his personality reveals itself in his prose: a firm realism which stands in sharp contrast to his vague poetry. It is as if the poet in him had no knowledge of the potentialities of his prose.

Disciple of Vogel: Baruch Katzenelson

Vogel created no school of poetry but he influenced one Hebrew poet to a very marked degree: Baruch Katzenelson (1900–1968). Like his master the disciple loved the short poem and the short line. And he preferred the birth of emotion to its elaboration in art. These are the obvious similarities.[6] But there are very important differences between the two poets. Katzenelson is more conscious of his Jewishness than Vogel. He identifies with the people, he admires its past and shares its hopes for a brighter future; Vogel knows only loyalty to himself. Katzenelson is haunted by the chimera of antisemitism, by its past outrages and present potentialities. In the nine lines of the little lyric "By Candlelight" which is also the name of his first book of poems, he managed to draw in minature what Bialik painted on the broad canvass of "Ha-Matmid": the loneliness of Jewish youth in the House of Study and the search for wider horizons.

By candlelight, between the walls of the House of Study,
My dream flickered sadly,
My soul yearned mutely.

The curtain gleamed on the ark
In whiteness like a veil on my youth,

Like trembling arms of a girl.

I often wished I were dead
Because the house had windows
Which looked upon a world so strange.[7]

The frustrated longing for life changed into longing for death. Storms of youth receded before contemplation in maturity. When, in later years, Katzenelson came to summarize his literary abilities in a poem, he vaunted his "understanding sorrow, yearning songs for visions and redemption."[8] Understanding sorrow is tranquil sorrow; it lacks despair, it often rises to faith.

Those who come after us,
The great discoverers, the masters of life,
Will not despise us though we stumbled.[9]

This would be misrepresentation if it were not poetic indulgence in weakness and an invitation to sympathy. If Katzenelson stumbled, it was not before dark gates like Vogel but in quest for the still, small light. Even the characteristic titles of his books of poetry which were published in Israel, *In the Crucible of Silence*[10] and *From Heart to Heart*,[11] record the soulfulness and sincerity of a poet who suffered in Slutzk, in New York and, since 1934, in the Land of Israel.

13
Cultivators of Introspection: Feierberg; Gnessin; Schoffmann

Fin de Siècle: Feierberg

Mordecai Zev Feierberg (1874–1899) reproduced the pangs of his education in a memorable passage of his story "In the Evening"[1]—a passage which illumines traditional techniques of Jewish teaching with awesome clarity:

> The teacher is seated at the head of the table, with his two assistants at his sides. Before him on the table lies the cane with its leather straps. The children are seated on benches around the table. The teacher's voice blends with those of the assistants and the frail children. The din is deafening. A boy is being caned; he cries. The teacher holds on to his cane. His face is wrinkled up and his eyes are ablaze with terrifying wrath. He is angry with the children, the assistants, his wife, the table, the cane, and the divine will for creating a world so terrible and so troublesome. A few minutes pass. Two children cry, then three, four, five. The teacher strikes, teaching and yelling on one side; the assistants strike, teaching and yelling on the other side.[2]

With similar sensitivity Feierberg enshrined the pain and confusion of a generation in his short novel *Whither.* In less than a hundred pages he translated the abstract discourses of Ahad Haam into the anxious, agonized moods of Nahman, the protagonist of his novel. Like Feierberg himself and thousands of nameless young men at the turn of

221

the century, he had lost that faith and certainty which religions so generously bestow upon their adherents. And he symbolized that loss by an heretical act in the synagogue, by blowing out a candle on *Yom Kippur*, the Day of Atonement. This offense marked him as a madman in the eyes of his co-religionists. But it was also used as an effective device in the novel to sandwich in, as it were, the life of Nahman in a series of reminiscent monologs between the incomprehensible act which is described a few pages after the beginning of the novel and mentioned again as a matter-of-fact occurrence a few pages before the end of the novel.[3] In infinite sadness Nahman groped for a new way of life and exchanged the talmudic and post-talmudic sages for Spinoza and Kant, Darwin and Buckle. But the modern masters were disappointing:

> Kant revived society for a hundred years, Darwin will, perhaps, stimulate thought for another hundred years.[4]

The ghetto-bred hero craved a steadfast creed which would survive thousands of years. That creed, we learn from the end of the novel, would be the Jew's future gift to the Orient and the world at large. But the Jew would have to become oriental again in his ancestral home. With a distrust of occidentalism which turned to aversion Feierberg— like Bialik[5]—idealized the traditional house of learning and prayer. But the enthusiastic and encomiastic attitude to that "world of cherished shadows,"[6] as Feierberg termed it, was conscious self-deception. For the house of study had lost its vitalizing vigor, Europe decieved or deluded her lovers, Israel was a distant hope. With a touching belief in the efficacy of the written word Feierberg urged Hebrew writers in his last essay "Our Belles-Lettres and their Tasks"[7] to rouse humanity to the Jewish need for Israel in order "to cure a people upon which it has inflicted so many wounds in vain."[8] Curiously, after the infliction of the almost deadly wound, the holocaust, humanity was roused and Israel was born. Whether the process of orientalization, urged by Feierberg, will be the salvation of Jewry or not—that will be determined in the future. Our nineteenth-century author worked with a pair of antithetical concepts: Orient and Occident. In the light of archeological discoveries in the twentieth century we tend to minimize the rigidities of that geographical polarity and view the peoples of the Mediterranean basin—Greeks and Jews and other ethnic groupings—as one cultural entity with many regional variations.

Gnessin: Embodiment of Sensitivity

An admirer of Feierberg and a short-story writer of extraordinary sensitivity, Uri Nissan Gnessin (1879–1913), lived outside the pale of literary coteries. Though he corresponded with some of his contemporaries—Anohi, Brenner, Fichmann, Lachower, Shimoni—he was alone. And in spite of more than a hundred essays on his work, he is still an enigma.[9] Equipped with deep insight into human nature, disillusioned and morbid like those *poètes maudits* of the latter half of the nineteenth century whom Verlaine immortalized in a book, he has garnered the rich store of his experiences in four main stories[10] which seem to be made of elusive allusions and subtle moods, snippets and gobbets of talk rather than full-fledged conversations. Those ethereal heroes of his—Hagzar, Berger, Efrat and Margalit—are multiple projections of Gnessin who has lived an anguished life in a world apart—almost out of time, out of space.[11] They do not revolt, they do not reform; they simply hint at their rich inner life and they try to be true to themselves.[12] Whether they converse or soliloquize, they have the strange capacity of creating a mood in a sentence:

> And tomorrow she will come again, this lovely girl with her beautiful sadness, she will come when the sun sets in gentle red, and the bells of the churches wail their lonely and restrained angelus.[13]

This is poetry which, afraid of metrical shackles, flows in naked, unadorned splendor. And this is wisdom—sure of itself and ageless as a river:

> Man is one and the same being forever—at home or in the street. . .Only for the street you have a different dress which is, most of the time, not more beautiful than the one you wear at home.[14]

Proximity and distance: Gnessin achieved both modes of narration; he lived inside and outside his characters. And he was the first Hebrew poet of womanhood—the writer who has created a gallery of women out of a passionate concern with their perennial absorption in love.[15]

In an early story "Genia" Gnessin has fashioned an unforgettable type: a young woman who devotes her life to organizational work and seeks, at the same time, a fulfilling relation with one man. It eludes her; she gives herself to many inferior men; and when she seems to find the one at last, he is not the one.

> "I had a few loves before I met you. . .and now I love you. Yes, I loved them all." She raised her moist voice: "All of them. I loved with all the ardor of my youth, with all the fire in my heart, in my youthful heart. I loved and I gave myself—all of myself—to them. . . But they did not want to understand me. They were stupid, inferior. . .Darling. Please. Don't be like them."[16]

But her last lover is like them—as far as she is concerned: an episode rather than an experience even though he protests in the final sentence of the story: "No. I am not like them, I am not like them."[17]

Genia is the eternal feminine: in quest of love which eludes her, aspiring to the pleasures of abiding togetherness, abused for the sake of ephemeral pleasures by incomprehensive, insensitive men.[18]

Though outside the canon of the four Gnessin stories "Genia" prefigures the young women in them. And not only in them. In a strange story "In the Gardens,"[19] Suli, the imbecile daughter, spends her semi-conscious days in the company of her widowed father—a Jew who tends his farm and makes a good living. Pious, crass, ignorant, he conceives a passion for her and despises her, at the same time, for her lasciviousness. The story ends with the cohabitation of father and daughter. After the act the father spits and growls in disgust:

> "Such scum. I'll murder her. . ." The whip in his hand whistled through the air and snaked across Suli's bare shoulder. . . She jumped up, sat upright and waited in terror. As he turned to leave, she took her hand from her flogged shoulder and cried out quickly in her coarse, toneless, masculine voice: "You son of a bitch. Bastard, dirty bastard." [20]

That Gnessin, the refined poet of womanhood, had also an understanding for the coarser aspects of life, comes as a surprise. Perhaps the story "In the Gardens" pointed to a new development which was not consummated in his brief life. Nor have other aspects of his creative personality come to full fruition. The handful of lyrical poems and the few sensitive translations of Chekhov and Obstfelder, Shestov and Wassermann, Nomberg and Spector, are interesting as revelatory documents of the author rather than autonomous creations.

They have helped to shape his noiseless style and his hushed vocabulary. The poems, in particular, are branded with an embryonic amorphism which reached its ripest expression in his last stories with their characteristically prepositional titles: "Before" and "At."[21] Vague yearnings at the beginning of spring, insecurity in loneliness, an almost hopeless stance inform line after line.

> I am not crushed by darkest night
> But by the desert of my life.[22]

This is Gnessin's resumé of man's lot, of his lot on earth.

Schoffmann: Master of Miniature

Gnessin's delicate sensibility was matched by Gershon Schoffmann (1880-1972) who may be regarded as the unique and unexcelled master of miniature in Hebrew literature. In the five volumes of his collected works the longest story, "Man on Earth,"[23] numbers twenty-eight pages, the shortest—a few lines. Thematically, too, he is an innovator. Modern Hebrew literature before him was correct to the point of prudishness. Schoffmann did not hesitate to introduce the *fille de joie* or the pervert as appropriate subjects to his stories. To accuse him of pornography, however, is to do him as little justice as charging D. H. Lawrence or Norman Mailer with obscenity.

Conscious nationalism, the obsession of most Hebrew writers in the beginning of the twentieth century, rarely colors his stories. Yet in the brief sketch "Wiener Neustadt"[24] the Jewishness and the solidarity with his people emerge with unexpected vigor:

> A small town, about an hour's ride from Vienna by express. At night one sees from the train window a lighted room in one of the houses opposite the railroad station—a very dismal room and an old sombre clock with black weights on the wall. And one is weighted down by an unbearable sadness. It is a relief, indeed, that the express doesn't stop here long and hastens to carry one away from that vale of tears. Only then one breathes freely. Still, for a long time, I was unable to account for the peculiar discomfort which I experienced whenever I stopped at that station on my way to Vienna. The conductor's call "Wiener Neustadt" in the night air used to sadden me much but I did not know exactly why.

Until. . .until I found in Bernfeld's *The Book of Tears* the story of persecution and slaughter that took place there seven hundred years ago: "Also the wives of our enemies spilled our blood," thus runs the lamentation commemorating the event of those days. "We were slaughtered like rams and lambs, all of us, boys and girls, widows and orphans. . .The sun above me grew dim and would not shine for the shining old master R. Meir was slain. . ."[25] And now I understand.

In Israel where Schoffmann settled in 1938 he applied his honed sensitivity to biblical landscapes and biblical characters. In his wanderings through the region of Gilboa he is eager to guess "on which crest, on which slope, Saul and Jonathan fell."[26] Near Mount Tabor, Deborah quickens his imagination.

> I pondered on that "mother in Israel. . ."[27] A dark girl in khaki trousers passed by with a smile, the sort of beauty I have not seen for many a day; and yet, at the same time, suffused with something of orphanhood that touched a cord of pity.
> "Who is that girl?" I asked my companion. . .
> "From Czechoslovakia."
> "Perhaps you will introduce her to me? . . ."
> He responded gladly and called after her: "Deborah."[28]

With ineffable artistry, by mere evocation of a common Hebrew name in ancient and modern times, Schoffmann bridges the generational gap of three thousand years. More than that: the beautiful girl of modern Israel is also the age-old heroine, a living embodiment of ancient glory. In his incipient confrontation with the ancestral land Schoffman Schoffmann artfully mixed the old and the new, romantic and realistic moods, Jewish and non-Jewish themes. And he achieved in one of his stories, "In the Circle,"[29] a sensitive juxtaposition: the depressing feeling of enslavement in Aryan countries and the exhilarating feeling of liberty in mandatory Palestine:

> The benches, in a circle around the fountain, are good, new and sturdy benches, not worse than those in the streets and parks of foreign countries, except that they do not bear the legend "for Aryans only. . ." School children pass by, their books under their arms, jolly and gay, just like gentile children in foreign countries.

Perambulators, one after the other, are being pushed by young mothers. The babies smile to the young sky that blinds them with its brightness—to the sky that looks as if it had just emerged from the hand of its Creator. And it is such an old sky, the sky of the Bible. Under it all the ancient things have happened, some of them full of meaning: Here both Jonathan and Michal fell in love with young David of the beautiful eyes. Michal, sweet daughter of Saul, proud and wonderful Michal, where are your traces here? Not in vain did Paltiel, the son of Laish, follow you, weeping as he went, when you were taken away from him—not in vain.[30]

In the evening lovers meet on the benches. Some remain until midnight and some even later than midnight. . .Still, happiness does not reign on every bench as it may seem at first glance. Some benches witness silent tragedies at night. Here is a couple whose affairs are not as they should be. Not at all what they should be. And that's why they came here for a final account. This is their last meeting before parting. These are the last flutters of a love-sick soul that wrestles with destiny and tries to hold on to a straw. But you cannot struggle against the truth. Just now, as if in spite, the beloved face shines in all its fearful glory under the cold and distant stars. But facts are facts; she does not love him.

To escape from her, not to see her again, to escape and forget her somewhere far away, in strange places. But where? From here, from this last refuge, there is no escape. As in the legend, the vulture preys on the flesh and the victim cannot budge.

Thus we move about in a circle.

As in most stories of Schoffmann, inessential trimmings are avoided with ascetic deliberation. And the bare structure projects the precarious equilibrium: the unloved lover cannot escape from the Land of Promise because "from this last refuge there is no escape." Neither can the people. We move in a circle—on a personal, on a national, on a universal level.

Though Schoffmann feels a keen affiliation with Jewry, he does not achieve his highest artistic effects in a specifically Jewish story. He is at his best when he sounds the depths of an important but seemingly insignificant moment in the life of a man or a woman, and floods it with unexpected insight. Only his story "Man on Earth" is sufficiently long to permit him a rather minute study of a rural community with its petty jealousies and cruelties throughout the changing seasons of the year. This he does with merciless exactitude and symbolic implication; the world at large seems to be a mere replica of the cruel village microcosm.

Even in his review of books and evaluations of personalities, Schoffmann contents himself with a page or two. He is not interested in a detailed analysis but rather in the impression which a sentence creates or a man makes in an unguarded moment. A fleeting glimpse of Ramsay MacDonald, prime minister of the first Labor government in England, elicits this comment from the pen of Schoffmann:

> There is brutality in his gestures; his hypocrisy is more provoking than that of other statesmen. . .Diplomatic cunning is in their eyes (Briand, Lloyd George) but his glance is straightforward, innocent, yet not convincing. Wile without a smile.[31]

Only the Austrian author Peter Altenberg whom Schoffmann loved and translated[32] had a similar gift for mini-writing. But while the former cherished the almost legendary Austria of waltzes and cafés, the latter who has lived from 1904 to 1938 in Vienna and in Wetzelsdorf, a village near Graz, reflected the fears, the anxieties and the murderous inclinations of individuals in a land which was ripe for rape by the Nazis. When Schoffmann settled in Haifa, he made no revolutionary break with his past; he entrusted his new observations of an almost alien land to his old genre. In his eighty-ninth year he received a belated honor for literary excellence: the Irving and Bertha Newman Literary Prize from New York University.

The three sensitive writers—Feierberg, Gnessin, Schoffmann— move in an atmosphere of impaired Judaism. They have more in common with contemporary writers in the West than with their predecessors in Hebrew literature. And they share a sombre magnificence; they heap the Pelion of despair on the Ossa of defeat.

14
Hebrew Literature Between Two World Wars

A. In Russia

The Bolshevist revolution spelled the doom of Hebrew literature in Russia. In the first victorious years the Communists maintained a policy of caution toward Hebrew writers. By the end of their first decade in 1927 they showed open enmity. Jewish Communists may have accelerated the process of dissolution; they did not influence the outcome.

Two men made an ill-fated beginning for Hebrew literature under the Soviet regime: the publisher Abraham Joseph Stybel who founded the most influential Hebrew periodical, *ha-Tekufah*, in Moscow in 1918 and its first editor David Frischmann. But the ambitious enterprise enjoyed—if that is the word—a brief career: In 1919 it had to transfer its activities to Warsaw where it led a precarious existence in independent Poland for a number of years.[1] The emigration of Bialik with an entourage of prominent Hebrew writers from Odessa in 1921 marked the beginning of the end for Hebrew literature in Russia.[2]

A few young writers hoped to revive literary creativity with Communist orientations. They made their new departures with the weak voice of sloganized epigones in a thin-leaved pamphlet *Loud Cymbals*.[3] In 1926 another collected effort of Hebrew writers *In the Beginning*[4] raised false hopes for a new literary dawn. The translation from Babel's famous cycle of stories "Red Cavalry" lent prestige to the volume which was more substantial in content and quantity than *Loud Cymbals*.

These two collective ventures were paralleled by two individual collections of poetry: *Eruption*[5] by Samuel Novak and *On a*

Ten-Stringed Instrument[6] by Ben-Zion Fradkin. But their revolutionary ardor was as misplaced as it was unrewarded. After the first decade of the Russian revolution the few Hebrew writers who remained in the Communist paradise had to publish abroad—chiefly in the periodicals of former Palestine and nascent Israel. Some of them, like the poets Borovitsh and Hanovitsh, have been completely forgotten. Some like Yokebed Bat Miriam and Abraham Kariv have emigrated to former Palestine and made names for themselves in poetry and criticism. Of the few who remained only Abraham Friemann, Hayyim Lenski and Elisha Rodin deserve serious consideration. Preigerson, an engineer by profession, never conquered his addiction to the *shtetl.* Yosipon penned incendiary sketches about Asian Jewry. Shimon Haboneh showed an ardent predilection for revolutionary Ukraine in prose and verse. But his Communist zeal did not save him from exile in Siberia. Nor did faith in red justice save Yosipon from banishment to that inhospitable land.

The life of Abraham Friemann (1890–1954?) is a grim accompaniment of his unfinished work. The Russian government punished him with twenty years in Siberia for his love of Hebrew. When he returned to his native Ukraine to die a premature death, he ended an individual destiny which, in a sense, symbolized the destiny of his people in the land of coercion. His voluminous novel[7] aims—as its title *1919* indicates—to translate the experiences of a fateful year into imaginative prose. It is an apocalyptic sequence of violence, destruction and death. The final phase of the First World War provides a nightmarish background; the Austrian army occupies Ukraine; the Russian army suffers disorganization; Ukraine aspires to statehood and its national hero, Simon Petlura, shows his greatest prowess in the organization of successful pogroms. The fate of Jewry amidst the bloody events is Friemann's paramount concern. That the Jews had been good neighbors to the Ukrainian peasants is a documented fact in the idylls of Tschernichowsky.[8] But the year 1919 changes the comforts of co-existence into sudden enmity. Solomon Stupashkover, the protagonist of the novel and the man of heroic proportions, organizes self-defense in spite of the bickerings of Zionists, Communists and Bundists who vie for the soul of the town and its Jewish inhabitants. With the tenacity of despair he half-succeeds in his impossible, ungratifying task of leadership.

Like the Polish Nobel prize winner Władyslaw Stanisław Reymont (1868–1925) who organized his novel *The Peasants*[9] around the seasons of the year, Friemann chose summer, autumn and winter for the grim events of the novel. The season of spring is missing—perhaps fortuitously, perhaps by design: spring and the bloody plot of the novel are contradictory rather than complementary events. The macabre milieu projects one statistical fact with uncommon strength: the valuelessness of human life. Shootings are common; instinctual drives prevail; barbarization is inevitable. The Jews are accused as friends of Bolsheviks by Ukranians; as friends of counter-revolutionists by Bolsheviks. Between hammer and anvil they are beaten to shreds. The old story of scapegoatism and persecution enjoys the penultimate rehearsal before the great holocaust.

The brief life of Hayyim Lenski (1905–1942) unrolled in the most pregnant decades of the century. It was a *vita dolorosa* from birth in Lithuania to death in Siberia. In early youth the poet acquired an undying love for the Hebrew language and its literature. And that love—unwavering and unremitting—earned him imprisonment in Leningrad and exile in Siberia.[10] Before imprisonment, in relative freedom in Leningrad, he worked in an iron foundry. But he did not accept his situation with stoic resignation; he was bitterly unhappy with the government which exacted ceaseless toil for a rotten wage.

Amid cruel circumstances he wrote his poems—always uncertain of his fate and their destination. The revolutionary presence was on the outside. Inside a non-revolutionary existence charted an independent course for Lenski. His defiant conservatism of expression was matched by his use of conservative genre and metres and forms: ballads, sonnets, traditional stanzas and rhymes dominate his poetry. Even his literary gods—Pushkin and Hölderlin—belong to former times.

The Jewish townlet, as it existed in the Pale of Settlement, the fields and forests on its fringe, the Sabbaths and the holidays as they were celebrated in the ramshackle houses and synagogues—these are the objects of his chief love.

On the fringe of my town ten birches play
A hundred white flutes every day:
Tri-li-lee. . .Tri-li-lee. . .
A hundred flutes—lay upon lay—
And all for me.

On the fringe of my town the north winds cry,
The north winds cry and prophesy:
It's a mystery. . .It's a mystery. . .
Woes upon woes come nigh, come nigh—

Also for me?

On the fringe of my town a shack falls apart,
On the well near the shack the swipe gives a start.
Oh bucket! Oh well! Oh spree!
She comes with her pitcher, her song and her heart
And waits—not for me.[11]

The delicate indication of the suburban landscape, the fear of the future and the longing for love which will not be consummated—all these elements have combined in the poem to fashion a miniature work of art. Lenski seemed to love his *shtetl* with that nostalgic zest which is reserved for the loves of one's youth. He had his preferences—the poor and the insignificant and, especially, the children who resemble somewhat the little Mo's and the little Sols in Bialik's folksongs. Like their prototypes in life they lead a less childlike, a less carefree, a less happy existence than gentile children.

Exile in Siberia did not crush Lenski's spirit. His love for Hebrew sustained him and fortified him against the snow and the ice which appear with uncomfortable profusion in poem after poem. The loss of personal liberty was, in a sense, a sort of liberation of the spirit from a repression which almost wrecked his poetic talents:

Far beyond the Ural hills
The days of youth are setting slow.
What am I to bear tomorrow? . .
What have you decreed, my fate?[12]

Fate had decreed for him a minimum amount of food, a maximum amount of hard, road-building labor and, ultimately, death by hunger.

The translation of the Siberian epic *Yangal Maa*[13] by the exiled Hebrew poet was more than a labor of love. The Vogul hunters who led a nomadic existence in the vast tundras east of the mountains of Ural had been subjected by Czarist Russia and christianized by force. But the tribe kept its customs, its pagan faith and its superstitions. The tempting theme inspired Lenski to brilliant rendition. Did not his own people, a small tribe in the wilderness of exile, groan under the yoke of the oppressor? Was not the elder of the tribe, Oyka Kuksa, a poet who imbued his unfortunate brethren with hopes of a better future by keeping the vital past alive? The verses of *Yangal Maa* sound like the farewell of the poet who, like his people, suffered the miserable lot of exile for reasons of political exigency. For Lenski was indeed "the last of Hebrew poets on the step-motherly soil of Russia."[14] But the title of his last book, *Beyond the River Lethe,* is an epinikion rather than an epitaph: He will not be the victim of the River of Forgetfulness.

While Lenski flourished with folk-like simplicity even under the inhospitable Siberian skies, Elisha Rodin withered under the impact of the revolution. In lyrical, plaintive poems he expressed his unbounded loyalty to the ancestral language. As a poet of personal rather than communal emotion he mourned the loss of his son Grisha who served the Red Army and was killed during the Second World War. The sixty-one poems, dedicated to the experience of death, are his best: He managed to combine two loves in them—the love for his son and the love for the Hebrew language. When he attempted an objectivation of his namesake Elisha ben Abuyah in a two-page poem—his longest—he failed to create a credible image of the heretic sage or of himself. Similarly, his thoughts on the revolution and his essays on Bialik and Mendele, Heine and Tolstoy, rarely rise above ephemeral journalism.

Rodin was not unaware of the social implications of the October revolution. "The white gloves and the shining spurs"[15] which vanished in the first gust of the upheaval in Russia did not inspire him with elegies on dead elegance. But he could not and would not understand the "music of skull-bashing bullets."[16] And he was deeply disturbed that he had to wrap the Book of Books in a copy of *Pravda* in order to escape persecution for the possession of the counter-revolutionary classic: That was a desecration of the dignity of the Bible.[17]

Like Lenski, Rodin was assigned to a menial job which only exacerbated his sensibilities. And like Lenski he had the pathetic distinction to be among the last Hebrew writers in Russia.

B.   In Poland

During the First World War Jews in Poland suffered more than the indigenous population. Russians, Germans, Austrians or Austro-Hungarians deployed their armies in various sectors of the country and left damage and death in the wake of their multiple occupations and retreats. Antisemitism of the Polish and Ukranian masses aided and abetted defeated generals who used Jews as convenient scapegoats for their inefficiency or bad luck. It also permeated all strata of the population—from the downtrodden peasants to the colonels who were in the saddle in liberated Poland.

The twenty-odd years of Polish independence between the two world wars were the fullfillment of a people's dream which began with the loss of statehood in the three partitions of 1772, 1791 and 1796. But political freedom was not paralleled by economic prosperity. Mismanagement—*polnische Wirtschaft* in the ironic German phrase—persisted; the plight of Polish peasantry was as miserable as in pre-independence days; the wretched Polish roads remained in a wretched state.

Jews between the two world wars made up, roughly, 10% of the population: 2,855,318 out of 27,176,717 according to the census of 1921; 3,113,933 according to the census of 1931.[18] They engaged—first and foremost—in trade and in manufacturing enterprises.

The traditional antisemitism fed on the myth of deicide and on the reality of mass poverty which, ironically, affected Jews and non-Jews. The Jewish deputies in the *Sejm*, the Polish parliament—an Isaac Grünbaum or a Leon Reich—fought a losing battle on behalf of their people. Even Osias Thon (1870–1936), the excellent and prolific journalist, the gifted preacher, the brilliant rabbi of Cracow, was helpless. Like his rabbinic colleagues in the capitals of Europe—Moses Schorr in Warsaw, Marcus Ehrenpreis in Stockholm, Zevi Peretz Chajes in Vienna—he was a Hebraist. And like them he was a tower of strength to Jewry when the century was young. But he failed to provide the comforts of dignity to Polish Jewry.

In circumstances of want and misery Hebrew literature declined in Poland between the two world wars. The representative Yiddish writers of Poland died during the First World War: Isaac Leibush Peretz, Sholem Aleyhem, Simon Samuel Frug, Mendele; somewhat later Ansky, Hirsch David Nomberg. All of them also wrote in Hebrew; some of them had a decisive influence on Hebrew literature. Ansky who, through Bialik's translation of the *Dibbuk*, became one of the most popular dramatists in the era following the First World War, is still a *force majeure* in the repertoire of *Habimah*, the national theatre of Israel.

Between the two world wars poets like Jacob Cahan and thinkers like Maisels-Amitai did their best work outside Poland. Even Shoham, the poet and dramatist, wrote one play outside Poland—*Tyre and Jerusalem*.[19] And it was an accident of fate that he did not settle in former Palestine like his close friend, the poet Benzion Benshalom: He could not find work to support himself. Of the important poets between the world wars only Aaron Zeitlin, the son of the martyred Hillel Zeitlin, and Ber Pomeranc worked in Poland consistently. Of the social scientists the historian Menahem Edmund Stein (1895–1943) who died in the Polish concentration camp of Treblinka in the vicinity of Lublin and the sociologist Aryeh Tartakower who became Professor of Sociology at the Hebrew University after the Second World War lived and created their important tracts in Poland: Stein engaged in researches on Jewry in hellenistic and Roman times, Tartakower shed light on contemporary problems of Jewish sociology, especially on the history of the Jewish labor movement and on modern Jewish history.

The Zeitlins—father and son—were irresistibly drawn to journalism in spite of their multiple literary endowments. The father, Hillel Zeitlin (1871–1942) began his literary career with a monograph on *Good and Evil* which appeared in *ha-Shiloah* at the end of the century. That problem was central to his thought and action. It involved him in tensions and instabilities which enabled him to embrace and abandon organizational structures. For brief periods of time he was Zionist and territorialist à la Zangwill, socialist and freethinker. Finally, he seemed to have resolved his contradictions in strict adherence to tradition. In Warsaw where he spent the last thirty-six years of his life, he developed an intense journalistic career—mainly in Yiddish. The articles and books which flowed from his pen in profusion were tinged with a deeply felt but not commensurately articulated mysticism. The classics of Kabbalah and Hasidism were his constant intellectual fare in the last decades of his life. And they tinged his writings with ecstatic rhetoric and pseudo-poetical phrasing. In his long literary career he was at odds with Ahad Haam and Berdyczewski. But Brenner was a life-long friend and Herzl a life-long hero.

Aaron Zeitlin, who published a hagiographical account of the life and works of his father in a series of essays in the Yiddish *Morgen Journal,* scattered his talents in two languages—Hebrew and Yiddish—with prodigal recklessness. Poems, plays, novels, essays and feuilletons flowed in an endless stream from his pen. Journalistic assiduity in Poland and, later, in America, swelled his literary output. But, essentially and primarily, he was and remained a poet. In his predilection for mysticism—a partial inheritance from his father—he occupies the same position as William Butler Yeats in modern English literature: He is fascinated by the mystery of the world while the soul of mystery seems to elude his rational mind. Like his Irish contemporary he seems to believe that "the soul cannot have much knowledge till it has shaken off the habit of time and of place. . . ."[19a] In the dying and undying twilight he finds allusions to "the unrevealed twilight of the heart," and in the twilight of the heart he seeks an allusion to the Ineffable. But it is difficult to say whether the poet aims at the heart of mystery or simply mystifies a common experience. It seems that he wishes to convince himself with all the ardor of the mystic that the world is a chain of impenetrable secrets. While a few of its links may be seen by the naked eye and the observant mind, most of them remain hidden forever. In such a scheme of things man is "servant to Satan" and Satan is son of God.

For the Jew Zeitlin reserves a special rank in the hierarchy of the world: He is what Spinoza was according to the German poet Novalis—a God-intoxicated man.

> Every man is an Israel Baal Shem.
> Hidden, cave-dwelling.
> There is a forest in the cave
> Like the cave of Israel in the Carpathian mountains.
> Satan grew the forest.
> God grew Satan[20a]

Zeitlin could turn a word or a phrase into a delightful homily as his hasidic ancestors were wont to do. Unlike mystics who shun sensual perception as a vehicle of knowledge he believes in the reliability of the senses. For he possesses talents of a plastic artist which are quite uncommon in a mystic. And he uses them to great advantage in the more formal poems. In a sonnet on "The Poor"[21] he describes the great patience of the unpossessing multitudes whose lips move like the gentle grasses of the summer and whose fingers wither like autumnal flowers. True to the pattern of his thoughts, however, Zeitlin sees them as saints in rags, as "children of Buddha thinking deep thoughts."

In numerous lyrical poems he characterized the search for his own soul as an unsuccessful adventure:

> I loved Women,
> And my soul perished.
> I have not found my soul
> And I have not found love.
> I wrote books,
> And my word perished.
> I found words,
> But I did not find the word.
> Every book is
> An abyss which swallows words,

And the abyss is not full.
Every woman is
An abyss which swallows man,
And the abyss is not full.
The abyss of words, the abyss of woman—
They are empty, both abysses.[22]

The banality of love, the banality of the world, the banality of the word: this is a haunting mood which validates, in paradoxical commitment, sudden insights of the poet.

Ber Pomeranc (1900–1942)—village-bred, self-taught, musical, dreamy—was the classical blueprint for failure. In a country where even the ambitious had a difficult time to earn a living he simply could not succeed either as a clerk for the "Organization of the Hebrew Writers" or as a teacher in one of the *Tarbut*[23] schools. As a poet he was doomed to starve; as an aspiring violinist who struggled with his love for another art he made no headway:

Two angels struggled with me in my youth. The first played the violin, the second wrote poems. Had Jasha Heifetz's teacher, Professor Malkin, who taught me without remuneration how to play the violin in Vilna and who promised me a brilliant future, had he known that my violin was silenced without my fault, he would have certainly sighed as he sighed when he thought about the revolution.[24]

In 1935 Pomeranc published his first volume of poems: *With Lips to the Rock*,[25] in 1939 his second and last volume *Window in the Forest*.[26] The symbolic title of the first book needs no exegesis: Moses smote the rock with the rod and drew water,[27] Pomeranc sucked the living water of poetry out of the rock. As for the title of the second volume, the poet seems to emphasize his love for nature as a point of vantage on the man-made world.

To the heart of the city, resplendent in myriads of lights,
I brought a vision of forests in my eyes.[28]

That vision was nurtured by his own experiences and by the experiences of the poets whom he translated: the Yiddish Itzik Manger, the Russian Alexander Pushkin, the Polish Stanislaw Wyspiański.[29] The city was a constant reminder of natural and economic deficiencies. But poverty, a grim symbol of the Jewish masses in Poland, was transformed by Pomeranc into poetry which approximated "a prayer of the afflicted":[30]

> The yellow shell of the prosaic day
> Drops upon the pavement like an empty nut.
> The price of a meal is a coin or two.
> Father in heaven, what is it to you?
>
> My tattered coat shivers
> In the sharp shears' vise of the north wind.
> My timid gaze jumps
> From face to face in dangerous acrobatics.
> Near a show-window I linger and rest:
> The wonderful bamboo-cane has drawn me.
> Father in heaven, it is so cold to stand.
> Let me rejoice in the cane.[31]

In the beginning of the century such poetry could not have been written anywhere in the world. In its stark statement of feeling, in its immediacy of expression, in its bold imagery it appears as a new art which has retained only the measured line out of the conventional devices of poetry. Sometimes even the measured line disappears, the external décor vanishes. Bareness which intends to project the experience at its inception or in its fluid vagueness: that seems to be the poet's intent. Yet the themes are the recurring themes of lyrical poetry all over the world: love, bucolic rather than urban aspects of life, poverty, despair. Metaphors are drawn from the field rather than the street:

> Where did that cold clod come from—
> Thrown at me with the hoe of despair
> When evening wheels around me like some speckled fowl?[32]

Horses are transformed in urban surroundings; their natural joy changes into mechanical, city-trotting rhythms; their expression is an infinity of sadness.[33]

Rural experience and rural knowledge which have earned him the exaggerated sobriquet of "the Hebrew Virgil"[34] link the poet with his people in remote periods of history. From a window in his mother's house he feels how the wind combs "clouds of wool and flax. . .as in biblical times."[35] And his nostalgic longing for Zion endows him with a peculiar realism:

> You are stretched in desolate splendor by the Mediterranean Sea,
> Thorned, swarming with naughty swamps.
> The Bedouin has skinned the hyena,
> The hyena ate the skin of the Bedouin.[36]

Without rhetoric or pathos, in unrhymed verse which borders on prose but does not cease to be poetry, with the visionary anticipation of the impending catastrophe, Pomeranc wrote almost the last Hebrew poems in the unhappy country which was the most important citadel of Jewry in the last three hundred years. And he labeled his quiet desperation as the feeling of "a man who sends his letter in a flask in the heart of the foamy sea."[37] His sympathies with the poor, with the wandering, with the gypsies were almost familial. With morbid fascination he describes the hospital where women bring forth their offspring, the row of white beds like the row of clenched teeth, the visits of husbands who bring pathetic boxes of sweets.

> Before the pallor of your parturient body
> All of my expressions come to naught.[38]

Unlike the contemporary poets Shlonsky and Gruenberg who indulged in parental idealization Pomeranc described a parent of flesh and blood: not a generalized parent but a father who retained the qualities of kindness and goodness in spite of dire poverty. With touching tenderness the poet describes the multiple peregrinations of his father, his life in the forests of Polesia, his death in a metropolitan hospital at the age of forty-four.

> Neither whiskey nor obesity nor sexual disease
> Whittled down his strong roots.[39]

Economic and emotional deprivation in a stark environment aged the poet. "My grandfather at my age was younger than I."[40] And he died a martyr's death with millions of his people in Poland.

Before its annihilation Polish Jewry, in a final burst of creative energy, produced a Hebrew playwright and poet of uncommon stature. His name was Mattathias Moses Polakiewicz (1893-1937). In the very beginning of his literary career he abandoned the family name, which was identical with the people of his country, for the pen-name Shoham—"a kind of gem, onyx or sardonyx"—which, according to biblical tradition, adorned the garments of the High Priest and bore the names of the twelve tribes.[41] It was a deliberate, calculated change. The man Polakiewicz dissociated himself from the inhospitable and intolerant people of his native land and assumed a new identity which epitomized his personality: Shoham, a gemlike, pure, priestly consecration to Israel, its meaning and mystery enshrined in the beginnings of history.

In the brief span of eighteen years Shoham produced four plays, a few poems and a number of almost epigrammatic essays. Return to the original verse-form of the drama was an act of protest and revolt against the dullness of the modern theater and a reassertion of its ancient value.

With intuitive insight he recreated ancient Semitic civilizations rather than characters, and placed the rich contributions of biblical Jewry in a new perspective. Like Saul Tschernichowsky he endeavored to fathom the Canaanite and pre-Canaanite roots of the Jewish people. While the older contemporary sought to bridge the gap between Sinai and Olympus, Shoham stressed the incompatibility of ethical monotheism and profligate polytheism.

The four verse-plays of Shoham, *Jericho, Balaam, Tyre and Jerusalem,* and *Thou Shalt Not Make Gods of Iron unto Thyself,* seem to have been written according to a preconceived plan: They are meant to illuminate the mystery of Israel. And it is the plan that saps their strength. For a problem play begins with a disadvantage: The soul of the problem is abstraction; the soul of the play is concretion. The gods of the drama, if there be such, exact punishment from dramatists *à la thèse*: Ibsen, Shaw and Shoham age prematurely.

Our playwright lived with a tragic contradiction throughout his creative life. The ancient enemies of Israel attracted him with their sparkling vitality, the genius of Israel seemed to impose upon him the inaudible command of contempt for their excesses. This may explain the fact that the pre-eminent characters in his plays, Rahab in *Jericho,* Balaam in *Balaam,* Jezebel in *Tyre and Jerusalem,* and Hagar in *Thou Shalt Not Make Gods Of Iron Unto Thyself,* are either non-Jews or foes of Jews. Almost all of them are women of great beauty, symbols of the fatal attraction of pagan civilization.

In the very first play, *Jericho,* Shoham introduces the central theme which appears in variations in his other plays: the difference between the ancient Canaanite civilizaton and the emerging civilization of Israel. And in that play he also flaunts the appeal of paganism for the first time. Jericho, the city of gay temples and reckless debaucheries, stands on the edge of doom. Rahab, its perfect symbol of laxity and lasciviousness, stirs with uncontrollable desire. Priests and officers yearn for her in her presence and in her absence; the Hebrew spy, Achan, betrays his people for her sake. Sated with too much sensual adoration, she longs for the hero who would fight for her sake "with God and kin, with the whole world".[42] In the Hebrew man of the desert, Achan, she seems to sense the strong-armed miracle which she has sought all her life in vain. Unfortunately she finds him only to lose him irrevocably. The Jews ravage the city, Achan who has vainly struggled with his love is sentenced to death by the harsh priest and judge Phinehas, the hypocrite of the play whose zeal for God is a mere pretext for the acquisition of the beautiful Rahab as a captive of war. It is in vain that the friends of Moses, the judges Eldad and Medad, seek to soften the sentence of Achan. Hypocrisy gains the upper hand, the true spirit of the law of Moses is sacrificed for the letter of the law:

His word of fire froze in stony tablets.[43]

The luxurious and soft metropolitan civilization on the one hand, the harsh zeal of desert tribesmen on the other hand: This is the dramatic contrast between Israel and Canaan in its embryonic stage in *Jericho*. The youthful Shoham is still quite frank in his sympathy with the inimical force, in his exultation of the pagan and refined beauty of Rahab. Even betrayal was not too heavy a price for such magnificence as the courtesan of Jericho. But Shoham was too much of a playwright to portray all Jews as desert barbarians. Another spy, Othniel, and the two judges Eldad and Medad, seem to realize the implications of the law of Moses, the law of wise understanding and sympathetic kindness. But they are reduced to pointless ineffectuality; they are minor characters on the periphery of the play. Their voice of compassion is drowned in the tumult of war, not unlike the voice of pity, mingled with self-pity, of the courtesan for the ruined dovecote in the demolished temple of Astarte:

Cedar-ceiled, seraphic stood your cote
In the shrine of love where you were born.
First-fruits of corn and lentils Canaan's ladies,
Bereft of fruit of body, brought you hither
To placate the implacable Astarte.
Here incensed-laden hands of courtesans

> Patted tenderly your purple crop. . .
> The goddess left, like you, this holy place.
> We are her orphans in an abandoned nest,
> Captured by a strange, avenging God.[44]

The mission of Moses was bastardized by a vengeful priest in *Jericho*. But in *Balaam*, the second play of Shoham, Judaism was glorified through the father of prophecy. This was accomplished by a subtle dramatic device. Instead of making Moses the central character of the play, Shoham threw a sharp, clear light on Balaam, the antithesis of Moses. Envy, resentment and jealousy marred his life. No'ah, Balaam's daughter, who is also endowed with the gift of prophecy, endeavors to influence her father with exemplary sweetness and goodness. When the Hebrew spies, Phinehas and Zimri, come to him in the guise of messengers of Moab and Midian in order to wrest from him the magic blessing which is to prevent the bloodshed of the Jews and their enemies, No'ah realizes the import of their mission with her prophetic gift. But Balaam, who cannot extricate himself from the overpowering passion of jealousy, suspects that out of fear and not out of a desire for peace a wily Moses attempts to trick him with a treacherous embassy. And when he learns from his daughter that Zimri, the spy, and Kozbi, the Midianite princess, are in love, he decides to corrupt the leaders of Israel with the fatal daughters of Peor. The superior charms of the Canaanite women ease the task of Balaam considerably. The sensuous Phinehas expresses the attitude of most Jewish leaders of his time when he praises their beauty:

> The vestals of Peor are soft; in temples
> Their bodies mellowed; how unlike the women
> Of Israel who knew the desert heat,
> Whose breasts have shriveled from long wanderings,
> Whose round and unanointed thighs have thinned
> And lost their smoothness under hairy cloaks. . .[45]

Yet the old sorcerer is somehow prevented from carrying out his diabolic plan. At the sight of the armies of Israel, "the pioneers of God to the desert of nations,"[46] he changes, almost involuntarily, his curse into blessing. In a visionary trance he compares the Jews to comtemporary and future nations: the former carry the torch of redemption, the latter grope in terror of war, in lust for loot, in hunger for blood.

The sudden metamorphosis of Balaam has not been sufficiently motivated either in the Bible or in the play. An inexplicable insight, a mystical experience, inaccessible to cold logic and unplumbed in its depth, transformed the sorcerer into a prophet and facilitated the victory of the Jews over Balak, king of Moab. Balaam himself succumbed to the sword of Phinehas who also killed Zimri. Kozbi, the Midianite princess, committed suicide with the sword of Zimri which pierced her unloved lover Avi, son of Zur, prince of Midian.

The deaths which occur in the play with Elizabethan profusion cast a bloody shadow upon the main characters. Yet the plot in *Jericho* and in *Balaam* centers around the tender love of an Israelite for a foreign woman. And it is rather significant that in both plays wrath yields to kindness.

The struggle between pagan laxity and Jewish asceticism is the central theme of *Tyre and Jerusalem*. In this play Shoham reached the full maturity of his dramatic talent. His characters have attained tragic stature in the sense that Oedipus or Antigone are tragic in their entrapment in a fatal concatenation and sequence of events. Though the Bible remained his chief source of word-material, he neither abused nor plagiarized its language: he simply transformed it in the spirit of Semitic syntax and invigorated it with his semantic sensitivity. And from the Bible he also drew his chief characters— Jezebel, Elijah, Elisha—and illuminated them with unexpected and unsuspected traits.

Jezebel is true to the type of woman Shoham loved to portray in his plays. She is as attractive and as seductive as Rahab or Kozbi. Like Rahab she longs for the unconquerable hero although, conscious of her feminine force, she rules the world of men with her imperious beauty. That unconquerable hero, that beloved enemy is Elijah who dares to spurn her virgin body on the day of her consecration to Astarte, the goddess of love:

By my desecrated womb upon
The day of dedication to Astarte
I have sworn revenge upon the prophet
And his God till I erase my shame.[47]

These are the words of a pagan woman whose enemy is a member of an unimaginable race. Desire and magic, slyness and sweetness and, above all, the domineering self-assertion of a wounded queen are pitted in powerful array against the impervious might of Elijah:

> . . .And all the flames of my full summer
> I will kindle for him, ecstasy
> Of flesh which rises with the vintage, all
> My paints and perfumes, pride and expectation
> Of harvests of revenge I'll gather for him.[48]

She seduces Micha out of the band of prophets, Elisha out of her entourage of nobles, and Salu, the son of Naboth, out of his environment. Even Joram, the son of the neighboring king of Judah, cannot resist the atmosphere of debauchery which surrounds the queen like a seductive scent. Only Elijah succeeds in abstaining from the temptations of pleasure with the fantical zeal of an ascetic.

If Jezebel personifies feminine charm, Elijah represents spiritual charm. While she seduces men to the worship of physical love and its presiding goddess Astarte, he leads the people to the worship of a spiritualized deity.

Elisha, the friend and lover of the queen, experiences a profound transfiguration in the course of the play. The assassination of his relative, Naboth, opens his eyes to her trickeries and cruelties. Through association with Elijah, whom he was supposed to deliver into her hands, he becomes impregnated with the spirit of prophecy. And it is one of the ironies of the play that Elijah vanquishes her with the aid of Elisha. As for her husband, he is a mere tool in the hands of the two historic architects of fate, a defender of temporal royalty. It is Elijah who sets the course of the Jewish mission of peace and love on earth.

In *Tyre and Jersualem* Shoham contrasted the power of royalty with the power of prophecy. In the period of enlightenment Judah Leb Gordon touched upon the same antithesis in a fine dramatic monolog "Zedekiah in Prison." There the last king of Judah expresses contempt and anger for the prophet Jeremiah and his spiritualizing mission among the people. But Shoham's Ahab shows understanding and appreciation for Elijah and his visionary interests in humanity.

There is a minor character in the play, a gentile prophet by the name of Ahikar, who endeavors to reduce the contrast between Judaism and paganism, and advises the queen to effect a marriage between Astarte and Jahve, and adopt a syncretistic faith which would neutralize the power of the Invisible Deity. But the attempted compromise vanishes in victory for Elijah and in the consequent embarkation of Israel on a unique career of spiritual exaltation and physical privation.

The glory of the pagan world on the one hand and the grandeur of

Israel on the other hand constitute the theme of Shoham's last published play *Thou Shalt Not Make Gods of Iron unto Thyself.*[49] The central female character, the Egyptian Hagar, possesses the great beauty of Rahab and Kozbi and only a few of the wiles of Jezebel. The representative of Israel, Abraham, appears as a rich, peace-loving prince in the play. This is, in the case of Shoham, a new departure. In *Jericho* Achan succumbed to the charms of Canaanite civilization, in *Balaam* Zimri fell in love with Kozbi, in *Tyre and Jerusalem* the representative of Israel abstained from the pleasures of the flesh in order to conquer the temptation of pleasure. Only in *Thou Shalt Not Make Gods of Iron unto Thyself* Shoham dared to portray a man of civilized refinement as a representative of Israel. The kings of Canaan, Aram and Egypt intend to win him over to their little nostrums of separatist statesmanship but Abraham sacrifices his loyalty to the land of his birth, Aram, to the land of his sojourn, Canaan, and to the land of his ally, Egypt, on the altar of a higher loyalty to humanity. It is the dawn of allegiance of man to a world-state composed of brotherly units instead of warring tribes.

The mystery of the stranger among nations assumes a new meaning in the play of Shoham. National ties have to be loosened, blood relationships have to be discarded, racial allegiance has to be denied because they tend to foster parochial interests. Man owes a debt of brotherhood to the totality of men rather than to segments of humanity. No one is better qualified to represent this revolutionary concept than Abraham, the voluntary exile and guest in a foreign environment. And it is only natural that his wife Sarah becomes the first convert to the new idea though she cannot wholly renounce her native country and the memories of her youth.

Against the lofty conceptions of Abraham stands the youthful son of the king of the North, Gog, who only heeds the law of the God of iron and war, and the law of blood and race. These command ultimate spoliation of the neighbor and total destruction of the stranger. Gog, in short, is the prototype of the Nazi who dreams of wings of steel while Abraham imbues his household with a vision of peace. These two elemental forces, the Nazi concept of "culture" and the Hebrew aspiration to a golden age, form an arc of unusual tension in the play. Between them stands the genius of mediocrity, Lot, who differs *toto coelo* from both of them: He does not indulge in luxurious visions of the future but accepts the trifles and trivialities of the day with becoming humility and satisfaction. Suffering humanity speaks through him when, caught in a vise of grandiose rivalries, he realizes with dismay that the indifference of the ordinary man to abysmal evil and to lofty aspirations ends in premature extinction.

There is symbolic significance in the love of Gog for Sarah: The North is swayed by the powerful attraction of the East. But the friendly rivalry of Hagar and Abraham has historic rather than dramatic interest.

The timeliness of the play mars its ancient flavor. While the past suffers from the intrusion of the present, the present suffers from the intrusion of the past. Thus, dramatically, *Thou Shalt Not Make Gods of Iron unto Thyself* is weaker than the earlier plays. But the future historian of world literature will have to point to this play as one of the first, if not the first important literary evaluation and condemnation of Nazism. Though it was published in Warsaw in 1937, it was written not only before the rape of Austria and Czechoslovakia but also before the civil war in Spain.

The last two plays, *Tyre and Jerusalem* and *Thou Shalt Not Make Gods of Iron unto Thyself,* together with the unpublished *Jesus and Mary* which seems to have been lost in Warsaw during the Nazi occupation, were to form a dramatic trilogy with the genius of Israel in its triple aspect as the true protagonist: the prophet in *Tyre and Jerusalem,* the patriarch in *Thou Shalt Not Make Gods of Iron unto Thyself,* the creator of religion in *Jesus and Mary.* The two parts of the trilogy which have come down to posterity adumbrated a climax of dangerous possibilities. Two contemporary Jewish novelists, Asch in *The Nazarene* and Kabak in *In the Narrow Path,* stirred a hornets' nest with their portrayal of the founder of Christianity. Whether Shoham succeeded in his attempt will remain a subject of tantalizing speculations for the lover of Hebrew literature.

An almost sensual love for the past fired the verses of his plays as well as the lines of his poems which were essentially plays in miniature. One of his earliest poems, *Shulamit,* presents the eternal antinomy of youth and age. *East,*[50] perhaps his best achievement in poetry, takes the form of a dramatic vision. The characters are not human beings but the great civilizations of the East. One by one they emerge from the past with a wild beauty and an ancient glamor: Egypt, Babylonia, Persia, Judea. The poet succeeds in assembling the traditional foes of his people with a touching love because time healed the wounds of hate. And the yearning for eastern wisdom which was prevalent in Europe a generation ago contributed its share toward the strange evocations of the Hebrew poet. For imperial Germany's unsuccessful *Drang nach Osten* which culminated in the defeat of

1918 changed into a cultural "push toward the East" in the twenties of this century. In republican Germany and in other European countries the stage was flooded with biblical plays while the mysteries of Buddhism, the verses of Tagore and the political essays of Gandhi were studied with an almost sacred veneration. In Anglo-Saxon countries the most important poets of the period—Eliot and Yeats—were profoundly affected by the recrudescence of the East in their work. Thus Shoham's interest in the Orient was but an aspect of a cultural trend which influenced Europe and America.

In *Erez Yisrael* Shoham devoted pages of great beauty to the land of his dreams. The erotic passages are as powerful as in the plays. The comparisons of Palestine to a virgin-mother are highly effective in their persuasive suggestiveness:

> My land, my virgin-mother! When for a while you wrinkled
> Your womb before me, wild and barren like your riven rocks,
> I thought the splendid buds of your breasts withered
> In the sorrow of your virgin widowhood.
> Suddenly you loved me and desired me—your son—
> Mirthfully and modestly, a bridal land,
> Pregnant with the scented spring and hiding
> Her pregnancy in her white almond sheen.[51]

In one of the few essays which appeared under the collective title *To Scatter and to Winnow*,[52] Shoham praised Bialik for "the echo of biblical vision which flowed in his blood and in his poetry."[53] While this evaluation has dubious critical value, it characterizes Shoham with admirable exactitude. For he, with his fanatic sympathies and antipathies, was the closest approximation to a biblical poet among modern Hebrew writers.

In two epitaphs a fellow-poet, M. Lusternick, enshrined his memory: The poet was not really the citizen in his land; "he wandered among the planets, he made his covenant with someone far—the judge, the prophet, the messiah."[54]

For a few years after the First World War the newly created State of Poland, with its large Jewish population, seemed destined to inherit and develop the literary traditions of the defunct Russian center. Some of the most important Hebrew publishing firms like *Tushiyyah* and *Ahiasaf* had been established in Warsaw when it was still part of the Russian empire. After the First World War the Stybel Publishing

Company reorganized its activities in the capital of Poland. Periodicals like *Seneh* under the editorship of Jacob Cahan and *Tehumim*[55] under the triple editorship of Malkiel Lusternick, a young poet, Dr. Nathan Eck, a journalist and memoirist, and Ber Pomeranc, attracted budding and established writers. But the Hebrew revival in Poland had spent itself by the end of the twenties. Most Hebrew writers, Hebrew teachers and Hebrew-speaking individuals emigrated to former Palestine. They were driven from their native homeland by a combination of idealism and economic hopelessness. And there were not many new Hebrew writers to fill the depleted ranks. Before the Nazis overran Poland Hebrew literature was dying a slow death throughout the country. When they seized the unhappy land, they destroyed—often with the connivance of the indigenous population—Polish Jewry and the remnants of its millennial culture. And they made Poland—the quantitative and qualitative core of global Jewry—the burial ground of all European Jewries. But the few writers who remained in the ghetto of Warsaw planned—even on the threshold of death—the publication of a collective volume.[56] It was not published; but the will to write was not crushed.

With the occupation of Warsaw by the Nazis Jewish printing houses were closed, their presses confiscated and shipped to Germany. The last Hebrew book was published under the imprimatur of Abraham Joseph Stybel and printed before the German invasion of Poland.[57] It was a Hebrew translation of Caius Suetonius Tranquillus's *The Lives of the Caesars*[58] by Menahem Edmund Stein, the last rector of the Institute of Jewish Studies in Warsaw and one of the leaders of the Hebrew cultural organization *Tekumah* which conducted courses, lectures and seminars in the ghetto. It is a chilling coincidence of symbolic import that the eighth book of Suetonius deals with Vespasian and Titus, the emperors who destroyed the Jewish State but could not prevail against the Jewish soul.

15
Minor Center of Hebrew Literature in America

A. The Period of Oddments

There appear to be three distinguishable phases of Hebrew literature in America. The first, beginning with the settlement of twenty-three Jews in New Amsterdam in 1654 and ending in 1860 when the first Hebrew book was published in the United States, may be conveniently called The Period of Oddments. The second and intervening phase—from 1860 to 1909—may be called The Period of Belated Beginnings. The third, starting with the publication of Silkiner's epic poem *Before the Tent of Timmurah,* may be called The Period of Emergent Achievements. But a caveat is in order: All literary classifications are more or less arbitrary attempts to introduce order into chaotic and unmanageable masses of heterogeneous material.

Like the Puritans who reached the coast of New England in 1620 in order to live according to their own conscience, the Jews who arrived in Manhattan in 1654 on a Mayflower of their own, the St. Charles,[1] hoped to lead an unmolested life according to their ancestral traditions. Though they were to remain few in number in the next few centuries,[2] they established congregations along the eastern seaboard as early as the middle of the seventeenth century: Shearith Israel in New York in 1656, Jeshuat Israel in Newport, Rhode Island in 1759—though Jews of Newport probably held services as early as the 1670's—Mickva Israel in Savannah, Georgia in 1733,[3] Mikveh Israel and Rodeph Shalom in Philadelphia in 1745 and in 1795 respectively, Beth Elohim in Charleston, South Carolina in 1750 and Beth Shalome in Richmond, Virginia in 1789.[4] These were seven pioneering congregations which exercised a lively influence on the religious pattern of Jewry in America.[5] It is estimated that, although many Jewish communities sprang up subsequently on the Atlantic Coast between Massachusetts and Georgia and, somewhat later, on the Pacific Coast in San Francisco, there were in the United States fifty thousand Jews out of a total population of twenty-three million in the middle of the nineteenth century. As many as ten thousand were peddlers: basket peddlers at the bottom of the economic ladder, trunk carriers, pack carriers who often bent their backs to one hundred and fifty pounds of merchandise, and the aristocrats among peddlers—the horse-and-buggy peddlers and jewelry peddlers.[6] Presumably they had an elementary Hebrew education: They recited their prayers and they probably read the Pentateuch in the original. But their separatist ways aroused suspicion—as they have done throughout the centuries in Asia, Africa and Europe. During the Civil War a Jew of Cincinnati was arrested at Corinth, Mississippi. He was accused of spying because he had phylacteries which an officer examined minutely and found in them the customary Hebrew texts of *Exodus* 13:1–16 and *Deuteronomy* 6:4–9; 11:13–21. The incident was brought to the attention of General William S. Rosecrans who asked a priest to examine the strange writing. Luckily the priest knew Hebrew, was familiar with Jewish customs and recommended acquittal.[7]

The new patterns of American life did not stimulate scholarship, learning or growth of Hebrew letters. The physical and spiritual ghetto which made for cohesion of Jews in Europe and Asia gave way to unlimited horizons which favored decentralization and disruption. The student and the scholar were superseded by the peddler and the trader who enjoyed previously unattained freedoms of opportunity. Restrictions were rare and ineffectual. The Dutch governor of New Amsterdam in mid-seventeenth century, Peter Stuyvesant, may have been unfriendly and inhospitable to the Jews. But they settled on the tip of Manhattan Island and acquired almost equal rights with other citizens. The Puritan governors and divines of New England may have hoped for the quick conversion of the Jews to Christianity. But, on the whole, they were not inimical to the people who created the Bible.

Colonial America had a religious interest in the Hebrew language. The Old Testament, so dear to the Puritans, was more to them than a divinely inspired document; it was the alpha and omega of knowledge and wisdom, the guide in personal habits and social relations, the inspirational force in just government. Austere respect for the Sabbath,[8] the concept of New England as a society "in covenant with God like Israel of old,"[9] references to New England as the "New

English Canaan" or New Canaan,[10] names of towns like Salem, names of persons like Israel and Samuel, Abner and Melchizedek, attest to love for the Bible—love which was fostered by temporal and spiritual rules, by schools and colleges.[11]

The early poets meditated on biblical verses. Edward Taylor (1645?–1729), grandfather of the eminent Christian Hebraist Ezra Stiles, based several poems on verses of the Song of Songs. And even when poets satirized the habits of their co-religionists, they referred to them in biblical terms. Peter Folger, the maternal grandfather of Benjamin Franklin, wrote in 1676:

> New England they are like the Jews
>   as like, as like can be,
> They made large promises to God,
>   at home and at the sea.
> They did proclaim free Liberty,
>   they cut the Calf in twain,
> They passed between the part thereof.
>   O this was all in vain.

Governor William Bradford of Plymouth studied Hebrew because he would see with his own eyes "something of that most ancient language and holy tongue in which...God and angels spoke to the holy patriarchs of old time..."[12] And the old lady, who is said to have learned Hebrew in the ninth decade of her life in order to converse in the inevitable meeting with her Maker in his native tongue, is merely a humorous illustration of a predominant interest. Henry Louis Mencken quotes William Gifford as authority for the story that "at the close of the Revolution certain members of Congress proposed that the use of English be formally prohibited in the United States, and Hebrew substituted for it."[13] The fascinating prospects of a Hebrew-speaking, Hebrew-centered and Hebrew-oriented America can only be contemplated with visionary reservations.

Though Hebrew did not become the official language of America, it was studied assiduously. A spate of Hebrew grammars testifies to their need. John Smith, "Professor of the Learned Languages at Dartmouth College," published in Boston *A Hebrew Grammar Without Points: Designed To Facilitate The Study Of The Scriptures Of The Old Testament In The Original; And Particularly Adapted To The Use Of Those Who May Not Have Instructors.*[14] Martin Ruter published in Cincinnati in 1824 *An Easy Entrance Into The Sacred Language,*

Being A Concise Hebrew Grammar, Without Points.[15] Like John Smith's grammar it was "compiled for the use and encouragement of learners, and adapted to such as have not the aid of a teacher."[16] James Seixas, a convert, published A Manual Hebrew Grammar For The Use Of Beginners in Andover in two editions in 1833 and 1834.[17] It was based on Moses Stuart's grammar to a very large extent—a work that has been rightly evaluated as "the first modern Hebrew grammar."[18]

Manuals of Hebrew also appeared in New York. Some of them did not advance Hebrew studies in the United States. This may be said of A Key To The Hebrew Language And The Science Of Hebrew Grammar Explained (With Points)[19] by Joseph Aaron, "Hebrew Professor and Teacher of Hebrew Grammar."[20] But some had real merit. This may be specially said of A Critical Grammar of The Hebrew Language in two volumes by Isaac Nordheimer.[21] It showed knowledge of Semitic languages and it made good use of German forerunners in the field, Wilhelm Gesenius and Heinrich Ewald.

The study of Hebrew in Pennsylvania dates back to the eighteenth century. James Logan, a Quaker and friend of William Penn, studied Hebrew and acquired the lexical compendia of Johann Buxtorf and Johann Leusden,[22] an edition of the Mishnah, the Shulhan 'Aruk and the mystic Book of Reincarnations[23] by Hayyim Vital.

Though Philadelphia was the center of the book-publishing trade in colonial America and in the early decades of the nineteenth century, no Hebrew books were published in the city before 1812. It was in that year that James P. Wilson's work on the Hebrew language appeared in the city of brotherly love: An Easy Introduction To The Knowledge Of The Hebrew Language Without The Points. Easy it may have been; it was a mine of "grammatical and etymological fallacies."[24] In 1815 a grammar by E.N. Carvalho,[25] a Jewish immigrant from England, attracted the attention of students and scholars. But the interest in Hebrew studies was fanned mainly by Jonas Horwitz, a native of Poland who had lived in Germany, Holland, England and arrived in Philadelphia in the beginning of the previous century. He seemed to have a wide knowledge of biblical and rabbinic Hebrew and applied to Jefferson for a professorship at the University of Virginia in Charlotteville.[26] The Gratzes—with their wide literary and social associations—had also an interest in Hebraic studies.[27] But the Horwitzes and the Gratzes were ultimately to leave the Jewish fold and merge with their Christian neighbors.

The most active promoter of Jewish studies in the first half of the nineteenth century was undoubtedly Isaac Leeser (1806–1868). Born in Neuenkirchen in Westphalia, he arrived in Richmond, Virginia in 1824 and became associated with the congregation *Mikveh Israel* in 1829. As founder and editor of the influential periodical *The Occident* he shaped the attitudes of nascent Jewry in America. And he fostered Jewish education on all levels—from Sunday School to Maimonides College.[28] He may be said to have inaugurated The Age of Leeser which lasted roughly till the end of the Civil War. For there was hardly a literary, organizational, institutional, congregational or educational activity which he did not inaugurate or stimulate. Leeser was not only the most significant Jewish leader in America during the first half of the nineteenth century; he was the prototype of the intellectual and spiritual man of communal affairs. He was even a proto-Zionist who advocated sound methods of agriculture and industrial enterprises for the Jews in order to elevate them "from the low degree of unlaboring idleness. . . to the rank of independent, industrious freemen."[29] He may not have been the man who, since Mendelssohn, "did more to promote the study of Judaism than any follower of the Law of Moses, either in Europe or America."[30] But neither was he "a specimen of a lost type,"[31] a superannuated antique.

Leeser was among the first to attempt a Hebrew text for children which was popular with the generation that studied Hebrew from the late thirties to the late sixties of the previous century.[32] And his translation of the Bible was an achievement of importance in those days; it was used in school and synagogue and home till it was replaced by the version of the Jewish Publication Society in 1917.[33]

Yet, in spite of Leeser's multiple activities on the cultural level and in spite of unrestricted contacts between Jews and Christians, there was almost no Jewish awareness of the passionate preoccupation with Hebrew among non-Jews. Jews seem also to have been ignorant of the great Jewish upheavals in other countries. The messianic movement of Sabbataism and the mystic confraternity of early Hasidim, the rationalist revolution of Spinoza and the enlightened impact of Mendelssohn passed them by without leaving discernible traces on their thinking and writing.

No memorable poem, story or essay in Hebrew appeared in America before the nineteenth century. No major contribution to biblical or talmudic exegesis illumined the intellectual night which settled on Jews in the New World. For two hundred years, from the middle of the seventeenth to the middle of the nineteenth century, Hebrew literature in America perpetuated documentary curiosities which survived in manuscript or in print or in stone such as James Logan's

Hebrew vocabulary in manuscript, preserved in the Library Company of Philadelphia[34] or Judah Monis's unpublished nomenclator, preserved in the Library of Harvard University[35] or the circular letter of Congregation Bnai Jeshurun, printed in 1826[36] or the rhymed epitaph in double acrostic on the tomb of Samuel Zanvill Levy.[37] It is a sad reflection on Hebrew literature in America that in the eighteenth century epitaphs are among the best and the most skillful efforts of the Hebrew muse. At a time when Moses Hayyim Luzzatto invigorated Hebrew letters with remarkable plays and idyllic poems, with genuine mysticism and piety, anonymous Hebrew versifiers in America were courting the families of eminent merchants with tombstone poetry. Like Samuel Zanvill Levy who was president of the congregation Shearith Israel in the early years of the eighteenth century, Isaac Adolphus, president in the later years of the century, was praised in stone for his philanthropic pursuits.[38] Seldom, too seldom, one encounters genuine inspiration among graves in a cemetery. The Greeks cultivated the art of the epitaph and developed it to a high level of poetry. The Greek Anthology alone contains hundreds of inspired lyrics on the transitoriness of all life. And these are but a tiny fragment of the thousands of recovered epitaphs which were moldering under the soil of Greece. Edgar Lee Masters (1869–1950), the American poet, imitated the Greek Anthology with his *Spoon River Anthology* which had a transitory fame after its publication in 1915. Among the epitaphs, collected by David de Sola Pool in a massive volume *Portraits Etched In Stone,* there is perhaps one inspired poem on the death of Walter J. Judah who died in 1798 at the tender age of twenty. In a sort of rhythmic, partially rhymed prose, the anonymous epitaphist extols the healing virtues of the deceased who was a medical student and contracted yellow fever in his ministrations to a stricken community. He even coined a Hebrew equivalent for yellow fever—*Eshta Zehubta*—a rare occurrence of a neologism on a tombstone.

The sparseness of literary documents in Hebrew between the middle of the seventeenth and the middle of the nineteenth century can only be excused by the paucity of Jews and the rarity of learned Jews in colonial America and in the first decades after the establishment of the United States. Hebrew Bibles, grammars, prayer books, almanacs and broadsides with Hebrew titles appeared in fitful intervals. And the reprint of a Hebrew translation of an English missionary tract saw the light of day in Philadelphia in 1821.[39] That was all.

B. The Period of Belated Beginnings

First Hebrew Tract

In 1860 there appeared in New York a commentary on the *Sayings of the Fathers*—the first original Hebrew book in America with an unfulfilled promise of a second to come. It was called *Book of the Stones of Joshua*[40] and it was authored by Joshua Falk, an adventurous traveler and scholar. "If my book will find favor in your eyes"—we read on the title page—"and you will buy it from me for the full price, I will publish, with the help of God, another book." The book was to be merely a preparation for the *Building of Joshua*[41] which was to contain a second part *The Wall of Joshua.*[42] The narcissistic title was an obvious choice:

> For my name is Joshua and this house which I built for myself. . .will be my intercessor. . .when my soul comes before the God of Hosts. If I am asked there about my activities. . .these words of mine will be my intercessors before my God.[43]

The medievalism of the title and the preface is matched by the medievalism of the content: Halevi, Maimonides and Albo are cited, allegory is used, rabbinic sources are frequently adduced. As a commentary, the book is a homiletical discourse on moral and devotional themes with the text of the *Sayings of the Fathers* as mere pretext. Yet the author, somewhat immodestly, thought that its one hundred and eight pages[44] made a book "small in quantity but great in quality."[45] And he indulged in self-congratulatory assertions about his excellent interpretations or solutions to complicated problems. Though he seemed to be conscious of the inhospitality of the American milieu to Hebrew learning, he comforted himself with a delusion:

> I shall disregard what people say: what's the use of a new book in this country? Even the old are neglected. . .People wish to see something new. . . . Just as fish, though they grow up in the water, whenever they are aware of a drop of rain, they imbibe it avidly, so Jews who grow up in the study of the Torah, when they hear a new interpretation, they receive it thirstily as if they never had savored the taste of Torah.[46]

It was an unreasonable hope. In the sixties of the previous century there were only few learned rabbis in the United States.[47] Among the non-orthodox there was probably none. The Jews of America had no faith in their leaders, and the leaders had no faith in their knowledge. In the first half of the nineteenth century a responsum was solicited from Rabbi Eliezer Bergman in former Palestine by a leader from Cincinnati: Can a Jew who had joined the Freemasons and decided to leave them expiate his sin?[48] And when, in 1861, the Jews of New Orleans resolved to erect a monument in honor of Judah Touro who had resided in that city for fifty-three years, they turned to European rabbis of eminence—Dr. N.M. Adler of London, Samson Raphael Hirsch of Frankfurt on the Main, Zacharias Frankel of Breslau and Solomon Judah Rapoport of Prague—to ask whether such an action was not in conflict with Jewish law.[49]

The paucity of Jewish intellectuals in America in the last decades of the nineteenth century can partly be explained by lack of opportunities and incentives. Hebrew books were ignored, Hebrew periodicals —with few notable exceptions—were short-lived. Indifference of the reader induced apathy in the writer. This, in turn, lessened the receptivity on the part of the reader. It was a vicious circle of failure and futility.

Eleven years after the publication of the *Book of the Stones of Joshua* the first Hebrew periodical, *ha-Zofeh be-Erez ha Hadashah,* appeared in America under the editorship of Zevi Hirsch Bernstein.[50] Although no complete set is known to exist here or elsewhere,[51] it is fairly certain from the extant issues that no extraordinary talent blossomed in the periodical which appeared irregularly for five years—from 1871 to 1876. What the writers lacked in talent, they endeavored to make up with devotion. Eliassof, an ardent contributor who never received compensation for his literary efforts, confesses pathetically:

> I believed firmly that the world begins and ends with the Hebrew language and that the salvation of Israel will come only through the study of the Hebrew language.[52]

That belief and that devotion were characteristic of most contributors. Yet every successive periodical aroused new and often unjustified hopes. Thus, *Ner ha-Ma'aravi* (1895–1897) carried on the first page in the very first issue a poem which expressed the hope, not unmingled with despair, that Jewish learning—and this included also Hebrew literature—would bloom in the wilderness of American Judaism. And the talmudic motto, preceding one of the articles, is indicative of faith in renewal and revival: "Wherever they were exiled, the Presence of God went with them."[53]

First Hebrew Book of Poetry

This intense belief, amounting to religious fervor, drove the pioneering generation of Hebrew writers in America to quixotic enterprises. In 1877 an immigrant published the first volume of Hebrew poetry in the United States: *A Golden Hymn In Honor of Age-Old Israel.*[54] It was a quaint book with a quaint title-page in Hebrew, a twelve-line poem in Yiddish and a four-line stanza in German. Only the name and address of the printer appeared in English: M.Toplowsky, Book & Job Printer, 112 Canal Street, N.Y. The poet, Jacob Zevi Sobel (1831–1930) or as he liked to call himself in his adopted country James H. Soble, came to America from his native Russia where he had been head of a Yeshivah in Kovna, a rabbi in Slobodka, a preacher in Vilna and, finally, one of the enlightened literati in Odessa. He had even published a book of poems in that city. But he rose to historic significance in America with his pioneering hymn. After a brief introduction in dialog form between author and bee similarities in their work are extolled: both feed humanity with sweetness. Then follow twenty-three laborious six-line stanzas—favorites of Hebrew writers for two centuries: They form a coherent but dull monolog of self-praise by age-old Israel who revels in his Torah, his language, the prophets, "the proclamation of liberty to the world." Contempt for the contempters of Hebrew—be they orthodox or reform Jews—and blessings for the cultivators of Hebrew: This is the grand finale of the hymn which gives the book its title. The other poems in the book—some with satirical overtones, some with pathetic outcries —hurl the usual accusations against the American milieu: the insensitivity to scholarship, the arrogance of the boor, the vagaries and vulgarities of worship. But they also reflect the virtues of the new environment: freedom, equality, opportunity for all. Sobel was the first Hebrew poet in America to describe a Jewish peddler in the hills of Pennsylvania "with a pack on his back." In one of his poems—in "Bridegroom and Bride"[55]—he deplored the homelessness of the Jew by translating two lines from Byron's "Hebrew Melodies":

The wild-dove hath her nest, the fox his cave,
Mankind their country—Israel but the grave.

Though the poetic value of Sobel's book is slight, its historical significance cannot be doubted. As a paean in praise of Jewry and the Hebrew language, as a panegyric on liberty in the United States, as a criticism-in-verse of the ignorance and spiritual emptiness of Jewish immigrants it deserves a place of honor in the history of Hebrew literature.

Pioneers of Journalism and Bibliography

Hebrew writers in America in the seventies of the previous century suffered from an historical imbalance. Some were making desperate attempts to integrate with the cultural life in the New World. The apostate[56] Zevi Gershuni (1844–1897)—Henry Gersoni in the Anglicized form of the name—attempted to translate American poetry into Hebrew. His version of "Excelsior"—the first American poem to be translated into Hebrew—elicited a courteous letter from Longfellow:

> I am sorry to say that my ignorance of the grand old Hebrew tongue makes it impossible for me to read your translation. . .[57]

Gershuni's prose sketches of Jewish life in America have not lost their historic significance. The difficulties of adaptation led him to believe that agriculture might be a more profitable occupation for the immigrant than business. This proved to be a prophetic advocacy of a new profession in the light of later valuations of farming as a means of salvation for Jewry. With many other Hebrew writers Gershuni shared a belief in the eternality of the Jewish people and the Hebrew language. But he was also a pioneer of Yiddish journalism in this country. Together with Zevi Hirsch Bernstein who founded the first Hebrew periodical he edited the Yiddish weekly *Di Post* in 1870. In 1878 he founded an Anglo-German weekly *The Jewish Advance* and in 1882 the monthly *The Maccabean*. These were short-lived ventures by a tortured, unhappy individual who never abandoned his connections with Hebrew journalism in Russia. And he was a devotee of the leading Hebrew writers of his time—from Abraham Ber Lebensohn to Ahad Haam. As a correspondent to *ha-Meliz* he brought information and enlightenment on American Jewry to Jews in eastern Europe. For he reacted to the burning problems of his times: orthodoxy and reform, persecution and defense, immigration to America and to Palestine, ethical culture, organizational fragmentation of Jewry. His subjective observations of the American scene lent an aura of urgency to his articles. It was not a historic role; but it was an expiatory service of dedication. And Naphtali Herz Imber, author of the national hymn of Israel, praised him in his elegy on "The Death of Gershuni" for the sturdy fight on behalf of human rights "against the Russian government"[57a]

Other writers who were active in the seventies of the nineteenth century were not of high caliber either morally or intellectually.[58] Even in the following decade the situation did not improve. Ephraim Deinard (1846–1930), the well-known bibliophile and bibliographer, asserted[59] that, when he arrived in America in 1888, he found no Jewish library and no Hebrew writers except the restless journalist Wolf Schur who was later associated with the periodical ha-Pisgah (1889–1899) and ha-Tehiyyah (1899–1900) which was a continuation of ha-Pisgah.[60] This was carelessness or falsification of facts. Collections of Hebrew books were available at Harvard University in the seventeenth century and in some Jewish homes in the eighteenth century.[61] Hebrew writers, though not many, were scattered in various cities.[62] In 1877 a Hebrew library existed at Temple Emanuel—perhaps the first Hebrew library in New York.[63] In 1880 another Hebrew library was established in that city: the library of the society Shohare Sefat 'Eber—the first Hebrew-speaking society in the United States. More libraries were established in the eighties and nineties and in the first decade of the twentieth century in New York, Chicago, Philadelphia, Baltimore, Boston, Rochester and probably in other cities. Important collections of Hebraica and Judaica were concentrated in the library of the Jewish Theological Seminary and in the Jewish section of the New York Public Library where its first librarian, the genial and kindly A.Z. Freidus served scholars and students with exemplary devotion.[64]

As for Wolf Schur who, like Deinard, arrived in America in 1888, he was a pioneer in Hebrew journalism and an indefatigable defender of his people. In his main work The Eternality of Judaism[65] he deduced the eternality of the people from the divine origin of the Torah and asserted the superiority of Judaism to Christianity. On Reform Judaism, on socialism, on anarchism he looked with a jaundiced eye. In his ardent advocacy of Zionism, he leaned heavily on ideas of Smolenskin and Ahad Haam. He was the first to react ardently and favorably to political Zionism.

Americanism of Hebrew Writers

It was not only Schur who commended a future-oriented outlook on life. In prose and poetry Hebrew writers and journalists of the nineteenth century appealed to readers to turn from the "tombs of the past" to the better days that lie ahead, to love America and not to neglect the Hebrew language. An intense patriotism animated them. Moses Aaron Schreiber, cantor of the congregation *Shaare Tephillah* in New York, wrote for the centennial of American independence in 1876 a long and graceful poem "Gift of Judah."[66] In its passionate love of liberty and loyalty to America it set the tone for many similar compositions. But is was more happily worded and more esthetically satisfying than succeeding poems on the theme of Americanism. In quietly moving historic vignettes and in gracefully rhymed lines the poet recounted the historical accomplishments of the American people, the pre-revolutionary leaders as well as the surge of stricken humanity to the shores of the new world:

> Unto these coasts. . .
> Migrated hosts.
> Jew and gentile. . .
> Braved the sea
> To be free.[67]

There were Hebrew poets who glorified American statesmen. Abraham Luria [Lewis] acclaimed the naval heroism of Richmond Pearson Hobson, a member of Congress, dedicated a poem to President McKinley and ended an acrostic poem "Remember the Maine" with the couplet:

> Retribution came to Spain.
> Take revenge. Remember the Maine.[68]

The fabric of traditional life changed under the impact of America. The literature of responsa which originated in the Gaonic period in seventh century Babylonia was flooded with American place-names. Ritual questions from Kalamazoo and Leavenworth found erudite answers in a legalistic work of Shalom Elhanan Joffe.[69]

The factional squabbles, the vulgarism, the optimism, the shallow panaceism of the American milieu—all these were mirrored in verse and essay, sketch and story. All America, it seemed, was the province of the tanners[70] who had usurped the place of honor held by the erudite in Jewish life. Stature and status were no longer co-valent.

The Jewish *Kulturkampf* was fought out with an intense bitterness in the United States. The second Hebrew book to be published here was a twenty-eight page tract by M.E. Holzman, "scribe of Courland, Russia," against Reform. In crude, ungrammatical language the author mounted his attack: "The reformists. . .are thoroughly evil. . . men and women sit in Temple side by side as in the playhouse."[70a] The war of Reform and Orthodoxy aroused another writer, Mayer Rabinowitz, to publish *The Two Camps*.[71] And Abraham Moses Shershevsky, who was Rabbi in Portland, Maine, at the turn of the century, had scathing words of criticism against American Jewry in the third section of his work *The Brook of Abraham*[72] which was published in 1896. He decried Reform, he deplored the lack of learning and neglect of education:

> Just as our forefathers. . .crossed the sea and made the golden calf, so do their sons after them in this country: After crossing the Atlantic they bowed and prostrated themselves before the golden calf. . .Snow and frost settled on their hearts like the terrible ice on the summits of the Alps in Germany and the Rocky Mountains in America.[73]

Insensitivity to Jewish values became the standard complaint; the golden calf—the standard metaphor. M.M. Dolitzky—a protegé of Judah Leb Gordon—used it in his introduction to *Poems of Menahem*.[74] In pathetic helplessness he asked who will bring salvation to Israel: the Messiah, the dispensers of charity, the worshippers of God, the devotees of Satan, the kissers of the Western Wall, the Utopian visionaries? And he answered: The dollar will bring salvation.[75] Small wonder that he became disillusioned: "In America, the Hebrew poet has no one to fight against, no one to fight with and nothing to fight for."[75a]

Another early author complains:

> The basis of all things in America is the dollar. . .it's the method, it's the aim, it's the glory, it's the power, it's the one true document according to which most people evaluate their deeds in this city and in this country.[76]

Benjamin II (1818–1864) though not as perceptive an observer as Alexis de Toqueville, had remarked:

> "America worships. . .Mammon who is deaf, dumb and blind,

before whom the multitude of the land bow humbly and kneel down, forgetting all honor, thinking only, day and night, how to heap up riches. . .[77]

Time and again Benjamin II reverts to the theme of all-powerful Mammon in America:

"Money makes a man respected here. . .An honorable man without money is not respected at all; he is considered a nobody. . .On the other hand, we heap all honors on a rich scoundrel, on a well-to-do blockhead, on a wealthy ignoramus. . ."[78]

Though brash materialism, "the dangerous cancer that undermines American society," has been castigated by Jew and non-Jew, it was Benjamin II who drew the startling conclusion:

"The neglect of learning is the principal cause of all the misfortunes in which the United States has. . .found itself."[79]

It is surprising that Hebrew writers had the leisure to write at all in the land of unlimited opportunities. Most—if not all—of them gained a precarious living.

Their lot—writes an author in 1887—was like the lot of the majority of Hebrew writers from time immemorial: some of them were teachers; some, store attendants; some, peddlers; some, merchants. But the majority were merely poor. . ."[80]

The land of opportunities presented no opportunities to the Hebrew writer. Education—his traditional occupation—offered slight rewards. Compensation in the eighties for Hebrew lessons reached the august sum of ten cents per week per boy in a *Heder*.[81] Every failure, every misfit taught. "A shoemaker, tailor, furrier, harness-maker, village school master, butcher. . .has on occasion been transformed into a shepherd of souls."[82] The goals were minimal, the achievements almost nil.[83]

Judah David Eisenstein (1854-1956), who lived to be more than a hundred years old, arrived in the United States in 1872. In that year he earned the princely sum of eight dollars a week peddling shirts.[84] Though he wrote numerous essays in English and though his one hundred and fifty-nine articles for the Jewish Encyclopedia[85] earned him the title "a walking encyclopedist" from the editor Joseph Jacobs, he eked out a precarious living. But he prided himself on his American citizenship and on his loyalty to the Republican party. It was his patriotism which prompted him to translate the Declaration of Independence and the Constitution of the United States into Hebrew.[86]

In 1880 he founded together with Zevi Hirsch Bernstein, the editor of the first Hebrew newspaper in America, *ha-Zofeh be-Erez ha-Hadashah*, a Hebrew-speaking society: *Shohare Sefat 'Eber*.[87] It was almost one hundred years after a similar society with the identical name had been organized in Königsberg. And just as the society in Königsberg marked the beginning of an era, so the Hebrew-speaking society in New York presaged new developments. Members—there were one hundred of them—met in their quarters on 105 East Broadway and heard a lecture on a Hebrew theme in Hebrew at least once a month. They read newspapers of Jewish import and even published in 1881 *ha-Meassef be-Erez ha-Hadashah*. Somewhat later another society—*Mefize Sefat 'Eber we-Sifrutah*—undertook to propagate the Hebrew language, to foster knowledge of Hebrew periodicals and books, to promote lectures,[88] to interest wider circles of Jews in Hebrew literature. But the results were inconsequential and ineffectual. Discussion often revolved around the merits of Hebrew style with an appositeness that has lost nothing of its actuality. How should Hebrew writers write? Should they imitate the Bible or the so-called neo-Hebraic style of the Mishnah and the Midrash? Hillel Malachowsky came to a sane conclusion: The talented writer creates a style of his own: Gordon wrote à la Gordon and not like a prophet of old, Smolenskin used the language of Smolenskin, and Frischmann created Frischmann's style.[89] But he shared the pessimism of his confrères about the future of the Hebrew language and its devotees.

Yet Dr. Bernard Drachman, Rabbi of the Congregation *Zichron Ephraim* and Dean of the Jewish Theological Seminary at the turn of the century, stated in the year 1900 that "with the exception of the physical and technical sciences, every brand of literature is today represented by Hebrew works of importance written and published in America."[90] This was enthusiasm carried to exaggerated lengths. Hebrew literature cannot boast a single drama, a single novel of importance in the beginning of the century. It certainly cannot represent the best intellectual efforts of American Jewry. The works of Hebrew authors at the turn of the century not only do not substantiate Drachman's assertion; they refute it. Another unwarranted note of optimism was sounded from abroad by Solomon Mandelkern, the author of the well-known biblical concordance: The tailor and the cobbler might yet build "the house of Israel" in the United States.[91] Such sentiments were the exception. The rule was despair and disappointment. Dolitzky observed that the people of the book have no literature in this country; they are in perpetual pursuit of imaginary honors; between the dissensions of the orthodox and the reformed Judaism is being torn into shreds.[92] And Malachowsky predicted in 1895 that "in a little while the name of the Jew will be nonexistent in America. . .Instead a new generation will arise–Americans of Mosaic faith. . ."[93] This dark prediction voiced by the enlightened in the nineteenth century—from Shalom Cohen to Mapu to Judah Leb Gordon—was a persistent theme. That it proved unjustified was a freak of history or an act of Providence.

At the turn of the century there was a distressing lack of humor among Hebrew writers in America. While Mark Twain and his Jewish counterpart, Shalom Aleyhem, were creating classics of comic grandeur, the Hebrew writers in America made the feeblest attempts at none too hilarious fun. "Breach of Promise," written in a mixture of poor Hebrew-Yiddish-English, was a characteristic product of the nineties: a ludicrous, almost fantastic tale of pre-marital complications. The narrator, in search of a bride, arrives in an apartment on one hundred and twenty-first street in New York and finds that the landlady, Becky, has received a Christmas present from her husband.

> When I asked her the meaning of the word Christmas, she answered that it was a Jewish holiday. I laughed at her and told her that I was a scholar and well-versed in all the holidays—Pesah, Shabuot, Sukkot, Days of Awe, Hanukkah, Purim, Lag be-'Omer. But she, in turn, laughed and called me greenhorn.
>
> Christmas, you know, she said laughingly, is a great holiday for American Jews, a holiday greater than Purim. Instead of Purim gifts in Europe, we have Christmas gifts here. Whereupon she showed me a small *Sefer Torah* which the rabbi gave her husband for a Christmas present. When I asked her husband Ike about it, and he is not an ignoramus, he answered: Sure, it is so, Christmas is a greater holiday than *Yom Kippur*. And this is the proof: On *Yom Kippur* all artisans are allowed to work, but on Christmas there is solemn rest, not a single Jew in America works on Christmas.[94]

Seventy-five years earlier Joseph Perl, the Galician satirist, castigated the vices of Hasidism in an intentional mixture of bad Hebrew and Yiddish. His American counterpart copied the method with poor results: He succeeded in cataloguing the crass blasphemies of American Judaism but he failed to transmute them into art.

In the faceless literature, preceding the First World War, two men—Rosenzweig and Imber—endowed with a bit of wit and poetry, pursued a definite trend, a definite direction.

Rosenzweig: First Hebrew Satirist in America

Gershon Rosenzweig (1861-1914), who settled in this country in 1888, was the typical immigrant in the New World; he managed to starve or nearly starve as peddler, bookkeeper, restaurateur, editor, teacher. His poetic talents rarely rose above the jingle, his linguistic abilities rarely violated conservative patterns. But his genuine flair for satire was given full scope in this country. And it earned him a secure place in the history of Hebrew letters in America. Already his contemporaries dubbed him "Sweet satirist of Israel."[95] And the sobriquet was richly deserved.

Elegy preceded satire in the development of Gershon Rosenzweig. The needle trade and the trade of the peddler elicited lachrymose effusions in verse from his heart: dull, ineffective, stillborn lines in innumberable stanzas which praised America and flailed American Jewry. For the land of plenty and freedom merely accentuated the meagre accomplishments of the Jewish spirit; factionalism became a curse, faith a business. America, in felicitous Hebrew spelling *Amireka*, was made to mean my people is a hollow people.[96] Thus Rosenzweig stumbled—through a fortuitous accident of language—on the haunting symbol of destitution and desiccation which T.S. Eliot discovered for modern poetry: "The Hollow Men."

In prose-parodies he attained literary stature. His *Yankee Talmud*[97] which appeared in book form in 1907 made a genuine contribution to the unabundant treasury of Hebrew humor. This mock-talmudic genre enjoyed popularity for the past six hundred years—since Kalonymos ben Kalonymos wrote his *Purim Treatise*[98] in the first half of the fourteenth century. It reached its heyday in the latter half of the nineteenth century.[99] It was then that Jewish intellectuals, former alumni of talmudic academies, developed their favorite verbal sport: savage ridicule of the intricacies of talmudic discussion. The *Beraitot* of R. Isaac[100] which were fathered by the popular Hebrew poet, Dr. Isaac Kaminer (1834–1901), must have made an impression on Rosenzweig. Certainly their style and their diction influenced the *Yankee Talmud.*

> It is taught: there are four kinds of writers—he who speaks little and says much is wise; he who speaks much and says little is the florid kind; he who speaks much and does not say anything is the preaching kind; he who does not speak at all and says much is the one who knows how to keep silence in days of evil.

This is a sample of Kaminer's parodies. But it could have been written by Rosenzweig. There was a difference, of course, between Hebrew parodists in the Old World and the Hebrew parodist in the NewWorld. In Russia they concentrated their verbal attacks on social injustice. Gershon Rosenzweig ridiculed and castigated essential aspects of Jewish life in America: the greenhorn with his uncouth manners and awkward gestures, the peddler, the teacher, the rabbi. And the barb was sharp, pointed, poisoned—like an Indian arrow.

The peddler was Rosenzweig's *bête noire.* This favorite occupation of the greenhorn—springboard to future fortune and graveyard of hopes—he castigated with pitiless abandon. In poetry he bewailed his lot, in prose he laughed at his shortcomings. In the classic form of the Talmud—in a brief *Mishnah,* followed by a long *Gemara* and by supporting biblical texts—he presented the portrait of the profession.

> *Mishnah:* What does a peddler peddle with? With a basket and a sack and a coffer and a valise and a chest. . .
>
> *Gemara:* Our Rabbis have taught: A greenhorn who has spent seven days in this country and does not know how to earn a living is helped to become a peddler. How? Friends buy him a basket and a bit of merchandise. They reveal to him the mysteries of peddling.They tell him: go from door to door. And they bless him twice: Blessed art thou in thy going out and blessed art thou in thy coming in. Blessed art thou in thy going out—that the rogues may not harm him. And blessed art thou in thy coming in—that his coming shall be as his going out. If he succeeds he bends his shoulder to carry bundles of merchandise like a large-boned ass. If he does not succeed, his basket wastes away and he becomes a worker, for it is written (*Genesis* 49:14): And he bowed his shoulder to bear and became a servant under taskwork.[101]

The unsuccessful peddler becomes a tutor. This is the second link in a chain of metamorphoses.

"Jewish women pity the peddler who has been proven unfit or the worker who has been disqualified. They engage him as Hebrew teacher for their children. For teaching Hebrew in America is neither an art nor a science. . ."[102]

There is a third link: peddler turned author.

He who writes a Hebrew book in America or arrives with his book from Europe is a madman. . .If David, king of Israel, who has only scribbled a few unnecessary letters was thought to be mad (*Samuel* I, 21:14-15), the man who wrote or brought with him a whole book for which there was no need whatever must certinly be deemed mad.[103]

The real culprits in Jewish life are the rabbis. They are interested in honor and wealth. The spiritual welfare of their people is neither their concern nor their worry.

There is he who pretends to be rich yet has nothing; there is he who pretends to be poor, yet has great wealth (*Proverbs* 13:7). There is he who pretends to be rich yet has nothing—this is the European rabbi, rich in Torah, disgraced by poverty. There is he who pretends to be poor, yet has great wealth—this is the American rabbi, poor in Torah, enriched by his rabbinate. Any rabbi who studies the Torah from left to right attains riches and glory as it is written (*Proverbs* 3:16): In her left hand are riches and honor.[104]

Rosenzweig was merciless in his denunciation of the vulgarisms of the country—the love for money, the worship of success.

Rabbi Know-All preached: What is the meaning of the biblical passage (*Psalms* 104:25): Yonder sea, great and wide, therein are creeping things innumerable, living creatures, both small and great? Yonder sea—that is America which is like a sea. As the sea receives and covers everything people throw into it, so America receives all who come here and covers all their transgressions.

Therein are creeping things innumerable—these are the people who resemble creeping things; the bigger swallow up the smaller. Living creatures, both small and great—these are men of small wealth who become men of great wealth. And why are they called beasts? Because all who act like beasts that trample upon others and stuff themselves succeed in preserving their money.[105]

Rosenzweig vents savage humor on individuals and institutions.

Ten types of distinguished men came first to America: murderers, thieves, informers, firebugs, counterfeiters, slave-dealers, false witnesses, bankrupts, ban-breakers, and the stubborn and the rebellious. And there are those who say: also girls who were enticed. Why, then, are they called people of distinction? Because all the unfit of other lands, when they come to America, become distinguished there.[106]

Even anarchists are not forgotten: "What is the difference between a convert and an anarchist? A convert denies what he believes and an anarchist believes what he denies."[107] And, in summation of American Judaism, he repeats the perennial dirge on neglected learning: "By two things is America sustained: by worship and by deeds of loving-kindness. . .but not by Torah for it is written (*Deuteronomy* 30:13) 'And it is not beyond the sea."[108]

Since the Hebrew reader of that time—most likely a recent immigrant from eastern Europe—had a nodding acquaintance with rabbinic literature, Rosenzweig chose the traditional format of the Talmud as the proper vehicle for his stinging attack on American Judaism. The pages of his *Yankee Talmud* resemble the pages of the Talmud: the text is printed in large letters, the commentary in Rashi script wreathes the text. Six small tracts instead of the traditional six orders of the Talmud fill the contents of his book.

There was an epigrammatic terseness about Rosenzweig. Like Solomon who is said to have composed a thousand and five songs,[109] he produced a book of original epigrams.[110] In them, as in his Talmud, he was the carping critic of folly in any shape or form. Only for the social malaise of his adopted country—such as the fate of the Negroes—he showed that compassionate understanding which was born of centuries of persecution:

In our South the Negro's grief

Will not decline, will not abate.
In all the lands, in all the isles
The Jew and Negro share one fate.[111]

Rosenzweig had a touching faith in America: He praised Columbus, Washington, Lincoln with uncritical approval. In the English preface to his Hebrew translations of "America," "The Star Spangled Banner" and "Columbia, the Gem of the Ocean," he maintained that their American authors must have "mused in Hebrew."

The oldest and the youngest nations thinking in the same vein, in the same measure, in the same tongue: There must be some significance in this. Perhaps, nay, assuredly, the youngest nation is the heir of the oldest, and all that was best in the Jewish nation is now the possession of the American nation to be developed and cultivated for the benefit of all humanity.[112]

As a humorist Rosenzweig did not exempt his own lot from his satire. Before he died from cancer of the tongue, he jested at his own expense: life and death are at the mercy of the tongue.[113] It was no mere caprice that he likened the epigram to the bee whose body is small, sweet and stinging. In that simile he compressed his schizoid essence.

Bohemian Poet: Imber

While Rosenzweig introduced satire into Hebrew letters in America, Naphtali Herz Imber (1856-1909) became the first Jewish bohemian in the New World. He arrived in the United States in 1892 but he made his reputation in Europe and in Palestine with a slender book of poems, *Dawn*.[114] Hatikvah,[115] one of the poems in the book, was adopted as the national anthem by Zionism and, with slight modifications, by the State of Israel. Zangwill translated it into English and molded Melchitsedek in his rambling novel *Children of the Ghetto* on the personality of the poet.

In America Imber traveled the length and breadth of the land, from New York to San Francisco, from Phoenix to El Paso. In a poem, written in Denver in 1899, he says truthfully of himself:

I sailed the rivers and the seas.
I made my way in desert lands.[116]

In St. Louis, he was seriously ill and wrote his humorous confessional which he himself translated into English in *The Third Dawn:*

> There are still handsome maidens
> Whose lips I have not pressed;
> There are still lovely flowers
> Which I did not caress.[117]

But he recovered, went back to London for a brief time and then returned to America where he spent the remainder of his days in squalor, misery and an orgy of alcoholism.[118] Future fame was no consolation for the poet who addressed himself to his muse with realistic despair:

> "Tell me, Muse of my heart,
> Fountain of song that assuages:
> What will you pay for my art,
> When I come to ask for my wages?"

> "When you come to ask for your wages,"
> She whispered, "I promise, your name
> Will adorn history's pages.
> You will die full of years, full of fame."

> "What good, what good will they do me—
> The letters of gold on my tomb?
> Only the worms will woo me
> In earth's inescapable womb.

> Give me bread, give me clothes give me shelter,
> Give me these as wages of song,
> And I'll live content in the welter
> Of assailable right and wrong."[119]

Fortunately, the poet attracted a man of uncommon attainments— Judge Mayer Sulzberger, whose monthly subventions alleviated his poverty. Though he was frequently chided that he didn't influence the poet to neglect the cup and conform to accepted conventions, he never presumed to interfere—a laudable trait in a tolerant Maecenas.

Imber's colorful personality could not but attract the wise-in-heart and the wise-in-mind. One such was Dr. Amanda Katie, a Protestant lady-physician of high intellect and unusual charm who accepted Judaism and married him. For some reason or another Imber dissolved that union after a brief interval of happiness. But in the second volume of his poems, *The New Dawn*, he dedicated his "Song of Songs"[120] to Dr. Amanda Katie-Imber. The poem, an uneven catalog of physical attributes of his wife, verges on pornography.

The Second Dawn bristled with gaucheries in language, in style, in sentiment. The impish divertissements such as the cycle of poems on seven graces—Hope, Faith, Love, Brotherhood, Knowledge, Song, The Cup—were no more than charming trifles. The book was hardly an improvement on the first *Dawn* which dazzled with youthful exhilaration and refreshing wit. Imber was never too careful a writer, and his brother who published the book was even less attentive to facts in his introduction and to the typography of the poems. The result was a volume which became a curiosity rather than a book. Absurd theories of the Hebrew calendar based on untenable etymologies and fickle emendations, were pathetically squeezed into verse-molds. At its best, the volume lashes the apostates who apostatize for personal gain, the rabbis who wait helplessly for the messiah, the smooth-tongued preachers who have neither knowledge nor wisdom nor Torah and who ensnare their God-forsaken audiences. It is rather characteristic of Imber that *The New Dawn*, largely composed in America and dedicated to the fate of Palestine, was published in his native town in Galicia.

In 1904 there appeared as strange a book as was to emerge from the pen of this strangest of poets: *The Third Dawn*.[121] It carried a dedicatory epistle in English to the Mikado Mutsuhito of Japan:

> "Your Majesty—The horrors of Kishineff which took place a year before the outbreak of the present war, has (*sic!*) inspired me to prophesy the punishment of the Russians in the victory of your Majesty's arms.
>
> "There was another inspiration—the poem which your Majesty has published in three stanzas, which has inspired me to render them into the sacred language of the oldest nation of the world—the Hebrews.
>
> "I lay before the throne of your Majesty this poem, with the closing words that our hope is not yet forlorn."

Beside the translation of his august contemporary and a poem in Yiddish entitled "To the Japanese,"[122] Imber reprinted the originals and English translations of "Hatikvah" and "The Watch on the Jordan," some youthful poems and a few satirical pieces. This melange was his last book of poetry. It merely accentuated his own need for translations of his own verses—a need which revealed itself at the end of the very first *Dawn* where the poem "Palms and Psalms"[123] also appeared in German. Imber's translations of Omar Khayyam from Fitzgerald's English version into Hebrew was published in 1905 under the significant title *The Cup* [124] which was one of the seven graces in Imber's mythology.[125]

Imber's bizarre tracts on mysticism, written in English, were merely a continuation of a wide literary activity in Chicago, in Boston, in Washington, in New York. An editorial venture in Boston collapsed after a brief existence. The first issue of *Uriel*, "a monthly magazine devoted to cabbalistic science," was published in August in 1895 and died immediately. The September issue which was planned to contain an English rendition of *Sefer Yezirah*, the *Book of Creation*, never saw the light of day.[126] Future generations were also mercifully spared Imber's seven-volume work *The Battles of Jehovah* which was to inaugurate a new era in biblical research. But they were not spared his pseudo-scientific disquisitions on music and money which were beyond his intellectual reach and research.[127]

Two tracts of Imber—*Education and the Talmud* and *The Letters of Rabbi Akiba or the Jewish Primer As It Was Used in the Public Schools Two Thousand Years Ago*—were incorporated by the U.S. Commissioner of Education in the fourteenth chapter of his report for the year 1895/6. They earned him $250 from the U.S. Government and publication at government's expense. And they encouraged him in the ostentatious use of the title "professor" in his publications.

Imber's two ventures into the arcana of post-biblical literature were as disastrous as his misuse of biblical criticism. *Education and the Talmud*, a brew of ill-blended and superannuated pronunciamentos on education among ancient peoples including Jews, was republished in Imber's *Treasures of Two Worlds*—probably from his original manuscript. It retained the inept phrasing which was deleted or changed by adroit hands in the offices of the U.S. Commissioner of Education. A sample of his style and content—almost any sample—is apt to expose Imber's insensitivity to English usage and his incompetence which borders on charlatanism. Thus speaking about the two Talmuds, he says that

Like the Hebrew religion, which is divided into two, the Elohistic and the Jehovistic cult, so the Talmud is divided into two, the Talmud of Jerusalem and the Babylonian Talmud. . .Both Talmuds are prototypes of the two kinds of Jews we have, corresponding to the two kinds of religion. The Talmud of Jerusalem has a Jehovistic color, with a liberal toleration toward the Elohists, especially toward the early Jewish Christians, of whom many were in the ranks of its contributors.[128]

Imber seems to have reached the height of irresponsibility in the introduction to his translation of *The Letters of Rabbi Akiba* reprinted as a booklet in 1897: "I discovered an ancient Jewish text-book, which was written for the public schools by the great educator Rabbi Akibah." [*Sic!*][129] All that can be said charitably of this mixture of vanity and naiveté is that Imber's imagination was as untrammeled as his knowledge was limited. To ascribe *The Letters* to Rabbi Akiba is about as profitable an undertaking as to associate the *Zohar* with Rabbi Simeon Bar Yohai. Since, according to the talmudic tradition,[130] Moses was told by the deity on Sinai that Akiba ben Joseph was to heap mounds upon mounds of halakic interpretations on each letter-stroke, there was a plausible connection between the midrash on *The Letters* and the sage of the second century. But Imber should have known that the work was composed many centuries after the tannaitic period.

The real theme in Imber's writing, the master-idea in his heart was Zion. His homelessness only served to intensify nostalgic yearnings for a Jewish homeland. Spiritually, he was an Israeli long before Israel was established. For no one in modern Hebrew literature has been so completely dominated by the idea of a Jewish homeland as he was. In a constant stream of lyrical poems which, at their best, strike the reader with their vernal exuberance, he poured out his heart to Zion. If *Hatikvah* and *Barkai*, Hope and Dawn, were his favorite words in the Hebrew language, it was because they symbolized for him imminent restoration and redemption of Israel.

A limited imagination sent him sometimes scurrying to other poets for themes and forms which he imitated slavishly. His "*Three Jews*" is Heine's "*Die Grenadiere*" in Hebrew dress. Even his long poem "*Don Yehudah Halevi*" bears traces of Heinesque ideas. But his lyric gift was dissipated, his satiric vein not sufficiently mined, his scholarly imagination not disciplined and not buttressed by vast learning.

Untamed rhetoric and inordinate length vitiated his poetry.

Even if little were known about Imber, the last will and testament, written with Heinesque irony on his deathbed, would be eloquent documentation of a life which had its origin on *Hanukkah* (which is tragedy turned into miracle) and its finale on *Simhat Torah* (which is the acme of spiritual hilarity):

> To the Rabbis I leave what I do not know and do not understand.
> It will be useful to them for many long years.
> To my enemies I leave my rheumatism.
> To Republicans and Democrats I leave that delusion which they haven't hatched yet.
> To Jewish editors I leave my broken pen. Let them write slowly and correctly.
> As executor of my will I name an expert in Barnum and Bailey's philosophy.
> Witnessed by Pluto, Master of the Underworld, and his assistants, the physicians.
> In a codicil I leave to my publishers my last I.O.U. They can frame it and guard it as a talisman in order to protect themselves from similar debt-ridden authors.[131]

In its Monday issue of October 11, 1909, the New York Times reported that "the body of Naphtali Herz Imber. . .who died on Friday in want, was followed from the Educational Alliance Building on East Broadway to the Mount Zion Cemetery by 10,000 sincere mourners." The sincerity may be arguable but not the notoriety of the poet who was addicted to Bacchus and Zion.

C.   The Period of Emergent Achievements

In the years immediately following the First World War Hebrew literature in Palestine and in America was the product of immigrants whose roots were not in their respective places of sojourn.

In Israel Hebrew literature drew its sustenance from the soil and the sky, from the language and the life of the land. In America it was an exotic growth; it satisfied primarily the needs of the writer and a comparatively small Hebrew-speaking group. Hence a marked degree of introspection and a preponderance of poetic output in America—not necessarily a disadvantage. In Israel there was an overwhelming concern for the immediate; in America a leisurely yearning for the eternal. A "realistic," soil-bound literature dominated Israel; in America, Hebrew literature was "romantic," soul-bound.

There is also a marked difference in the Hebrew language as it is being spoken and written in Israel and in the United States. There, the Hebrew language already boasts a healthy, picturesque slang and some not very healthy barbarisms and colloquialisms which have been imported in unabashed literal renditions from Yiddish, German, Arabic and other languages. In America the Hebrew language tends to be more bookish and more classical. It could and should serve as a corrective for the untamed flights of lingual irresponsibility in Israel.

A comparison of Hebrew literatures in Israel and America will disclose the melancholy fact that, after the death of Bialik, no man of similar stature usurped the vacant seat of his recognized eminence. Uri Zevi Gruenberg, lone poetic prophet of doom in Israel and nearest pretender to the throne, is too isolated, too self-centered to win the unchallenged admiration and affection of the Hebrew public. Yet poets predominate—as they always have—in Hebrew literature both in Israel and in America. Even the foremost prose writers in Israel —Hazaz and Agnon—lapse into a poetic lilt. And this can also be said of such Hebrew prose-writers of America as Twersky who spent his formative years in New York and Boston and developed a staccato style for romanticized biographies à la Maurois and Ludwig; Blank who in his novels preferred the idyllic life of the Bessarabian Jews to the hectic drive of American Jews; and Sackler whose re-creation of the past imparts lyric lucidity to his style. Even criticism was charged with poetic overtones.

One of the most significant contributions of the Hebrew writer in America was this: Anglo-American literature has become a factor of importance in Hebrew prose and poetry. Until the emergence of a center of Hebrew literature in this country, the influence of English literature was small, that of American literature almost non-existent.[132] Ahad Haam drew deeply on English scholars such as Lecky and on English moralists such as Carlyle. Frischmann popularized the dramatic poems of Byron with his translations and Tschernichowsky created the proper meters and vocabulary for his renditions of Longfellow's *Evangeline* and *Hiawatha* as well as for the rhythmic extravagances of Shelley and Francis Thomson. English poems on Hebrew themes, such as Byron's *Hebrew Melodies*, [133] were repeatedly translated into Hebrew. But these were isolated instances. It was left to the Hebrew writer in this country to introduce into Hebrew literature the great wealth of Anglo-American classics either in translation or in critical appraisal or in subtle absorption in his own works. It was he who rendered into Hebrew Wordsworth and Tennyson, Yeats and Eliot, Frost and Amy Lowell, Melville and Walt Whitman. It was he who first apprized the Hebrew reader of the existence of the new poetry, the avant-garde criticism, the stream-of-consciousness fiction. And Hebrew poets, especially Silkiner and Lisitzky, Ginzburg and Bavli, Halkin and Regelson, Feinstein and Friedland, Grossman-Avinoam and Preil cannot be properly evaluated without constant reference to English and American literature.

It may be said, then, that the Hebrew writer in America conquered wholly new ground for modern Hebrew literature: to the German and Slav influences which dominated Hebrew literature for the past two hundred years he added a new factor—the literature of the English-speaking countries and all their wealth of moods and attitudes, images and ideas. In Israel today, poetry is the most sensitive refractor of light that is beamed from modern English and American literature.

Choice of subject-matter was also influenced by the new domicile. Native ores of poetry and prose were eagerly exploited by Hebrew writers who were attracted by the fate of the exotic Indian and Negro, the native American and the American Jew. These were the four dominant themes in American-Hebrew literature between the two world wars.

Silkiner: Hebrew Poet of the Native American

Since the Negro and the Indian were the poor and the down-trodden, it was natural that the Hebrew writer should first turn to them. B. N. Silkiner (1882–1933) was aware of the vast cultural potentialities of the New World. Like many immigrants and many observers before him, he was fascinated by the native Indian. Almost a century before him, Alexis de Tocqueville made this superannuated observation about the Negro and the Indian in 1830:

> The Negro would like to mingle with the European and cannot; the Indian might to some extent succeed in that, but he scorns to attempt it. The servility of the former delivers him over into slavery; the pride of the latter leads him to death.[134]

That was not the stance of Silkiner. As a poet—rather than the cool chronicler of ethnic psychologies—he was charged with sympathy for the Indian. In the year 1909, which will be remembered as a turning point in the history of Hebrew literature in the United States, he presented the Hebrew-reading public with the first native epic of importance, *"Before the Tent of Timmurah."*[135] It was cast in the form of a poetic story told to an Indian girl by her father Timmurah—hence the name of the poem. Composed at the age of twenty-nine and published in Jerusalem, it struck a bold note and a new theme. No Hebrew poet before Silkiner ventured into the realm of the intertribal quarrels of the Indians and their fights with the Spaniards. With a fine sensitivity to the early injustices of the white man and with an excellent command of the Hebrew language, he succeeded in portraying the noble savage against the background of primitive religion. In his poem human sacrifices to the Great Spirit clash with the tender cult of the God of Peace and Purity, the Soul-God; the wiles of chiefs jar on the wisdom of priests. And, above all, the American landscape in all its glory comes into its own.

High mountains of flint to the east—these are for eagles,
The hoary sea to the west—for the whales, the spawn of the deep,
The ancient woods in the south—for the lions, the roaring
[leopards,
The desert of awe to the north—for the storms and the
[whirlwinds.[136]

Neither Longfellow's *Hiawatha*, thematic kinsman of Silkiner's narrative poem, nor the noble savage of Chateaubriand, dominate contemporary literature. Still, *Before the Tent of Timmurah* is a milestone in Hebrew literature: an epic which a Hebrew poet fashioned out of Indian folklore, the Spanish conquest of America, veiled allusions to early Jewish history and—the inevitable ingredient of every poem—personal vicissitudes. Structurally and thematically it resembles the great poetic prototypes of Gordon who loved to depict decisive moments in Jewish history. Silkiner also chose a crucial time in the life of an Indian tribe: struggle with an invader and ultimate defeat. Gordon's dramatic monolog "Zedekiah in Prison" is a clash of two wills: the will of the king who, as the realistic statesman, wishes to protect his country with equitable laws and strong fortifications, and the will of the prophet Jeremiah who preaches a spiritualization of life which, in his opponent's view, is attenuation of life and fatal state-policy. That dichotomy of might and right Silkiner again invokes in his poem: the warrior Mugiral serves war, the priest of the Soul-God Ezima practices the gentle art of peace. While Gordon sympathizes with the symbol of power—the king, Silkiner shows his preference for the symbol of pity and kindness—the priest.

Rosenzweig may be regarded as the father of Hebrew satire, Silkiner as the father of the Hebrew narrative poem in America. The former held to the deluded belief that he was a poet, the latter never seriously strayed into prose and never swerved from his poetic vocation. It was his personal tragedy and the misfortune of Hebrew poetry that his potential ability exceeded his actual performance. Extremely sensitive to the biblical idiom and excessively erudite in biblical studies, he seemed to be the ideal interpreter of ancient insights in verse. But his "Ruth" and "There is no King in Moab"[137] are merely unfulfilled promises of larger undertakings. Endowed with a historical imagination and enamored of the Golden Age of Jewish culture in Spain, he seemed to possess the right empathy for spiritual heroism. But he succeeded in merely composing a beautiful fragment "Manoah Franko"[138] rather than a great poem: a torso on the theme of redemption. Episodic discontinuity distorts the plot which centers around Manoah. As a boy he receives instruction from Rabbi Joseph who "with his fine voice. . . with the light of his soul reflected in alert and dreamy eyes, with his commiserate, sad smile bears a marked resemblance to the author himself. Under his tutelage in the academy of Barcelona Manoah spends several years. An unhappy love affair undermines his spiritual equilibrium. Peninah, the daughter of the principal of the academy who is attracted to him at first, slowly falls under the spell of the Palestinian stranger Immanuel who inspires men and women with glowing messages of impending redemption. Even the students of the academy, not unlike the students of the Yeshivot in Russia, who felt the powerful attraction of nationalist ideals, follow his activities with unequivocal sympathies.

In a stormy night which reflects inner turbulence Manoah returns to his parents. Doubt which, according to a posthumously published note of the author, is the soul of the poem,[139] destroys his peace of mind. The parents feel his distress but they cannot help him. Manoah then turns to the teacher of his youth Rabbi Joseph but he is equally ineffectual in stemming the tide of his emotions. When, finally, Peninah, Immanuel and their friends sail for Palestine, and Rabbi Joseph disappears mysteriously, Manoah is left alone in his restlessness. In vain he turns for guidance to the sages and saints of old. From the lips of the archheretic Elisha ben Abuyah, he receives partial illumination:

Incline your ear, my son, and listen with your heart:

All mankind cries, not only your own people.
The world is soaked in tears from the birth of time
Until this time—from end to end. Ask the passing minute
If there is an eye that has not wept in its passing.
Ask the fading hour in its flight to eternity
If it does not carry the sighs of suffering hearts. . .
And darkness spreads its cloak on the hesitant light
Till all is covered by darkness and all is mantled by cold. . .[140]

This, then, is the message of Elisha ben Abuyah: The sufferings of the Jews are a drop in the sea of mankind's sufferings; the death of God enables man to become a temple of the living God. With the fervor of the convert Manoah embraces this new religion of the deification of man which resembles the religion of the Soul-God in *Before the Tent of Timmurah*. The result is excommunication. But a thousand ties bind Manoah to the past: parents, love, devotion to his former teachers. On the Day of Atonement which the Spanish authorities have chosen with deliberate cruelty as the day of an *auto da fé* Manoah joins the Marranos at the stake. The divine soul of the people conquers the idolized soul of the individual.

Most of the characters in *Manoah Franko* search for redemption. Rabbi Joseph pursues it in mystical speculation. The head of the academy of Barcelona, Rabbi Baruch, strives for it in the traditional mode of life, Immanuel and Peninah choose the realistic way of settling in Palestine, Manoah almost attains it in the tortuous paths of doubt. It is this passion for redemption which lends dramatic tension to the poem and unity of purpose to the characters. But it lacks *couleur locale*: Barcelona resembles Odessa. The Spanish Jews are Russian Jews who receded a few centuries to a familiar environment.

It was in that environment that Silkiner experienced the heady spell of Bialik and the linguistic pull of the Bible. But Bialik and the Bible were not his only sources of inspiration. The literatures of Europe also contributed to his inner growth: the Elizabethans and their chief exponent Shakespeare, the romantics and their *enfant terrible* Byron, the classic poets of Germany, Goethe and Heine. Even Maeterlinck's cult of silence claimed him as devotee:

Are there mysterious sounds,
  Ancient and young,
Which tell heart's sorrow to heart
  In unsung song?[141]

As a man of unimpeachable integrity Silkiner tapped the source of innocence: childhood. And he dedicated to children a poem which combines unaffected grace with the serious theme of redemption:

Watch the little ones,
The darlings of fate.
Love them and steel them
Against the world's hate.
Wash them and cleanse them
In rebirth's dew,
Clothe them with garments
Of our spirit's hue.
Remember: they are
The stuff we dream.
One is the Messiah
Born to redeem.[142]

This blend of innocence and nationalism reappears in the poem *Before the Tent of Timmurah*. For it was the love of romanticized savages for the land of their fathers which turned Silkiner, a Hebrew poet, to the legends of the Indians and which converted the chief character of the poem, Mugiral, into a symbol of protest against redemption by brute force.

Nobility of character stamped Silkiner's life and work. Purity of language which dominated his poetry also permeated the best endeavors of his contemporaries and successors. The world of the past which charmed him also exercised a fatal attraction over most Hebrew writers in America.

Enamored of the genius of Shakespeare, he dreamed of translating, in cooperation with a few Hebrew poets in America, the entire Shakespearean corpus of plays and lyric poems. But he only succeeded in producing a Hebrew version of *Macbeth* which appeared posthumously in Warsaw in 1939—one of the last Hebrew books to be published in the Polish capital before the grand debacle.[143]

Tantalizing incompleteness characterizes Silkiner's entire work. Yet he charted new vistas for his contemporaries and for his successors. Not only were native themes cultivated after him by most Hebrew poets in America, but historical personages and periods were brilliantly exploited—especially by the eminent playwright and novelist Harry Sackler.

Silkiner may be regarded as the progenitor of Hebrew literature in America. What preceded him was—with the exception of some poems by Imber and some satires by Rosenzweig—either mediocre or macabre: a fatuous effusion in florid poetry, a well-turned epitaph on the tombstone of a leader, an occasional commentary on a biblical book or talmudic treatise, a tract on the literary or nationalist aspirations of Jewry. What succeeded him was one of the manifold miracles of Jewish history: a half-century of growth and flowering of Hebrew letters in America.

Virtuoso of Hebrew: Lisitzky

Ephraim E. Lisitzky (1885–1962), like his older contemporary Benjamin N. Silkiner, was a virtuoso of the Hebrew language. Disparate ages seem to have deposited their lingual crop on his doorstep. His voracious memory assimilated such enormous amounts of Semitic philology from his predecessors that it is difficult to isolate his contributions from the mass of heterogeneous material. That he has been able to compose, in spite of his unusual scholarship, songs of touching, folk-like simplicity, remains an inexplicable process of creation which must defy the investigations of the most indefatigable psychologists.

> My beloved is a lily
> Blooming out of walls of blue.
> Heaven, heaven, bless my lily
> With the blessings of your dew.
>
> My beloved is a pond
> Dreaming dreams by mountain streams
> Beam, bright sun, upon my pond,
> Splendors of your golden beams.
>
> My beloved is a dove
> Cooing for her only love.
> Vulture, vulture, keep your claws
> From the heart of my sweet dove.[144]

In spite of the simplicity of the poem there is an obvious weakness in its structure: There is no logical end and no logical beginning, stanzas can be added between the stanzas, at the end of the poem, before the beginning of the poem. The beloved can be compared to a garden, a forest, a brook, a meadow. This catalogization of images and similes rather than the logical evolution of one from another is one of the gravest faults in the poetry of Lisitzky. It vitiates many poems and destroys their potential effectiveness.

The poet may have known his weakness. His dissatisfaction with his own achievements which erupts in the form of regrets and complaints in his poems can perhaps be traced to his conscious or unconscious awareness of a fundamental deficiency which he is unable to remedy. Otherwise it is difficult to account for the numerous comparisons of his life to a desert and his attempts to create characters which are far removed from the poet by modes of living and thinking.

In the narrative poems Lisitzky achieved a greater integration of his talents. In his idyll "Upon the Blowing of the Trumpet"[145] he recreated Jewish life in a small town of the southern United States and compared it with Jewish town life in Russia and Poland. Against the feverish preparations of body and soul for the high holidays on the other side, Lisitzky notes a complete absence of spiritual elevation among the Jews in the southern United States. The synagogue is empty on Sabbaths and holidays; the Sabbaths and the holidays are workdays like ordinary days. With every additional grave in the cemetery an unfillable place becomes vacant in the synagogue. The indifference of the younger generation to Judaism is only matched by the willingness of the immigrants to forget, together with the unsavory aspects of the old country, the traditional precepts and commandments. The Jewish communities become ripe for the blandishments of the Reform Rabbi who is short on learning and long on rhetoric. This harsh critique of Reform Judaism must be attributed to the traditionalism of the poet who knew orthodoxy in its full glory and Reform in its brash beginnings. Traditional Judaism has meanwhile undergone such modifications that even Conservative Judaism looks like a mild case of Reform while Reform Judaism endeavors to draw its sustenance *ex fontibus*.

Lisitzky has created the longest poetical work of this generation in modern Hebrew literature: *Struggles of God*.[146] In five hundred pages of poetry he sought to unload his ideas on God and man. It was to be an ambitious project on the scale of Goethe's *Faust*, but it lacked the soaring imagination and the grand conception of the German poet. A central theme informs both parts of *Faust* from beginning to end: The soul of Faust, sick with knowledge and science, stands on the threshold of utter collapse. Satan revives it with fresh promises of happiness which, in the end, prove to be as elusive as the quest of intellectual fulfillment. The dramatic poem of Lisitzky lacks clarity. No central theme, no central idea informs its misty pages. Vision is heaped upon vision, song is heaped upon song. The net result is utter bewilderment and confusion. The supernatural world jostles with the natural world but the conflict and the interdependence baffle the imagination of the reader. Nymphs and salamanders and a host of invented spirits flit through the pages of *Struggles of God*. For the place of action, we manage to learn, is infinity; the time—eternity. In such a setting the impossible becomes possible and the possible—absurd or impossible. All the great religions of the world are summoned to yield their essence: Judaism, Christianity, Mohammedanism, and Buddhism. All of them strive to achieve the victory of good over evil, the redemption of man from sin. And the redemption of man from evil—from the evil of man and fate—seems to be the theme of the poem.

As in the entire corpus of his poetry, Lisitzky shows an astonishing knowledge of Hebrew in his *Struggles of God*. But he remains an addict of his cataloging propensities. One of the characters, for example, compares himself to the forest, to the eruption of a volcano, to a storm, to a layer of snow. As in the folk-poem on the beloved he uses a stanza for each simile and achieves a conglomerate of images rather than a poem.

The failure of the whole does not mar the beauty of the parts. Passages with intensity of feeling and loftiness of aspiration can be garnered from the *Struggles of God*. Individual lyrics attain a rarified atmosphere of tranquillity and compare favorably with the best verses that have been produced by Lisitzky:

> Earth is wrapped in shadows' might—
> Night, night.
>
> The world's asleep, all life's asleep—
> Sleep, sleep.
>
> Sorrow's gone and laughter's zest—
> Rest, rest.[147]

But the loveliness of the individual passages, lost in an ocean of innocuous verse, fails to redeem the value of the book which is too great in scope and incommensurate with the capabilities of the poet.

In *Dying Campfires*[148] Lisitzky achieved the best integration of his poetic qualities. This book of Indian legends which have been carefully paraphrased and woven into an epic reflects the influence of Silkiner's *Before the Tent of Timmurah*. There is more than a superficial resemblance between the two books. Both tell the story of the destruction of Indian civilization out of love and sympathy for the Indian rather than the white man. Both tend to idealize their way of life and gloss over the unsavory aspects of their barbarous cruelties. Lisitzky has undertaken a more ambitious project than Silkiner. To the trochaic metres of *Hiawatha* and *Kalevala* he entrusted the story of two tribes: the sons of the vulture and the sons of the serpent. This monotonous rhythm which pervades the greater part of the book makes for a certain drabness which Silkiner avoided by cleverly changing his metres at set intervals. In *Dying Campfires* there is also a far greater idealization of the Indian than in *Before the Tent of Timmurah*. In some passages, as in the dirges of the Indians, Lisitzky composed memorable poetry:

> Woe is me! I am the shrub that
> Vintage robbed of sweetest fruit and
> Autumn robbed of leaves of glory.
> Winds howl through the balder branches
> And the shrub sighs in remembrance
> Of the sweetest fruit that rotted,
> Of the fallen leaves of glory.
> Woe is me! The spring will cover
> Shrubs with leaves again and summer
> Will again hang fruits upon them.
> Woe is me! I am bereaved of
> My fair daughter, fairest jewel,
> And I part from life in sadness.[149]

This is the lament of Hototon over his daughter. The mother and the medicine-man add their own wails of mortification and create a minor symphony of sorrow.

Apt descriptions of the American landscape combine with the beautiful legends into an artistic pattern of unusual grace. While in his other poems Lisitzky tended to reflect idyllic scenes of nature, he chose to paint harsher landscapes in *Dying Campfires*. Thus, in the description of the drought, he creates a picture of utter desolation which settled upon the forest and its inhabitants, upon the plain and its birds and beasts, upon the swamp and its fowls.

Stalk is dry and root is withered,
Fruit is rotten.[150]

Graceful rendition of Indian legends and original composition in *Dying Campfires* brought to the fore the happier aspects of Lisitzky's talents which, in philological equipment and ease of paraphrase, seem to have been predisposed for the work.

It was inevitable that the poet should also explore the world of the black man, his legends, his habits, his flair for spirituality which found its maturest expression in spirituals. In his book *In the Tents of the Black Men*[150] Lisitzky has woven a vast cycle of poems around Negro themes. As a resident of New Orleans he had unusual opportunities of observing colored people:

> When I became acquainted with the southern Negroes, they impressed me with their primitivism, their childish innocence and cunning, and their simple religious outlook. . . I have gone to their meetings, their clubs and their get-togethers for many years. I have heard the speeches of their spokesmen and the sermons of their preachers in their churches. I have listened to their prayers and their spirituals which are sung by their congregations and choirs with the enthusiasm and absorption of *Hasidim*. When I understood the life of the Negro, as much as a man who is not a member of their church and their race can understand it, I said to myself: Here is poetic stuff that can have a beneficent influence on Hebrew poetry in America.[152]

The book hovers on the brink of greatness; it never achieves it. But what it lacks in depth, it compensates in latitudinal dimensions: it not only lets the Negro sing his songs and tell his poetic tales; it pursues him down the lanes of history to his serfdom and to his free origins in Africa.

Lisitzky has recreated the more articulate Negro who was only once removed from his primitive counterpart: the Negro preacher. In a charming sermon "Israel in Shittim"[153] he retells in verse the temptations of the people in the wilderness and their "harlotry with the daughters of Moab." The Moabites are the snakes in the grass according to the Negro version: they open saloons and sell moonshine in all the streets; they invite the Israelites to dice-games and card-games, to dances and jazz; they expose them to the seductive charms of dancers and singers. The cards are marked, of course, the dice are loaded and the girls are painted hussies. But Moses finds the right remedy: He orders his brother Aaron to call a revival meeting. In a sermon, not exceeded by any former preacher, Aaron exposes the terrible sins and predicts the more terrible punishments: lynching and burning in the depths of hell. Eleazar helps out when the High Priest tires. But after the preachments the people sin again. Moses is perplexed, but Phinehas son of Eleazar comes to the rescue. He is a fine young man, tall and handsome; he has a way with women-folk, and he promises his uncle Moses to get all the lost sheep of Israel back to the fold. With the organizing ability of an American he mobilizes an army of Israelite women who invade the saloons, break all the mirrors and bottles and cups and cut all the Moabite whores with razors. After that gory experience all is set right: The Israelites perform their work in the pasture; they hunt quail and gather manna and hold revival-meetings every night for one full month. Phinehas gets his reward from uncle Moses: He becomes a preacher of the Lord because a stubborn mule like the Israelite people needs the whip and the sword rather than the honeyed word.

"Israel in Shittim" is undoubtedly the best example of a Negro sermon in Hebrew. It has the charm of simplicity; it has the sovereign inattention to history; it elevates anachronism to a poetic principle and it applies the moral with full force. It is no mere accident that most Negro sermons of Lisitzky are patterned on biblical themes: they are imbedded in his imagination and they are readily transformed into poetic stuff. In a weird marriage with Negro songs, sermons, folkways and folktales, the biblical stories have yielded poetic offspring which will have a permanent place in Hebrew literature.

Compassion was the dominant note in the poems on Negro themes from Rosenzweig to Lisitzky as it was in Negro writings from W.E. Burghardt DuBois to Langston Hughes. And compassion characterized the ablest Negro leadership from Booker T. Washington to Martin Luther King. Black militancy as expressed by LeRoi Jones was alien to Hebrew poetry. His bloody brand of revolutionism evoked revulsion. For in his book of essays *Home* he not only advocated the end of white domination in America and beyond America; he postulated the burning of the white man to cinders. In marked contrast to this aggressive nihilism Léopold Sédar Senghor, the poet of *Négritude*[154] and President of the Republic of Senegal, envisions civilized blackness which harks back to the deep roots of African vastness and wildness. This is a sane attitude to a precious patrimony. The establishment of independent states in Africa has already given a new impetus to literary efforts of black and white men all over the world. Alexis de Tocqueville has observed that

> oppression has deprived the descendants of the Africans of almost all the privileges of humanity. The United States Negro has lost even the memory of his homeland; he no longer understands the language his fathers spoke; he has abjured their religion and forgotten their mores. Ceasing to belong to Africa, he has no right to the blessings of Europe.[155]

The Negro is no longer a slave; but he is not yet possessed of all the privileges of the white man. And his plight is a contributing factor to the contemporary malaise in American cvilization. Hebrew writers in America have been aware of the disequilibrium between the white and the black man; they identified with the misery of the black man and, with their ingrained libertarian ardor, they anticipated a new dawn for him and for all the oppressed minorities in the world.

Efros: Master of Simplicity

Like Silkiner and Lisitzky, Israel Efros was stimulated by the Indian. But he cast a wider net than his predecessor: In search of epic material he ransacked the ancient civilizations of the Jews, the Greeks and the American Indians. Out of the Bible he borrowed characteristics for the portrayal of Moses, out of Greek mythology he revived Pan and Syrinx. In his poem "Hellas" which, paradoxically, shows strong influences of modern Hebrew poetry, he mourned the death of gods who succumbed to the power of Christianity.

It was in his narrative poem *Silent Wigwams*[156] that he struck a rich vein of native ore and created, against an early American background, a tender love story of a white man and a half-Indian girl. It was not his first attempt to portray the inner life of an artist. In "The Dream of the Artist"[157] he endeavored to delve into the soul of a sculptor, in *Silent Wigwams* he sketched the soul of the painter Tom. And the half-Indian girl Lalari is the very image of simplicity, innocence, vitality. Silkiner and Lisitzky portrayed the end of Indian civilization on a broad canvass; Efros depicted the clash between the white man and the red man in a region which was to become the State of Maryland. He described the early American landscape with feeling and felicity and he achieved a greater concentration of plot than

Silkiner and Lisitzky. His central thesis which, in its obvious application to the Jewish people, was not startlingly new or original, repeated effectively what so many Hebrew publicists and essayists —including Aaron David Gordon and Hayyim Joseph Brenner— have been preaching since the second half of the nineteenth century: Man must strike roots in the soil and possess it with the sweat of his brow.

Efros made another discovery: Primitive culture does not imply a primitive mind. While his Indian girl Lalari shares simple tastes and simple ways with tribal brethren, she is a refined and even sophisticated lover. From her surrender to Tom till her suicide she articulates her love experience with a complicated ardor worthy of as civilized a woman as Lawrence Durrell's Justine. Yet Lalari's wigwam in the county of Wicomico in southern Maryland and the palatial home of Justine in Alexandria are not only thousands of miles but aeons of civilizations apart.

From American history Efros extracted a story-in-verse *Gold*[158] about the feverish days of the gold rush in California. The protagonist of the poem—the peaceful landowner Ezra Lunt of Salem—becomes involved in a melodramatic career and infected with the mad greed for gold. He embarks on a life of adventures and privations. By day he rides at the head of a group of emigrants, by night he wards off attacks of the ever-present and ominous Indians or listens to stories about the legendary princess of California, Calafia, who drew men into captivity and killed them at leisure. As he travels on and on, he forgets his wife Abbie and his son Danny, and succumbs to the charms of Lola whose hair is a cascade of "black waves." This girl persuades him to acquire land for farming.

After the death of her guardian she marries Ezra. They venture out again into the fields of gold. True to the melodramatic pattern of the story, their happy sin is followed by inevitable punishment. Lola and her horse slide down an abyss. Meanwhile, the abandoned wife Abbie comes to California in search of her husband. She cannot locate him; she marries again. Ezra succeeds in finding his former wife and son; he hears her voice, he listens, in hiding, to her conversation with the new husband but he does not dare to approach her. With his son he manages to exchange a few words. Then he resumes his sad pilgrimage in the sunkist landscape.

As in all the poems of Efros the lyrical passages, not the narrative or the dramatic, produce an unforgettable effect. Thus, in *Gold*, the wistful lullaby is one of the most beautiful lyrics which the poet created in his long career. It is Abbie's song to her child about the father who wrenches gold out of the rocks while the children grow up like orphans and the farms decay. Neither high mansions nor streams of gold will compensate them for the desolation of family life. This, in simple words, is the most effective statement of the unsavory results of the goldrush.

In the lyric which verges on the folk-song Efros has achieved skill and mastery. While in the narrative poems his imagination moves with pedestrian pace, in the lyric it sparkles with an effervescent originality. There the sunset writes with the ink of twilight, death pens the three dots at the end of life. There he creates the exquisite image of the bridge of dreams which stretches along the Mediterranean Sea and leads to the Land of the Fathers:

There is a bridge to Palestine
Upon the Western Sea:
The planks are made of dreams of silver
The nails—of gold of poverty.
You pay your toll on every bridge:
A slice of life, a bit of soul.
You pay your toll with laughing mien
And with a wounded soul.
But on the bridge of brightest gold
Which leads to Palestine
My soul flames up in sheerest joy,
My thoughts like sunrays shine.
And my fathers who stand guard
On that bridge on either side
Look with love upon the son
Who returns from far and wide.[159]

Efros is the singer of movement in space. The vagabond or the brook: they meander in leisure or in a hurry to an unknown destination.

We are wanderers
With a singing heart.
We forget our goal,
We forget our start.
Forward or sideward,
Without grief, without sorrow.
All paths are straight.
No yesterday, no tomorrow.[160]

For Efros identification with a wanderer is as easy and natural as identification with a brook.

My life is a winding brook
On the mountain slope,
A brook that stumbles on stones
But sings its song of hope;
A brook that runs to the ledge,
And from the ledge to the lea,
And breaks its waves and sings
A song of life and glee.[161]

Even the flowers in his poetry *ascend* from the depths of the earth and *go forth* to the light of the world. Thus the static world of vegetation assumes functions of movement which are not ordinarily associated with it. Movement and song are the twin stars that guide Efros on the graceful paths of his poetry. Pain is a rare guest in his works.

This youthful approach to life results in environmental awareness. That is why his poetry so often reflects the American scene. The Hudson River,[162] the trains and the cars of New York and, above all, the whole strange and unwieldy conglomeration of races and nationalities sing with an alert vigor in his poetry. The train is the beast of iron; it presages the arrival of the man of iron whose thought will be formed by the din of the hammer on the anvil and not by the pallor of the lilies. The automobile is the poetry of tomorrow. In such a mechanical civilization life loses meaning and death its sting. A caravan of black cars follows the hearse that bears the casket, the people wonder for awhile at "that black riddle" and return to their habitual pursuits.

The superficiality of modern life, however, did not change Efros into a prophet of evil but only strengthened him in his preoccupation with the singing landscape. As a poet Efros is a master of simplicity, as a scholar he delves into abstruse scholasticism. His *Philosophical Terms in the Moreh Nebukim* in English earned him a doctorate in philosophy. His *Studies in pre-Tibbonian Philosophical Terminology* and his *Ancient Jewish Philosophy*[163] earned him the respect of scholars. Though his researches into Jewish thought in ancient and medieval times fill three out of the eight volumes of his collected works, they do not burden his poetry; he keeps a reasonable distance between his interest in philosophy and his poetic gift. Deceptive innocence and an almost complete absence of intellectualism in his lyrical poetry charm his readers. Such disparity in two fields of intellectual endeavor was matched only by A.E. Housman in English literature. This literary fact is not intended as a comparison of their poetic and scholarly abilities. Housman was a classical scholar, one of the renowned Latinists of his age; Efros devoted his studies to Hebrew philosophy. Their poetical works also differ enormously: Housman left a small body of lyrical work—*The Shropshire Lad, Last Poems* and the posthumous *More Poems*. In the classic conception of death and disappointment he achieves an unusual pitch of intensity. Efros concentrates on the brighter aspects of life. But grace of feeling and expression characterizes both poets who have been peculiarly uninfluenced by their scientific work.

Bavli: Poet of Maturation

There was a spiritual consanguinity between Silkiner, Lisitzky and Efros: They were addicted to native themes. Indians interested all of them; Negroes attracted Lisitzky's attention. In general Hebrew poets in America tended to delve deeply into the lot of the black man. Already in the beginning of the century Gershon Rosenzweig called attention to the plight of the Negro in his verse. But it was Hillel Bavli (1893–1961) who first interpreted their rich folk-songs and folk-poetry. Stimulated by James Weldon Johnson's *The Book of American Negro Poetry* he studied individual Negro poets. In the translation of "The Negro Poet," a sonnet by James D. Corrothers, "The Prayer from Atlanta" by W.E. Burghardt Du Bois and "Blood for Blood" by Claude McKay, he found emotional equivalents for the exotic style of the Negro in Hebrew.[164] Yet it was not the Negro *per se* who interested Bavli but the Negro as a symbol of Jewish destiny.

Other Hebrew poets followed and even improved on Bavli who also pioneered interest in non-Jewish types in America. In "Mrs. Woods" he depicted a charming old woman, young in spirit, fresh as the mountain winds which blew upon her humble shack. The cities, in the assertive monolog which bears her name, bring premature wrinkles to the faces of people; they teach everything, but they fail to instruct humanity in the wisdom of life. Not so the mountains; they are the true repositories of happiness and repose and innocence for Mrs. Woods. A little dog like Princie can lighten the burden of her solitude; memories of the past can brighten her present; finally, the Book of Books never fails to delight and to instruct her simple soul. "Mrs. Woods" is the American version of the pure and innocent characters which entered Hebrew literature via the plays of Moses Hayyim Luzzatto and the contemporary idylls of Tschernichowsky and Shimoni.

Bavli's proselyte in "Sergeyev from Kefar Tabor"[165] is also an embodiment of simplicity. As a Russian in Astrakhan he heard rumors about the new life in Palestine; and he decided to see it for himself. The twenty-five years in the new environment strengthened his love for the soil and his delight in the exotic landscape:

> . . .Mother earth!
> She gives us happiness; she also gives security.

It is significant that Bavli, so markedly Jewish in his poetry, peopled his idyllic poems with non-Jewish characters. Perhaps he was unconsciously driven to show that innocence and purity know no national boundaries and belong to no specific race. And innocence and purity are the true protagonists of Bavli's idyllic poems.

While Sergeyev looked upon Palestine as a man of the soil, Bavli saw it with the avid eyes of the tourist. The landscape, starred with ancient places and new settlements, exercised an irresistible attraction on every fibre of his being. As an unhappy lover he parted from the country:

> From the heart of this soil a fountain flows to my heart,
> And the sinuous veins of the land, knotted and twined within me,
> Embrace my whole being.
> There were times when I prayed: Would that the wonder occurred
> And my body were chained to the heart of this land.

Love for woman and for Palestine were among the deepest experiences in the personal life of Bavli. And they left a correspondingly deep mark on his poetry. In his love for woman the poet rebelled against the magic of tradition, in his love for Palestine he identified with national aspirations. If he showed a marked preference for autumn in his poetry, it was because autumn always represented abundance and sorrow. It was the unconscious symbol of his soul bent under the weight of its maturation.

The short lyrics were the mainstay of Bavli's strength. Admiration for his father lent uncommon lustre to Bavli's choicest lyrics.

You are the ancient tree of many roots.
Daily you drink at the primeval source.
Daily you bend anew beneath your fruits
And bloom and grow in ever-youthful force.

Under your heavy shadow I recline
And listen how your soothing murmur mounts.
I seem to hear the rustle of the pine
In pristine forests and the song of founts.

Oh give me both the shadow and the sound
Of your pure voice! My soul's athirst for all
That's great. The beauty of your soul is bound
To surge within me like a waterfall.[166]

In Bavli's relationship to his father there is, over and above the biological bond, a deep admiration for the national values which are embodied and idealized in his personality. And, by the force of ambivalence, the love for his father is charged with a will to rebellion against the shackles of tradition. The peculiar charm of Bavli's poetry manifests itself in the tension that results from parental love and his people on the one hand, and the will to rebel against that love on the other hand. His poems turn and return to this central theme in numberless variations. Sometimes they speak of the "wick of generations" which has to be cut by the poet, sometimes they mourn the "autumned epochs" which weigh upon him, sometimes they raise their voice in protest against "the mummified generations" which are stored up in his soul and which direct him, "beyond the veil of times," to the inevitable goal. Bavli is the battlefield "where ancient wars are waged again in silence."

The will to rebel assumes various forms in the poetry of Bavli. When in the days of early youth he alighted from the home of his parents in Lithuania on the alien soil of America, he was captivated by alien poetry though the song of his native land and the God of his fathers accompanied him in all his ways. His fine poetical eulogies on Edwin Arlington Robinson and William Butler Yeats, his essays on the poetry of the Negroes, on Robert Frost and Edgar Lee Masters, on Carl Sandburg and Amy Lowell show beyond a shadow of a doubt that he succumbed to the charms of American and English literature though he did not renounce his own culture.[167]

This preoccupation with non-Semitic literatures is the mildest aspect of Bavli's will to rebel. His love poetry which is his best gift to modern Hebrew literature is another and acuter form of his latent disaffection with the "burden of inheritance." There are three stages in his love poetry: youthful love, mature love and a third love which partakes of "the mercy of morning and the flame of noon." The poems "To Helen"[168] are undoubtedly the first-fruits of the first love. Their innocence and folk-like grace seem to be derived as much from the image of the beloved as from the poet himself.

> A black butterfly
> Flew to my heart
> And stirred its strings
> With innocent art.
>
> A black butterfly
> Spread its wings
> And encompassed my world
> With invisible rings.
>
> Oh black butterfly,
> Oh wings of might!
> Fly away, lest my soul
> Be burned in your flight.

The urgent anxiety in the last stanza reflects the inner struggle between love of woman and love of tradition which is so strong a component of Bavli's personality. In that first skirmish of major porportions tradition won its painful victory.

In his mature love, represented by the cycle of poems "Veil of Sorrows"[169] Bavli grew in erotic awareness. Not as a black butterfly but as the regenerative earth in spring the beloved enveloped him in her ubiquitous being. "Primeval foundations shook within me, but did not totter"—this is the summation of his mature love.

The memory of a young girl from the early days of his life shed a tender light on the third love, became identified with it in its initial stages, but receded into the background as the reality of the new love grew in intensity.

> You are no orphaned sound in the music of the past,
> You are no memory that beckons from my youth.
> You are a new beginning, a splendid revelation,

The roots of my whole being burrow into yours.
Perhaps you also are an end, and I don't know,
The high finale of my song, the sunset in its glory.
Whatever you may be I hedge my life with love,
I walk in paths of beauty crowned with light of wonder.[170]

Meeting with love often means parting from love. In Bavli's case parting assumes a new symbolical meaning: his entire life appears to him in the guise of "one parting melody."

This is my fate: to leave that which I love,
To feel the bars of solitude even in a kiss.[171]

This confession sheds light on the personality of the poet which is made of the stuff of rebels but not of their fateful daring. Never did Bavli burn the bridges between the past and himself. The beauty of tradition captivated him and held him like a prison. The alien charms were powerless to break the magic of the indigenous splendors. This conflict explains the elegiac tenor of his poetry. Only his non-lyrical, narrative poems, with the sole exception of "Eli,"[172] sound notes of unadulterated composure and peace of mind.

Intellectual Authors: Halkin and Regelson

There was familial intimacy in Bavili's poetry. Simon Halkin's poetry, on the other hand, inclined from the very beginning toward philosophical and even metaphysical problems. In a youthful essay he announced that "only cerebral poetry will sustain man in our time."[173] And this credo fed his pioneering work in intellectual poetry; it sought to understand rather than to sing the sorrows of the world; above all, it revolved around the concept of the evolving deity.

The philosophical and metaphysical foundation of poetry did not harmonize with Halkin's talent for lyricism which was tinged with an ancient, almost pre-human anxiety. That disharmony of poetical anitinomies aspired at times to heights beyond its great reach.

Anglo-American and German influences prevailed in Halkin's first poems. Upon his long youthful poem "Among the Rocks"[174] he grafted, not without originality, Heine's lyric of the pine and the palm:

. . .I shall not complain
My solitude is complete.

Why should the northen pine complain of longing
For the palm that swoons in farthest south?
God has decreed that men should suffer
Together without knowing one another.

The curse of solitude and silence closes in upon mankind; the blessing of poetry is powerless against the isolation of the individual. That is why the poet turns to God in his loneliness.

Open, soul, your gates, admit the light of spring!
Listen, God of Life knocks stealthily and sings:
Let my love sojourn in your unfathomed depths,
Let me spread my wings on your uncharted paths.

This lovely prayer is typical of Halkin's youthful poetry which echoes lines and imagery from Keats, Shelley and Tennyson. The limpid ripple of waters rises softly in the lines of three poems–in "Prayers"[175]—which were written in the Lake Kiamesha region in the Catskills. Like a young priest the poet serves his evolving deity which appears only to disappear again and leave him in uncertainty, doubt and wretchedness. The traditional God was the object of Bavli's will to rebellion; he lost his hold on Halkin, but another was slow in coming.

The apogee of Halkin's youthful achievement is the long and lofty poem "On the Shore of Santa Barbara."[176] The four parts have a symphonic structure: *leitmotifs* occur and recur, incidental *motifs* merge with the central themes. The heat and the light of the Californian landscape are the *leitmotifs*. "Gales of light," "seas of light" and "storms of light"—these are merely a few metaphors from the heap of hyperboles. The intellectual lives of men—and these are the incidental *motifs* of the poem—are blurred by the glory of light. Animalic contentment and the majesty of the sea act as powerful deterrents to the inner strivings of the poet.

In the second part of the poem, a sort of an *allegro* following the *andante* of the first part, the poet glories in his discovery of the phenomenal world: "Oh earth! You, only you." In the past he had viewed the earth as a mist that envelops and hides his emerging God and as a hint of his presence; he even wished to die in order to lose his material sight and gain insight "into the heart of God." Now, in the land of light, he seemed to divest himself of the burden of brooding and fruitless search; now there was no longer any God. "You alone are, oh earth!" The ephemeral seems to have conquered the eternal. Yet the heart hesitates: "Will it cease to listen to the song of God?" On this questioning note the second part of the poem comes to a sudden end.

The third part, the *scherzo,* describes a detail in the vast panorama of the earth: Santa Barbara, a Venus of Botticelli in urban form.

> Santa Barbara, daughter of waves, nurtured by wonderful wines!
> Trembling in beauty, she sprung from the foam of the ocean
> And stood in her gleaming nakedness, on the gleaming sands of
> [the shore.
> Desiring, desirable woman, you are flooded with terrible splendors.
> Your pink blood shines in your cool, marblelike flesh.
> You are flooded with terrible splendors, and your azure veins seem
> [to yearn.
> In your pink and transparent flesh, a cup full of wine in the sun.

The poet feels refreshed and recharged. Like "a pale monk" he came to Santa Barbara and rekindled his lust for life.

The briefest and last part of the poem, the *finale maestoso* of the symphonic composition, is a sonnet. The yearnings of youth reassert themselves: the poet does not want to search for God; he strives to be like God for one brief moment, to suffer and die like a god. The poem which opened on a note of victory ends in despair:

> No more prayers. Pain appears and disappears.
> Even so, in man, shine God's tears.

The Shakespearean sonnet at the end of the long poem was no accident. To this form which the great English poet invested with the complications of his love life, Halkin entrusted the history of one of his loves. The thirty-six Shakespearean sonnets which make up his little volume *In Six Days and Seven Nights*[177] are the best documents of abortive love in modern Hebrew literature. The broken heart of a girl who gives all to her love and the strange heart of the poet who cannot, in spite of his ardent desire, give his soul to his love—this is the twin theme of the sonnets. The feeling of solitude, first encountered in the narrative poem "Among the Rocks," reemerges in a deeper variation:

> God decrees that souls shall never kiss
> Sister-souls, not even in the brief
> Embrace; that they shall yearn in lonely grief,
> In love-calm and in hurricanes of bliss.

Each soul, even the soul of the beloved, is wrapped in invisible veils. The poet lifts a veil sometimes, sinks in its folds but never reaches the focal center. An anterior life presses on our lives with all its fatal cruelty, disrupts intimate relationships and welds disparate entities. That individual memory is fed by springs of ancient life is no hasty thought on the part of the poet but rather a central belief. Not only in the sonnets but in a later poem "To Tarshish"[178] he expresses the conviction that he is "a vat overflowing with ancient wines." Memories of thousands of years are taken for granted as they were taken for granted by Baudelaire in his sonnet *"La Vie Antérieure"* and by William Butler Yeats in his *Essays.*

Like "On the Shore of Santa Barbara" the sonnets end on a note of defeatism:

> I am weak and sick. Soon I shall fall
> And never see my dazzling God forsooth.
> Thirsting for him I spent my spring, my youth,
> And calling for him with a wounded call.

But unlike "On the Shore of Santa Barbara" the sonnets do not celebrate an intoxication with light nor do they exult in an intoxication of love. They are poems of fatigue; the poet despairs of love and does not come nearer to his God. In his autobiographical poem "Baruch Son of Neriah"[179] and in his autobiographical novel *Yehiel the Hagrite*[180] the poet split his personality into the man of God who is in search of greatness and into the disciple of the man of God. The novel is a poor example of this dichotomy. Rabbi Dov, the *alter ego* of Halkin, is a Hasid who spends his days in search of God while Yehiel, the counterpart of Dov, suffers from his lust for Lorraine and strives, at the same time, to divest himself of his humanity and lose himself in God. But the characters are obscured by a mist of verbosity. They are the component parts of an essay on God rather than protagonists in a novel. The background of *Yehiel the Hagrite,* New York, is sketched in barest outlines. Bronx Park, the Hudson River, Greenwich Village are incidentally mentioned but not organically woven into its texture. Instead of plot there is self-analysis and self-torment.

There is a more successful division of personality in "Baruch Son of Neriah." Jeremiah, the man of God, is the unsophisticated and uncomplicated character of the poem. He is the harp on which God plays his divine melodies. The wilderness howls at his displeasure, the people weep when he shows wrath. Baruch feels the life of nature with an intense sympathy but he cannot express its diversified moods. This is the contrast between the two men: Jeremiah articulates the grief of man and God, Baruch feels everything and expresses nothing. Envy and hate torment the disciple who thirsts for the redeeming word. These feelings merge, not unreasonably, with a strong feeling of love for Jeremiah. Like a dog the disciple follows the master and copies faithfully whatever he chooses to say in divine inspiration. And toward the end of the poem, love and hate dissolve in overwhelming admiration for Jeremiah's greatness.

In his fragmentary novel *To the Edge of Crisis*[181] Halkin has created a caricature of greatness. The hero, Professor Reuben G. Fowler, is the rabbi of an important congregation in New York, a member of the faculty of the Jewish Theological Seminary, an author of a number of books on Judaism, a reformer and a philosopher. But failure stalks all men including Professor Reuben G. Fowler. The young and lovely wife is in love with her southern accent but not with her husband. And the eminent professor who is not free from the call of the flesh suffers agonies of deprivation. Their wayward daughter Lena Fowler alias Elaine Novikova is an alcoholic and an habituée of a night club—"The Black Colt." The pompous professor may ascend the empyrean heaven; reality forces him to lower depths.

Spiritual oscillation also characterizes the poem "To Tarshish." The asceticism of the earlier years appears to the poet as downright folly. While he eschewed the society of men, he lost God and the faculty to appreciate the immanent godliness of men. He even lost the way to himself and to his future. Yet every man has his refuge. Jonah found it in Tarshish, the poet longs for the northern woods. But this longing becomes the source of guilt: The poet imagines that his rightful place as a good Jew is in Palestine. In a moving stanza he begs forgiveness from the land of his fathers and from its glassy light that stands like a partition between him and his innermost self. "To Tarshish" is not the light-intoxicated paean of the singer of Santa Barbara. The verses move in weary cadence; the interminable periods, after the manner of Proust but without their psychological subtlety, hamper the understanding and the enjoyment of the massive poem.

Though Halkin has published a few stories,[181a] scores of articles on Hebrew and foreign literature, numerous translations from Maeterlinck and Lagerlöf and Jack London, beside the novel *Yehiel the Hagrite*, fragments from novels in progress, he is essentially a poet. And he has rendered his cherished poets in Hebrew: Shakespeare and

Shelley, Arnold and Tennyson, and Walt Whitman's *Leaves of Grass*. Like one of his favorite authors, D.H. Lawrence, he searches for a new deity. The English novelist has found the object of his search in sexual mythology; the Hebrew poet, conditioned perhaps by the burden of his race and by individual difficulties, can never complete his spiritual odyssey. His God is an evolving God, his pain is the pain of his growth.

More than any other Hebrew poet in America Abraham Regelson is possessed of an intimate knowledge of English and American poetry. Yet to stamp his work with the seal of literary influence or worse than that, plagiarism, is to do it grave injustice. Regelson is an original poet in spite of his excessive debt to English poetry. Robert Browning guided him toward a poetic form which was most congenial to his talents: the dramatic monolog. John Milton taught him the use of pathos and the use of the long phrase; John Keats lured him into the world of mythologies; Percy Bysshe Shelley introduced him to Promethean themes. Fragments of philosophies from Thales to Bergson also found their way into his writings which succeeded in preserving their peculiar Jewishness.

Poetry was not merely a thing of beauty in Regelson's estimation but also a way to higher ethics:

> As man's imagination develops, the force of his ethics grows. He who can imagine himself in the place of others will also be able to make their sorrows and their joys his own. An untrammeled imagination lifts the veil which hides the inner life of other people.[182]

The triumph of pity and love is, according to Regelson, the goal of life, "the immanence of God in man." This conviction lends strength to his work. In its intellectualism it resembles the poetry of Halkin, in its rejection of philosophical doubt it reflects a less differentiated mind. The identification of divinity with pity and love leaves the poet one goal: to help establish the reign of pity and love on earth. As a Jew he did not condone severance of morals from poetry, ethics from esthetics. And he even developed a Jewish poetical technique. Most of his poems are *Midrashim* in verse: simple questions and not very simple answers, rich in interpretations of biblical and talmudic phrases, overflowing with homilies, parables and legends.

In his first printed poem, in "Rape of Love" Regelson revealed his unmistakable talents for poetic *Midrash:*

What does the flower do before it wilts?
It sows the seeds. Oh song of mine, be wind
And scatter all the seeds of my heart's flower
And plant the sparks of my unfathomed love
In the sunset, in the crimson rose,
In the blue of noon and violets,
In the pallor of the moon and dawn.[183]

In his autobiographical poem "Abiel"—a poetical sermon on the soul
of Abiel-Regelson—the hereafter which is tantamount to the "world of
truth" in Hebrew is explained in terms of an imaginative *Midrash:*

Man is enemy to man on earth.
Man sees man as tool for his advancement
Or as obstacle upon his road.
Therefore man knows not his brother man
And loves him not. The hand of death, however,
Lifts the soul above the petty contests
And bares its beauty and divinity.
That's why our world is called the world of truth.[184]

This is a homily after the manner of the ancient story-tellers in the
Talmud; it is lifted onto the plane of poetry by the special gift of
Regelson.

In the earlier stages the poet inhabits superhuman, ethereal planes.
Moses in "Moses on Mount Nebo"[185] sees from the height of Pisgah not
only the land of Canaan but also the future generations. Ahijah the
Shilonite and Israel Baal Shem Tov in the poem "Ahijah and Israel"[186]
converse in incorporeal bliss. The philosopher of Königsberg in
"Immanuel Kant" makes a resumé of his life in the presence of friends
and speaks of the two great gifts which were given to him: "the moral
law within and the starry skies above." This preoccupation with the
non-terrestrial world deprived Regelson's poetry of the tang of reality.
In ancient myths it endeavored to touch the roots of existence. The
long poem "Cain and Abel"[187] is the outstanding example of a
primitive tale of horror and grandeur in abstract modernization. Cain
and Abel, Adam and Beer represent forces of life rather than people of
flesh and blood. Adam is the battlefield of two passions: the passion for
mere existence and the passion for sheer annihilation. The passion for
mere existence was inherited by Cain, the passion for annihilation
clung to Abel. Thus Cain becomes the blind will in the Schopenhauer-

ian sense or the Dionysian impulse in the Nietzschean sense: the builder and architect who knows no respite in his untiring work. Abel, on the other hand, represents the thinker, the critic, the skeptic whose impotence in action is matched by a sovereign consciousness of the vanity of all things. When Cain kills Abel, it is will which kills thought. In a magnificent curse which accompanies the first murder on earth the elder brother invokes all the powers of nature to help him in his act of destruction:

> Founts of night and darkness, curse Cain!
> Gates of dawn and gaps of evening, curse him!
> Hate him, hate him, flocks of heavenly stars!
> Give no solace to him, rains and rainbows.
> And withhold your blessing from him earth,
> For he cut down your comforter, your Abel!
> Woe to Cain!
> His plow will lord the soil; a little while
> She will give him strength but she will close
> Her womb again because he raped her. He'll
> Build cities but they'll rise against each other
> To crush and to destroy till they lie waste.
> His right will strike his left,
> His passions will consume him,
> All his labors will have come to nought.

The curse had a devastating effect. Cain married Beer, the daughter of Abel: Will mated with the daughter of thought who undermined his absolute reign. But she, too, was not victorious though she poisoned Cain:

> Between the ninth and tenth dimension sleeps
> An atom of sheer strength, a wave of energy
> Which, being small, was not destroyed by Cain,
> And lay somewhere unknown to Beer.
> That's why, when earth fell at her bidding
> And the canopy of sky dissolved, it stayed.
> It will serve as seed
> That will burst into bloom of being.

"Cain and Abel" is merely a mature, complicated paraphrase of an earlier poem "Yehiel and the Netherworld."[188] There two forces also vie with each other for supremacy: the force of life and the force of death. And just as the victory of Cain is no complete victory, so the victory of the Netherworld lacks finality. It is Yehiel, the force of life, who cheats the netherworld out of its vaunted fruits of victory:

> I am your labor and your pain within
> And enemy without. You conquered—not
> Forever. If you kill me thousandfold,
> I will rise to plague you in your womb,
> Till I return to victory in battle.

In an incisive essay on "Cain and Abel"[189] Moses Feinstein demonstrated Regelson's dependence on Keats and Shelley. The brotherly antithesis of Cain and Abel is paralleled by mythical antithesis—Jupiter and Prometheus, Jupiter and Hyperion—in "Prometheus Unbound" and in "Hyperion." But Feinstein also asserted that Regelson's "imagination. . .is not kissed by emotion."

This is critical harshness. Some poems by Regelson are charged with lyrical emotion and some seem to explode with unsuspected passion:

> I feel the sap of spring in me,
> The intoxication of the great creators. . .
> From the beds of burning poppies
> Which burst in scarlet stream. . .
> And from the scents of night which fill the sleeping bush
> And whirling constellations with intoxication
> I shall weave a solitary flower. . .[190]

It is true that even the lyrical poems of Regelson bristle with philosophical maxims and metaphysical ideas. In the beautiful elegy on the death of Bialik the poet presents an evaluation of a great contemporary and combines it with thoughts on death and eternity. Even a small lyric like "Anemones"[191] does not merely extol spring flowers.

> One or two fingerlengths deep your roots lie in the earth
> But your true roots are far deeper than that.
> They are also my roots. . .
> When my time comes to leave the pasture of the living and descend
> To earth, I shall not go down in mourning. For I know:
> I have a rendez-vous with you in the earth's depths.

The seeming coolness of Regelson robs his poems of lyrical intimacy, but it strengthens their texture with objectivity. They are singularly free from introversion and full of dramatic situations which do not—like Browning's *Dramatic Lyrics, Dramatic Romances* and *Dramatis Personae*—combine into real drama. Unlike Browning, Regelson prefers the legendary and the mythical to the actual and the real in the ordinary sense of the word. Chinese, Hebrew and Indian lore supplied him with ancient tales which he retold and reshaped in poetry and prose.

In *Shawlful of Leaves*[192]—a mélange of essays and feuilletons—Regelson reveals the more human aspect of his personality. It seems that he reserved metaphysical flights for his poetry, the commoner things for his prose. For the critical essays on the sonnets of Shakespeare, on kabbalistic ideas in the poetry of Milton, on Freud, the myth-maker of this generation, and on Henri Bergson rarely rise above the level of popular and informative lectures.[193] The feuilletons, on the other hand, are little poems on little trifles: problems of the hour jostle with problems of philosophy; self-characterizations vie with happy characterizations of friends, acquaintances and strangers. A sense of humor informs Regelson's sketches which are not entirely free from the influence of Schoffmann. One of the most graceful and delicate exercises in self-commiseration is perhaps the short sketch entitled "Beggars":[194]

> The reason why I don't like beggars is because I am one of them. They are beggars without camouflage, experts in the profession and quite successful, too. But I am a beggar in hiding, an eternal recruit to the profession and unsuccessful, too. . .And even when I work, I cannot quite rid myself of the disgrace of begging.
>
> Two people teach in a school: Mr. Mixer and myself. Mr. Mixer takes his salary proudly. To me it is given as an alms. . .Even if I give my best to teaching, the principal always suspects my motives. . .because my innermost self. . .is somewhere else; because the geometric structure of the spiderweb interests me more than the cheating of the pupil in the examination. . .
>
> Two people translate a book for the publisher: Mr. Mustachio and myself. My translation is being praised by critics and readers. The translation of Mr. Mustachio is not even mentioned. Yet Mr. Mustachio enters the offices of the publisher as a welcome guest. He is sure of them, and they are sure of him. I come with a feeling

of insecurity. For the publishers know that because of the work which they give me and which I have not selected or because of the work which I have selected and they have given to someone else, my artistic soul is restless. Mr. Mustachio has no artistic soul; he is not required to sell it. . .

The short sketch reads like an autobiographical account of the unsuccessful ventures of the poet into the field of battle for a livelihood. Instead of complaining about his bitter lot, he uses the more impressive method of self-mockery and achieves a remarkable effect of graceful profundity.

Like the exegete and poet of the middle ages Abraham Ibn Ezra who was commemorated by Robert Browning in his poem "Rabbi Ben Ezra," Abraham Regelson is the happy beggar who knows how to laugh at himself and others. He never abandons his faith in the ultimate victory of love and pity. And this faith is the golden link which connects his prose with his poetry.

The Romantics: Simon Ginzburg and Moses Feinstein

Simon Ginzburg (1890–1944) can be characterized as the poet of unabashed romanticism. The din and the fury of the contemporary world do not compel acceptance but they do not incite rebellion. Death, an inconvenient phenomenon, exercises no devastating effect on the essential contentment with life.

Even when Ginzburg seems to rebel against contemporary civilization, he manages to impart an air of tranquillity to his poetry. If favorite expressions point to predilections, then the frequent occurrence of the word "eternity" in the work of Ginzburg must be taken as an indicator of his interests. Artists are "orphans of eternity." The soul of the poet is "a star among thousands of stars." Nature is a refuge of immutable innocence.

I shall go to the grove and search for my soul
In the nets of light and shade.
I'll take sweet counsel with mushrooms and listen
To the murmur of leaves in the glade.
I'll hear the forgotten tale of the wind
And the sailing cloud with the silver oar.
Perhaps I'll discover the soul
Of my innocent youth once more.[195]

Romantic overtones from Bialik's "In the Field" seem to have dominated the poem. And it was not only a debt of admiration but a deep debt of gratitude which prompted the poet to dedicate his book of poems to Bialik.[196]

In his reaction to the American scene Ginzburg also remained an inveterate romantic. Faces of Negroes evoked a sympathetic response in the poet: "We are brothers, bound by invisible ties."[196a] The American landscape attracted him, but he preferred the peacefulness of an Ukrainian village to metropolitan confusion. In his long poem on New York he failed to produce memorable passages. The theme was too alien to his idyllic soul to inspire him with good poetry. The abundance of legendary entities in the poem reeks with artificiality: the genius of the metropolis, the genius of light, the genius of clouds, the genius of thunder fail to infuse poetic vitality into the interminable verses of "New York."

In his love for Jewry, Ginzburg is as naïve as in his attitude to nature.

> God of Israel! Pity your own nation!
> You are his burden, he is your revelation,
> The tree of your own planting!
> You are his burden, he is your revelation.
> For thousands of years he bore your ranting
> To the uttermost ends of the earth without a pause.
> All the crocodiles and all the adders lopped
> Your burning tree wherever it was dropped
> And all the demons whirled upon it with their claws.[197]

This prayer—an attempt to break the shackles of commonplace Zionism and say words of indignation on the fate of Jewry—stands in solitary splendor among his ordinary Zionist poems. But it demonstrates an ability to treat a hackneyed subject with poetic power.

The prayer is Ginzburg's demonstration of hymnal ability; *Love of Hosea*[198] is his demonstration of dramatic ability. In spite of the title, the character of Gomer, the wife of the prophet, is the chief concern of the poet. Hosea moves on an angelic rather than human plane. With uncommon empathy the poet has treated the love affairs of Gomer and traced the factors of heredity and environment which preconditioned her for a debauched life. Her beauty incited the desire of men, her passion threw her into their arms. Already her mother, the daughter of a prince, showed an inclination toward illicit love. Before the birth of Gomer she was driven from the house together with her paramour who eventually became her legitimate husband. Gomer was hardly fifteen when she became enamored of a worker who robbed her of her virginity. When her region was invaded, she fled with her parents to Bethel. The lot of refugees was as precarious in the past as it is today. Gomer found employment as a servant of temple prostitutes. For a brief interval she evaded the trap of fate with a short-lived love for Hosea. But she left him for his evil friend who proved to be the chief misfortune in her checkered career. It was he who took her into his house after her marriage to Hosea and it was he who sold her to her former husband, the prophet, as a withered prostitute.

This profound experience inspired Hosea with the great vision of doom and salvation for Israel. For he realized that his personal vicissitudes represent, in miniature, the fate of his unhappy people. Like Gomer they debauched their innocent charms. Sanation will come to them through rededication to the God of Israel. Amidst the confusion which followed the death of Jeroboam II and which ended with the complete destruction of the kingdom of Israel Hosea regains in the poem, at least, a faithful companion in his wife. Regret and love which marked her later life symbolized the reconstituted people.

Ginzburg followed the biblical source and deprived the long poem of the rich background which was uncovered by archaeology on the site of Samaria. This is not the only deficiency in *Love of Hosea*. In character-drawing he imitated the early Hebrew novelists and poets who divided people into two broad categories: good and evil. Thus Hosea is the incarnation of good and his friend Hildai the symbol of evil. What appears as an even greater fault in the poem is its length. Against these obvious shortcomings it must be pointed out that the *Love of Hosea,* like the biblical plays of Shoham and Sackler, represents a serious attempt in contemporary Hebrew literature to revive or rather to reinterpret biblical Judaism in terms of modern significance. In this twilight age of many gods the twilight of the northern kingdom and the regeneration of the Jews on the eve of doom point to a significant lesson for contemporary humanity.

Not only with unaffected lyrics and the dramatic *Love of Hosea* but also with untiring research into the life and work of Moses Hayyim Luzzatto, Ginzburg enriched the field of Hebrew poetry. He published the biography [199] and the three plays of the Hebrew-Italian poet of the eighteenth century including *Story of Samson*[200] out of a manuscript in the New York Public Library. His critical notes in the edition throw light on obscure passages; the critical introductions help toward a greater understanding of the meaning of the plays. In his edition of the letters of his admired poet[201] and in the poem *Ramhal* [R. Moses Hayyim Luzzatto] *in Akko*[202] he deepened our appreciation of a commanding figure in the history of Hebrew literature. In his translation of Coleridge's "The Rime of the Ancient Mariner," Robinson's *Tristram*[203] and of lyrics of Tennyson, Hood, Byron and Poe he brought to bear English and American influences on his own poetry and on the works of his contemporaries.

Like Simon Ginzburg, Moses Feinstein (1896–1964) learned much from Victorian literature. English poets of the nineteenth century penetrated into the structure, the slow rhythms and figures of speech in his verses. In narrative poetry—in his lines "To Baruch Spinoza,"[204] in his two books *Dream and Fate* and *Abraham Abulafia*[205]—he tried to combine epic with lyric elements. The Spanish mystic who sought to convert Pope Nicolaus III in 1280 fascinated Feinstein throughout his creative life. But he only produced a fragmentary *vita* in poetic form—an account of restless voyages which yield no solution to the mystery of meaning in a meaningless world.

In *Dream and Fate* the amount of poetry is negligible; the prosy account of a sea-voyage from Palestine to America and the meeting of the two chief characters on board ship is the poem. In a long soliloquy, politely interrupted here and there by an interested fellow-passenger, a woman tells the sentimental story of her life as a kindergarden teacher and her marriage to a doctor who was claimed by sudden death. The story is an exercise in cerebration rather than in emotion; it is planned with such thoroughness that it leaves no room for the reader's imagination.

There is poetic boldness in some lines:

> The sealed cups of his soul awakened
> At the touch of her myrrhic palm.

And some lines even combine to form an autonomous poem:

> Inebriated with the wine of the sun the gull
> Flew into the blue vistas of the sky and sea
> And paved his path with white and black vainglory.
> He did not turn his head to strips of beach which melted
> In the mysterious veils. And when the wind

Rose in fury, the gull dream disappeared
In the storm. The dance of death whirled on;
And like a leaden shaft the gull fell into the sea.
Into the gaping gullet of the foam. . .
. . .Is not like this gull's fate
My fate, your fate, everybody's fate?

The song of the gull is better than most lyrical poems in the book of *Songs and Sonnets* which flow with a sleepy tranquillity and delight in calculated equanimity.

Friedland: The Narrative Poet

Hayyim Abraham Friedland (1891-1939) who, during his lifetime was a sporadic guest in the halls of literature, revealed his full talents on the brink of death when he published a volume of poetry and a volume of short stories, and after his death, when his widow published a posthumous volume of his poems.[206] In modest self-appraisal he defined his work as "a meager sheaf of fruits, yieldings of a minor talent."[207] But there is genuine gold in the sheaf and in the unusual gifts of narration.

Such was his story-telling talent in poetry that it shaped the sonnet to its own use and recreated it as a tale in miniature. Change of content in a form which was designed for lyric and philosophic poetry modified the metre. Friedland had to disregard the iambic pentameter, combine the rhyming schemes of Shakespeare and Petrarch and still preserve, somehow, the form of the sonnet. "Man and Book"[208] is a happy example of his narrative aptitude as well as his original metre in a sonnet:

I saw a book of poems in the hands of a man and blessed
The man and the book alike. For he had an uncouth shape.
Broad shoulders, strong muscles and wrinkles on the nape
Told of winds and rains and storms that pressed
On his youth. His hands, shovel-wise and sovereign,
Blushed to hold a volume, pure and frail,
As peasants do at the touch of city girls' pale
Hands, as strong men do in sight of weaker men.
For the man was like a tree whose roots extend
To the bowels of the earth among stones without end
And underneath them, lower, till it clings

To the mother of all living things.
And now in the hour of rest, in the silence of the night,
He bends his head to the poem like the tree-top to heaven's light.

It was not the exotic but the pathetic touch which stamped
Friedland's poetry with vigorous originality. A woman who commits
suicide in order to vanquish the indifference of the beloved, a
discharged gardener who offers his services without hope of
compensation because he feels that his flower-beds will miss him, the
good-natured dog who barks his greetings to every stranger but finds
only misunderstanding—such are the themes of his poetry. In endless
variations Friedland tells about the rebuff of kindness—the main
theme of his narrative poetry.

What is true of the sonnets is also true of the ballads and lyrics.
Titles such as "The Death of the Librarian"[209] and "The
Bookkeeper"[210] indicate the story rather than the reflection, the epic
rather than the lyric element. But excursions into other forms of
poetry did not deflect his attention from the sonnet. Not only did he
find complete satisfaction in the fourteen lines which served Dante
and Petrarch, Shakespeare and Milton as a vehicle of expression but
he extracted, somewhat artificially, a daring figure of speech from its
very narrowness: Was not Palestine itself a sonnet wherein an ancient
people hatched a vision of peace and foisted it upon the entire world?
An almost unconscious feeling of nationalism burst from time to time
into sonnets like "Spain"[211] and "Let Us Light Candles"[212] which
vaunt a proud defiance and suppress the budding anger at the memory
of Jewish martyrs.

In the short stories Friedland did not achieve the originality which
marked the narrative sonnets. Both in form and content they adhere to
the conventional type. In three stories, "With Myriads of People,"[213]
"An Expert from Without"[214] and "Letters,"[215] Friedland attempted to
describe Jewish community life in America. In the first story he
showed the influence of the federation of Jewish philanthropies on
Jewish institutions. The statistician became the *spiritus rector* of all
activities; statistics were the soul of all enterprises. With exquisite
irony Friedland lodged the statistical hero of his story in an insane
asylum.

In "An Expert from Without" Friedland recreated the Bureau of
Jewish Education and the Talmud Torah which derive their financial
assistance from the federation of Jewish philanthropies. The honest
and learned principal has to submit to the humiliating experience of

evaluation by one of his students who, as director of Jewish education in Chicago, receives the invitation to inspect the status of local education from a jeweler who happens to be also a trustee. The fear of the aging principal and the arrogant assurance of the inspector who lacks wisdom and knowledge create a miniature work of art which mirrors cultural frivolities of Jewry in America with stark realism.

But Friedland was also capable of seeing the brighter side of Jewish leadership in the local community and in the country. In "Letters" he depicted a Reform rabbi with sympathetic understanding and endowed him with erudition and gentleness. In the relationship to one of the female congregants who acquired from him some knowledge of Judaism and paid him back with deep admiration the rabbi found that personal happiness which his home failed to give him. When she died in the flower of her youth, she left the tell-tale letters of the rabbi which might have caused a scandal in the community. While the rabbi wavered in indecision about his next step in life, he learned with a mixed feeling of relief and gratitude that she asked to bury a sealed box of letters with her body.

There are too many dead and too many suicides in the prose and poetry of Friedland. In the sonnets the poet attained stature; in the stories he succumbed to realism which was rarely tempered by poetic distortion or enhancement.

Abraham Samuel Schwartz: The Traditionalist

In common with Silkiner and Lisitzky, the patriarchs of Hebrew poetry in the United States, Abraham Samuel Schwartz (1876–1957) did not escape Bialik's influence. From his first appearance in print he never swerved from loyalty to tradition and a concomitant, almost pathetic adherence to accepted patterns of metre and rhyme. This extreme conservatism clipped the flight of his imagination. The poems resemble the pre-impressionistic paintings of brown and red sunsets which have faded in color and appeal. Thus a poem on the Sabbath combines the usual ingredients which go into the making of the day of rest: a soft twilight and tranquil evening, a holy yearning and an atmosphere of modesty.

In the historical poems in general and in "Rabbi Yohanan ben Zakkai"[216] in particular Schwartz followed tradition with unquestioning and uncritical ardor. When the great teacher was carried out of Jerusalem in a casket and requested Yavneh from the Romans in order to build a spiritual center for Jewry, he not only behaved as the talmudic legend prescribed but he also saved Judaism as the traditional historians taught.

With his romantic love for the sunset Schwartz succeeded in creating a memorable lyric:

> In this divine resplendence, among the pines
> That drip with purest gold and show the lines
> Of years, I stand a golden captive in the sun,
> In the magic of the golden setting sun.
> Among the scarlet branches and the ridges
> The sun has hung a thousand golden bridges
> And paved between the world's heart and its own
> Dusty paths with gold dust—all alone.
> In the path of gold to the setting sun
> That celebrates its parting my longing soul must run,
> Kiss in trembling bliss its bright-red wing
> And draw, before it's gone, the gold and sing.[217]

Like "Silver" of Walter de la Mare, Schwartz's poem on the sunset derives its strength and originality from a single word which, in endless variations on the same theme, imparts its elixir of meaning to the individual verses and to the whole poem. In spite of the hackneyed theme, the poem bears the stamp of true inspiration.

In the narrow mold which Schwartz cultivated with fatal persistence he managed to create few lyrics of imperishable beauty. And in "Little Fish" he relinquished the prescribed recipes of thematic choice.

> A little form of life, a point in liquid black,
> The dark sea underneath, the dark sea on its back—
> Who has banned it thus, who has robbed its light
> To live the ephemeral life in the prison of the night,
> To have as its whole world, for its small use,
> A narrow hole in the primeval ooze. . .
> To have as its whole work—perennial motion
> In the mighty and mysterious ocean,
> To have as its whole work—a sinister and stark
> Search for food and dodging of the foe in the dark.[218]

The little creatures of the sea are as important repositories of the mystery of life as the most exalted specimens: That is the message of the poem. In spite or because of his Jewishness, Schwartz seems to stress the universal rather than the ethnic springs of poetry in Hebrew literature. An aspiration to an idealized existence, tinged with ascetism and romantic *Weltschmerz*—this was Halkin's verdict on Schwartz's poetry.[219]

Grossman-Avinoam: First Native Hebrew Writer in America

Reuben Grossman-Avinoam, (1905–) one of the very few native Hebrew writers in America, devoted his talents to the glorification of Israel. But his numerous translations from English and American literature, his numerous sonnets about English poets, his anthologies of English and American poetry in Hebrew, betray his origin. The Victorian Era which was especially dear to his heart points to romantic tendencies in his personality and work. The fine translations of Tennyson's *Enoch Arden* and Zangwill's *Dreamers of the Ghetto*, Thoreau's *Walden* and three Shakespearean tragedies are more than negligible contributions to Hebrew literature; they widen the scope of Anglo-Saxon influences on modern Hebrew writers.

In his own work Grossman-Avinoam surrounds himself with an unruffled, almost anachronistic air of calm. With the exception of the poems dedicated to the memory of his son Noam,[219a] nothing seems to stir his soul from its Chinese peace of mind. Though he speaks of pain and longing, the reader is kept in complete ignorance of the nature of his pain and longing.

> I see no vision of light,
> I sing no songs of gloom.
> I do not shout my joy
> To the sun.
> I do not, at the end of night,
> Fill with prayers of light
> Nor do I overflow
> With feelings of doom.
> I desire but one single thing:
> A holy hour of twilight.[220]

This is a confession which fails to reveal the individuality of the poet. It is escapism which, in a later phase, delights in creating spirits and ghosts in the vein of Ginzburg and Lisitzky.

Of all the forms of poetry Grossman-Avinoam cultivated the idyll with singular predilection. He even wrote an idyll in praise of the idyll.

But he did not escape the danger of excessive narration which turns poetry into prose. Of his entire book of idylls the best is undoubtedly "Who Rejoice in Their Lots":[221] The story of two elderly widows who have come from Poland to Palestine and found complete happiness in the new surroundings. In the other idylls he neither reached the simplicity and warmheartedness of Shimoni nor exploited the artistic potentialities of his own imperturbability.

Aaron Domnitz and Abraham Zevi Halevy: Forgotten Poets

Aaron Domnitz (1884–   ), a resident of the United States, collected his lyrical poems, essays and memorabilia in a slender volume of his writings. The lyrics are old-fashioned, romantic descriptions of natural phenomena and emotional outpourings of individual sorrows. They are influenced by Bialik's diction and Shneour's pose. Bialik's diction permeates the nostalgic poems of childhood like "My Generation,"[222] Shneour's influence envelops "Evening Melodies"[223] where the opening line echoes the opening line of "With the Strains of the Mandoline." Domnitz's stories are Schoffmannesque in brevity though not in quality. His memoirs throw an uncertain light on early beginnings of Hebrew and Yiddish literature in America.

Abraham Solodar (1890-1936) who spent the last decade of his life in the United States, was a genuine lyricist. The posthumous volume of his poems teems with folk-like motifs and deeply felt—though not deeply realized—sentiments. Palestinian place-names abound; the American environment is almost totally absent.

In lyric endowment, in dedication to the younger generation, in love for children, Elhanan Indelman resembles Abraham Solodar. Both are guests in the realm of poetry; both have cultivated pedagogical activities to a much greater extent than literary work.

Abraham Zevi Halevy was the singer of New York, especially lower Manhattan with its concentration of Jewish masses. In contradistinction to Simon Ginzburg, who wished to capture the city in a grandiose poem, Halevy contented himself with lyrical vignettes of the metropolis, its streets and its people in the vicinity of the East River.

In Pursuit of Originality: Gabriel Preil

Gabriel Preil, one of the most original Hebrew poets in America, vaunts deliberate prosiness, festive restraint, an almost autumnal sadness in his work. But precise, realistic imagery imparts poetry to his prosaic utterances. The buried father rises in green metamorphosis from his grave.

> His organs speak the language of herbs and see God
> In the low Lithuanian skies.
> His organs understand the slow gait of winters and the speed of
> [summers
> And listen to the flow of time.[224]

Preil uses metaphor and simile with the caution and economy and sobriety of Robert Frost who has influenced his power of observation and his indulgent humor. He has also drawn on other resources of American literature. As a translator of Sandburg's "Prairie" and an admirer of Whitman's verse, he used blank verse with exclusive abandon.

As an introspective lyricist in pursuit of the poetic fact rather than the artifact, Preil is unique in Hebrew literature. In his proselike idiom he seeks to establish the inner identity of the petty things which are the raw stuff of man's associative powers: a map, a mailbox, a picture of Vincent van Gogh or an original juxtaposition of the desperate colors of the Dutch painter with the Job-like face of a Jew.

> My afternoons froth now
> With desperate colors of van Gogh.
> Sunset drums upon the window pane.
>
> Tomorrow I shall be drawn to the trembling skies of
> [Williamsburg. . .
> Perhaps in the mirror in my room I shall not recognize
> The face of a Job-like Jew anymore.[224a]

It is no mere chance that Preil is attracted to the landscape of New Hampshire and Vermont; the cool sobriety of the northern regions corresponds to his temperament which never ventures into grand flights of pathos.

Only Brandwein who grew up in Israel and Band who was born and educated in America move in a poetical milieu which is reminiscent of Preil's milieu. A deliberate, non-traditional diction suffuses their poetic work. Both have produced formidable critiques of Hebrew literature: Brandwein concentrated on Gnessin and biblical forms of poetry, Band on Agnon. Brandwein also cultivated the short story—particularly the hasidic environments of Jerusalem.[224b] In poetry he concentrated on the short lyric with an avantguardist abandon. Search for the novel expression and skillful use of novel techniques impart an enviable freshness to his all too meager output.

Dramatists, Novelists and Short Story Writers in America

The Hebrew dramatists, novelists and short-story writers in America never forged a novel around a gentile American. Their protagonists were often the Jewish, rarely the gentile immigrants in the early stages of Americanization: the greenhorn or the first-generation American bewildered by his new home. In a later stage they enjoy success in business but they are not compensated for the absence of spiritual elevation: Holidays are almost ordinary workdays, temples resemble social clubs rather than religious meeting places. Worst of all, the children are guided by untutored rabbis whose inadequate knowledge of Judaism is matched by empty rhetoric and safe ideas.

While the theme of the Hebrew novelist was monotonously repetitive, the variations were endless. The talent expanded on that theme ranged from sensitive to senseless, from first-rate to tenth-rate. The short stories which had a century-long European tradition predominated; the novels about American Jewry were few and far between. Two authors managed to transmit fascination and repulsion of the immigrant with superb artistry: Isaac Dov Berkowitz and Harry Sackler.

Isaac Dov Berkowitz (1885–1967), son-in-law of the Yiddish humorist Shalom Aleyhem and his translator into Hebrew, commanded an exemplary Hebrew style. With empathy rooted in centuries of alienation he dwelled on the bafflement of the newcomer in the new land and on his pathetic longing for "the other side." One of his best short stories "Uprooted"[225] involves an old mother transplanted from a poor Lithuanian milieu to her son's spacious apartment in New York. The long voyage from Europe to America by train and ship is seen through the eyes of a woman whose cultural referrent is the Yiddish commenting translation on the Pentateuch. The Babel of tongues, the journey of Jacob's sons to Egypt, the exiles bound and led into captivity by Nebuzaradan, the captain of the guard—these ancient events acquire a new reality from her experience, and her experience, in turn, is enriched by biblical tales. But her son, his Americanized wife and their two children who are totally ignorant of Judaism—these make adjustment difficult if not impossible. Thus the story of the "Uprooted" unrolls as gradual withering of a human being in an inhospitable environment, a living death with a constant prospect of bleak despair.

The story "From Far Away"[226] is the perfect counterpart to "Uprooted." It relates the vicissitudes of a man who lived ten years in America and returned to visit his native town, his wife and his two grown-up children. The primitive environment is a shock: no electricty, no plumbing, no comforts which are taken for granted among the poorest in America. Adjustment is impossible; the man is a failure in America, a greater failure at home. The native's return is a convergence of sentimental or pathetic sorrow. And like "Uprooted" it is an unrelieved tale of woe.

The author of "Uprooted" and "From Far Away" was not a hunter of the macabre. He translated Shalom Aleyham out of choice and not out of necessity. And, in imitation of his father-in-law, he wrote a pathetic and witty monolog: "Greenhorn."[227] In a comedy In Distant Lands[228] he showed an impish love for the older and unadjustable type of Jewish and gentile immigrant.

For most of Berkowitz's immigrants, America is no more than a station or a stopover on the way to the ancestral home of the Jew. The title of his story "America Leaves for the Land of Israel"[229] is emblematic and ironic: American Jewry is on the way to its ancestral homeland. Berkowitz himself left America for Israel at the end of the twenties. Like their author his heroes fail to embrace the American environment.

In Israel the talents of Berkowitz reached their full maturation. In an epistolary novel Menahem Mendel in the Land of Israel[230]—a clever imitation of the styles of Mendele Moker Sefarim and Shalom Aleyhem—he succeeded to depict the corrupt profiteers of Tel Aviv after the First World War; in an excellent short story like "The Driver"[231] he poured out his love for the ancestral land as the car passed through historical sites and the driver chattered on and on in an imitable potpourri of shrewd observations and personal vicissitudes; in his novel The Days of the Messiah[232] he succeeded to transplant a gallery of young and old immigrants from America to Israel and lend a new dignity to their new lives.

Though Berkowitz never struck roots in America, he had a profound influence on Hebrew writers in America. His editorial imprint on the periodicals ha-Toren,[233] which he edited before Brainin and on Miklat (1919–1920) which appeared after the First World War, educated a generation of Hebrew writers during their formative years.

318   EISIG SILBERSCHLAG

In contradistinction to Berkowitz, Harry Sackler (1883-   ) struck deep roots in America. Like Berkowitz he was addicted to the immigrant. In a long novel *Between Earth and Heaven*[234] he traced the history of a family from its departure from Europe through its expectant voyage to its painful years of adjustment in America. Sackler was endowed with a gift which no other writer in America possessed in such abundance and maturity: a historical imagination. It was this gift which served him in his plays, in his novels, in his stories.

In the most characteristically American artifact of Sackler, *Messiah American Style*,[235] the hero Mordecai Emanuel Noah (1785-1851)—journalist, politician, playwright, diplomat, adventurer—acquires Grand Island in the Niagara River and renames it Ararat. This is to be the penultimate resort of the Jews before the ultimate salvation. With this abortive political project Noah becomes a precursor of Herzl. Partly charlatan who manipulates current events to his advantage, partly dreamer who outruns reality and misleads his followers, he is motivated by the distress of his people, by ignorance of Jewish tradition and by a deeply-felt messianism, by a mixture of dilettantism and missionary zeal. In Sackler's play Noah is characterized as a man who lives simultaneously in the land of dreams and in the land of reality. To build a bridge from New York City to Staten Island, to convert the Mikado to the Jewish faith or to settle the Jews in a land of their own—these are the dreams. But to a Noah who has imbibed the heady drink of American freedom, no phantasy is too daring, no impulse impossible. And when a swindling emissary from Palestine arrives to ask for aid and succor to poor Jews in the Holy Land, Noah is ready—not as a philanthropist but as a deliverer:

> I feel that God brought us to this land because here we Jews will learn how to win for ourselves a free life again. Here is the last station of the diaspora, here—the last lesson. . .

The rabbi, the notables of the community are ranged against Noah. But new friends are won: Christians, Jews, and even Black Vulture, an elder of an Indian tribe and an alleged descendant of the Ten Tribes—according to a favorite and exploded theory in the early years of the nineteenth century. But the Jews do not respond to Noah's pseudomessianism. The farcical adventure ends in Noah's marriage to a young lady who believes in him and mothers him and anchors him in a weightier reality.

Messianism—a dominant idea in Jewish history—is the *bête noire* of

Sackler. Since it implies redemption at all cost and since it bears a heavy weight of supernatural intervention, it antagonizes his rationalist attitude to life. Another false Messiah, the half-legendary Joseph della Reyna in the play *Incense to the Nose of Satan*[236] fails in his mission; he is conquered by the very symbol of evil and his helpmate Lilith because he lacks the sacral fire and the childlike innocence of the religious leader. It was not arid historicism that impelled Sackler to seek his heroes—real and imaginary—in the past. It was his sober imagination which needed the challenge of characters who have grown to superhuman dimensions in lore and legend: King Solomon, Honi the Circle-Drawer, Simeon Bar Yohai, Abraham Abulafia, Joseph della Reyna, Solomon Hurwitz, the Seer of Lublin, Mordecai Emanuel Noah.

On a more modest scale Yohanan Twersky (1900–1967), who settled in Israel in 1947, produced a prodigious number of historical stories and novels: a multi-volumed novel *Uriel Acosta*,[237] a novel on the Second Commonwealth, *Height and Depth*,[238] three short stories with seventeenth century backgrounds—"Descartes," "Leibnitz and Spinoza," "Leone de Modena," stories on Saadia, Moses Hayyim Luzzatto, novels on *Ahad Haam*[239] and *Alfred Dreyfus*,[240] stories on "Dr. Herzl," "Rathenau" and "Mordecai Emanuel Noah."

Twersky was the first Hebrew writer to explore and exploit depth-psychology. Freud and Adler were not only his masters; they guided his pen. This addiction to psychologism, coupled with insatiable historicism, made Twersky what he was: a writer who held the interest of his reader through an endless repetition of a successful formula.

In his work on Hasidism, Twersky recreated and reconstructed—out of his own observation and intimate knowledge—the exciting innovations of the founders of the movement and its latter-day epigones. The fictional biography of Hannah Rachel Berbermacher under the title *The Virgin of Ludmir*,[241] the novel on R. Nahman of Bratzlav, *The Heart and the Sword*[242] and the fictionalized autobiography *The Inner Court*[243] bear witness to insightful empathy with a vanishing world.

What Sackler and Twersky have in common is a preoccupation with the inner rather than the outer life. They are both, to use a Riesmanism, inner-directed and tradition-directed. A comparison between Sackler and Twersky, based on two historical characters in their works, would be unjust to both of them: Sackler is an addict to the weighty period, Twersky's style is febrile and quick-moving.

Sackler wrote a short story on Rashi, Twersky—a novel. Sackler wrote a play on Mordecai Emanuel Noah, Twersky—a story. The different genres used by them—play and story and novel—necessitated different techniques and different approaches. Sackler's story about the outstanding medieval commentator is a study in contrasts: Rashi, gentle and modest, speaks to Godfrey de Bouillon on behalf of his people with the authority of learning and spiritual prowess. Godfrey de Bouillon confronts Rashi with the authority of the sword, with the pride of power. Twersky's Rashi, on the other hand, is a skillful reconstruction of a medieval milieu and a medieval hero. Similarly his Mordecai Emanuel Noah is an episode which recreates a nineteenth century adventurer. Sackler's play is a study-in-depth of a false Messiah. That both authors were worlds apart in their portrayal of Hasidism is too obvious to need documentation. Was the preoccupation with history—in America, in Israel—an inability to cope with the present and a feverish search of the past as possible guide or mentor? In the literatures of Europe André Maurois, Lytton Strachey and Emil Ludwig had succeeded in creating a literary hybrid which was neither history nor novel but slick and exciting rendition of a historical period or personage. Twersky was not unaffected by their techniques. But Sackler ransacked bygone ages with conscious calculation; he shored up the shaken present with the firm values of the past.

The hasidic plays *par excellence* were written in our generation by Harry Sackler. Possessed of unique gifts—historical empathy and dramatic imagination—he recreated on a vast canvass Canaanite civilizations and early American civilization, rabbinic and hasidic Jewry. In essay, story and play he attempted to fathom the eternal mystery of Judaism and reconstruct mystics with a certain sobriety which distanced him from them. Like Buber he was fascinated by the personality of Rabbi Jacob Isaac, the Seer of Lublin. Unlike Buber, who devoted a novel to the saintly man, Sackler chose a crucial episode in that life and fashioned it into a playlet in three scenes.[244] The Seer is about to be married to a beautiful girl. But with innate psychological and parapsychological powers of observation, with an incipient talent of penetrating sight he notices her captivating vivaciousness which betrays sexual experience. And he expresses it by implication: "This is my bride. But that other—that shadow. . .There will be no wedding." In spite of the bridegroom's unwillingness there is a wedding with unhappy consequences: divorce, father's shame and rage, the prospective marriage with the young squire of the Manor House. The bridegroom's master, aware of the penetrating sight of the Seer and its awesome possibilities, hopes that the children will not inherit "the terrible and ominous power." His parting words to the man who in turn will be master and saint: "You shall be the first and the last of your line. . ."

Sackler managed to impress dramatic delicacy and intensity on three scenes of extraordinary tension. The natural and the supernatural: they are also delicately balanced in an earlier playlet *Eastward*,[245] a dramatization of events which force the young Rabbi Nahman of Bratzlav to undertake an arduous trip to the Holy Land. Three days of incessant rain had imposed gloom on him and his surroundings. Why the flood when he prayed for dew? The friend who is about to offer a simple explanation of natural phenomena is impatiently interrupted; there are no simple interpretations. Self-incarceration deepens the melancholy of the young saint. The seekers of advice and the sick in need of soothing promises have been turned away. Dialog with a mysterious stranger points to a change of mood and a fateful decision. The wall that rises between him and his Maker indicates a journey to the Wailing Wall: "I have to direct my steps to the top of the mountain which rims the heart of the world." And he leaves his family to the tender mercies of strangers because in reality "there are no strangers in the world." It is incumbent upon him to fulfill the command which was given to Abraham to leave his native land. And when it is pointed out to him that his grandfather, the Baal Shem Tov, had attempted the trip to the Holy Land unsuccessfully, he parries the thrust of the objection with a witty phrase: "Grandfather had no grandfather like my grandfather."

With the art of a watercolorist Sackler painted his gentle playlets on hasidic themes. The more ambitious full-length play *Journey of the Zaddik*[246] is a study in contrasts: the spiritual and the workaday world clash in antithetical antiphony. The choice of a saintly heir by the Zaddik, the struggle of the heir with his instinctual drives, the victory of the powers of holiness over the powers of defilement—these are dramatized with technical skill and with delicate irony. It is an artistic achievement of first rank, perhaps the best hasidic drama of our generation. But it could not compete in popularity with *The Dibbuk* which was written by Solomon Zanvil Rapoport under the pseudonym S. Ansky(1863–1920).[247]

The minor story-tellers, Blank and Markson, Soyer and Damesek contributed slight variations on the theme of the *Shtetl* and some new insights into the soul of the immigrant. Samuel Leb Blank

(1891–1962), the most prolific of these, spent his formative years in Bessarabia. In 1922 he emigrated to the United States, but mentally he never left the land of his youth. In early stories he stressed erotic urges of individuals who cultivated the virgin lands of Bessarabia. In his tetralogy *Sheep, Earth, Inheritance, Settlement*[248] he patterned his hero Boaz after the biblical prototype in the book of *Ruth*. Though not a psychologist of subtle insights he depicted the Jewish peasant and the Jewish shepherd with a sure brush. And he was careful to note the slow-paced life in primitive surroundings in an infinite variety of detail. This thematic novelty stood in sharp contrast to the *Shetl* of his contemporaries. And critics sought to detect influences of Knut Hamsun or William Henry Hudson in his work.[249] But he can be evaluated, with equal justice, in the context of a long idyllic tradition in Hebrew literature—a tradition that originates in the Bible and continues through the ages to the novels of Mapu and the rural vignettes of Tschernichowsky and Shimoni. As a landscape painter Blank has few equals among Hebrew writers in America.

The harsher realities of life after the First World War were not in consonance with Blank's literary equipment. When he attempted to portray the pogroms in his native Ukraine in a novel like *In the Hour of Ravage*[250] or the maladjusted immigrant in America in *Mr. Koonis*[251] or in *Island of Tears*,[252] he veered to melodrama. He was at his best in descriptions of the idyllic life of Bessarabian Jews. In them he achieved freshness and novelty. In dialog and plot he was frequently a clumsy artificer.

In contradistinction to Blank's idyllic stance, Arieli's literary posture is veined with pessimistic bitterness. His stories are stories of disaster, his protagonists sneer at poetic idealizations of life. The only ray of light, the only revelation of beauty in that gloomy universe is woman. Some stories of Arieli reflect the Palestinian milieu with its pioneers and artists and exotic Yemenites in the early decades of the century. But the stories with American backgrounds—especially "How I Became an Antisemite"[253] and "New York"[254]—are invariably and devastatingly critical of the Jewish immigrant and of the communal life. In Arieli's vision a hallow, shallow veneer of oratory and philanthropy covers Judaism in the present. And there is no hope for the future.

The stories of Aaron David Markson (1882–1932), the translator of Mark Twain's *The Prince and the Pauper*, and the stories of Bernard Isaacs, the stories of Abraham Shoer [Soyer] and the stories of

Solomon Damesek are conservative, realistic vignettes of the drabber aspects of Jewish life in eastern Europe and in America.

Markson, sensitive to the niceties of the Hebrew language and to music, made his mark with a very meager output: a few stories and essays which were collected in a volume by his friends. Isaacs traced the metamorphosis of a poor Jewish boy in Poland to a rich manufacturer of orthopedic shoes with compassion, skill and without due regard to the land of limitless opportunities. And by adroit juxtaposition of Vilna and New York, he achieved effects of memorable artistry. Abraham Shoer (1868–1940), the father of the three painters—Isaac, Moses, and Raphael—made a modest contribution to the treasury of Hebrew short stories with a two-volume collection of stories A Passing Generation.[255] It is almost entirely devoted to Jewish life in the old country.

Like Blank, Solomon Damesek (1896–1963) was a prolific writer of sketches and stories, essays and art criticism in Yiddish and in Hebrew. With a Schoffmannesque brevity though not with his insight he reminisced about his native town, Nesvizh, about Lakewood, New Jersey, about his long sojourn in hospitals and convalescent homes, and about his fellow sufferers in the world of the unrecuperative. There was warmth in his writings in spite of the meagerness of endowment.

The stories and novels of Wallenrod present types and individuals in the tradition of Berkowitz: suffering, unadjusted and frequently unadjustable. Their usual milieu: New York with its teeming neighborhoods of lower Manhattan and Brooklyn and the non-plush hostels in the Catskills one or two generations ago. Their occupation and relaxation: the sweat shop and the T-Model Ford. It is the time when Hearst's New York American was at the peak of power and popularity; when a salary of thirty-five dollars a week was a better-than-average salary. It was the time of The New Masses for the pink intellectual and the Saturday Evening Post for the non-intellectual. It was the time of "Yes Sir, She's My Baby" and "Red–Hot Mama." Even the poolroom and the speakeasy cast their furtive shadows on Wallenrod's inventory of the twenties and early thirties.

The protagonists of Wallenrod's novels and stories start at the bottom and never reach the top. They listen to advice; but it comes from people who have not benefited by it: "In America you have to begin from the ground up, you have to suffer a bit and to wait for an opportunity." Thus begins the story "Opportunity" in the collection of stories titled On the Third Floor.[256] And Wallenrod sympathizes with the petty lives which ebb away in colorless monotony. Even their names are drab and dun: Jack and Joe, Sam and Louis, Sylvia and Mary, Millie and Lillian, Helen and Jeannette. The quick and nervous tempo of metropolitan New York is almost audible in Wallenrod's fiction; there is a perpetual rush, a constant whirr of automobiles, a noise of subways, a surging crowd. His people manage to transfer their tensions even to the mountains.

The element of sex—not in the extreme form of the seventies but in the muffled tones of the early decades of the century—dominates the fictive world of Wallenrod. The triangle with the usual complications appears and reappears in endless variations. And man and woman talk on the appetitive rather than on the psychological plane. Though most of Wallenrod's characters are Jews—drifting, aimless, humorless Jews—they are not too aware of their Jewishness. And the non-Jews are not indigenous Yankees; they are Russian immigrants as in Berkowitz's stories; they have not learned English and they have not forgotten their past; their present is too often a nightmare or a mirage.

Like most Hebrew writers in America Wallenrod made a living out of teaching and not out of writing. And education was more than an economic necessity in his life. His thesis on John Dewey which led to a doctorate was veined with reformist zeal. In one of his stories, in "Shelter,"[257] he recreated a pathetic man who has experienced nothing but disillusion in education; he has been a one-time *Haluz* in Israel, a one-time member of the Labor Party, a one-time student of Columbia University and, finally, a Hebrew teacher in an elementary Hebrew school. Even the young and tender love of Beatrice cannot revive him; she leaves him, understandably, and plunges him into his last disillusionment.

Wallenrod was the first Hebrew writer in America who deliberately and almost totally forgot the past: the townlet in Russia, the traditional values, the religious tone and tenor of life. The immigrant in his new milieu: that was the central theme in his fictional oeuvre.

Though he ventured into criticism with *The Literature of Modern Israel*[258] in English, he was more interested in the native American writer. His series of essays on John Dos Passos and Thomas Wolfe and James Farrell can be read as background for his own *education sentimentale.*[259]

Early in his literary career Wallenrod wrote stories about Jews in Russia or in Israel. But they are few in number and not characteristic of his literary output which revolves around the emigrant. Even in a travelog like *Ways and A Way*,[260] a series of touristic impressions in

Europe and in Israel, he carried the memories of American Jews with him. And he sought out his favorite types in Paris, in an American *Kibbutz* or in Tel Aviv. His permanent gift to Hebrew letters in America was his portrayal of the greenhorn in New York in the first three decades of this century.

Representatives of Criticism and Philosophy in America

In critical work Hebrew America showed unusual awareness. The birth and demise of New Criticism in the country, the comparitist achievements of René Wellek and the conservative massiveness of Edmund Wilson, the original theories of Northrop Frye and W. K. Wimsatt, Jr. created a keen interest in criticism. No Hebrew critics can compare with the fertile achievements of their American mentors, but they have confronted literary artifacts with honed tools of analysis and synthesis. Their thematic wealth is a matter of common knowledge and uncommon achievement.

Concentration on Hebrew literature in America was a regional innovation which was practiced by a number of critics: Jacob Kabakoff searched and researched early and contemporary Hebrew writers in America; Abraham Epstein devoted a two-volume monograph to the study of the outstanding Hebrew writers in America; Mikliszansky traced the history of Hebrew literature in America in an extensive volume; Ribalow, in a series of books of essays, wrote enthusiastic appraisals of Hebrew writers in America; Simon Halkin and Simon Ginzburg, Maximon and Ovsay, Max Raisin and Frischberg, Leaf and Orlans, Steiner and Yinnon also devoted some of their criticism to Hebrew literature in America. Almost all of these essayists were helped in their critical work by the original researches and bibliographies of E. R. Malachi. What they shunned—with the exception of Isaiah Rabinovitch and Naphtali Brandwein and Arnold Band—was academic criticism and academic documentation. But what they lacked in scientific precision, they compensated with charged enthusiasm.

Philosophical thinking was represented by three Hebrew writers in America: Simon Rawidowicz, Misha Maisels and Zevi Diesendruck. Simon Rawidowicz who spent the last decade of his life as Professor of Jewish Philosophy at Brandeis University in Waltham, Massachusetts, had made his reputation in Europe with the massive monograph which served as an introduction to the critical edition of Krochmal's *The Guide of the Perplexed of Our Time*. His studies on

Maimonides, Mendelssohn and Feuerbach had earned him recognition; he was regarded as one of the important philosophical thinkers in Hebrew between the two world wars. As co-editor of *ha-Tekufah* in Berlin and editor of *Mezudah* in England he imparted weight and depth to Hebrew letters. Before his death he finished a two-volume study *Babylon and Jerusalem*[261] on the twin aspect of Jewish destiny. Babylonia, symbol of Diaspora, he regarded as the fountainhead of Jewish spirituality; Jerusalem, symbol of independence, as a perennial reminder of political aspirations for redemption. First Commonwealth and Second Commonwealth were for him concepts charged with emotive overtones. The former included the biblical period up to 586 B.C.E.; the latter the period from the Babylonian exile to the present. The First Commonwealth stressed faith; the Second Commonwealth deeds, dedication to oral law, interpretation of the written law; determination to practice that law anywhere in the world, to study it, to understand it; ideal statehood was relegated to a remote period of implementation. According to Rawidowicz the two concepts—First and Second Commonwealth—struggle for supremacy in Jewish life. In the eighteenth century they clashed violently. And they have not been able to harmonize in the last two hundred years. Enlightenment, Reform, Zionism—these are movements with biblical inspiration. But the Third Commonwealth in Israel—will it be dominated by the spirit of the First Commonwealth, the Second Commonwealth, an admixture of the two or by a new concept? Israel tends to aspire to hegemony over Jewry. But Jewry outside Israel resents such pretense at domination. Here is divergence which must be turned to convergence. The Diaspora and the State can serve Jewry through complementary harmonization.

Misha Maisels (1903–   ) also attempted to present a philosophy of Judaism in the two volumes of *Thought and Truth.*[262] In the first volume he surveyed the history of philosophy in the West and interpreted it in terms of will and law. Even the highest human activities—science and religion and art—are products of man's will and ambition to master the universe. And it follows—in the second volume—that also Jewish history must be interpreted in terms of human volition. What is basic, however, to Jewish history alone is the preponderant role of man, his ethical drive and his ethical consciousness. In contradistinction to Greek civilization with its emphasis on esthetics, Judaism stresses the primacy of ethics. This superannuated antithesis can only be excused by the author's lack of sympathy with Hellenism. His ardent Judaism posits a focal point of humanity at its best in prophecy. And prophecy is illumined by the idea of the Divine, the source of spirituality, the "will of wills." It also invests man—particularly Israel—with a mission. The chosenness of Israel implies will to moral duty toward humanity.

After prophetic Judaism Pharisaism dominated Jewish life according to Maisels. In his conception Pharisaism was a deviation from original Judaism; it emphasized study as the prime human activity. But the masses of the people, despised by Pharisaism, were the true keepers of ancient traditions. Throughout the exile they revolted against the exile. The apogee of the revolt was reached in Zionism which has provided possibilities of linkage with early Judaism.

While Rawidowicz and Maisels conceived grand systems of Jewish philosophy, Diesendruck (1890–1940) cultivated the refined philosophical essay. It was not an accident that he was befriended by Schoffmann; both were writers with an original slant. And both edited, briefly, the periodical *Gebulot* in Vienna immediately after the First World War. Most of Diesendruck's work was done before he came to America. In the last decade of his life in the United States he studied Maimonidean problems with his customary acuity and he published results of his studies in English and in German. But his name will be primarily associated with the all too few Hebrew essays. Some of them like "Metaphysics of Leisure" and "The Grotesque"[263] possess a brilliance which age has not dimmed. In his translations of *Phaedrus* and *Crito, Gorgias* and the *Republic,* he showed perceptive empathy for Platonic thinking. The precise, somewhat cumbersome style of Diesendruck was not in disharmony with the Athenian philosopher.

In the field of education and educational psychology, Hebrew writers like Touroff and Scharfstein and, later, Zevulun Ravid, explored modern theories and practices. Scharfstein not only guided the Hebrew writer through the maze of new educational theories but developed in later years an urbane type of feuilleton.

Judaic studies were pursued with commendable assiduity by Hebrew writers in America. Hayyim Tchernowitz, the sage of Odessa, bridged two worlds with his massive contributions: his researches into legal literature—beginning with Joseph Karo and ending with a history of codifiers—were supplemented by his memoirs of Odessa and Zionist essays.

The edition of halakic texts by Mirsky, biblical and post-biblical studies of Feigin and Churgin, Federbusch and Orlan, Rosenthal and Szulwas, the researches in medieval poetry by Israel Davidson and Simon Bernstein, the scholarly essays and books by Rivkind and

Waxman and Birnbaum enhanced the thematic wealth of Hebrew literature in America.

The light-hearted, witty essay boasted few practitioners: Yekuthiel Ginzburg and Abraham Goldberg in the early decades of the century, Abraham Regelson and Daniel Persky in the latter decades. The serious essay and the scholarly monograph encompassed the entire field of Judaism; it was the favorite of numerous Hebrew writers in America.

Hebrew style and diction was geared to high standards which were set by Brainin and Berkowitz. As joint and separate editors of Hebrew monthlies and weeklies in the early decades of this century they set the tone and the standard for their successors. Brainin advocated clarity of thought and universality of subject matter in light and graceful prose which covered a wide range of literary predilections in Hebrew and non-Hebrew literatures; Berkowitz commended addiction to purity of style and its application to modern exigencies. The tradition of excellence in editing was continued by Ribalow who became identified with *ha-Doar* and Tchernowitz who founded the monthly *Bizaron*. They have the distinction of having guided the longest-lived Hebrew periodicals on the American continent.

Amid temptations of vulgarity in the art of writing and kaleidoscopic changes in the other arts, Hebrew literature in America managed to retain a dignity commensurate with its ancient lineage and an oriental flavor inseparable from the Hebrew language. But almost all the writers who created a minor renaissance of Hebrew literature in America are dead. The few who survive here and in Israel are old and past their literary prime. And the young are yet to come. The rigorous logic of events would necessitate a prognosis of demise. But Jewish history is replete with miraculous resurgences of the spirit. And a miraculous resurgence of Hebrew letters in America is not an impossibility.

Notes to *New Approaches to the Study of Hebrew Literature*

1   Shiratenu ha-Zeirah" in the Dvir edition of *Kol Kitbe Bialik* (Tel Aviv, 1956), p. 230.

2   "Ha-Bahur mi-Padua," *ibid.*, pp. 228-229.

3   *Dibre Shalom we-Emet*. A series of four essays in the form of letters to the Jewish communities in the Austrian Empire. For a convenient summary of the first letter in English see Isidore Fishman, *The History of Jewish Education in Central Europe* (London, 1944), pp. 129-130.

4   Joseph Klausner, *Historiyyah Shel ha-Sifrut ha-'Ibrit ha-Hadashah I* (Jerusalem 1929/30). pp. 1-3.

5   See Abraham Shaanan, *ha-Sifrut ha-'Ibrit ha-Hadashah li-Zeramehah I* (Tel Aviv, 1962), pp. 13-19.

6   See Dov Sadan, *'Al Sifrutenu* (Jerusalem, 1949/50), pp. 5-6.

7   Franz Delitzsch, *Zur Geschichte der jüdischen Poesie vom Abschluss der heiligen Schriften Alten Bundes bis auf die neueste Zeit* (Leipzig, 1836), p. 95.

8   Hayyim Nahman Schapiro, *Toledot ha-Sifrut ha-'Ibrit ha-Hadashah* (Tel Aviv, 1939), pp. 43-58. Schapiro's *History* was to be a twelve-volume work. Some manuscript material disappeared with his death in the ghetto of Kovna in 1943. See *Genazim* II ed. B. Karu (Tel Aviv, 1965), pp. 61-62.

9   Baruch Kurzweil, *Bialik u-Tschernichowsky* (Tel Aviv, 1967), p. XIV. He devoted his *Sifrutenu ha-Hadashah-Hemshek O Mahapekah* to his pet theory on the discontinuity in Hebrew literature or rather on the de-Judaization of Hebrew literature. See also his *Ben Hazon le-Ben ha-Absurdi* (Jerusalem-Tel Aviv, 1966), pp. VII-VIII.

Notes to Humanism and Mysticism
1492-1750

1   C.S. Lewis, *English Literature in the Sixteenth Century Excluding Drama* (Oxford, 1954), p.56.

2   Some students of the period speak of a renaissance and renascences. See Erwin Panofsky, *Kenyon Review* VI (Spring, 1944), pp. 201-236.

3   Heinrich Graetz, *Geschichte der Juden IX* (Leipzig, 1891), p. 1.

4   See *Mayene ha-Yeshuah in Abrabanel, Perush 'Al Nebiim u-Ketubim* (Tel Aviv, 1959/60), p. 421.

5   Abrabanel, *Perush 'Al Nebiim Rishonim* (Jerusalem, 1954/55), p. 422.

6   *Shebet Yehudah.* Quotations from the critical edition with notes by Azriel Shohet and with introduction by Fritz Baer (Jerusalem, 1947).

7   See Fritz Baer in his introduction to *Shebet Yehudah*, p.7.

8   *A Jewish Reader* ed. Nahum N. Glatzer (New York, 1946), pp. 204-205. The translation was slightly altered in a few passages. The original of the excerpt in *Shebet Yehudah*, p. 122.

9   *'Emek ha-Baka* (Cracow, 1895), pp. 102-103. The title of the book is based on *Psalms* 84:7.

10   *Ibid.*, p. 100.

11   *De-Be Eliyyahu.* Interestingly, even contemporary Spanish historians —Gaibrois, Luis de Arminan, Felipe Torroba Bernaldo de Quiros, F. Soldevila—sought to justify the edict of expulsion.

12   Jacob Loans, the court-physician of Frederic III, was the first to instruct Reuchlin in Hebrew; Sforno was his second teacher. See Heinrich Graetz, *op. cit.*, IX, pp. 83-85.

13   See Cecil Roth, "Leone de Modena and the Christian Hebraists of his Age" in *Jewish Studies in Memory of Israel Abrahams* (New York, 1927), p. 385. Jews must have helped artists in the renaissance with Hebrew inscriptions which appear in the paintings of Sebastiano del Piomo and the brothers van Eyck, in a woodcut portrayal of Saint Jerome, the translator of the Bible into Latin and in the woodcut illustrations to the allegorical novel *Hyp-*

nerotomachia Poliphili. See Moses Barash, *"Ketobot 'Ibriyyot be-Yezirot ha-Omanut shel ha-Renaissance* in *Scritti in Memoria di Leone Carpi* (Jerusalem, 1967), pp. 141–150.

14   See Giorgio Vasari, *Lives of the Most Eminent Painters, Sculptors and Architects* V tr. by Mrs. Jonathan Foster (London, 1864), p. 249. This hyperbolic statement on Jews' admiration of *Moses* parallels Vasari's estimate of the statue's worth: "Never will any modern work approach the beauty of this statue; nay, one might with equal justice affirm, that of the ancient statues none is equal to this." *Ibid.*, p. 248.

15   Moritz Steinschneider, *Jewish Literature* (Hildesheim, 1967), p. 1. The edition of the English translation is a reproduction of the London edition of 1857.

16   *Orah Hayyim* 307:16.

17   The name is also spelled Hanau—an indication of the German city of the family's provenance. It may be a corruption or derivative of the Hebrew *'Anav* (=modest). See *Iggerot S.D. Luzzatto* (Przemyśl, 1881/2), p. 613. Bologna must have been dear to Samuel's heart for he curses the day he had to leave the city. See his poem beginning with *"Yobad Yom"* in Simon Bernstein, *Mi-Shire Yisrael be-Italiyyah* (Jerusalem 1939), p. 9.

18   See the poem *"Shime'u 'Ammim Kullam,"* *ibid.*, pp. 13-18.

19   *"Telunah 'Al ha-Zeman"* in *Leone Ebreo: Dialoghi d'Amore; Hebräische Gedichte* ed. Carl Gebhardt (Heildelberg, 1919), pp. 3-6; German prose translation *ibid.*, pp. 7-17; the text is also reproduced in S. Bernfeld, *Sefer ha-Dema'ot II* (Berlin, 1924), pp. 262-275.

20   On the confusion of authorship regarding the elegies see *Mi-Paolo ha-Rebi 'i 'Ad Pius ha-Hamishi* ed. Isaiah Sonne (Jerusalem, 1954), pp. 17-18, n.2. The burning of the Talmud in 1554 was not the principal factor in the publication of the *Zohar.* R. Immanuel of Benevento collected manuscripts in the east for the publication of the book which interested Christians in the age of the renaissance. See I. Tishbi, *"ha-Polemos 'Al Sefer ha-Zohar ba-Meah ha-Shesh 'Esreh be-Italiyyah, Perakim* I (Jerusalem 1967/68), p. 182. On R. Immanuel of Benevento, see *ibid.*, pp. 143-148.

21   For poems on these events see: S. Bernfeld, *op. cit.*, III (Berlin, 1926), pp. 52-89; 164-175; 178-184.

22   See Joseph ha-Cohen, *Sefer Dibre ha-Yamim le-Malke Zarfat u-Malke Bet 'Ottoman ha-Togar* ed. David A. Gross (Jerusalem, 1955), p. 79, n.38.

23   *Kol Shire Jacob Frances* ed. Peninah Naveh (Jerusalem, 1969), p. 355.

24   *"Soneh ha-Nashim".*

25   2 *Kings* 11:1.

26   *Kol Shire Jacob Frances*, p. 344.

27   *Ibid.*, p. 346.
28   *Ibid.*, pp. 348-349.

29   *Magen Nashim.* On Jewish misogynous and philogynous poetry in Italy see J. Schirmann, *Ha-Mahaze ha-'Ibri ha-Rishon* (Jerusalem, 1946), pp. 145-148.

30   *Shilte ha-Gibborim.*

31   *Tragicomedia de Calisto y Melibea.* For convenient reference, see *The Celestina—A Novel in Dialogue* translated from the Spanish by Lesley Byrd Simpson (Berkeley and Los Angeles, 1955).

32   See M.D. Cassuto, *"Mi-Shire Yosef ben Shemuel Zarfati: ha-Komediyyah ha-Rishonah be-'Ibrit"* in *Jewish Studies in Memory of George A. Kohut* ed. Salo W. Baron and Alexander Marx, *Hebrew Section* (New York, 1935), p. 123.

33   *Zahut Bedihuta de-Kiddushin.* Edited with notes and introduction under the title *Ha-Mahaze ha-'Ibri ha-Rishon* by J. Schirmann (Jerusalem 1945/46). See note 29. Second edition: Jerusalem, 1965.

34   The play, under the name of *Tofte 'Aruk* was imitated by Jacob Daniel Olmo (1690-1757) who composed a mystery on paradise under the title *'Eden 'Aruk* (1743).

35   *Yesod 'Olam.* It was published with a valuable introduction by Dr. Berliner in 1874.

36   See J. Melkman, *David Franco Mendes* (Jerusalem and Amsterdam, 1951), p. 27.

37   *Asire ha-Tikvah.* On the date of publication see *idem,* p. 28; pp. 129-130, n.44. On plays and performances of plays see J. Schirmann, *Shemuel Romanelli, ha-Meshorer we-ha-Noded* (Jerusalem, 1969), pp. 51-55.

38   In Hebrew: *Azaryah Min ha-Adummim;* in Italian: *Bonaiuto de Rossi.*

39   In Hebrew: *Meor 'Enayim.* Quotations from the edition published in Vienna in 1829.

40   See *The Jews in the Renaissance* (Philadelphia, 1959), p. 321.

41   See *Meor 'Enayim,* pp. 4b-5a. For a slightly different translation see Leo W. Schwarz, *Memoirs of My People* (New York-Toronto, 1943), p. XX.

42   *Meor 'Enayim, p. 10a.*

43   *Ibid.,* p. 10b.

44   See Salo Baron, "Azariah de Rossi's Attitude to Life" (*Weltanschauung*) in *Jewish Studies in Memory of Israel Abrahams* (New York, 1927), p. 12.

45   *Ibid.*

46   See his *Rhetoricum Libri V* (Leyden, 1547), p. 512.

47   See his *Epistolarum Libri III* ed. L. Juhasz (Budapest, 1931), pp. 60-64.

48   *Poetics IX.*

49   *Discorsi.*

50   *Storia d'Italia.*
51   *Mazref la-Kesef.* The title is based on *Proverbs* 17:3; 27:21.

52   *Iggeret Orhot 'Olam.* At the request of the Duke of Ferrara Ercole d'Este I, Farissol wrote a book on his disputations with two monks. It bore the title *Magen Abraham* or *Wikkuah ha-Dat* and it has not been published.

53   *Shebet Yehudah,* p. 90; Baer in his introduction, *ibid.,* p. 16.

54   *Ibid., p. 85.*

55   *Ibid.,* p. 88.

56   See Baer in the introduction, *op. cit.,* pp. 13-15.

57   *Le cento novelle antiche.*

58   *Nathan der Weise.*

59   See Baer in the introduction to *Shebet Yehudah,* p. 15.

60   The English translation of C.H.F. Bialloblotzky is unusable because of its many inadequacies. Already in the title page the translator renders *Dibre ha-Yamim* with *The Words of the Days* instead of *Chronicles.* And this is merely one of many samples of the translator's art.

61   *De-Be Eliyyahu.* A portion of the book was published by Dr. M. Lattes in 1869.

62   *'Emek ha-Baka.* Joseph ha-Cohen subjected the book to the final recension in 1575. An anonymous author added historical material up to the year 1605. See *'Emek ha-Baka* ed. M. Letteris (Cracow, 1895), p. 5.

63   In the original Portuguese, *Consolaçam as Tribulaçoens de Israel.* An English translation by Martin A. Cohen was published by the Jewish Publication Society in 1964.

64   The translation is mine. For the original of the passage see *'Emek ha-Baka,* p.10.

65   *Sefer Peles ha-Shemot.*

66   *La Historia General de las Indias.*

67   For the Hebrew title see note 20.

68   *Shalshelet ha-Kabbalah.* First edition: Venice 1586/7.

69   *Shalshelet ha-Shekarim.*

70   *Shalshelet ha-Kabbalah* (Warsaw, 1889), pp. 65-66.

71   *Ibid.,* p.

72   *Sefer ha-Kabbalah.*

73   *Sefer Zemah David.* First edition: Prague 1592/3.

74   *Pene Yehoshua.*

75   For a slightly different translation see Jacob R. Marcus, *The Jew in the Medieval World–A Source Book* (Cincinnati, 1938), pp. 323-324; for the original, *Sefer Zemah David* (Sudzilkov, 1834), p. 26a; Yehiel Heilprin copied the passage almost verbatim. See his *Sefer Seder ha-Dorot* (Warsaw, 1883), p. 250.

76   See Introduction to the second part of *Sefer Zemah David.*

77   *Sefer Yuhasin ha-Shalem* ed. Herschell Filipowski, Second edition (Frankfurt am Main, 1924), p. 232a.

78   Not five as Waxman maintains in *A History of Jewish Literature II* (New York/London, 1960), p. 466.

79   *Sefer Yuhasin ha-Shalem,* p. 15.

80   In the original: *dulce bellum inexpertis.* On the adage see Margaret Mann Phillips, *The Adages of Erasmus* (Cambridge, 1964), pp. 308-353.

81   *Yeven Mezullah.* An English translation by Abraham J. Mesch, with a preface by Solomon Grayzel, appeared in New York in 1950 under the title *Abyss of Despair.*

82   For a different translation, see *Abyss of Despair,* p. 51. For the original see *Sefer Yewen Mezullah* ed. *Ha-Kibbuz ha-Meuhad* ('En Harod, 1945), pp. 37-38.

83   For a different translation see *Abyss of Despair,* p. 53. For the original see *Sefer* etc. p. 39.

84   For a different translation see *Abyss of Despair,* pp. 110-111. For the original see *Sefer etc.,* p. 83.

85   *Megillat Efah* not *Megillah 'Afah* as in *Jewish Encyclopedia* XI, p. 217. It is easily available in Abraham Kahana, *Sifrut ha-Historiyyah ha-Yisreelit* II (Warsaw 1922/3), pp. 320-325 and S. Bernfeld, *Sefer ha-Dema'ot* III (Berlin, 1926), pp. 133-141.

86   *Dibre Yosef.* Dr. Philip Grossman, the translator of the *Book of Holiness* by Maimonides for the *Yale Judaica Series* worked on a new and complete edition of *Dibre Yosef.* His death in 1964 interrupted completion and subsequent publication. See Leon Nemoy in his review of Gerson Cohen's edition of *Sefer ha-Kabbalah* by Abraham Ibn Daud in *Jewish Social Studies* XXX (January, 1969), p. 51.

87   See *Medieval Jewish Chronicles* ed. Neubauer, p. 121; 124.

88   *Seder ha-Dorot.* First edition: Karlsruhe 1769.

89   For a different translation of the passage, see Jacob R. Marcus, *The Jew in the Medieval World—A Source Book,* pp. 419-420; for the passage in the original: *Sur me-'Ra* (Vilna, 1903), p. 26.

90   See Cecil Roth, "Leone de Modena" in *Jewish Studies in Memory of Israel Abrahams* ed. George Alexander Kohut, p. 384.

91   *Ibid.*

92   See Leone Modena, *Hayye Yehudah* ed. A. Kahana (Kiev, 1911), pp. 64-65. For an English translation of the passage enumerating Modena's occupations, see Leo W. Schwarz, *Memoirs of My People,* p. 83.

93   *Hayye Yehudah,* p. 9; *Genesis 47:9.*

94   Moses Hayyim Luzzatto, the poet and mystic, believed that Modena was

an anti-kabbalist. And he attacked him and his *Ari Nohem* in a special tract *Maamar ha-Wikkuah*.

95   *Kol Sakal.*

96   The original—a transcription of the manuscript which had been copied by Rabbi Moses of Baiersdorf, the son of the author—was published by the well-known scholar, Dr. David Kaufmann, under the title *Die Memoiren der Glückel von Hameln* (Frankfurt am Main, 1896). It was translated into English and edited by Beth-Zion Abrahams under the title *The Life of Glückel of Hameln* (London, 1962).

97   *Die Memoiren*, pp. xxxv-xxxvi; *The Life*, p. xv.

98   *Die Memoiren*, p. 1.

99   *Ibid.* p. 4; *The Life*, p. 2.

100   *Tosefot Yom Tob.* It was the Maharal, the great teacher of Heller, who emphasized the importance of the *Mishnah* in the Jewish curriculum. See Aharon Fritz Kleinberger, *ha-Mahashabah ha-Padgogit Shel Maharal mi-Prag* (Jerusalem, 1962), pp. 136-138.

101   *Megillat Ebah.* The word *Ebah*–enmity is composed of initials of the first four Hebrew words in *Lamentations 1:1.* For an interesting excerpt from the autobiography, see Leo W. Schwarz, *Memoirs of My People*, pp. 68-74.

102   See C. Roth, *The Jews in the Renaissance*, p. 156.

103   The book, *Sefer ha-Bahur*, was published in Rome in 1518. The author deemed it to be a choice book, and choice means *Bahur* in Hebrew; it was designed for all youth: *El Kol Bahur;* the author was known by the surname *Bahur* which also means someone distinguished, adolescent or bachelor (and he was not even a bachelor at that time). The three reasons for the name of the book are given at the end of the author's unpaginated introduction. See *Sefer ha-Bahur* (Prague, 1789). The grammar is divided into four parts, each dealing with verbs, vowels, regular nouns, irregular nouns respectively. Each part is subdivided into thirteen sections in reminiscence of the thirteen articles of Jewish faith. The total number of sections, equaling fifty-two, represents the numerical value of Elijah in Hebrew.

104   The surname is mentioned in 1 *Kings* 17:1; 21:17; 21:28; 2 *Kings* 1:3; 1:8; 9:36.

105   Peretz records another instance of mutual vilification. "We called Shrebreshin Jews *Plachtes* which means lengths of coarse cloth . . . to the citizens of Shrebreshin, we were the Zamosczer *Fressers* (gluttons). J.J. Peretz, *My Memoirs* translated from the Yiddish by Fred Goldberg (New York, 1964), p. 67.

105a   In French: *l'étudiant aventurier.* See David Kaufmann's article on Jacob Mantino, "Une page de l'histoire de la Renaissance," *Revue des Études Juives* XXVII (1893), p. 30.

106   See Gérard E. Weil, *Élie Lévita-Humaniste et Massorète (Leiden, 1963),* p. 42.

107 *Ha-Tishbi,* s.v. *Kabbel.* Also in the same book in explaining *Nabal, Pardes Zaraf, Shaken,* he either professes ignorance of Kabbalah or dismisses it with the curt phrase: I don't deal with these matters.

108 The knowledge of these three languages was the way to perfection. In his dedicatory introduction to the *Book of Remembrance (Sefer Zikronot)* Elijah Levita praises George de Selve, Bishop of Lavour, as a true representative of the new learning: "You have acquired fame through knowledge of the sacred Hebrew language, the rich Greek language and the elegant Latin language in order that you may become perfection itself and, indeed, my Lord, you shine among the sages as the sun among the stars. . ." See Jacob ben Chajim Ibn Adonijah's *Introduction to the Rabbinic Bible. . .and the Massoreth ha-Massoreth of Elias Levita. . .*(Published in 1867 and republished in New York, 1968), pp. 23-24. My translation differs somewhat from the translation in the New York edition.

109 Gérard E. Weil *op. cit.,* p. 321.

110 *Sefer ha-Bakur.* The title is a tantalizing mystery: See note 103.

111 *Pirke Eliyyahu.* It appeared in 1520 in Pesaro; in a bilingual edition—Latin and Hebrew—in 1527 in Basle.

112 *Sefer ha-Harkabah.* In the publication of the book see Gerard E. Weil, *op. cit.,* pp. 96-98.

113 *Masoret ha-Masoret.* First edition: Venice, 1548.

114 *Tub Ta'am.*

115 *Sefer Zikronot.*

116 Its Hebrew title: *Shemot Debarim.*

117 *Ha-Tishbi*–the numerical equivalent of 712. The title is an allusion to the author's name but it has also messianic overtones: Elijah the Tishbite.

118 *Ha-Meturgeman.* In this work as in *ha-Tishbi* the last word to be explicated is *Tishbi.* And both works were issued in two editions: one for Jews and one for Christians with a Latin title and a Latin introduction.

119 Gérard E. Weil, *op. cit.,* pp. 286-343.

120 See Jacob ben Chajim Ibn Adonijah's *Introduction to the Rabbinic Bible. . .and the Massoreth ha-Massoreth of Elias Levita . . .* p. 103. My translation differs somewhat from the translation in the aforementioned book.

121 *Weiber-Loshn* in the Yiddish phrase composed of one German and one Hebrew word. See Gérard E. Weil, *op. cit.,* p. 172.

122 An allusion to *Ecclesiastes* 7:28.

123 *Serefah Lid.*

124 *Pitron Halomot.* In the first edition it is called in Aramaic *Mefasher Halmin.* In the Constantinope edition: *Pitron Halomot u-Mefasher Halmin.* In the edition published by Menasseh ben Israel: *Pitron Halomot.* See Aaron Grünbaum, "*Pitron Halomot: Korot u-Mekorot,*" *Areshet IV* (Jerusalem, 1966), p. 182.

125   *Mikneh Abram.* It was completed by Kalonymos ben David.

126   *'Arugat ha-Bosem.* The title is based on the *Song of Songs* 6:2.

127   *Leket Shoshannim.*

128   On Spinoza the grammarian see the luminous pages of Wolfson, *The Philosophy of Spinoza* I (New York, 1969, First Schocken Paperback Edition), pp. 44; 54-55.

129   *Talmud Leshon 'Ibri.* On the book see J. Klausner, *op. cit*, I, pp. 159-160.

130   This is the contention of S. Eidelberg in his brief article on Luther's distortion of a Maimonidean passage. See his *"Silluf Dibre ha-Rambam be-Sefer mi-Martin Luther,"* Tarbiz XXXVIII² (December, 1958), p. 182.

131   *Or 'Ammim.*

132   See Joseph Almanzi, *Higgayon be-Kinnor* (Vienna, 1839), p. 103.

133   Leo Strauss in his essay "On Abravanel's Philosophical Tendency and Political Teaching" in *Isaak Abravanel* ed. Trend and Loewe (Cambridge, 1937) and Fritz Baer in his essay *"Don Yizhak Abrabanel we-Yahaso El Ba'ayot ha-Historiyyah we-ha-Medinah"* in *Tarbiz* VIII (1937) assessed and endeavored to solve the difficulties each in his own way. For a discussion of their points of view see B. Netanyahu, *Don Isaac Abravanel-Statesman and Philosopher* (Philadelphia, 1968), pp. 150-194.

134   *Numbers* 17:27. For Schwarz's different translation of the passage see his *Memoirs of My People Through A Thousand Years* (New York-Toronto, 1943), p. 47.

135   *Torat Mosheh.*

136   His commentaries on *Psalms, Job, Proverbs* are still in Ms. in the Bodleian.

137   *Mezudat Ziyyon.*

138   *Mezudat David.*

139   *Arba Turim.*

140   *Bet Yosef.*

141   See R.J.Z. Werblowsky, *Joseph Karo–Lawyer and Mystic* (Oxford, 1962), p. 87.

142   Meir Benayahu, *"Hiddushah Shel ha-Semikah bi-Zefat"* in *Yizhak F. Baer Jubilee Volume* (Jerusalem, 1960), p. 252.

143   *Maggid Mesharim.* The words of the title are taken from *Isaiah* 45:19.

144   See R.J.Z. Werblowsky, *op. cit.*, p.2.

145   *Ibid.*, p. 13-14.

146   The quotation is from *Proverbs:* 31:1. For the interesting passage see *Maggid Mesharim* (Vilna, 1857), p. 4a.
147   *Ibid.*, p. 10a.

148   Graetz, *op. cit.*, IX, p. 546.

149   See *Joseph Karo, op. cit.*, 99-121.

150   On the dates of Maharal's birth and death, see Frederic Thieberger, *The Great Rabbi Loew of Prague* (London, 1955),
pp. 12-13.

151   Thieberger, *op. cit.*, p. 21. *Tiferet Yisrael* (Lemberg, 1859), Chapter 56, pp. 71-72 and numerous other passages in the writings of Maharal.

152   See *Seder ha-Dorot*, p. 250.

153   Thieberger, *op. cit.*, p. 100.

154   *Ibid.*, pp. 123-124. The translation has been slightly altered in a few passages.

155   Aharon Fritz Kleinberger, *op. cit.*, p. 80; 148.

156   *Netibot 'Olam.* First edition: 1595.

157   The exact meaning of *Derek Erez* is merely adumbrated in rabbinic sources; it is not clarified in the writings of Maharal. For a discussion of the phrase see Aharon Fritz Kleinberger, *op. cit.*, pp. 103-107, also the last chapter of Maharal's *Netibot 'Olam.*

158   *Golem*, synonymous with fool in Yiddish, is a talmudic expression signifying a lump of lifeless mass. The first man, in rabbinic lore, was allegedly a *Golem* till God breathed life into his nostrils. Raba created a man who was returned to dust by R. Zera (*Sanhedrin* 65b). But *Golem*, in the sense of being created by incantation or magic, does not appear in Hebrew literature before the beginning of the thirteenth century in Eleazar's of Worms commentary on *Sefer Yezirah*. Immanuel of Rome banishes Avicenna to hell because he created an artificial being. See *Mahberot Immanuel ha-Romi* II ed. Dov Yarden (Jerusalem, 1957), p. 515 and an inexact rendition of the passage in *Tophet and Eden* tr. by Hermann Gollancz (London, 1921), p. 200. Men of extraordinary saintliness like Maharal also succeeded to create and animate a body made of clay or wood. Even the Baal Shem Tov and his opponent the Gaon of Vilna were credited with the creation of a *Golem*. In our own day a German and a Yiddish writer subjected the legend of the *Golem* to literary treatment: Gustav Meyrink in a novel *Der Golem* and H. Leivick in a dramatic poem. In English literature Mary Shelley's Frankenstein shares elements with the *Golem* legend. But the classics also knew men created by man: Lucian mentions an Egyptian priest who could create a servant for himself out of a bar of a door or a broom or a pestle. See *Philopseudes ē Apiston* in *Lucian* III, p. 372 (Loeb Classical Library). Popular imagination tended to endow popular men with godlike creativity.

159   *'En Ya'akov.* A bilingual edition in the original Hebrew or Aramaic and in English appeared in New York. The translation by Rabbi S.H. Glick in five volumes went into its third edition in 1919/20-1921/22.

160   *Behinat 'Olam.*
161   *Hobot ha-Lebabot.*

162   See *Tzeenah u-Reenah—A Jewish Commentary On the Book of Exodus* by Norman Gore (New York-Washington-Hollywood, 1965), p. 29. Gore's is a partial translation into English from the original.

163   *Shene Luhot ha-Berit.*

164   For a different translation see *In Time and Eternity* ed. Nahum Norbert Glatzer, pp. 114-115. The original in *Sefer Kab ha-Yashar* (Vilna, 1873), pp. 247-248.

165   *Sefer Kab ha-Yashar*, p. 57. The translation is mine.

166   *Trionfo della Fama.*

167   *Theologia Platonica.*

168   Gershom G. Scholem has proved definitively that Giovanni Pico della Mirandola was the first Christian, of non-Jewish extraction, but not the first Christian to point out affinities between Kabbalah and Christianity. Jewish converts to Christianity have pointed out such alleged affinities already in the thirteenth century. See G. G. Scholem "Zur Geschichte der Anfänge der Christlichen Kabbalah" in *Essays Presented to Leo Baeck on the Occasion of his Eightieth Birthday* (London, 1954), pp. 164 ff. Paul Oskar Kristeller who cited the essay has cautiously asserted that Giovanni Pico della Mirandola was "probably the first Christian scholar to make use of Cabbalistic literature." See *Eight Philosophers of the Italian Renaissance* (Stanford, California, 1964), p. 61.

169   *Princeps Concordiae.*

170   Kaufman's article "Jacob Mantino" in *Revue des Études Juives* XXVII (1893), pp. 30 ff. is still an important source of information on this colorful representative of Jewish humanism in the period of the renaissance.

171   *Minhat Kenaot*—not *Kanaut* as in Cecil Roth's *The History of the Jews of Italy* (Philadelphia, 1946), p. 218. The two words appear in *Numbers* 5:15; 18:25.

172   For a convenient selection of Moses ben Joab's poetry see J. Schirmann, *Mibhar ha-Shirah ha-'Ibrit be-Italiyyah* (Berlin, 1934), pp. 236-240.

173   *Behinat ha-Dat.*

174   See especially Julius Guttman "Elia del Medigo's Verhältnis zu Averroes in seinem *Bechinat ha-Dat*" in *Jewish Studies in Memory of Israel Abrahams* (New York, 1927), pp. 195-208.

175   The title is based on *Exodus* 15:27: "And they came to Elim where there were twelve springs of water and seventy palm trees. . ."

176   *Torah Or.* It appeared in Bologna in 1538.

177   See especially Harry A. Wolfson on the concept of fear (*Yirah*) and love (*Ahabah*) in Judaism from biblical times through the seventeenth century in *Philosophy of Spinoza II*, pp. 275-288.

178   See Kristeller, *op. cit.*, pp. 47-48.
179   The title of the English translation by F. Friedberg-Seely and Jean H.

Barnes is *The Philosophy of Love* (London, 1937). On a thorough list of the translations and editions of the *Dialogues*, see Leone Ebreo, *Dialoghi d'Amore* ed. Carl Gebhardt (Heidelberg, 1929), pp. 111-119.

180   *Il Cortigiano.*

181   In the original the sentence reads as follows: *affetto volontario de l'essere o di havere la cosa stimata buona che manca.*

182   *The Philosophy of Love, p. 12.*

183   *Ibid., p. 13.*

184   *Ibid., p. 16.*

185   *Ibid., p. 24.*

186   *Ibid., p. 31.*

187   *Ibid., p. 50.*

188   *Ibid., p. 64.*

189   *Paradiso XXXIII,* 145: *L'amor che move il sole e l' altre stelle.*

190   G.G. Scholem, *Major Trends in Jewish Mysticism* (Paperback edition, 1967), p. 246.

191   *Idem, "Le-Ahar Gerush Sefarad"* in the Literary Supplement to *Davar,* June 22, 1934.

192   *Tomer Deborah.* The title is based on *Judges* 4:5.

193   On the printing press in Safed see Abraham Meir Habermann, *Toledot ha-Defuse be-Zefat* (Safed, 1962) and Naftali ben Menachem, *"Sheloshah Defuse Zefat Bilti Yedu'im"* in *ha-Zofeh* (October 10, 1969), p. 4.

194   *Mori.*

195   *Lekah Dodi.*

196   See especially Alexander Scheiber and Meir Benayahu, *"Peniyyat Hakme Mizrayim El ha-Radbaz we-Hakme Zefat le-Hashkit Mahaloket she-Parzah bi-Kehillatam* in *Sefunot VI* (Jerusalem, 1962), pp. 125-134.

197   See David Conforte, *Sefer Kore ha-Dorot* (Venice, 1746), p. 40 b.

198   *Pardes Rimmonim.* Of the other printed works of Cordovero these are of special importance: *Elimah Rabbati* (the first word of the title is based on *Exodus* 15:27); *Shi'ur Komah*—on the doctrine of *Sefirot; Or Ne'erav*—an introduction to the Kabbalah; *Sefer Gerushin*—on mystical peregrinations; *Tomer Deborah*—an ethico-mystical manual of conduct.

199   *Elimah Rabbati,* p. 24d. Quoted in the original by Gershom G. Scholem, *op. cit.,* p. 409., n. 19.

200   *Pardes Rimmonim,* p. 55 a. Quoted in *Jewish Encyclopedia X,* p. 371.

201   Rabbi Moses Cordovero, *The Palm Tree of Deborah* tr. by Louis Jacobs (London, 1960), p. 46.

202   *Ibid.,* pp. 47-48. (Slight changes in translation).

203 Solomon Schechter, *Studies in Judaism* II (Philadelphia, 1908), Appendix A, pp. 292-294.

204 *Sefer Gerushin.* It was first published in Venice in 1648 and then republished many times. Last edition: Jerusalem, 1962. See also note 198.

205 The practice of celebrating *Lag be-'Omer*, the thirty-third day of the counting of Omer, developed at a later date. See M. Benayahu, *Hanhagot Mekubble Zefat be-Miron"* in *Sefunot* VI (Jerusalem, 1962), pp. 14-20.

206 *Reshit Hokmah.* First published in Venice in 1578/9. The title is based on *Psalms* 111:10; *Proverbs* 4:7.

207 This attitude has its source in *Psalms* 100:2: Serve the Lord with joy.

208 See Spinoza's *Ethics* and *De Intellectus Emendatione* tr. by A. Boyle with introduction by G. Santayana in Everyman's Library (London, 1934), p. 128. The translation of the sentence has been slightly altered.

209 *Sefer Haredim.* First edition: Venice 1600/01.

210 Hebrew title: *'Asis Rimmonim.*

211 Gershom G. Scholem, *op. cit.*, p. 254.

212 *'Ez Hayyim.* First edition: Koretz 1781/2.

213 *Zimzum.*

214 *Shebirat ha-Kelim.*

215 *Tikkun.*

216 Gershom G. Scholem, *op, cit.*, p. 261.

217 *Ibid.*

218 *Adam Kadmon.*

219 Gershom G. Scholem, *op. cit.*, p. 13.

220 *Bereshit Rabbah* ed. J. Theodor (Berlin, 1912), p. 68.

221 *Kelippot.*

222 Gershom G. Scholem, *op. cit.*, p. 268.

223 *Parzufim.*

224 *Azilut.*

225 *Beriah.*

226 *Yezirah.*

227 *'Asiyyah.*

228 *Kawwanah.*

229 *Yom Kippur Katan.*

230 Solomon Schechter, *Studies in Judaism* II, p. 222.

231 The characterization by Farissol in a lengthy passage on Reubeni in *Iggeret Orhot 'Olam* has been translated by B. Halper, *Post-Biblical Hebrew*

Literature II (Philadelphia, 1921), pp. 230-234.

232   For a different translation see *Masterpieces of Hebrew Literature* ed. Curt Leviant (New York, 1969), p. 514.

233   *Shibhe ha-Ari.* The intricate question of the relationship of *Shibhe ha-Ari* and *Toledot ha-Ari* has been thoroughly discussed by Meir Benayahu, *Sefer Toledot ha-Ari* (Jerusalem, 1967), pp. 79-90. Such was the popularity of *Sefer Toledot ha-Ari* that fifty-nine manuscripts of the book are known to exist. *Ibid.,* p. 125.

234   *Sefer Toledot ha-Ari,* p. 166.

235   *Ibid.,* pp. 188-189.

236   See I. Zinberg, *Di Geshihte fun der Literatur by Idn* IV (Vilna, 1933), p. 341.

237   The poem, part of which was known from the book *Reshit Hokmah* by Elijah de Vidas, has been published *in toto*—with an introduction—from a manuscript, Ginsburg 694, by R.J.Z. Werblowsky. See his *"Tikkun Tefillot le-Rabbi Solomon ha-Levi Alkabez"* in *Sefunot* VI (Jerusalem, 1962), pp. 146-153.

238   *Yah Ribbon 'Olam we-'Olmaya.*

239   See   Aaron Mirsky, *"Shire Naggar u-Bar Naggar"* in *Sefunot* VI, p. 262-263.

240   *Zemirot Yisrael.*

241   Rudolf Otto (1869-1937), the author of the seminal book *Das Heilige,* influenced all major scholars of religion in this century. It is no accident that "his solid grasp of the concept of the holy was first evoked as he heard the chanting of Isaiah's three holies—*Isaiah* 6:3—in a dilapidated Tunisian synagogue. See Edward J. Jurji, "Religious Convergence and the Course of Prejudice," *Journal of the American Academy of Religion* XXXVII (June, 1969), p. 121.

Notes to The Apocalyptic Age

1   See his *Philosophy of Spinoza I*, pp. 17; 245; 314-316. Earlier historians of Hebrew literature have attributed an inordinate influence of kabbalism on Spinoza. The first historian who perceived kabbalistic influences on Spinoza in rightfully limited perspective was Israel Zinberg. See his *Di Geshihte fun der Literatur bei Yidn IV*, p. 411.

2   Aboab memorialized—in litanies and prayers—the fateful events and sufferings of the Jews in Brazil. See M. Kayserling, "Isaac Aboab, the First Jewish Author in America," *Publications of the American Jewish Historical Society V* (New York, 1897), pp. 129-136.

3   The title in Spanish: *Puerta del Cielo*; in Hebrew: *Sha'ar ha-Shamayim*. The book in Latin condensation exercised considerable influence on Christian views of the Kabbalah. See Gershom G. Scholem, *Major Trends in Jewish Mysticism*, p. 258.

4   *Nishmat Hayyim*. First edition: 1651/2.

5   Cecil Roth, *A Life of Menasseh Ben Israel* (Philadelphia, 1934), p. 75.

6   *Peregrinando Quaerimus*.

7   Roth, *op. cit*, pp. 87-88.

8   *Nishmat Hayyim* (Warsaw, 1876), p. 86b.

9   *Piedra Gloriosa o de la Estatua de Nebuchadnesar*.

10   Nishmat Hayyim p. 4a.

11   *Ibid.*, 4a-4b.

12   See *Nishmat Hayyim*, p. 62a. Menasseh ben Israel uses the terms incubus and succubus and adduces rightly—as proof of said copulations—St. Augustine's *The City of God*, Book XV, Chapter 23 and *Zohar* (*Bereshit*, Section 176).

13   *Ibid.*, p. 62b.

14   *Ibid.*, pp. 55-57, 62b, 63b.
15   *Spes Israelis*.

16   *Deuteronomy* 28:64.

17   *Daniel* 12:7.

18   Scholars seemed to detect paranoia or hysteria in the personality of Sabbatai Zevi. But Gershom G. Scholem was the first to pose the well-documented theory that Sabbatai Zevi was a manic-depressive. See his *Major Trends*, p. 209 and especially his book *Sabbatai Zevi* (Tel Aviv 1956/7) pp. 100-110. On dating Sabbatai Zevi's year of birth see *ibid.*, pp. 83-85.

19   The enthusiastic poem by a follower of Sabbatai Zevi in Zinberg, IV, p. 514. For other enthusiastic poems see Scholem, *op. cit.*, p. 113; 116; 261; 405; 445-447 *et al.*

20   See Scholem's *Major Trends.* p. 316.

21   *Księga Słów Pańskich.*

22   *Zizat Nobeł Zevi.* The title of the work was based on *Isaiah* 28:4: And the fading flower of his glorious beauty.

23   The full text was published by Isaiah Tishbi in 1954. Abbreviations appeared in Amsterdam in 1737, in Altona in 1757, in Odessa in 1867.

24   *Zizat Nobel Zevi,* p.1.

25   *Ibid.*, pp. 23-24.

26   *Ibid.*, p. 17.

27   *Ibid.*, p. 48.

28   *Ibid.*, p. 17.

29   *Ibid.*, p. 55.

30   *Ibid.*, pp. 115; 131.

31   *Isaiah* 53:3; 7.

32   *Zizat Nobel Zevi,* pp. 200-201.

33   See Tishbi's analysis of Sasportas's personality in the introduction to *op. cit.*, pp. 16-23.

34   *Ibid.*, p. 47.

35   No less a personage than Moses Zacuto celebrated the double marriage with an epithalamium. See *Kol Shire Jacob Frances* ed. Peninah Naveh, pp. 36–38. And Jacob Frances wrote a sonnet about Moses Zacuto. *Ibid.*, p. 204.

36   *Zevi Muddah* in *Kobez 'Al Yad* (1885), p. 116.

37   *Kol Shire Jacob Frances,* p. 449.

38   *Zevi Muddah,* p. 101.

39   *Kol Shire Jacob Frances,* p. 449.

40   *Ibid.*, p. 450. The second verse is based on *Job* 21:33.

41   *Ibid.*, pp. 195-198.
42   *Sippur Ma'aseh Shabbetai Zevi we-Nathan ha-'Azatfi be-Kizzur.*

43   *Kol Shire Jacob Frances*, p. 441.

44   *Diwan le-Rabbi 'Immanuel ben David Frances* ed. Dr. Simon Bernstein (Tel Aviv, 1932), p. 177.

45   *Ibid.*, p. 180.

46   *Ibid.*,

47   *Ibid.*, p. 184.

48   *Ibid.*, p. 191.

49   *Leshon Limmudim.* The title is based on *Isaiah* 50:4. The context is important for the didactic tendencies of Luzzatto: The Lord God has given me the tongue of them that are taught (*Leshon Limmudim*) that I should know how to sustain with words him that is weary. . .

50   *Ma'aseh Shimshon.* The best edition of Luzzatto's plays: Moshe Hayyim Luzzatto, *Sefer ha-Mahazot* ed. Dr. Simon Ginzburg (Tel Aviv, 1927).

51   Before Luzzatto, Abraham Sabbatai paraphrased psalms; after him and under his influence, Isaac Halevi Satanov composed fifty psalms.

52   *Migdal 'Oz.* The phrase occurs in *Psalms* 61:4; *Proverbs* 18:10; and with a conjunction in *Judges* 9:51.

53   Twenty Italian editions were published by 1602; the number of editions totaled over one hundred in the eighteenth century. The French, German, English, Spanish, Greek, Swedish, Dutch and Polish translations were also very popular. The play was even translated into Latin and several Italian dialects. Luzzatto knew Guarini's play and its better poetic prototype, Tasso's *Aminta* which was performed in 1573. See Walter F. Staton, Jr. and William E. Simeone, *A Critical Edition of Sir Richard Fenshawe's 1647 Translation of Giovanni Battista Guarini's Il Pastor Fido* (Oxford, 1964), pp. IX-X.

54   On Luzzatto's borrowings from Guarini: see Sergio J. Sierra, "The Literary Influence of G.B. Guarini's *Pastor Fido* on M.H. Luzzatto's *Migdal 'Oz*" in *Jewish Quarterly Review L* (January, 1960), pp. 246-255; 319-336.

55   *La-Yesharim Tehillah.*

56   *Mesillat Yesharim.* It was translated into English by Mordecai M. Kaplan.

57   *Yam we-Yabashet.*

58   See J. Melkman, *David Franco Mendes* (Jerusalem and Amsterdam, 1951), p. 23; 126, n. 21.

59   On the relationship between Luzzatto and Mendes see Melkman, *op. cit.*, pp. 30-37.

60   See J. Melkman, *op. cit.*, p. 19.

61   *Gemul 'Atalyah.*

62   *Gioas re di Giuda.*

63   *Ahabat 'Olam.*

64   *Kinnor David.*

65   *Sukkat David.*

66   They should be published—separately and in an edition of Mendes's collected works: the ingathering of books is as necessary—if not as urgent—to the future of Israel as the ingathering of exiles. For many years Bialik urged a massive ingathering—*Kinnus*—of Hebrew classics. His pleas were only partially heeded.

67   *Teshu'at Yisrael bi-Yede Yehudit.*

68   *Kaftor wa-Ferah.* First edition: Basle, 1580/1581.

69   *Discorso circa il stato degl' Ebrei* (Venice, 1638).

70   It is Romanelli's phrase: *"Efraimo Luzzatto, ebraico Petrarca."* See J. Schirmann, *Shemuel Romanelli, Ha-Meshorer we-ha-Noded,* p. 12. On new biographical details which illumine Ephraim Luzzatto's personality see Cecil Roth, *"Kavvim li-Demuto Shel Ephraim ˥Luzzattoˌ,"* in *Sefer J. Schirmann* ed. Shraga Abramson and Aaron Mirsky (Jerusalem, 1970), pp. 363-370.

71   He translated *"La Primavera"* by Metastasio into Hebrew and he wrote a bilingual epitaph in Hebrew and in Italian. See *Ele Bene ha-Ne'urim,* pp. 26-33; 48. For the full title of the book see note 72.

72   *Ele Bene ha-Neu'rim, Yelide ha-Rofe Ephraim Luzzatto be-Nuah 'Alav Ruah ha-Shir bi-Yeme 'Alumav me-Az be-Erez Italiyyah wa-Abihem Hetel Bam wa-Yashlikem El Erez Aheret ka-Yom ha-Zeh we-Hemmah Bokim u-Meshottim be-Huzot London we-Gam Zedah Lo 'Asu Lahem.* The five last words of the title are lifted *in toto* from *Exodus* 12:39. The first edition—limited to one hundred books—was published in London in 1768. The second edition—introduced and prepared by Letteris—appeared in Vienna in 1839. A recent edition with a preface by Fichmann appeared in former Palestine in 1942. Quotations are from the Palestinian edition which is more readily available than others.

73   *Ele Bene ha-Ne'urim* (Tel Aviv, 1942), p. 64.

74   *Ibid.,* p. 88.

75   *Migdal 'Oz,* Act III, Scene I.

76   *"Neged Zehok ha-Karti" in Ele Bene ha-Ne'urim,* p. 93.

77   Half of the collected poems is written in sonnet form. See Isaac Luzzatto, *Toledot Yizhak* ed. D. Eckert and M. Wilensky (Tel Aviv, 1944), pp. 5-68.

78   It appears in the original Italian and in the Hebrew translation in Isaac Luzzatto, *Toledot Yitzhak,* pp. 98-109.

79   *Ibid.,* p. 64.

80   *Ele Bene ha-Ne'urim,* p. 54.

81   *Ibid.,* p. 25.

82   *Ibid.,* p. 65.
83   *Toledot Yizhak,* pp. 121-129.

84   *Ibid.*, p. 133.

85   *Ibid.*, p. 134.

86   '*Ugab Rahel.*

87   See Nahum Slouschz, *The Renascence of Hebrew Literature* (Philadelphia, 1909), p. 84. For an English prose translation by Henrietta Szold, *ibid.* For a verse translation, see Nina Salaman, *Rahel Morpurgo and Contemporary Hebrew Poets in Italy* (London, 1924), p. 47. For an Italian translation of Vittorio Castiglioni, see '*Ugab Rahel*, p. 96.

88   For a panegyric in the form of a sonnet on Moses Hayyim Luzzatto see *Higgayon be-Kinnor*—Almanzi's volume of lyrics (Vienna, 1839), p. 25.

89   The fable "The Wolf and the Fox with the Monkey as Judge" (*Lupus et Vulpis iudice Simio*) appears in Latin and in Hebrew, *ibid.*, pp. 30-31.

90   *Ibid.*, pp. 42-43—in Latin and in Hebrew.

91   *Ibid.*, p. 19.

92   *Ibid.*, pp. 40-44; 44-51.

93   The dates of Romanelli are known with precision: he was born on the 19th day of September 1757 in Mantua, the birthplace of Virgil, and died on the 17th of October 1814 in Casale Monferrato.

94   He may have known as many as twelve languages: Hebrew, Aramaic Arabic, German, Italian, French, English, Spanish, Portuguese, and perhaps Dutch, Polish and Latin. But his philological and etymological knowledge is hazy. And his erudition is more show than reality. On his knowledge of languages, see especially Schirmann, *op. cit.*, pp. 12-15.

95   Its Hebrew title—*Massa ba-'Arab*—is lifted from *Isaiah* 21:13. And though Romanelli uses the word in the Isianic sense of "burden," he also alludes to the similarity of sound which, in a changed spelling, would mean "travel." The popularity of the book is attested by eight editions. See Schirmann, *op. cit.* pp. 73-74.

96   Shemuel Romanelli, *Ketabim Nibharim* ed. J. Schirmann (Jerusalem, 1968), p. 42.

97   The author of "*Sefer Kinat Adonai Zebaot*" (The Book of the Zeal of the Lord of Hosts), first published in 1852, is full of invective against Romanelli and his heterodox life and opinions. See the relevant passages in Schirmann, *op. cit.* pp. 76-77.

98   *Shemuel Romanelli, Ketabim Nibharim*, p. 52.

99   *Ibid.*, p. 125.

100   *Ibid.*, p. 55.

101   *Ibid.*, p. 65.

102   See Schirmann, *Shemuel Romanelli-ha-Meshorer we-ha-Noded*, p. 14.

103   *Ibid.*, pp. 80-82.

104   The Hebrew title—*Ha-Kolot Yehdalun*—is taken from *Exodus* 9:29.

Interestingly the action takes place in Cyprus which is hebraized as the talmudic *Sippori*.

105   Romanelli complains that in the entire Bible he found no equivalents for *Fortuna* and *Constanzia*. An so he translated them *'Osher* (Wealth) and *Hosen* (Force). See S. Romanelli, *Ha-Kolot Yehdalun* (Berlin, 1791), un paginated introduction. It did not occur to the author to explore extrabiblical sources or to coin words for his needs.

106   The title *'Alot ha-Minhah* is based on 1 *Kings* 18:36.

107   Merope was a favorite subject of tragedy from Euripides to Voltaire. In his translation Romanelli hebraized the *dramatis personae* and endowed them with biblical names which approximated the Italianized names. Merope became Merab, Polifonte—Piltai, Equisto—Azgad, Adrasto—Yitran, Euriso—Perez, Ismene—Zilpah, Polidoro—Pildash. The translator even hebraized names of cities: Corinth became Kinneret, Sparta—Sefarad (sic!) and Argos—Erech. See *Merab* ed. Dr. Thomas Aquinas Weikert (Rome, 1903), p. 13. Romanelli's dramatic nomenclature is also interesting: tragedy is *Taaniyyah*, Act—*Helek* or *Dibbur*, scene—*Dibbur* or *Wikkuah*.

108   The translation, a manuscript in the library of the Jewish Theological Seminary in Budapest, has never been published. For a description and discussion of the manuscript, see Schirmann, *op. cit.*, pp. 60-62.

109   On translations from Metastasio see the important article of J. Schirmann on theatre and music in Jewish Italy: *"Ha-Teatron we-ha-Musikah bi-Shekunot ha-Yehudim be-Italiyyah," Ziyyon* XXIX (1964), p. 63, n.3.

Notes to Leaders of Enlightenment:
Mendelssohn and Wessely

1 *Si Dieu n'existait pas, il faudrait l'inventer.*

2 See Frank Manuel, *"Newton As Autocrat of Science," Daedalus* (Summer, 1968), p. 971ff.

3 Arthur Hertzberg, *The French Enlightenment and the Jews* (New York, 1968), p. 313.

4 *Reasons for Naturalizing the Jews in Great Britain and Ireland,* p. 60.

5 Full Title: *Discorso circa il stato de gl'Hebrei in particolar dimoranti nell' inclita Citta di Venetia, di Simone Luzzatto, Rabbino Hebreo. Et e un appendice al Trattato dell' openioni e Dogmi de gl' Hebrei dell' universal non dissonanti, e de Riti loro piu principali.*

6 On the influence of Luzzatto on Toland, see Isaac E. Barzilay's penetrating essay "John Toland's Borrowings from Simone Luzzatto," *Jewish Social Studies* (April, 1969), pp. 75-81. Toland was not the first Englishman to advocate tolerance for Jews. Many Englishmen—Leonard Busher, Joanna and Ebenezer Cartwright and others—preceded him. See Joseph R. Rosenbloom's letter to the editor, *Jewish Social Studies* (October, 1969), p. 359.

7 See the hortatory remark of Rab in *Hagigah* 10a: as soon as man turns from Halakah to Scripture, he no longer has peace.

8 *Lesebuch für jüdische Kinder.* David Friedländer (1750-1834), silk manufacturer, radical reformer and friend of Mendelssohn, was regarded as a "stubborn, passionate, half-crazy individual." See J. Raphael, "Die Zeitschrift des Dr. Leopold Zunz" in *Zeitshrift für die Geschichte der Juden* (1970), p. 36, n.10.

9 *Kohelet Musar* cited in Joseph Klausner, *Historiyyah Shel ha-Sifrut ha-'Ibrit ha-Hadashah I,* (Jerusalem, 1930), p. 43.

10 Among the epistolary treasures of Mendelssohn there is a respectful letter to the English prelate Robert Lowth who established the principle of parallelism in biblical poetry in his *De sacra poesi Hebraeorum praelectiones academicae.* The missive announces Mendelssohn's gift of *Genesis* and *Exodus* to Lowth.

11 In a letter to N.H. Wessely, assigned to August-September 1768, Mendelssohn declared that he originally wanted to write his tract on the immortality of the soul in Hebrew. See Moses Mendelssohn, *Gesammelte Schriften* XVI (Berlin, 1929), p. 119.

12 On Sonnenfels see Jacob Katz, "Judaism and Christianity against the Background of Modern Secularism," *Judaism* (Summer, 1968), p. 302; 308f. Also note 16.

13 *Nathan der Weise.*

14 *Ritualgesetze der Juden.*

15 *Jerusalem oder über religiöse Macht und Judentum.*

16 Mendelssohn was challenged personally and impersonally to defend Judaism as a religion at a time when Christianity was on the defensive and when Jewish converts sought to bolster their adopted religion. Josef von Sonnenfels, for instance, sought a common base for Christianity and Judaism in a religion of reason. This he hoped to accomplish by divesting Christianity of dogma and mysticism, by divesting Judaism of ritual observances. It was this challenge of Sonnenfels which prompted Mendelssohn to write *Jerusalem*. See the fascinating article of J. Katz, *"Le-Mi 'Anah Mendelssohn bi-Yerushalayim Shelo?"* *Ziyyon* XXIX (1964), pp. 116-132.

17 See Max F. Schneider's descriptive booklet of the *Mendelssohn Archiv*, p. 7.

18 *Kol Kitbe Ahad Haam* (Tel Aviv and Jerusalem, 1949), p. 269.

19 The famous poem which is part of the liturgy for *Tish'ah be-Ab* and which begins with the line *Ziyyon ha-lo Tishali bi-Shelom Asirayik.*

20 *Biur.* Mendelssohn wrote the interpretation to part of *Genesis*—from 1 to 6:6—and to *Exodus*. The rest of *Genesis* was interpreted by Solomon Dubno, the tutor of Mendelssohn's children, *Leviticus* by the Hebrew poet Naphtali Herz Wessely, *Numbers* by Aaron Jaroslaus and most of *Deuteronomy* by the educator Herz Homberg. The entire edition of the Pentateuch was designated as *Paths of Peace (Netibot Shalom)* and the Mendelssohnian introduction appeared under the title *Light for the Path (Or le-Netibah)*. A prospectus for the public with samples of the translation and interpretation of the *Pentateuch* and, irrelevantly, a translation of Yehudah Halevi's *Zionide* appeared under the title *Therapeutic Leaves ('Alim li-Terufah)*. On the translation and interpretation of the *Pentateuch*, see Klausner I, *op. cit.*, pp. 52-63.

21 *Philosophische Gespräche.*

22 *Pope ein Metaphysiker!*

23 *An die Freunde Lessings.*

24 *Die Juden.* As for Mendelssohn's reaction to the play and the unfavorable criticism of the play see his letter to Gumpertz in *Juden und Judentum in deutschen Briefen aus drei Jahrhunderten* ed. Franz Kobler (Vienna, 1935), p. 56-57.

25 See his letter to his bride Fromet Gugenheim dated Berlin, June 5, 1761

in Moses Mendelssohn, *Gesammelte Schriften XVI*, p. 12.

26 *Briefe über die Empfindungen.*

27 In a beautiful essay on "Moses Mendelssohn, Leibniz and Spinoza," Professor Alexander Altmann argues that "Spinoza had been his [Mendelssohn's] first thought as a young writer. Spinoza was also his last." See *Studies in Rationalism, Judaism and Universalism in Memory of Leon Roth* ed. Raphael Loewe (London, 1966), p. 39. Lessing, somewhat exaggeratedly, regarded Mendelssohn as a second Spinoza without the latter's "mistakes" (*Irrtümer*). See *Juden und Judentum in deutschen Briefen*, p. 57.

28 In the French original: *un philosophe mauvais catholique supplie un philosophe mauvais protestant de donner le privilège à un philosophe mauvais juif. Il y a trop de philosophie dans tout ceci que la raison ne soit pas du côté de la demande.*

29 Schutzjude.

30 *Phadon.*

31 Über die Evidenz in metaphysischen Wissenschaften.

32 *Morgenstunden oder Vorlesungen über das Daseyn Gottes.*

33 A few admirers of Mendelssohn—Samuel Romanelli among them—linked his name with Moses the Lawgiver and Moses Maimonides the philosopher. See Klausner, *op. cit. I*, p. 274. But it was the Hebrew translator of *Jerusalem* who was responsible for the appelation. See Abraham Dov Ber Gottlober, *Yerushalayim* (Zhitomir, 1867), p. xxx.

34 Isaac Barzilay contends—with a great deal of justification—that the worship of Maimonides was neither a monopoly of the enlightened nor an imitation of the Christian regard for the Jewish philosopher. See his review of Arthur Hertzberg's *The French Enlightenment and the Jews* in *Conservative Judaism XXIII²* (Winter, 1969), pp. 91-92.

35 The term *Wissenschaft des Judentums* has inexact equivalents in other languages: *Hokmat Yisrael* and even *Mada'e ha-Yahadut* in Hebrew, *Études juives* in French, *studi ebraici* or *studi rabbinici* in Italian, "Jewish lore" or "Jewish learning" or "Jewish research" in English where the word "Hebrew" is sometimes used as a substitute for "Jewish." Laymen in France use *science juive* and laymen in English-speaking countries use "science of Judaism" or "Jewish science." The German term was undoubtedly coined by Zunz, but it gradually changed its meaning from systematic research in Judaism as a classical and dead literature to a scientific study of Judaism as a living entity. See Ismar Elbogen, *Ein Jahrhundert Wissenschaft des Judentums* (Berlin, 1922), pp. 5-10; 43.

36 N.H. Wessely, *Shire Tiferet* (Warsaw, 1858), notes to the fifth canto, p. 101.

37 *Emet we-Emunah.*

38 Not Hufeland as in M. Kayserling's *Die jüdische Literatur von Moses Mendelssohn bis auf die Gegenwart* in J. Winter and A. Wünsche, *Die jüdische Literatur III* (Berlin, 1897), p. 893.

39   *Dibre Shalom we-Emet.*
40   *Yen Lebanon.*

Notes to the Pioneering Generations
of the Enlightened: 1783–1832

1   Mendel Stern tried in 1844 to resuscitate the annual and published one volume under the same name. Then I.S. Reggio and I. Busch together published one volume of *Bikkure ha-'Ittim ha-Hadashim*. Neither attempt had a sequel. See Bernhard Wachstein, *Die hebräische Publizistik in Wien* (Vienna, 1930), pp. xxxviii-xxxix, xcix.

2   H. Graetz, *Geschichte der Juden*, 3rd ed. (Leipzig, 1897), X, p. 289.

3   Dates of birth and death of Hebrew writers in the eighteenth and nineteenth centuries offer a hopeless maze of inaccuracies. The paucity of official documents leaves wide room for speculation. Thus Graetz gives 1822 as the date of Löwisohn's death. See his *Geschichte der Juden, 2nd ed., XI*, p. 453. And so does Wachstein, *Die hebräische Publizistik*, p. 202, n.3. But the year 1821 is explicitly mentioned in the epitaph which is reproduced in Ruben Fahn, *Solomon Löwisohn* (Lemberg, 1922), p. 21 and *idem, Pirke Haskalah* (Stanisławów, 1937), p. 68. On the dates of Efrati and Letteris see Joseph Klausner, *Historiyyah Shel ha-Sifrut ha-'Ibrit ha-Hadashah* (Jerusalem, 1930-50), I, p. 169, and II, pp. 366–367.

4   *Melukat Shaul*. First edition: Vienna, 1794.

5   On influences which might have shaped some scenes in *Melukat Shaul*, see Gershon Shaked's introduction to a new edition of the play (Jerusalem, 1968), pp. 17–21.

6   See Shaked's edition, *op. cit.*, p. 75.

7   *Sihah be-'Olam ha-Neshamot*.

8   *Melizat Yeshurun*.

9   *Vom Geiste der hebräischen Poesie*.

10   *Melizat Yeshurun* ed. Jacob Fichmann (Tel Aviv, 1943), p. 9.

11   It appeared in 1865 under the title of *Ben Abuyah* who was a rabbinic renegade in the second century!

12   *Yonah Homiyyah*.
13   *Galle ha-Mayim*.

14   Jewry as an innocent dove is, of course, an old motif in Hebrew poetry. It is based on rabbinic interpretations of biblical verses. Thus, the beginning of the poem by Letteris resembles, in vocabulary and intent, *Song of Songs* 2:14; "O my dove in the clefts of the rock." And the phrase is meant to apply to Jewry hiding from the enemy. Already the Aramaic translation of the verse likens the dove to the Jewish people. And the medieval and renaissance commentators develop the theme—each according to his ingenuity. Letteris, in his first stanza, applies "the clefts of the rock" to the original mountainous home of Jewry and not as Sforno, the teacher of Reuchlin, to the terrains of the diaspora which are mere refuges and hiding places from inimical persecutions.

15   Literary tastes change radically. Luzzatto's *Kinnor Na'im* was held in high esteem by such poets as Meir Halevi Letteris, Micah Joseph Lebensohn and Judah Leb Gordon. And a German scholar of the nineteenth century thought that the book contained seeds for the flowering of a new period of Hebrew poetry: *"Kinnor Na'im enthält die Keime, aus denen eine ganz neue Periode jüdischer Poesie erblühen kann."* See Franz Delitzsch, *Zur Geschichte der jüdischen Poesie vom Abschluss der heiligen Schriften alten Bundes bis auf die neueste Zeit* (Leipzig, 1836), p. 94. For a new interpretation of Samuel David Luzzatto as a poet see Eisig Silberschlag, *"Shedal ha-Meshorer"* in *Bizaron* (October, 1966), pp. 19–26.

16   *Ha-Hemlah.*

17   The poem under the title *"Heshek Shelomoh"* appeared in *Kerem Hemed* IV (1839) pp. 253–256. A panegyric on *Kerem Hemed* was also cast in the six-line-stanza mold. See *Kol Shire Abraham Ber u-Mikah Joseph Lebensohn* (Vilna, 1895), p. 242.

18   See his *Massa Zafon 'Im Ma'aseh Rokeah* (Lemberg, 1848).

19   See his *Nit'e Na'amanim* (Warsaw, 1868), pp. 7–10, 13–18, 20–27, 29–33.

20   See Jacob Eichenbaum, *Ha-Kerab* (Lemberg, 1860). There is an earlier bilingual edition in Hebrew and Russian. It appeared in London in 1840. See William Zeitlin, *Bibliotheca hebraica post-Mendelssohniana* (Leipzig, 1891–1895), p. 75. Eichenbaum may have been inspired by Abraham Ibn Ezra whom he studied and cherished. See *Kerem Hemed* IV (1839), pp. 113–121. A poet with a biting tongue and a self-taught mathematician, Eichenbaum also solved a geometric problem in one of Abraham Ibn Ezra's works, *Yesod Mora*, and incurred the wrath of Samuel David Luzzatto who grappled with the same problem unsuccessfully. See Reuben Goldberg, *"Wikkuah Ben Shedal le-Eichenbaum"* in *Tarbiz* XXXVIII[2] (December, 1968), pp. 175–180. It is interesting to note that Isaac Samuel Reggio (1784–1855) complained about the dearth of writings on chess when he reprinted Abraham Ibn Ezra's poem and furnished it with a scholarly introduction. See *Iggerot Yashar El Ehad mi-Meyuda'av* II (Vienna, 1836), p. 77.

21   Leopold Zunz, *"Etwas zur rabbinischen Literatur,"* *Gesammelte Schriften* I (Berlin, 1875), p. 4.

22   Yet Micah Joseph Lebensohn tells us in his introduction to *Shire Bat Ziyyon* that Zunz persuaded him to abandon foreign themes and devote himself

to Hebraic motifs. There was a close relationship between scholar and poet in the eighteenth and nineteenth centuries. Thus the philosopher Nachman Krochmal befriended the poet Meir Halevi Letteris. And though Zunz may have been the father of the *Wissenschaft des Judentums*, poets were its loyal partners and popularizers. It has not been sufficiently stressed that poets preceded and perhaps stimulated scholars in the choice of important subjects for research. Thus Shalom Cohen's article on liturgy in *Bikkure ha-'Ittim* (1820/21), pp. 38–48 (reprinted from his *Seder ha-'Abodah*) preceded Zunz's massive studies on the subject.

23 The periodical appeared with interruptions in the following years: 1783/84–1796/97, 1808/09–1810/11, 1828/29.

24 Delitzsch, *op. cit.*, p. 101. In spite of his critical exaggerations he correctly estimated that "Hebrew poetry is the most faithful image [*das treueste Abbild*] of the psychological history of that people [the Jews]." *Ibid.*, p. VII. Delitzsch deserves the gratitude of all students of Hebrew literature: he was a pioneer who undertook to write a history of Hebrew poetry from the conclusion of the Bible to his own days at a time when there were few books on the various ages of Hebrew poetry and, for his own period, no bibliographies, no anthologies, no monographs of consequence, no history of the neo-Hebraic language and not even a genre inventory. *Ibid.*, p. V.

25 See his *Essai sur la régénération physique, morale et politique des Juifs* (Metz, 1789), note to p. 262—the last page of the book: "*Ils aideront à la régénération de leur peuple; c'est peut-etre l'aurore d'un beau jour.*"

26 See his *Geschichte der Juden*, 2nd ed., XI, p. 240.

27 *Ha-Shalom.*

28 See Israel Zinberg, *Toledot Sifrut Yisrael* IX (Tel Aviv, 1959), p. 261.

29 See Klausner, *op. cit.*, I, p. 288.

30 *Mahalal Re'a.*

31 Shalom Cohen edited the three volumes of *ha-Meassef* which was published from 1808/09 to 1810/11 and the first three volumes of *Bikkure ha-'Ittim* (1820/21–1822/23) which had a less checkered career than *ha-Meassef*: it expired in 1831/32. The two periodicals are so similar in tone and content that *Bikkure ha-'Ittim must be considered as a repetition of rather than a continuation of ha-Meassef.* See Wachstein, *op. cit.*, p. 15. Wachstein, incidentally, assigns the date of Cohen's birth to the year 1770. *Ibid*, p. 30.

32 *Mishle Agur.*

33 *Matta'e Kedem 'Al Admat Zafon.* So considerable was the influence of Shalom Cohen that the first periodical—really an annual—to appear in Russia in 1841 was called *Pirhe Zafon.* See Joseph Lin, *Die hebräische Presse* (Berlin, 1928), p. 18.

34 *'Amal we-Tirzah.*

35 Klausner, *op. cit.*, I, p. 248. It is not the first play by Cohen. The third and final section of *Matta'e Kedem 'Al Admat Zafon* contains a biblical play under

the title of *Ma'aseh Nabot ha-Yizre'eli*. In a note to the dramatis personae—they are called *Gufim* and not *Nefashot* as they would be in modern Hebrew—the author apologizes because he has invented characters which do not appear in the Bible. He regarded it, apparently, as an act of daring.

36   *Nir David*. It appeared in 1834, not in 1837, as stated erroneously by Graetz, *op. cit.*, 2nd ed., XI, p. 241, n. 3. On the same page, in the same note, there is an erroneous spelling of *Bikkure ha-'Ittim* in Hebrew.

37   *Der Messias*. The augmented edition of *Matta'e Kedem 'Al Admat Zafon* (Żółkiew, 1818), pp. 15–17, contains a poem which amounts to an apotheosis of Wessely. It is, of course, written in the six-line stanza so dear to Wessely.

38   *Shire Tiferet*.

39   *Shir Tiferet*. Since Cohen uses the German *Epopee* for *Shir Tiferet*, it is apparent that the latter had become a technical term: epic. Is it possible that Wessely had already used it in that sense? At the end of the unpaginated introduction to the epic he claims that the term contains the idea of *ha-Gedolot:* the Temple, the miracles, prophecy, Torah are characterized in Scripture as *Tiferet*.

40   See his introduction to the third edition of Shalom Cohen's *'Amal we-Tirzah* (Warsaw, 1861), p. XIX–XX.

41   *Nit'e Na'amanim Minni Erez Kedem ha-Netu'im be-Admat ha-Ma'arav*. The title may also be a reminiscence of Cohen's *Matta'e Kedem 'Al Admat Zafon* though it is obviously based on *Isaiah* 17:10. The phrase *Nit'e Na'amanim* attracted the enlightened—see note 19—who did not and could not, at the time, suspect its strange meaning. *Na'aman* is most probably identical with Adonis. See Yehezkel Kutscher, *Millim we-Toldotehen* (Jerusalem, 1961), pp. 59–61.

42   The two languages were usually Hebrew and German. But Joachim Rosenfeld has two poems "Diogenes" and "Lot's Wife" in Hebrew and French—perhaps because of the dedication to Montefiore and Crémieux in French. See his *Tenubot Sadeh* (Breslau, 1842), pp. 78–79, 88–89. In the seventies of the nineteenth century we find a trilingual poem in Hebrew, German and Hungarian. See Simon Bachrach, *Muzal me-Esh* (Budapest, 1879), pp. 94–95.

43   *Bikkure ha-'Ittim* I (Vienna, 1820/21), p. 4.

44   *Resise Melizah*.

45   Graetz, *op. cit.*, XI, p. 498.

46   This assumption skirts the barren dispute about the relative importance of matter and form. For Matthew Arnold matter is all important; for a French critic like Brunetière form is everything: *C'est la forme qui est tout.*

47   *Hebrat Dorshe Leshon 'Eber*.

48   It appeared in Warsaw in 1857 under the title *Neweh ha-Zedek*. A later translation in hexameters was published in Berlin in 1922/23. In the postscript on p. 115 the translator, S. Ben-Zion, mentioned the earlier translation but he had forgotten the name of the translator.

49 See *Kinnor Na'im* II (Padua, 1879), p. 167. See also S. Spiegel, *"Tashlum ha-Hakdamah le-Sefer Kinnor Na'im le-Shedal"* in *Jewish Studies in Memory of George Alexander Kohut* ed. Salo W. Baron and Alexander Marx, Hebrew section, pp. 132, 140.

50 See the augmented edition of *Matta'e Kedem 'Al Admat Zafon*, p. 14.

51 See his *Tofes Kinnor we-'Ugab* (Vienna, 1860), p. 58.

52 In Hebrew: *Haskamot*. See, for example, Hayyim Joseph Pollack's *Haskamah* in the unpaginated introduction to Pappenheim's *Legend of Four Cups—Aggadat Arba' Kosot* (Vienna, 1863); also *ibid*, Lippman Fuchs's *"El ha-Lashon."*

53 Delitzsch, *op. cit.*, pp. 111–113.

54 *Lehrer der Moral u. hebr. Sprache bey der jüd. Freischule in Berlin.* The famous school existed for forty-eight years—1781–1829—and introduced into its curriculum modern methods of pedagogy, German and French, mathematics and natural sciences, geography and history in addition to Jewish studies. On the place and importance of the school in Jewish education, see Mordechai Eliav, *Ha-Hinnuk ha-Yehudi be-Germaniyyah bi-Yeme ha-Haskalah we-ha-Emanzipaziyyah* (Jerusalem, 1961), pp. 71–79.

55 The original name of the school: *Israelitische Freyschule*. After official recognition and accreditation by the Austrian government it was called *Deutsch-israelitische Hauptschule*. On the school and its curriculum, see especially *Yosef Perl's Yidishe Ksovim* (Vilna, 1937), pp. XXII–XXIII.

56 See Samość, *Resise Melizah*, (Dyhrenfurth, 1821), p. 122.

57 See *idem, Aggudat Shoshannim* (Breslau, 1827), pp. 13–14.

58 *Ha-Hashmonaim.*

59 *Ha-Meassef I* (Königsberg, 1783/84), p. 31.

60 It bore the characteristic title: *Nahal ha-Besor*. The brook Besor in the vicinity of Gaza is mentioned only in I *Samuel* 30:9; 10, 21. Since the root *bsr* means "announce," the name of the biblical brook was unhesitatingly used in the meaning of "announcement," "proclamation." It was immediately understood in its new connotation because thorough familiarity with the biblical text was taken for granted.

61 *Ha-Meassef* I, p. 1.

62 The monolog opens the fifth act of Joseph Efrati's *Melukat Shaul.*

63 See Gottlober, *ha-Nizanim* (Vilna, 1850), pp. 87–88.

64 *Shire Tiferet* I, p. 4 a.

65 *Ibid.*, p. 2 a.

66 *Ibid.*, III, p. 27 b.

67 *Ibid.*, XI, p. 3.

68 N.H. Wessely, *Lebanon* (Amsterdam, 1765), pp. 2 a–2 b.

69   Hebrew title: *Te'udah be-Yisrael.* The poem was reprinted in *Yalkut Ribal* (Warsaw, 1878), p. 86.

70   David Samość, *Resise Melizah,* p. 73.

71   On the irrationalism of rationalists, see Harold Nicolson, *The Age of Reason* (New York, 1961).

72   David Samosc, *Toar ha-Zeman* (Dyhrenfurth, 1821), p. 5.

73   See *Bikkure ha-'Ittim* IV (1823/24), pp. 170–172.

74   *'Alim li-Terufah* (Amsterdam, 1778), pp. 16 b–18 a.

75   Hebrew title: *Behinat 'Olam.* The fragment appeared in Dr. J. Heinemann's *Allgemeines Archiv des Judenthums* I (1842), pp. 286–288.

76   *Non versiones sed eversiones.*

77   *Bikkure ha-'Ittim* VIII (1827/28), pp. 279–280.

78   See Samuel Meisels, *Deutsche Klassiker im Ghetto* (Vienna, 1922), p. 10.

79   *Esther. . .Imitation après celle de Mr.* [sic!] *Jean Racine.* The Hebrew title of the imitation was *Shelom Esther.* It was published in Prague in 1843. The two previous translations of the play were made by Joseph Haltern in 1798 and Solomon Judah Rapoport who published the play under the title *Sheerit Yehudah* in *Bikkure ha-'Ittim* VIII (1827/28), pp. 171–254. Though Haltern actually preceded Rapoport, his translation appeared fourteen years after Rapoport's version. Dr. J. Heinemann received the manuscript from the author and published it in his *Allgemeines Archiv des Judenthums* I, pp. 293–298. Haltern's name, incidentally, has often been misspelled: twice in Zeitlin's *Bibliotheca hebraica*—on p. 234: Holtern; on p. 454: Haltem. In the introduction to Letteris's *Shelom Esther,* p. 11, it is spelled Halern. Klausner seems to have forgotten Haltern's existence altogether. He mentions only two known translations of Racine's *Esther:* Rapoport's and Letteris's. See his *op. cit.,* I, p. 17. For a brief chapter on Haltern, one of the early contributors to *Ha-Meassef,* see A. Shaanan, *'Iyyunim be-Sifrut ha-Haskalah* (Merhavyah, 1952), pp. 27–31.

80   *Goethe's Faust—Eine Tragödie in einer hebräischen Umdichtung.*

The Hebrew title of the translation—*Ben Abuyah*—refers to the well-known apostate sage of the second century. The translation was published in Vienna in 1865.

81   The book, translated by M.E. Stern, appeared in a bilingual edition in Vienna in 1845.

82   See Samuel Meisels, *op. cit.,* p. 9.

83   It was, interestingly, his poem *"Frau Sorge"* which was rendered into Hebrew by Selig Allerhand of Żurawno in Galicia under the title *"Bat ha-Deagah."* See *Kokebe Yizhak* XVIII (1853), pp. 62–63. Worry was a favorite theme in Hebrew poetry. Herder's *"Das Kind der Sorge"* was translated by Eisik Benjacob (1801–1863) in *Bikkure ha-'Ittim* XI (1830/31), pp. 162–163.

84   In his book *Heshbon ha-Nefesh*—the first Hebrew contact with American

literature—Mendel Lefin paraphrased some sections of Benjamin Franklin's *Sayings of Poor Richard;* he also translated the list of thirteen virtues as they appeared in Franklin's autobiography. See Eisig Silberschlag, *"Ha-Gorem ha-Anglosaksi be-Sifrutenu ha-Hadashah: Maga'im Rishonim"* in *Fourth World Congress of Jewish Studies* II (Jerusalem, 1968), pp. 72–74.

85   See *Ha-Meassef* I (1784), pp. 141–142. The translation is reprinted in *Bikkure ha-'Ittim* II (1821/22), pp. 72–73. John Gay (1685–1732), better known as the author of *The Beggar's Opera,* published his *Fables* in 1727. On the merits of the translation see my article, cited in note 84, p. 71f.

86   *Bikkure ha-'Ittim* I (1820/21), pp. 104–106.

87   *Ibid.,* XI (1830/31), pp. 177–178.

88   An interesting fragment of Ovid's *Metamorphoses,* translated from an Italian translation by an earlier Hebrew poet, Sabbato Vita Marini (c.1690–1748), under the title *"Shire ha-Halifot,"* appeared in J. Schirmann's *Mibhar ha-Shirah ha-'Ibrit be-Italiyyah* (Berlin, 1934), pp. 391–394.

89   The title is an imitation of Schiller's *Die Zerstörung von Troja.* See Eisig Silberschlag, "Tschernichowsky and Homer," *Proceedings of the American Academy of Jewish Research* XIV (1944), p. 256, n.7.

90   *Bikkure ha'Ittim* V (1824/25), pp. 38–42.

91   Schlesinger had a weakness for Greek literature. Not only Lucian but also Pythagoras claimed his attention. *Ibid.,* XII (1831/32), pp. 84–111.

92   There is a well-known talmudic dictum: "Why use Syriac in the Land of Israel? Either the holy tongue or the Greek language should be used." *Baba Kamma* 82 b–83 a. Rapoport, the bitter foe of Hasidism, paraphrased thus: Why use Yiddish in Poland? Either the holy tongue or Polish should be used. See *Bikkure ha-'Ittim* VIII (1827/28), p. 11.

93   According to Max Weber the charismatic leader is a sort of superman in the eyes of his followers because of his gifts of grace [charisma] by which "he is set apart from other men and treated as endowed with supernatural, superhuman, or at least specifically exceptional powers or qualities." See Max Weber, *Theory of Social and Economic Organization* tr. by Henderson and Parsons (New York, 1947), p. 358. The German sociologist exercised a powerful influence on political, economic and sociological thinking of the West. His concept of the charismatic leader and charisma colored many tracts in the social sciences. And he defined charisma as "the one great revolutionary force in epochs bound to tradition." *Ibid.,* p. 214.

94   For a rare instance of a positive interest in hasidic proverbs see *Kerem Hemed III (1838),* pp. 191–193. The editor, Samuel Leb Goldenberg, quotes with approval six proverbs of "the great preacher, the famous Maggid of Dubno of blessed memory."

95   A possible exception: an early anti-hasidic tract *Zemir 'Arizim*—one of the most vitriolic vilifications of the new sect. On the tract and on its presumable author see S. Dubnow, *op. cit.,* pp. 127–131; 417–419.

96 See Raphael Mahler, *Der Kampf zwischen Haskalah un Hasidut in Galizie in der ershter Helft fun 19ten Jahrhundert* (New York, 1942), p. 206. The book has been translated from Yiddish by the Hebrew poet Avigdor Hameiri and considerably enlarged by the author. It appeared under the title *Ha-Hasidut we-ha-Haskalah* (Merhavya, 1961).

97 See note 35 in the chapter on Leaders of Enlightenment: Mendelssohn and Wessely.

98 In Hebrew: *Moreh Nebuke ha-Zeman*. All students of Krochmal are indebted to Simon Rawidowicz who published a massive monograph on the philosopher as a preface to his critical edition of the work. See *Kitbe Rabbi Nachman Krochmal* by Simon Rawidowicz, Second Edition (London-Waltham, Massachusetts, 1960/61), pp. 17–225.

99 See Ahad Haam's essay *"Lashon we-Sifrutah"* in *Kol Kitbe Ahad Ha'am* (Tel Aviv-Jerusalem, 1956), p. 96.

100 It is not entirely correct to state—as Barzilay does in his excellent monograph—that Rapoport surpassed Krochmal "as historian and master of the critical method." See Isaac Barzilay, *Shlomo Yehudah Rapoport Shir and his Contemporaries* (Ramat Gan, Israel, 1969), p. 12. Krochmal had no ambitions to pose or let alone to excel as a historian. As for the critical method: for purposes of historiosophy Krochmal's method was rigorous, objective, precise; it compares very favorably with Rapoport's method.

101 See Rapoport's letter to Samuel David Luzzatto in *Iggerot Shir* (Przemyśl, 1885), p. 19; also Weiser's article *"ha-Wikkuah 'Al Rabbi Abraham Ibn Ezra be-Sifrut ha-Haskalah"* in *Sinai* LXI (Iyyar-Tammuz, 5727 [1967]), p. 112.

102 *Ibid.*, p. 115.

103 See Heine's *Werke* VIII ed. Oskar Walzel *et al.*, p. 360.

104 See the epilogue to Moses Hess, *Rom und Jerusalem* (Leipzig, 1899), pp. 110–111: *Die Sprachen derjenigen Völker, aus welchen unsre Civilisation hervorgegangen ist, gehören mindestens zwei primitiven Stämmen an, den indogermanischen und den semitischen. Die antike Cultur der ersteren culminirte in Griechenland, wie jene der Semiten in Judäa. . . ihre grundverschiedenen Lebensanschauungen sind uns in den klassischen Werken der Hellenen und Israeliten überkommen. Wir ersehen daraus, dass die Einen von der Mannigfaltigkeit, die Andern von der Einheit des Lebens ausgingen, dass Jene die Welt als ein ewiges Sein, Diese als ein ewiges Werden auffassten. Dort will der Geist das räumliche Auseinander, hier das zeitliche Nacheinander durchdringen. Im griechischen Geiste spiegelt sich die vollendete Schöpfung, im jüdischen die unsichtbare Arbeit des Werdens, das schöpferische Prinzip, welches im socialen Leben erst seine Werktage anfing als es im Naturleben schon zu seiner Sabbathfeier gelangt war.*

105 *On doit à Athènes la philosophie, les arts, les sciences. . . l'ordre, l'amour du beau et du grand, la morale intellectuelle et calculée. On doit au Judaisme la religion, la morale du coeur. . . l'amour du bon.* See *Ozar*

Nehmad IV (1863), p. 131.

106   On the date of Schorr's birth see Ezra Spicehandler, "Joshua Heschel Schorr: Maskil and Reformist," *Hebrew Union College Annual* XXX (1960), pp. 185–186, n.12.

107   See *Ozar Nehmad* IV (1863), pp. 117–118; 130.

108   *Iggerot Shedal* VIII (Cracow, 1891), p. 1093.

109   *Kerem Hemed* IV (1839), p. 135.

110   See the unpaginated introduction to his *Nit'e Na'amanim Minni Erez Kedem ha-Netu'im be-Admat ha-Ma'arab* (Vienna, 1814). The reader was mercifully spared a second and larger volume which was promised in Berger's introduction and which was to contain "three cantos on the war of Amalek and the giving of the Torah after the manner of the cantos of Ben Issachar [N.H. Wessely]." Berger cannot have referred to his play *Moses and Zipporah* which appeared earlier in *Ha-Meassef* (Altona, 1809/10), pp. 3–9, 79–85, and *Ha-Meassef* (1810), pp. 65–68. The play is listed in the bibliographical work of Abraham Yaari, *Ha-Mahzeh ha-'Ibri ha-Mekori we-ha-Meturgam me-Reshito we-'Ad ha-Yom* (Jerusalem, 1956), p. 34.

111   The title of the poem is *"Hotam Toknit."* It appeared in book form with a few of Moses Mendelssohn's letters in Vienna in 1797. On the author see Zeitlin, *Bibliotheca hebraica*, p. 200. Graetz has uncomplimentary things to say about Levi. See his *Geschichte der Juden* XI² p. 586.

112   These cardinal theses are developed with a wealth of illustrations in the work of Thorleif Boman, *Das hebräische Denken im Vergleich mit dem Griechischen*, Second edition, (Göttingen, 1954). They were subjected to a scathing criticism by Albright in his *New Horizons in Biblical Research* (London-New York-Toronto, 1966), pp. 18–19.

113   See William Barrett, *Irrational Man* (New York, 1958), p. 68.

114   For another summation of the contrast between Greek and Hebrew thought see James Barr, *The Semantics of Biblical Language* (London, 1961), pp. 8–20.

Notes to Flowering of Enlightment
In Eastern Europe

1 Under the Hebrew title *Te'udah be-Yisrael:* it first appeared in Vilna, 1827/28.

2 In Hebrew: *Bet Yehudah.* First Edition: Vilna, 1839.

3 See his tract *Efes Damim* which appeared in Vilna in 1836/37 and which was translated by Dr. L. Loewe under a detailed and descriptive title: *A Series of Conversations at Jerusalem between a Patriarch of the Greek Church and a Chief Rabbi of the Jews Concerning the Malicious Charge Against the Jews of Using Christian Blood* (London, 1841).

4 Mordecai Aaron Günzburg, *Abiezer* (Vilna, 1863), pp. 67–86.

5 Hebrew title: *Hatot Ne'urim.* First edition: Vilna, 1876.

6 The first issue of *Razsvet* appeared on May 27, 1860, the last on May 19, 1861. Fifty-two issues were published altogether. Yet the impact of *Razsvet* on the Jewish *intelligentsia* in Russia was vast and far-reaching. Hebrew writers of note like Judah Leb Gordon, historians like M. Jost and non-Jews like Professor Alexander Georgievsky contributed to the periodical. On *Razsvet,* see the excellent article by Moshe Perlmann, "Razsvet 1860–1861: The Origins of the Russian Press," *Jewish Social Studies* (July, 1962), pp. 162–182.

7 Hebrew title: *Tiferet li-Bene Binah* (Zhitomir, 1867).

8 Klausner, *op. cit.*, III, p. 247.

9 *Ibid.*, p. 210.

10 See chapter on The Pioneering Generations of the Enlightened, n. 89.

11 Hebrew title: *Shire Bat Ziyyon.* First edition: Vilna, 1868/1869.

12 Hebrew title: *Nikmat Shimshon.*

13 Hebrew title: *Ya'el we-Sisera.*

14 Hebrew title: *Mosheh 'Al Har ha-'Abarim.*

15 Hebrew title: *El ha-Kokabim.*

16 Klausner III, *op. cit.*, p. 287.

17   *Idem, op. cit.,* IV, pp. 366–367.

18   Hebrew title: *Zidkiyyahu be-Bet ha-Pekudot.*

19   Hebrew title: *Ben Shinne Arayot.*

20   Hebrew title: *Bi-Mezulot Yam.*

21   See Eisig Silberschlag, *Saul Tschernichowsky: Poet of Revolt* (Ithaca, New York, 1968), pp. 37–38.

22   Hebrew title: *Kozo Shel Yod.*

23   Hebrew title: *Shomeret Yabam.*

24   Hebrew title: *Ashaka de-Rispak.*

25   Hebrew title: *We-Samakta be-Hageka.*

26   Hebrew title: *Le-Mi Ani 'Amel.*

27   *'Ebed La-'Ibrit Anoki la-Nezah.*

28   Hebrew title of the poem: *'Eder Adonai.*

29   See *Iggerot Yehudah Leb Gordon* II³ (Warsaw, 1894), p. 4.

30   *Ibid.,* pp. 246–248.

31   The thesis was published by the Jewish Publication Society. See Abraham Benedict Rhine, *Leon Gordon—An Appreciation* (Philadelphia, 1910).

32   Hebrew title: *Mishle Yehudah.*

33   Hebrew title: *'Al Nehar Kebar.* The autobiography is a tetrapartite affair: 1. *'Al Nehar Kebar*—An account of the early years and of a visit to Berlin. 2. An Account of Gordon's imprisonment and exile in 1879—in Russian. 3. Memoirs of twenty years—1861–1882—in Russian. 4. A diary of the last year of his life in Hebrew under the title: *Debar Yom be-Yomo.* All parts—the Russian in the Hebrew translation of M.Z. Wolfovsky—appeared in *Kol Kitbe J.L. Gordon* I (Tel Aviv, 1928).

34   *Ibid.,* p. 51.

35   *Ibid.,* p. 117. According to one of his letters, written immediately after the banquet, there were sixty guests and six comprehending readers. See *Iggerot Yehudah Leb Gordon* II³, p. 7.

Notes to Interpretations and Reinterpretations of Hasidism

1   *Zaddik*—just, righteous in biblical Hebrew. In hasidic lore he is mediator between God and man; he is endowed with a special spirituality which enables him to see God when He is concealed from others. See *Toledot Ya'akov Yosef*, (Jerusalem edition, 1961/62), p.23. The Zaddik influences life on our planet and beyond our planet; he is a miracle-man and the embodiment of wisdom. Buber who correctly equates Zaddikim with the righteous adds that the term actually means "those who stood the test or the proven." See his *Tales of the Hasidim* (New York, 1947), p. 1. This is a leap into bold hypothetism. For a detailed discussion of the qualities of the Zaddik as reflected in the primary source of Hasidism—the writings of Rabbi Jacob of Polnoye, see the monograph on *The Zaddik* by Samuel H. Dresner (London-New York-Toronto, 1960), chapters V-IX. For the Zaddik in the writings of Elimelech of Lizensk, see Rivkah Shatz, *Le-Mahuto Shel ha-Zaddik ba-Hasidut, Molad 144-145* (1960), pp. 365-378.

2   See V.S. Pritchett's review of books by Singer and Wiesel in *The New York Review of Books* (May 7, 1970), p. 15.

3   This meaning s.v. *Hesed* II in Koehler and Baumgartner's *Hebräisches und Aramäisches Lexikon zum Alten Testament*, Third edition, with the participation of Hartmann and Kutscher (Leiden, 1967), p. 323. It is a better English equivalent than the vague *lovingkindness* in the biblical translations. On recent studies of *Hesed*, see Gerald A. Larue in his preface to Nelson Glueck's study of *Hesed in the Bible* tr. by Alfred Gottschalk (Cincinnati, 1967), pp. 1-32. The study by Glueck first appeared in 1927 as a published doctoral dissertation under the title *Das Wort hesed im alttestamentlichen Sprachgebrauche als menschliche und göttliche gemeinschaftsgemässe Verhaltungsweise.* Buber equates Hasidim with "The devout or more accurately those who keep faith with the covenant. See his *Tales of the Hasidim*, p. 2. The qualifying phrase "more accurately etc." is an unfounded assumption.

4   In a special unrelated meaning *revile* the verbal root appears in *Proverbs* 25:10; twice in identical meaning: *show yourself loyal* in 2 *Samuel* 22:26 and in *Psalms* 18:26.

5   In Greek: 'Ασιδαῖοι or συναγωγὴ 'Ασιδαίων

1 *Maccabees* 2:42; 7:13; 2 *Maccabees* 14:6. Apparently the Greek had no equivalent term.

6 Y. *Sotah IX,* 24 *et al.*

7 On Hillel as Hasid see Adolph Büchler, *Types of Palestinian-Jewish Piety From 70* B.C.E. *to 70* C.E. (London, 1922), p. 15-22; 25-26. The book was reprinted by Ktav Publishing Company (New York, 1968).

8 *Abot* 2:6. The treatise *Abot* discusses the Hasid on numerous occasions. Thus 5:13: He who says what is mine is yours and what is yours is yours is a *Hasid.* A few other interesting sayings concerning the *Hasid, ibid.,* 5:14; 5:16; 5:17.

9 *Tosefta, Sanhedrin* 13.

10 *Anshe Ma'aseh.* On the meaning of the term see Büchler, *op. cit.,* pp. 83-87.

11 The designation: *Hasidim Rishonim.* See Büchler, *op. cit.,* pp. 106-108. On the dates of these early *Hasidim, ibid.,* p. 78.

12 *Hasidut* in Hebrew.

13 *Sotah* 9:15.

14 *Sefer Hasidim.* A convenient and critical (second) edition by Jehuda Wistinetzki (Frankfurt, 1924). On the authorship, see J. Freimann's introduction to *Sefer Hasidim,* pp. 13-14.

15 On the development of mysticism among German Hasidim, see the first chapter of Joseph Dan's book *Torat ha-Sod Shel Hasidut Ashkenaz* (Jerusalem, 1968) pp. 9-45.

16 *Sefer Hasidim,* Section 1, p.1.

17 See his *Israel and Diaspora* (Philadelphia, 1969), p. 90.

18 *Levitcus* 19:1.

19 Literally: people of the land, rural population. In this sense it is used in the Bible, e.g. 2 *Kings* 24:14; in rabbinic literature: vulgarian, ignoramus, especially a person ignorant of Jewish law and lore. In that sense—and not in the Biblical sense—it is used today.

20 Literally: disciple of the wise. It denotes a scholarly person, well versed in Jewish law; and it is used as an antithesis to 'Am ha-Arez.

21 See, for instance, *Sefer Shibhe ha-Besht* ed. S.A. Horodetzky (Berlin, 1922), p. 25. Also *The Autobiography of Solomon Maimon* tr. by J. Clark Murray (London, 1954), pp. 81-84.

22 *Major Trends in Jewish Mysticism,* pp. 330-334. See also J.G. Weiss, "A Circle of Pneumatics in Pre-Hasidism," *The Journal of Jewish Studies* VIII[3]—[4] (1957), pp. 199-213.

23 See also the significant story in *Shibhe ha-Besht* ed. S.A. Horodetzky, pp. 124-125; in English: *In Praise of the Baal Shem Tov* tr. and ed. by Dan Ben-Amos and Jerome R. Mintz (Bloomingdale, Indiana—London, 1970), pp.

86-87. The Besht may have had scholarly ambitions: he claimed to have been a reincarnation of Saadiah. *Ibid.*, p. 106.

24   Apotropaic terminology is attested in the Gilgamesh epic and in the Bible. See Patrick D. Miller, "Apotropaic Imagery in Proverbs 6:20-22, *Journal of Near Eastern Studies* XXXIX (April, 1970) pp. 129-130.

25   *The Autobiography of Solomon Maimon*, p. 170.

26   *Ibid.*, p. 105.

27   *Abot* 1:5. The sages also stressed the connection between women and witchcraft. *Ibid.*, 2:7. For a spicy story, see *Shibhe ha-Besht*, pp. 163-164. In translation, *op, cit.*, p. 248.

28   *Hitpashtut ha-Gashmiyyut* in Hebrew.

29   *Sefer Likkute Maharan* (Ostraha, [Ostrog], 1820/21), p. 11 b.

30   Dobh Baer of Lubavitch, *Tract on Ecstasy* tr. from the Hebrew with an introduction and notes by Louis Jacobs (London, 1963), p. 48.

31   *Debekut* in Hebrew.

32   *Kawwanah* in Hebrew.

33   Martin Buber, *On Judaism* ed. Nahum N. Glatzer (New York, 1967), p. 92. See also J.G. Weiss, "The Kavvanoth of Prayer in Early Hasidism," *The Journal of Jewish Studies* IX (1958), pp. 163-192.

34   See *The Autobiography*, p. 166.

35   *Ibid.*, p. 167. On joy in Hasidism see A. Schochat, '*Al ha-Simhah ba-Hasidut, Ziyyon* XVI (1950/51), pp. 30-43. The author rightly refers to the verse which was constantly on the lips of the Hasidim: Worship God in joy (*Psalms* 100:2). And he traces the development of worship through joy in the writings of Cordovero, Luria and the moralistic literature of Jewry in the seventeenth century.

36   *Ibid.*, p. 172.

37   *Kol Kitbe Yehudah Steinberg* (Odessa 1912/13), IV, p. 163.

38   There is a well-known adage: The Holy One, blessed be He, the Law and Israel are one. Though it does not appear in the *Zohar*, it is derived from that book which maintains there are three levels tied to each other: The Holy One Blessed be He, the Law and Israel. (*Zohar* 3, 73). On the distinction between the two adages see Gershom G. Scholem, "*Demuto ha-Historit Shel R. Yisrael Baal Shem Tov, Molad* 144-145 (1960), p. 354. The article presents the best evaluation of the historical Baal Shem Tov as distinguished from the imaginary persona.

39   Quoted by Martin Buber, *On Judaism*, p. 81.

40   *Ibid.*, p. 93.

41   Hasidic music and Hasidic songs and Hasidic melodies with their multiple borrowings from Slav peoples still await the labors of musicologists in combination with Jewish scholars.

42   It is possible that, even before their publication, writings of Moses Hayyim Luzzatto influenced the mystical trends of Hasidism. See I. Tishbi, *"Darke Hafazatam Shel Kitbe Kabbalah Le-Ramhal be-Polin u-be-Lita,"* Kiryat Sefer XLV (December, 1969), p. 154.

43   Martin Buber, *For the Sake of Heaven* tr. by Ludwig Lewisohn (Philadelphia, 1945), p. 4.

44   *Ibid.*, p. 5.

45   *Gammatria*, among other connotations, can be defined to mean "the use of letters for their numerical value; homiletic interpretation based on the numerical value of letters." See Marcus Jastrow, *Dictionary* s.v. The pseudo-science, perhaps of Ionian origin, was practiced by Jews since Hellenistic times. See the interesting remarks and recent bibliography on *Gammatria* in S. Gervitz's article "Abram's 318," *Israel Exploration Journal* XIX[2] (Jerusalem, 1969), p. 110. *Notarikon* is an abbreviation, an acrostic method, a mere hint of a word. See Marcus Jastrow, *Dictionary* s.v.

46   *Mitnaggedim* in Hebrew.

47   On the persecutions of Hasidim, see Simon Dubnow, *Toledot ha-Hasidut,* pp. 107-169. Dubnow is still the best historian of Hasidism.

48   It was published in Koretz in 1779/80 under the title *Toledot Ya'akov Yosef.*

49   *Degel Mahane Ephraim.* It was published in Koretz in 1810/11.

50   The title: *Maggid Debarav le-Ya'akov.* First published in Koretz in 1783/4.

51   Published in Husiatyn in 1898/9 under the title *Or ha-Emet.*

52   *Haftarot*-Conclusions; portions of *Prophets* which are read in the synagogue after the pertinent sections of the week during the morning services on the Sabbath, holidays, the Ninth Day of Ab and on fast days.

53   *Toledot Yaakov Yosef* (Jerusalem, 1961/2), p.71.

54   Most of the stories of Rabbi Nahman of Bratzlav were transcribed by his amanuensis after they have been told to the disciples. How faithful are the transcriptions? One can only guess. Samuel H. Setzer has endeavored to establish a critical edition in his *Sippure Ma'asiyyot-Wunder Ma'asiyyot Fun Rabbi Nahman Braslaver* (New York, 1929). The sayings and stories of R. Nahman have been extensively anthologized. The personality of R. Nahman is the subject of a playlet by Sackler—see *infra*—and a poem by the author. See Eisig Silberschlag, *'Ale, 'Olam,be-Shir* (New York, 1946), pp. 82-85.

55   Agnon was born in eastern Galicia; Buber was educated there by his grandfather, Solomon Buber, a well-known scholar and editor of midrashic literature. Both in Galicia and Bukovina which, between 1775 and 1848, was a district of Galicia, Buber experienced Hasidism at the source. See Martin Buber, *Mein Weg zum Chassidismus* (Frankfurt am Main, 1918), pp. 10-13.

56   See the Introduction to Jiri Langer, *Nine Gates to the Chassidic* [sic!] *Mysteries* tr. by Stephen Jolly (New York, 1961), pp. 3-19.

57   See his *Autobiography*, p. 167.

58   *"Der Chassidismus, dieser hässliche Auswuchs des Judenthums. . ."* See Graetz, *Geschichte der Juden* XI² (Leipzig, 1870), p. 592.

59   *Kitbe R. Nachman Krochmal* ed. S. Rawidowicz, p. 416. A similar sobriquet "the hypocrites" (*ha-Mithassedim*) was used by S.J. Rapoport. See Samuel Werses, *"Ha-Hasidut be-'Ene Sifrut ha-Haskalah," ha-Molad,* 144-145 (1960), p. 382. On Rapoport's attitude to Hasidism, see also Isaac Barzilay, *Shlomo Yehudah Rapoport* [Shir] *And His Contemporaries*, p. 80.

60   On *The Visionaries—Hoze Hezyonot* in Hebrew—see especially J. Klausner, *Historiyyah Shel ha-Sifrut ha-'Ibrit ha-Hadashah III*, 1938/9), pp. 390-392.

61   The German phrase: *Religionsschwärmer.* See J. Klausner II, *op.cit.,* (Jerusalem, 1936/37), p. 265.

62   *Kol Kitbe Ahad Ha'am* (Dvir edition, Jerusalem, 1949), p. 466.

63   *Yalkut Ribal*, p. 31. "Men of God" were identified as Hasidim by Rabbi David Kimhi, *ibid.*, p. 85.

64   *Ibid.*, pp. 149-151.

65   The Hebrew title of the unpublished brochure—*Mahkimat Peti*—is based on *Psalms* 19:8. See *Yosef Perl's Yidishe Ksovim* with a biographical introduction by Israel Weinlös and a literary-linguistic analysis by Z. Kalmanowicz (Vilna, 1937), p. XXVII.

66   Perl was buried in his native Tarnopol alongside Lefin who preceded him and Krochmal who succeeded him. *Ibid.*, p. LXX.

67   See note 55 in chapter entitled "The Pioneering Generation of the Enlightened: 1783–1832."

68   Three types of Hebrew schools trace their origins to Perl's school: the so-called *Heder Metukkan,* The Day School and the afternoon Hebrew schools. His extreme dedication to educational reform can be attested by the following facts: his own annual salary of six hundred *gulden* was assigned to the purchase of books for the school library; the school building and the adjacent synagogue were donated by him to the community (*Yosef Perl's Yidishe Ksovim*, p. XXII); in his will he bequeathed half of his fortune to the school as well as his library of more than eight thousand items; and six thousand *gulden* for the education of artisans. *Ibid.*, p. LXIX-LXX. Over and above his own substantial contributions he succeeded in obtaining subventions for his school from Tarnopol and adjacent communities. For his educational and communal efforts he was bemedaled by the Russian government in 1815, by the Austrian government in 1821. *Ibid.*, p. XXIII. (Tarnopol was under Russian occupation between 1809 and 1815).

69   Title of Beer's book: *Geschichte, Lehren und Meinungen aller bestandenen und noch bestehenden Secten der Juden.* On the evaluation of Beer's work, see S. Dubnow, *Toledot ha-Hasidut*, pp. 379-380;

70   *Megalleh Temirin* in Hebrew. First published in Vienna in 1819. Original

title—*Megalleh Sod*—in manuscript copy in the former Perl library of Tarnopol. See *Yosef Perl's Yidishe Ksovim*, p. XXVIII.

71   It was Slouschz who contended that Abraham Mapu was the father of the Hebrew novel. See Henrietta Szold's translation of his pioneering study on *The Renascence of Hebrew Literature*, p. 134. Subsequent historians repeated his statement uncritically. That Slouschz was a superficial judge of Perl's achievement is evident from his article on Perl in the *Jewish Encyclopedia IX*, pp. 641-642. *Megalleh Temirin* was, in his evaluation, "a clever parody in the language of the Zohar." A parody in Aramaic or a parody of Zohar's mystical imagery? Slouschz was also wrong in assigning the date of Perl's birth to the year 1774 instead of 1773 and in thinking that Jost rather than Beer used Perl's German manuscript for his historical work.

72   It is Dubnow's contention that the tract refers to Beer's book. If this is the case then Perl who contributed the chapter on Hasidism to Beer's book, is the *cause célèbre* in *Megalleh Temirin*! In this connection it is, perhaps, right to remember that a contemporary rabbi regarded Perl as a dangerous apostate. See *Yosef Perl's Yidishe Ksovim*, p. XXVIII. Klausner regards Löbel's anti-hasidic tract in German as the one which exercises the Hasidim in *Megalleh Temirin*. See Klausner, *op. cit.*, II, pp. 299-300. On Löbel's book see Dobnow, *op. cit.*, pp. 285-286 and, especially, p. 377. It is also possible that Perl invented a tract as the center of his book's plot but had no known tract in mind.

73   See Introduction to *Megalleh Temirin* p. 6 a. Also *ibid.*, p. 49a.

74   *Ibid.*, p. 10a.

75   *Ibid.*, p. 7a.

76   *Ibid.*, p. 6a.

77   *Ibid.*, p. 8b.

78   *Ibid.*, pp. 57a-57b.

79   *Ibid.*, p. 62b.

80   In Hebrew: *Shibhe ha-Besht*. And Besht is the acronym of Baal Shem Tov.

81   *Megalleh Temirin*, p. 36b.

82   See *Yosef Perl's Yidishe Ksovim*, p. XXVIII.

83   See Israel Davidson, *Parody in Jewish Literature* (New York, 1907), p. 61. It was Davidson, the American scholar, who recognized—in contradistinction to subsequent critics—the great merit of Perl as a satirist and subjected the *Megalleh Temirin* to a searching analysis. *Ibid.*, pp 62-72. Only recently did an Israeli critic fully vindicate Perl's achievement. See Baruch Kurzweil, *Be-Maabak 'Al Erke ha-Yahadut* (Jerusalem-Tel Aviv, 1969), pp. 55-95.

84   Publication of the Yiddish version had to wait till 1937. It is now available in *Yosef Perl's Yidishe Ksovim*, p. 1-217. For a stylistic, linguistic and comparatist analysis, see Z. Kalmanowicz, *ibid.*, pp. LXXIX-CVII.

85   In Hebrew: *Bohen Zaddik*. It appeared in Prague in 1838.

86   See *Dibre Zaddikim* published as an unpaginated appendix to *Megalleh Temirin* (Lemberg, 1879).

87   The Yiddish story has a Hebrew title: *"Gedullat Rabbi Wolf mi-Czerny Ostrov."* It was published erroneously in *Yosef Perl's Yidishe Ksovim*, pp. 221-244. On the basis of a catalog entry by Zevi Hirsh Reitman, a teacher at Perl's school in Tarnopol, Katz drew the conclusion that the Yiddish story was authored by Malaga, not by Perl. See his *"Naye Materialn Fun Dem Perl-Archiv," Yivo Bletter XIII* (Vilna, 1938), pp. 561-563. For a letter from Malaga to Lefin, *ibid.,* pp 563-564.

88   See Isaac Erter, *Ha-Zofeh le-Bet Yisrael* (Tel Aviv, 1944), p. 57. The title is based on *Ezekiel* 3:17.

89   *Ibid.,* p. 19.

90   *"Kol Rinnah wi-Yeshu'ah be-Ohale Zaddikim"* in *ha-Shahar VI* (Vienna 1874/5), 157-158.

91   The translation is Patterson's. See *The Hebrew Novel in Czarist Russia* (Edinburgh, 1964), p. 208.

92   *Ha-To'eh be-Darke ha-Hayyim III* (Vienna, 1880), p. 58. The translation differs somewhat from Patterson's version in his article "The Portrait of the Saddik in the Nineteenth Century Hebrew Novel," *Journal of Semitic Studies* VIII (1963), p. 172.

Notes to *Heyday of Enlightenment*

1   In French: *Les Mystères de Paris.*

2   The medieval author of *Sefer ha-Shashu'im* is available in an excellent English translation by Moses Hadas, the late Jay Professor of Greek at Columbia University. It was published in New York in 1932 under the title *The Book of Delight.*

3   The earliest Greek romance *Dream of Nectanebus* is probably an adaptation or translation of an Egyptian original. See John W. B. Barns, "Egypt and the Greek Romance," *Acta of the Ninth Congress for Papyrology* (Vienna, 1956).

4   *Ahabat Ziyyon* in Hebrew.

5   *Ashmat Shomron* in Hebrew.

6   David Patterson's translation in his *Abraham Mapu: The Creator of the Modern Novel* (London, 1964), p. 114.

7   *'Ayit Zabu'a* in Hebrew.

8   David Patterson, *op. cit.,* pp. 163-164.

9   *Hoze Hezyonot* in Hebrew.

10   See *Kol Kitbe Abraham Mapu* (Tel Aviv, 1947), p. 457.

11   *Ibid.,* pp. 458-473.

12   On the fate of the manuscript, see Klausner, *op. cit.,* III, pp. 342-357; also Patterson, *op. cit.,* p. 23.

13   *Ibid.,* p. 19.

14   See *Kol Kitbe Abraham Mapu,* p. 456.

15   On the baffling meaning of *Amon,* see the notes in the recent translation of *Proverbs* in the Anchor Bible (New York, 1965), pp. 69-73.

16   *Bet Hanan* in Hebrew. See *Kol Kitbe Abraham Mapu,* pp. 477-490.

17   *Hanok la-Na'ar* in Hebrew.
18   *Pesahim* 3b.

19   A thesis at Harvard University in 1642 was announced under the title *Haebraea est linguarum mater.* See Samuel Eliot Morison, *The Founding of Harvard College* (Cambridge, Mass., 1968), Appendix D, p. 438.

20   *Les trois mousquetaires* in French.

21   *Le Juif errant* in French.

22   *Amon Padgog* (Fourth edition, Warsaw, 1876), p.4.

23   *Kitbe Yehudah Leb Gordon* (Tel Aviv, 1950), p. 304.

24   See David Patterson, *The Hebrew Novel in Czarist Russia*, p. 104.

25   *Ibid.*

26   *Ibid.*, p. 103.

27   *Ha-Dat we-ha-Hayyim* in Hebrew. First edition: 1876-1877.

28   *Shete ha-Kezawot* in Hebrew. First edition: Warsaw: 1888.

29   *"Ma'aseh Nora"* in *Kol Sippure M.D.* Brandstädter II (Cracow, 1895), pp. 169-200.

30   Patterson's translation in *The Hebrew Novel in Czarist Russia,* pp. 151-152.

31   *Ha-Niddahat* in Hebrew. It was published in Vilna-Warsaw in 1886.

32   *Hattat Horim* (Warsaw, 1884).

33   *Simhat Hanef* in Hebrew.

34   Patterson's translation in *The Hebrew Novel in Czarist Russia*, p. 179.

Notes to *Transition to Nationalism*

1   1 *Kings* 18:21.

2   The frontispiece of *Ha-Shahar* carries part of the verse of *Isaiah* 58:8: "Then shall your light break forth as the dawn and your healing shall spring forth speedily." The quotation implies a new dawn (*Shahar*) for Jewry.

3   *'Am 'Olam* in Hebrew. It was published in 1872.

4   *'Et la-Ta'at* in Hebrew.

5   *Nekam Berit.* The phrase is from *Leviticus* 26:25.

6   *Ha-To'eh be-Darke ha-Hayyim* in Hebrew.

7   The coinage is Patterson's. See *The Hebrew Novel in Czarist Russia*, p. 243, n. 24. The word in Hebrew: *Maafelyah.*

8   *Shakulah* in Hebrew.

9   *Zebuel* in Hebrew.

10   See *'Am 'Olam* in Smolenskin, *Maamarim* I (Jerusalem, 1923/24), p. 33.

11   *Ibid.*, pp. 48–52.

12   *Ibid.*, p. 162. These are the last words of *'Am 'Olam*. The two sequels to the book are entitled—interestingly: *'Et la-'Asot* and *'Et le-Daber. Ibid.*, pp. 164–220.

13   On nationalist trends in the nineteenth century see Eisig Silberschlag, "Zionism and Hebraism in America (1897–1921)" in *Early History of Zionism in America* (New York, 1958), pp. 327–328.

14   Smolenskin, *Maamarim* III, p. 226.

15   See *The Zionist Idea—A Historical Analysis and Reader* (New York-Philadelphia, 1960), ed. by Arthur Hertzberg, p. 105.

16   *Ibid.*, p. 107.

17   *Ibid.*, p. 114.

18   *Kitbe David Frischmann* V (Warsaw 1913/14) p. 9.

19   Smolenskin alleges piously that he does not fight Mendelssohn but his

philosophical system (ha-Shittah). See Maamarim II, p. 248, n.1. But in another passage he minimizes Mendelssohn's knowledge and wisdom: after all, he declares haughtily, he was "a mere merchant." Ibid., p. 196. In the same note Smolenskin states that he does not intend to fight the Baal Shem Tov. Yet he calls his predecessors Luria and Vital—with a biting allusion to the former's acronym and the latter's name "the dead lion" and "the living dog." Ibid. p. 186. And the Baal Shem Tov, in his opinion, did as much mischief in the east as Mendelssohn in the west. Ibid., p. 248. Smolenskin's war against Mendelssohn elicited counterattacks by Lilienblum and bitter blasts by the translators of Mendelssohn into Hebrew: Gottlober and Fünn.

20   Smolenskin was well aware of the Kulturkampf and called it "the war of knowledge and faith." See Maamarim II, p. 7.

21   The two Hebrew words from Ecclesiastes were given urgency by an additive from Abot 1:14: If not now, when? 'Et la-Ta'at we-Im Lo 'Akshav Ematai. See Maamarim II, p. 134. The dictum from Abot was also used as the title of an article against the Alliance Israélite Universelle. Maamarim III, pp. 200–226. The words 'Et la-Ta'at are used repeatedly in the book. See, for instance, Maamarim II, p. 149; p. 290 et al.

22   Ibid., p. 28, p. 19.

23   Ibid., p. 26.

24   Ibid., p. 28.

25   Maamarim IV, p. 105.

26   Maamarim III, p. 118.

27   Derek Teshuvah in Hebrew.

28   Kol Kitbe Moshe Leb Lilienblum IV (Odessa, 1912/13), p. 75; 85.

29   See his article "Shire Frischmann" in Ha-Shiloah XLV (Jerusalem, 1925), p. 173.

30   See Kol Kitbe David Frischmann II, p. 162.

31   This was Berdyczewski's opinion. See Kol Kitbe Micah Joseph Berdyczewski, Maamarim, Order 1, Part II, p. 31.

32   The youthful Abramowitsch was so impressed with an itinerant bookseller that he chose Senderl Moker Sefarim—Senderl the Bookseller—as a pseudonym and appended it to his Yiddish story "Little Man." The editor Zederbaum whose first name was Sender deemed it advisable to change the pseudonym into Mendele Moker Sefarim. Abramowitsch adopted it. See Rawnitzki, Dor we-Soferaw I, p. 55. Mendele's date of birth is still a matter of controversy. See S. Niger, Mendele Moker Sefarim—in Yiddish—(Chicago, 1936), p. 23; 293, n.2; Rawnitzki, op.cit., I, p. 35. On Mendele's gravestone in Odessa the following words were engraved by the Jewish workers of the city: "Dem Zaydn fun der Idisher Literatur Mendele Moker Sefarim, S.J. Abramowitsch, geboirn dem 20.XII.1836, geshtorbn dem 8.XII.1917. The same inscription appears also in Ukrainian. Near his grave are the graves of A.L. Lewinsky who died in 1910 and Simon Frug who died in 1916. See Hadoar (August 8, 1969), p. 593.

33 Interestingly, most novels of Mendele were first written in Yiddish and then translated into Hebrew by their author; most short stories were written by him in Hebrew—in the nineties—and translated into Yiddish. See Yehiel Shentuh, *"Sippurav ha-Kezarim Shel Mendele Moker Sefarim 'Al Nusheotehem"* in *Sifrut* (Summer, 1968), p. 391.

34 Quoted from "An Interview with Isaac Bashevis Singer" in *The National Jewish Monthly* (March, 1968), p. 19.

35 See Hone Shmeruk's *"Targume Tehillim le-Yiddish bi-Yede Mendele Moker Sefarim,"* *Sifrut I* (Summer, 1968), pp. 337–342. English summary, *ibid.*, p. 448.

36 *Limmedu hetev fun Shalom Yaakov Abramowitsch.* The text—a mere seventy-five pages—is preceded by an introduction, notes and four appendices in Yiddish by Professor Dan Miron of Tel Aviv University. There is also a facsimile of the title-page and a brief foreword in English.

37 *Ba-Yamim ha-Hem* in Hebrew.

38 *Kol Kitbe Mendele Moker Sefarim*[5] (Tel Aviv, 1935–1936), II, p. 6.

39 *Ibid.*, p. 15. For a slightly different translation see S. Spiegel, *Hebrew Reborn*, Paperback Edition (Cleveland—Philadelphia, 1962), p. 265.

40 A fine ironical effect is achieved in the sentence by the juxtaposition of a talmudic phrase—*Ketubot* 17 a—and a biblical quotation—*Proverbs* 31:30.

41 *Susati* in Hebrew. The novel in English translation: *The Hag* tr. by Moshe Spiegel (New York, 1955).

42 See *Kol Kitbe Mendele Moker Sefarim* I, p. 130. Different translations in Spiegel, *op. cit.*, p. 262 and Leo W. Schwarz, *A Golden Treasury of Jewish Literature* (New York, 1937), p. 335.

43 Klausner reports an interesting remark by Mendele in the course of a conversation: "I'd like to hang Ahad Haam and pronounce the eulogy myself. A spiritual center—is that all he needs? Does the Jew lack spirituality? A material existence, the joy of life, the love of work—that's what he lacks, not a spiritual center. Even the political aspirations of Herzl and Nordau will not detract an iota from the spirituality of the Jew. . . What the Jew lacks is ground under his feet, and political rights on that ground, and an economic and political life like that of all other nations in the world." See Joseph Klausner, *Yozerim u-Bonim* II (Jerusalem, 1929), p. 116. A similar remark is reported by Rawnitzki, *Dor we-Soferaw* I, pp. 103–104.

44 *Sefer ha-Kabzanim* in Hebrew.

45 *Be-'Emek ha-Baka* in Hebrew.

46 *Kol Kitbe Mendele Moker Sefarim* I, p. 29.

47 See Ilya Ehrenburg, "What I Have Learned" in *Saturday Review* (September 30, 1967), p. 31.

Notes to Ideologues of Nationalism

1 Literal meaning: one of the people. Ahad Haam explained the pseudonym: "With this signature I wanted to indicate that I am not a writer. . .and that only fortuitously do I express my opinion. . .like one of the people who is concerned with the affairs of the people." See *Kol Kitbe Ahad Haam*, p. 3.

2 In Hebrew: *"Lo Zeh ha-Derek."* The article had to be modified because it was not acceptable to the Russian censor. In its original form it was published in the literary supplement to *Davar* (January 15, 1937). The self-lacerating satire *"Ketabim Balim"* was written before *"Lo Zeh ha-Derek."* But it was published in the annual *Kawweret* in 1890 under his editorship. For the analysis of the *Ketabim Balim*, see Sir Leon Simon, *Ahad Ha-Am* (Philadelphia, 1960), pp. 36–39. On *Kawweret*, see *Kol Kitbe Ahad Haam*, p. 470.

3 His last article *"Sak ha-Kol"* was published in 1912. See *Kol Kitbe Ahad Haam*, pp. 421–430.

4 Reuben Asher Braudes, *Shete ha-Kezavot* II (Vilna, 1903), p. 6: *Avira de-Odessa Mafkir*—a paraphrase of the well-known adage in *Baba Batra 158 b: Avira de-Erez Yisrael Mahkim.*

5 Isaac Babel, *You Must Know Everything* ed. Natalie Babel, (New York, 1969), p. 28.

6 *Ibid.*, p. 26.

7 It was Babel who depicted in several stories the unsavory suburb of Odessa where draymen, thieves, pimps and gangsters thrived in lush profusion. He even projected a sort of Jewish Robin Hood among them—Benya Krik. See *The Collected Stories of Isaac Babel* (New York, 1960), pp. 203–222. The father of the gangster Mendel Krik is the protagonist of the story "Sunset" which was produced—in dramatized form—by the Second Studio of the Moscow Art Theatre. See Babel's *You Must Know Everything*, pp. 141–154.

8 Isaac Babel, *op. cit.*, p. 30.

9 In a letter to Klausner from Odessa (September 18, 1904) Ahad Haam writes: "You know that for about two years I have been dreaming about writing a book. . .which would clarify the essence of Judaism and the way of

its development. See *Iggerot Ahad Haam* III (Tel Aviv, 1924), p. 192.

10 *Ibid.*, p. 237. Israel Zangwill thought that Ahad Haam should be asked to write a history of Jewish philosophy. But Mayer Sulzberger, the patron of Imber, was a more perceptive critic of Ahad Haam. In a letter of June 15, 1902 he wrote to Zangwill: "Ahad Haam is a great Hebrew writer, but to write on Jewish philosophy even more than Ahad Haam's Hebrew. . . is necessary." See Isaac M. Fein, "Israel Zangwill and American Jewry: A Documentary Study" in *American Jewish Historical Quarterly* LX[1] (September, 1970), p. 18.

11 *'Al Parashat Derakim.* Originally this was the name of Ahad Haam's second article which, in the edition of collected articles, was changed to "*Lo Zeh ha-Derek, Maamar Sheni.*" See J.H. Rawnitzki, *Dor we-Soferav* II (Tel Aviv, 1938), p. 13.

12 See Romain Rolland, *Tolstoy* tr. by Bernard Miall (New York, 1911), pp. 3–4.

13 On foreign influences in general and on positivist influences in particular, see Aryeh [Leon] Simon and Joseph Eliyyahu Heller, *Ahad Haam—ha-Ish, Poalo we-Torato* (Jerusalem, 1955), pp. 140–150.

14 The society was founded by Eisenstadt and Lubarski in 1889 but Ahad Haam was the president from its inception in 1889. See *Kol Kitbe Ahad Haam*, p. 437. The birth of political Zionism in 1897 was the death-knell of *Bene Moshe.* See *'Al Parashat Derakim* IV, p. 227; *Kol Kitbe Ahad Haam*, p. 449.

15 *Hagigah* 13b.

16 *Hibbat Ziyyon.*

17 *Ten Essays on Zionism and Judaism* by Ahad Haam, translated from the Hebrew by Leon Simon (London, 1922), p. 5.

18 A gentle, almost touching attachment to friends and acquaintances is manifest in a sheaf of Ahad Haam's letters in *Sefer Touroff* ed. E. Silberschlag and Y. Twersky (New York, 1938), pp. 118–155. This warm-hearted trait is also emphasized in the novelized biography of Ahad Haam by Y. Twersky, *Ahad Ha'am* (New York, 1941).

19 *'Al Parashat Derakim* IV, p. 33; *Kol Kitbe Ahad Haam*, p. 368.

20 *Emet me-Erez Yisrael.*

21 *Ten Essays*, p. 46.

22 *Der Judenstaat* in the original German.

23 *The Complete Diaries of Theodor Herzl* I ed. by Raphael Patai; tr. by Harry Zohn (New York-London, 1960). p. 33. [Entry, June 5 1895].

24 *The Complete Diaries* II, p. 581. In German: *in Basel habe ich den Judenstaat gegründet. Ibid.*, p. 582.

25 *Joseph und seine Brüder I* (Berlin, 1933), pp. 324–325.

26 *Ten Essays*, pp. 44–45.
27 *Sheelah Nikbadah.*

28   *Ha-Shahar IX*, (Vienna, 1877/78) ed. Perez Smolenskin, pp. 364–365.

29   *Ten Essays*, p. 43.

30   "Not by might, nor by power, but by my spirit"—this dictum of *Zechariah* 4:6 is Ahad Haam's favorite biblical quotation. See *'Al Parashat Derakim* I, p. 8; IV, p. 73. *Kol Kitbe Ahad Haam*, pp. 14; 385. Frischmann asked—and many writers repeated the question—"How can a center of the minority be felt and sensed by the millions of Jews strewn and scattered on the face of the whole earth?. . ." Cf. *Kol Kitbe David Frischmann* (Warsaw, 1914), p. 8.

31   *Ten Essays*, p. 125.

32   *Ibid.*, p. 143.

33   "*Ha-Musar ha-Leumi.*"

34   It would have pleased Ahad Haam to read this statement by a twentieth century ethicist: "Religion is inadequately described as morality touched by emotion, for the elements of our ethical life are charged with emotion; and religion which did not originate as morality, developed as a spiritual realization not as an ethical code." Cf. M. A. R. Tuker, *Past and Future of Ethics* (1938), p. 94.

35   Quoted from the constitution adopted by the Second International Ethical Conference at Eisenach in 1906.

36   *Selected Essays of Ahad Haam* translated from the Hebrew by Leon Simon (Philadelphia, 1912), pp. 282–283.

37   *'Al Parashat Derakim* II, p. 5. *Kol Kitbe Ahad Haam*, p. 128. The negative attitude to nature is also emphasized in Ahad Haam's *Reminiscences:* "Though I have spent the best part of my youth in a village, I did not acquire any love of nature. . .But I was occupied with books and study, and paid no attention to the beauties of nature." The translation is Sir Leon Simon's in his book *Ahad Haam*, p. 16. Indifference to landscape and to the poetry of landscape permeated the influential Hebrew monthly *ha-Shiloah* which Ahad Haam founded and edited between 1896–1902. Ahad Haam was as immune to humor as to poetry: "And though Shalom Aleyhem speaks to the people in its language and according to its taste, there is no thought in his words except a pleasant jocularity." Cf. J.H. Rawnitzki, *Dor Ve-Sofrav* II, p. 31.

38   *Kol Kitbe A. D. Gordon I* (Tel Aviv, 1925), p. 43; also A. D. Gordon, *Selected Essays* tr. by F. Burnce (New York, 1938), p. 175.

39   *Kol Kitbe A. D. Gordon I*, p. 44; also A. D. Gordon, *Selected Essays*, p. 176.

40   His pseudonym Bin Gorion is derived from the alleged author of *Sefer Yosippon*—a popular history of the Second Commonwealth which was compiled in the middle ages and cherished by Berdyczewski.

41   *Abot* 3: 8. Translation by R. Travers Herford (New York, 1925).

42   *Kitbe Micah Joseph Bin Gorion* (Leipzig, 1921–1925), *Maamarim*, Order II, Part II, pp. 56–57.

43   L. Ginzberg, *Mekomah Shel ha-Halakah be-Hokmat Yisrael* (Jerusalem, 1931), pp. 12–34.

44   In fairness to Ahad Haam it must be said that he desired "our language to be sufficient unto all our needs." He thought, however, that there was a gap between the needs and the capabilities of the Jews. See *'Al Parashat Derakim II*, p. 11; *Kol Kitbe Ahad Haam*, p. 130.

45   *Kitbe Micah Joseph Bin Gorion, Maamarim,* Order II, Part I, p. 12.

46   *Mahanayim* in Hebrew.

47   Berdyczewski has written a series of poetical essays on Hasidism (*Maamarim*, Order II, Part I, pp. 15–32), a series of critical essays on the Kabbalah (*Ibid.*, Order III, Part II, pp. 13–60), and criticisms of books on Hasidism (*ibid.*, Order I, Part III, pp. 38–49).

48   Jacob Klatzkin, *Tehumim* (Berlin, 1925), p. 60.

49   *Ibid.*, p. 64. Klatzkin uses different nomenclature: a Hebrew group in the Land [of Israel] and a Jewish group in the Diaspora.

50   *Ibid.*, p. 98.

51   *Ibid.*, p. 35.

52   *Ibid.*, p. 46.

53   *Ibid.*, p. 54.

54   *Toledot ha-Emunah ha-Yisreelit mi-Yeme Kedem 'Ad Sof Bayit Sheni* (Jerusalem, 1953–1956). A one-volume abridgment and translation, "limited to the volumes treating of the preexilic age," is available in English under the title *The Religion of Israel from Its Beginnings to the Babylonian Exile* tr. by Moshe Greenberg (Chicago, 1960). A full translation of the first two chapters of the fourth volume by C.W. Efroymson appeared under the title of *The Babylonian Captivity and Deutero-Isaiah* (New York, 1970).

55   *Golah we-Nekar* (Tel Aviv, 1929–1930).

56   *Genazim* (Kisleb–Tebet 5724—1963/4), p. 14.

57   The book appeared in New York in 1965. Full title: *Jewish Identity—Modern Response and Opinions on the Registration of Children of Mixed Marriages. David Ben Gurion's Query to Leaders of World Jewry—A Documentary Compilation* by Baruch Litvin, ed. by Sidney B. Hoenig.

58   *Sefat 'Eber—Safah Hayyah*. It was published in Cracow in 1896 and, in a revised and enlarged edition, in Jerusalem in 1949 under the title *Ha-Lashon ha-'Ibrit—Lashon Hayyah*.

59   The saying is reported by one of his pupils, Baruch Karu, who translated Dubnow's massive *World History of the Jewish People* into Hebrew. See his article "*'Eser Shanim li-Petirato Shel Joseph Klausner*," *Moznayim* XXVIII[2] (January, 1969), p. 113.

60   *Historiyyah Shel ha-Bayit ha-Sheni* (Jerusalem, 1958).

61   *Historiyyah Shel ha Sifrut ha-'Ibrit ha-Hadashah,* (Jerusalem, 1929/30–1950).

62   *Da'at Elohim* (Warsaw, 1897).

63   *Sefer ha-Dema'ot* (Berlin, 1923–1926). It is a collection of poems, chronicles and stories of Jewish martyrdom—the best anthology of its kind to this very day.

64   *Toledot ha-Reformaziyyon ha-Datit be-Yisrael* (Cracow, 1900).

65   Hebrew title: *Dor Hakam* (Warsaw, 1896).

66   Hebrew title: *Bene 'Aliyyah* (Tel Aviv, 1931).

67   *Toledot Shir* (Berlin, 1898).

68   *Gabriel Riesser* (Warsaw, 1900).

69   The German title: *Geschichte der jüdischen Philosophie des Mittelalters nach Problemen dargestellt* (Berlin, 1907–1910). The Hebrew title: *Toledot ha-Pilosofiyyah be-Yisrael*, 2 vols. (Philadelphia, 1929). Both the German and the English edition are torsos. We know from the preface to the Hebrew edition that the work was to contain ten volumes. See his *Toledot etc. II*, p. III.

70   A bibliography of Neumark's writings and a selection of his articles in English appeared under the title *Essays in Jewish Philosophy* (Vienna, 1929).

71   In Hebrew: *Dorot ha-Rishonim.* Yizhak Isaac Halevi Rabinowitz began publishing his work in 1897. The sixth and last volume appeared in 1964.

72   See David Neumark, *"Kiyyum Yisrael"* (*ha-Shiloah I*, 1896/7), p. 376.

73   *Ibid.*

74   Unpaginated introduction to Hurwitz's volume of essays *Me-Ayin u-le-Ayin* (Berlin, 1914).

75   *Ibid.*, p. 11. Hurwitz refers to an exchange of letters between a would-be convert and Abraham Geiger in the latter's *Nachgelassene Schriften I* (Berlin, 1875), p. 238.

76   *Ibid.*, p. 53.

77   *Isaiah* 49:6

78   *Me-Ayin u-le-Ayin*, p. 13.

79   *He-'Atid V* (Berlin, 1919), p. 4.

80   See his *Ishim* (Jerusalem, 1958), p. 275.

81   Hebrew title: *Ha-Zofeh le-Bet Yisrael.* It is based on *Ezekiel* 3:17; 33:7. Sokolow was aware, of course, that Isaac Erter had used the phrase as a title for his book of satires against Hasidism.

82   Sokolow, *Ishim*, pp. 282–283.

83   Some of the pseudonyms are ordinary: *Lev 'Ivri, M. Balshan;* some are quaint: *Menahem Abot, 'Okef, Barkai, Kadma we-Azla, Rahash, Senappir.* See Sokolow, *op.cit.*, p. 174.

84   He was better known by his pseudonym Bukki Ben Yogli—a biblical prince of the tribe of Dan: *Numbers* 34:22. His contributions to the daily *Ha-Yom* included not only feuilletons under the collective title *Miktabim*

mi-Kiryat Ra'av but also medical books based on talmudic sources. See Sokolow, *op. cit.*, p. 177.

85   On Frischmann's feuilletons by the name of *Otiyot Porehot* in *Ha-Yom*, see Sokolow's *op. cit.*, pp. 285–286.

86   On Sokolow's ideas and implementations of a Hebrew daily, see *op. cit.*, pp. 153–158.

87   *Ibid.*, p. 86.

88   *Ibid.*, p. 145.

89   *Ibid.*, p. 130.

90   Sokolow calls himself "A sort of Benjamin the Third." *Ibid.*, p. 180. But that title had been preempted for a fictitious hero by Mendele Moker Sefarim. Benjamin I—Benjamin ben Jonah of Tudela—was the famous Jewish traveler in the twelfth century; Benjamin II—a German Jew—toured the U.S. in the middle of the nineteenth century and left an invaluable account of the early Jewish communities in the country.

91   Sokolow, *History of Zionism* 1600–1918 I (London, 1919), p. XV.

92   Arnold Toynbee, *A Study of History VI* (London, 1939), p. 63.

93   Hebrew title: *Mi-Mizrah u-mi-Ma'arav*. Only four issues were published at long intervals between 1894 and 1899.

94   Hebrew title: *Hayye Herzl*. It appeared in New York in 1919.

95   Title in the original German: *Das neue Ghetto*.

96   On Brainin's attitude to Tschernichowsky see Eisig Silberschlag, *Saul Tschernichowsky: Poet of Revolt*, pp. 12–14.

97   Hebrew title: *Kol Kitbe Reuben ben Mordecai Brainin*. They appeared in 1922, 1936 and 1940 respectively.

Notes to the Three Stars of
the Modern Hebrew Renaissance:
Bialik, Tschernichowsky, Shneour

1 *"El ha-Zippor."* A longer version of the poem appeared in *Iggerot H. N. Bialik I* (Tel Aviv, 1937), pp. 46–49. An extensive commentary on the poem by David Joseph Burnstein appeared in *Keneset I* ed. Jacob Cahan and F. Lachower (Tel Aviv, 1936), pp. 84–102.

2 The epithet, snowed under a flurry of exaggerations, was given to him by Ahad Haam: ". . .the national poet whose equal did not appear since the days of Judah Halevi and perhaps since the days of the prophets." See *Iggerot Ahad Haam VI*, p. 208. An American translator of Bialik echoes Ahad Haam: "Bialik is, without doubt, the greatest Jewish national poet since Judah Halevi." See Harry A. Fein, *Titans of Hebrew Verse* (Boston, 1936), p. 7.

3 *Iggeret Ketanah.*

4 *"Aken Hazir ha-'Am."*

5 *Birkat 'Am.*

6 *Ba-Sadeh.*

7 For a concise summary of the reasons which led to the pogrom, see Mark Vishniak, "Antisemitism in Tsarist Russia," pp. 98–100 in *Essays on Antisemitism* ed. Koppel S. Pinson (New York, 1942).

8 *"'Al ha-Shehitah."* A literary scandal surrounds its publication. The censor in Warsaw who had the authority to refuse or permit publication of Hebrew contributions to periodicals was afraid to exercise his rights and sent it to the censor in St. Petersburg—now Leningrad—together with a 25 ruble bribe. I. L. Peretz who had seen the poem in manuscript hastened to publish a parody—an alleged discovery in the library of Oxford University—of an additional Byronic poem in the series entitled "Hebrew Melodies." When Bialik's poem appeared in *Ha-Shiloah*, Frischmann—at odds with Peretz—published a condemnatory article on Peretz in the *Yiddishe Volkszeitung* under the editorship of Ben-Avigdor and Spector. Peretz who had suffered a heart attack—and Frischmann knew about his condition—almost lost his life from grief. See *Miktebe Klausner El Bialik, Moznayim XXVIII²* (January, 1969), pp. 120–122.

9 *"Be-'Ir ha-Haregah."*

10   An English version of the whole poem is given by Harry A. Fein, *A Harvest of Hebrew Verse* (Boston, 1934), pp. 101–108.

11   *Megillat ha-Esh.*

12   *Mete Midbar.*

13   Fein, *op. cit.*, p. 263.

14   *Ibid.*, p. 22.

15   *"Im Yesh Et Nafsheka la-Da'at."*

16   *Fein, op. cit.*, p. 61.

17   For the translation, see Sir Leon Simon, *Ahad Ha'Am*, p. 316.

18   The word does not lend itself to ready translation. It means "one who is at it always." Perhaps "The Alwayser" would do the word justice. On the purpose of the poem Bialik made some interesting remarks in his letters. See *Iggerot H.N. Bialik I*, pp. 100–102. On the gestation and variants of the poem, see F. Lachower, *H. N. Bialik* (Tel Aviv, 1937), pp. 33–40.

19   *Iggerot H. N. Bialik I*, p. 166.

20   Hebrew name of the commentary: *Ha'amek Shealah* (Vilna, 1861–67). The title is taken from *Isaiah* 7:11. The Hebrew name of R. Aha's work: *Sheeltot*—Questions. A critical and annotated edition by Samuel Kalman Mirsky (Jerusalem, 1959–63).

21   *Zohar.*

22   *"Ha-Berekah."*

23   *"Gammade Layil."*

24   *"Yehi Helki 'Imakem."*

25   *"Haknisini Tahat Kenafek."*

26   Respective Hebrew titles *Wa-yehi ha-Yom* and *Alluf Bazlut we-Alluf Shum*. Both were rendered into English by H. Danby.

27   In his work on the edition of rabbinic legends, on the poetry of Solomon Ibn Gabirol and Moses Ibn Ezra, Bialik was aided by Rawnitzki. On the method of collaboration, see Rawnitzki, *Dor we-Soferaw II*, pp. 126-135.

28   The conversations have been collected in two volumes under the title *Debarim she-be-'Al Peh* (Tel Aviv, 1935). They are a mixed bag of authentic and unauthentic material. See M. Ungerfeld "'Al Bialik she-be-'Al Peh" in *ha-Doar* (August 8, 1969), p. 587. It is his contention that only few of Bialik's friends caught the rhythms of his speech and reproduced them faithfully. Among them he singles out Zalman Shneour, Isaac Dov Berkowitz, Avigdor Hameiri and Hayyim Gliksberg, the painter. Mordecai Obadyahu, on the other hand, knew Bialik in the last four years of his life and transmitted his words in paraphrase rather than in authentic language. *Ibid.*, p. 588. Obadyahu's book *Mi-Pi Bialik* has achieved an enviable popularity: three editions were quickly sold out.

28a   One volume of a new series, under the editorship of the critic and poet

Abraham Kariv, appeared in 1960.

29 For the biography of the poet see Eisig Silberschlag, *Saul Tscherni-chowsky: Poet of Revolt*, pp. 3-35.

30 In Hebrew: *Sirtutim*.

31 In Hebrew: *Nokah Pesel Apollo.*

32 In Hebrew: *Ani—Li mi-she-Li En Kelum. . .*

33 See Schocken's edition of Tschernichowsky's poems (Tel Aviv, 1953), p. 590.

34 In Hebrew: *Ha-Pesel.*

35 See Schocken's edition of Tschernichowsky's poems, p. 462.

36 In Hebrew: *Be-Karme Agrippas.*

37 See *Israel Argosy VI* ed. I. Halevy-Levin (Jerusalem, 1959), pp. 41-42. The translator is Sulamith Schwartz.

38 In Hebrew: *Be-Palatin Shel Herodion.*

39 It is false, however, to assert—as some critics do—that Tschernichowsky's work is devoid of lyrical elements. See *Ha-Shiloah* XXXV (1918), p. 124.

40 In Hebrew: *Berit Milah.*

41 In Hebrew: *Hatunatah Shel Elkah.*

42 The Greek phrase is: $\dot{\eta} \ \tau \hat{\omega} \nu \ \pi \rho \alpha \gamma \mu \acute{\alpha} \tau \omega \nu \ \sigma \acute{\upsilon} \sigma \tau \alpha \sigma \iota s.$

See *Poetics* 1450 a 15.

43 See M. Croiset, *Histoire de la littérature grecque*[4] (Paris, 1928), pp. 17-19.

44 Dykman's unfinished version of the *Iliad* in Hebrew cannot hold a candle to Tschernichowsky's translation. See Benzion Benshalom's article in *Sifrut* (Summer 1968), pp. 386-390; English summary, *ibid.*, p. 445.

45 Homer made a theogony for the Greeks (Herodotus II, 53) and educated Greece (Plato, *Republic* X,606 E). Moreover, "he has made poetry about practically everything" (Dio Prusaensis, *Oratio* XXXIII, 11). The vitality of Homer is also attested by Aeschylus who admitted that his plays were mere slices from the great banquets of Homer (Athenaeus, *Deipnosophists* VIII, 347 E). The judgment of the ancients is corroborated by modern scholars: "Von den zwei Seelen, die im Herzen des Altertums wohnen, ist er [Homer] die eine; die andere ist die platonische." See J. Geffcken, *Griechische Literaturgeschichte* I (Heidelberg, 1296), p. 11.

46 In Hebrew: *La-Shemesh.*

47 Tschernichowsky authored a literary monograph—his only one—on Immanuel of Rome. Though there is an undoubted kinship between the two, the work lacks original research and critical penetration. Not a single page is devoted to Immanuel the eyegete and Immanuel the philosopher. Yet his commentaries on the Bible—most of them in manuscript, few in print—yield rich information on the encyclopedic range of his mind. His scientific, moral

and mystical interpretations of Holy Writ should have delighted Tscherni-chowsky whose intellect roamed over wide areas of knowledge. For the first study in depth of Immanuel's contribution to exegesis and philosophy see F. M. Tocci's publication and analysis of Immanuel's commentary on the first chapter of Genesis: *Il Commento di Emanuele Romano al Captio I della Genesi* (Rome, 1963).

48   In Hebrew: *'Al ha-Dam.*

49   In Hebrew: *Baruk mi-Magenzah.*

50   These lines are missing in Maurice Samuel's fragmentary version of "Baruch of Mayence" in Schwarz's *A Golden Treasury of Jewish Literature* (Philadelphia, 1946), pp. 621-624.

51   In Hebrew: *Hezyonot u-Manginot.* It was Tschernichowsky's first volume of verse and it appeared in Warsaw in 1898. The most important collections of Tschernichowsky's poetry include the one-volume edition published by Schocken in 1937 and republished several times; the two-volume edition published by Dvir in 1966. The ten-volume edition of Tschernichowsky's works, published between 1929 and 1934, does not contain all his stories, all his translations or even all his poems up to 1934. Nor does it include his feuilletons and his critical articles, his monograph on Immanuel of Rome, his children's poems and children's stories. A new multivolume edition of Tschernichowsky's prose and poetry is a desideratum.

52   In Hebrew: *Kir ha-Pele Asher be-Wormaiza.*

53   *Balladot Wormaiza.* On the historical sources of the ballads, see S. Eidelberg, *Ha-Balladah "Nerot ha-Almonim" le-Shaul Tschernichowsky* in *Bizaron* XLIX (November-December, 1963) pp. 115-116.

54   The word Dortmund is misspelled and mispunctuated in the Schocken edition on p. 615 and on p. 874. On the historical background of "Baruch of Mayence" and "The Dead of Dortmund" and on the thematic interrelation of the two poems, see S. Eidelberg, *Ha-Yesod ha-Histori be-Shirat Tscherni-chowsky* in *ha-Doar* (January 4, 1963), pp. 162-163. On the sources of "Baruch of Mayence," see also Meir Bosak, *Le-Mekorot Baruch mi-Magenzah* in *Moznayim* XVII (November, 1963), pp. 442-444.

55   In Hebrew, in the early editions: *Levivot Mevushalot.* In later editions: *Levivot.*

56   In Hebrew: *Ke-Hom ha-Yom.*

57   In Hebrew: *Berele Holeh.*

58   In Hebrew: *Simhah Lav Davka.*

59   The third half-line of "Eli" reads: *Yeshnam bi-Tefuzot ha-Golah. . .,* the first line of *Ha-Matmid* reads: *'Od Yesh bi-Tefuzot ha-Golah . . .*

60   In Hebrew: *Ha-Kaf ha-Shevurah.*

61   In Hebrw: *Kisme Ya'ar.*

62   In Hebrew: *'Amma de-Dahava.*

63   *Shene ha-'Orvim.* The final version—Schocken's edition of Tscherni-

chowsky's poems pp. 51-52—differs from the one in *Hezyonot u-Manginot*, pp. 78-79. Tschernichowsky revised his poems though not as endlessly and as elaborately as his great Irish contemporary William Butler Yeats. But Tschernichowsky's revisions have not been studied while Yeats's emendations have been subjected to careful scrutiny. See Marion Witt, "Yeats: 1865-1965" in *Publications of the Modern Language Association of America* LXXX (September, 1965), pp. 311-320.

64   In Hebrew: *Yohanan ben ha-Se'orah.*

65   In Hebrew: *Bi-Neot Harim Libi.*

66   In Hebrew: *Ha-Aharon li-Bene Koraitah.*

67   In Hebrew: *Mozae Shabbat.*

68   In Hebrew: *Ba-Shishi Ben 'Arbayim.*

69   In Hebrew: *Ha-Na'ar ha-Kushi.*

70   In Hebrew: *Sheloshah Ketarim.* The title is based on Abot 4:13.

71   In Hebrew: *Kezad Merakkedin.* The title is based on Ketubot 16 b.

72   On martyrdom in the poems of Tschernichowsky see the sensitive essay by Jacob Bahat, *"Kiddush ha-Shem be-Yezirato Shel Tschernichowsky"* in *Moznayim* XVII (November, 1963), pp. 432-437.

73   In Hebrew: *Ani Maamin.* Tschernichowsky parodied his own poem in *ha-'Olam* (1925). Hayyim Orlan republished the parody with a few enlightening paragraphs in *Ha-Doar* (January 31, 1969), pp. 217-218. The parody was published under a pseudonym. On Tschernichowsky's pseudonyms see Eisig Silberschlag, *Saul Tschernichowsky—Poet of Revolt*, pp. 89-90.

74   In Hebrew: *Manginah Li.*

75   Tschernichowsky was not uncritical about the play. He had serious doubts about its merits: he was anxious to read it to Klausner and to hear his opinion. See unpublished letter of February 13, 1925 from Tschernichowsky to Klausner in the Manuscript Collection of the National and University Library of Jerusalem.

76   On comparisons between Bialik and Tschernichowsky, see Eisig Silberschlag, *op. cit.*, p. 92, n.5.

77   Quotation from Marvell's verses prefixed to the 1674 edition of *Paradise Lost.*

78   In Yiddish: *Shklover Iden.* In Hebrew: *Anshe Shklov.*

79   *Shklover Iden*, pp. 6-7.

80   *"Shiratenu ha-Zeirah"* in the one-volume edition of Bialik: *Kitbe H.N. Bialik,* (Tel Aviv, 1933), p. 385.

81   In Hebrew: *Bialik u-Bene Doro* (Tel Aviv 1958). The book—a series of articles written over a period of several decades—tells more about Shneour than about Bialik. Gossip spices its pages: friendships and feuds between writers—including Bialik and Shneour—are chronicled with perspicacity but with pity to none. In spite of the minor misunderstandings between the two

poets, Shneour's attachment to Bialik was deep and lasting. For the fiftieth and sixtieth birthday of Bialik Shneour composed two poems respectively. On his death he wrote a moving poem *"Pesuke Ebel:"* *Bialik u-Bene Doro*, pp. 257-261. Both poets had fun in exchanging rhymed epistles. *Ibid.*, pp. 120-123.

82   *"Lule Tikvotai* in *Kitbe Zalman Shneour* I (Tel Aviv, 1960), p. 1. Some of the children's poems of Shneour for the children's magazine *'Olam Katan* also appeared in 1902 and preceded the publication of *"Lule Tikvotai."*

83   In Hebrew: *"Mavet"* *(Reshimot Shel Meabed 'Azmo la-Da'at)* in *Min ha-Hayyim we-ha-mavet* (Warsaw, 1910) pp. 11-95. The story was written in Vilna in 1905.

84   The poems, under the collective title *Luhot Genuzim* in *Kitbe Zalman Shneour* I, pp. 369-426.

85   In Hebrew: *'Im Shekiat ha-Hammah*. It appeared in 1906. Bialik, in unwarranted hyperbole, said of the book: "Our literature has not seen such poetry till to-day." *Bialik u-Bene Doro*, p. 186.

86   In Hebrew: *"Hayah Laylah,"* *Kitbe Zalman Shneour*, p. 29.

87   In Hebrew: *"Ha-Shemesh Shake'ah,"* *op. cit.*, pp. 11-12.

88   In Hebrew: *"Tahat Shemesh,"* *op. cit.* pp. 166-170.

89   Joseph Klausner, *Yozerim u-Bonim* III (Jerusalem, 1929), p. 77.

90   In Hebrew: *"'Al Hof ha-Seinah,"* *op. cit.*, pp. 164-166.

91   In Hebrew: *Hezyonot*. It appeared in Berlin in 1924. For the English translation of the poem, Harry H. Fein, *Titans of Hebrew Verse*, pp. 180-197. On the Strashun Library in Vilna, see the essay in Yiddish by Haikel Levinski, *"Di Strashun Bibliothek in Vilne"* (New York, 1935), pp. 273-287.

92   *Kitbe Zalman Shneour*, p. 244.

93   In Hebrew: *Ha-Gaon we-ha-Rav*. It appeared in Tel Aviv in 1952/53.

94   Kitbe Zalman Shneour, pp. 80-81.

95   In Hebrew: *"Peragim,"* *op. cit.* pp. 37-40. For English translations of the poem, see Yohai Goell, *Bibliography of Modern Hebrew Literature in English Translation* (Jerusalem and New York, 1968), p. 46.

96   In Hebrew: *"Marganiyyot,"* *op. cit.*, pp. 40-41. For an English translation of the poem, Goell, p. 48.

97   In Hebrew: *"Be-Harim,"* *op. cit.*, pp. 138-164.

98   *Op. cit.*, p. 34.

99   *Ibid.*, p. 64.

100   *Ibid.*, p. 103.

101   *Ibid.*, p. 119.

102   *Ibid.*, p. 34.

103   In Hebrew: *"'Im Zelile ha-Mandolinah,"* *ibid.*, pp. 182-194.

104   In Hebrew: *"Mi-Shire ha-Goral,"* *op. cit.*, pp. 197-210.

105   In Hebrew: "*Yeme ha-Benayim Mitkarvim*," *op. cit.*, pp. 42-44.

106   *Ibid.*, p. 68.

107   *Ibid.*, p. 69.

108   *Ibid.*, pp. 55-56.

109   In Hebrew: "*Mi-Shire Yisrael*," *op.cit.*, pp. 71-82.

110   *Ibid.*, p. 74.

111   *Ibid.*, p. 72.

112   *Feter Zhame* in Yiddish (Vilna, 1930).

113   The title has a long history. Originally applied to Jesus in rabbinic literature—in the form of Ben Pandera or Ben Pantere or Yeshu ben Pandera—it was perhaps a corrupt version of $\pi\alpha\rho\theta\epsilon\nu\sigma\varsigma$ = virgin. Thus Yeshu ben Pandera might mean Jesus son of the Virgin. In modern as in ancient times the name Pandre was given by Jews in mockery. On Pandre, see especially Joseph Klausner, *Jesus of Nazareth* (New York, 1944), pp. 22-24.

114   The English translation appeared in New York in 1944.

115   *Noah Pandre*, tr. by Joseph Leftwich (New York, 1936), pp. 7-8.

116   See *Restless Spirit—Selected Writings of Zalman Shneour* (London, 1963), p. 197. The translation of the passage differs slightly from Spiegel's version. The quotation at the end of the passage is from *Numbers* 15:39.

Notes to The Nimble-Winged Poets:
Jacob Cahan; Isaac Katzenelson

1 In Hebrew: "*Masat Nafshi.*" On the composition of the poem see the monograph—a reprint from *Moznayim*—by H. Toren, *Ha-Mezayyer Mane* (Tel Aviv, 1945/46), pp. 6; 14-15; 22. The clever acronym *Ha-Mezayyer—Ha-Bahur Mordecai Zevi Mane Yelid Radoshkowitz*—points to Mane's two loves: love for painting and love for the native town.

2 The Nazis who murdered Katzenelson also burned the entire Jewry of Radoshkowitz—Mane's birthplace and burialplace in the vicinity of Vilna. The ghastly event occurred on the grave of Mane: "In Radoshkowitz the Jews were driven to the cemetery, the trees were kindled, the [Jewish] populace was shot and later burned on the grave of the poet Mordecai Zevi Mane." See the Yiddish article by Uri Finkel, "*Di Shehiteh Baym Kever Fun Dem Bavustn Hebreishn Dichter Mordecai Zevi Mane,*" *Yidishe Kultur* (October, 1945), p. 53. On Radoshkowitz and its martyrdom, see *Sefer Zikkaron li-Kehillat Radoshkowitz* ed. Dr. M. Robinson, Dr. I. Rubin and B. Isaacson (Israel, 1953). A chapter of the book is devoted to the addictive admiration of the town for Mane. *Ibid.*, pp. 73-76. Reminiscences of townsmen about Mane, *ibid.*, pp. 143-155.

3 *Iggerot H.N.Bialik* I ed. F. Lachower (Tel Aviv, 1937), p. 212; II (Tel Aviv, 1938), p. 14.

4 Hebrew title: "*Helveziyyah*" in *Kitbe Yaakob Cahan* I (Tel Aviv, 1950), pp. 195-260.

5 Hebrew title: "*Hazon ha-Tishbi.*" *Ibid.*, II (Tel Aviv, 1948), pp. 43-78.

6 Hebrew title: "*Aggadot Elohim.*" *Ibid.*, II, pp. 287-333.

7 Hebrew title: *Kinnori.*" *Ibid.*, II, pp. 103-110.

8 Hebrew title: "*Mi-Shire 'Elem Bahir.*" *Ibid.*, I, pp. 137-140.

9 Hebrew title: "*Biryonim.*" *Ibid.* II, pp. 13-17.

10 *Ibid.*, II, p. 97.

11 Hebrew title: "*Ha-Nefilim.*" *Ibid.*, IV (Tel Aviv, 1945), pp. 7-124.

12   Hebrew title: *"David Melek Yisrael."Ibid.*, IV, pp. 125-204.

13   *Ibid.*, V (Tel Aviv, 1945), pp. 357-452.

14   Hebrew title: *Ha-Herpah ha-Gedolah.* It was changed in the collected edition of Cahan's works to *Viduyo Shel Tarno. Ibid.*, VI (Tel Aviv, 1945), pp. 209-237.

15   Hebrew title: *Ha-Berit ha-Aharonah. Ibid.*, VI, pp. 5-69.

16   Hebrew title: *Koso Shel Eliyyahu." Ibid.*, pp. 179-208.

17   Interestingly, Mane had translated a fragment of *Faust* toward the end of the nineteenth century. See *Kol Kitbe Mordecai Zevi Mane* II (Warsaw, 1897), p. 84.

18   Asher Barash, *Mibhar ha-Shirah ha-'Ibrit ha-Hadashah* (Tel Aviv, 1938), p. 231.

19   Hebrew title: *Bi-Gebulot Lita.* First edition: Warsaw, 1908.

20   *Ibid.*, pp. 68-69.

21   Hebrew title: *"La-Menazzeah 'Al ha-Meholot," Kol Kitbe H.N. Bialik* (Tel Aviv, 1959), pp. 70-71. English translation by I.M.Lask in his introduction to *Aftergrowth and other Stories by Hayyim Nahman Bialik* (Philadelphia, 1939), pp. 13-15.

22   Jacob Fichmann, *Isaac Katzenelson* in *Ha-Tekufah* XXIV (Berlin, 1928), p. 528.

23   Hebrew title: *Ha-Nabi* (Łódź, 1922).

24   *Ibid.*, pp. 194-195.

25   Hebrew title: *Ha-Ma'agal* (Warsaw, 1910-1911).

26   606 or salvarsan was discovered by Paul Ehrlich (1854-1915) and used for the treatment of syphilis. The number 606 is the numerical order in Ehrlich's experimental series.

27   Translated as *Damaged Goods* by John Pollock in *Three Plays by Brieux* (New York, 1913), pp. 185-254.

28   *Tehumim* I (Warsaw, 1936/7), p. 44.

29   Only two acts appeared in *Tehumim.* The third was set up in 1939 but the invasion of the Nazis prevented the publication of the issue. Some pages—including the third act—were rescued by the poet and co-editor of *Tehumim*, M. Lusternick. See Nathan Eck, *Ha-To'im Be-Darke ha-Mawet* (Jerusalem, 1960), p. 38; 195-196.

30   In Hebrew: *Ba-Mizbaah ha-Rashit* in Isaac Katzenelson, *Ketabim Aharonim*, pp. 299-336.

31   The title in the original: *"Dos Lid funm Oisgehargetn Yidishn Folk," Ketabim Aharonim* (Israel, 1956), pp. 337-383. For the Hebrew translation by

M.Z. Walfovsky, *ibid.*, pp. 385-431. On the fate of the poem and on its publications, see Nathan Eck, *op. cit.*, pp. 161-165.

Notes to Poets of the Monochord:
David Vogel; Baruch Katzenelson

1   Hebrew title: *Lifne ha-Sha'ar ha-Afel* (Vienna, 1923). Reprinted in David Vogel, *Kol ha-Shirim* (Israel, 1960), pp. 71-146. The book, edited by Dan Pagis, includes earlier and later poems by Vogel as well as the editor's biographical and evaluative essay on the poet.

2   In the original edition p. 69; in Pagis's edition, p. 138.

3   In German: *Der Ketzer von Soana.*

4   Hebrew title: *Be-Bet ha-Marpe* (Jerusalem, 1927/8).

5   Hebrew title: *Hayye Nissuim* (Jerusalem-Tel Aviv, 1929-1930).

6   In his introduction to Baruch Katzenelson's volume of verse *Le-Or ha-Ner* (New York, 1930), Menahem Ribalow drew attention to the kinship between Vogel and Katzenelson. *Ibid.*, p. 11. But Berkowitz denied the kinship. In an unpublished letter of June 20, 1930 he wrote to Baruch Katzenelson: "The similarity which Ribalow found between you, Vogel and Temkin is, in my opinion, a false similarity. Vogel beautifies himself, you are pureminded. Temkin is tonguetied, you are fluent. In beauty of Hebrew style you are superior to both of them." I am indebted to the officials of *Genazim*—especially to Ben Yaakov—for letting me excerpt the letter from Berkowitz's archive which is in their possession.

7   *Le-Or ha-Ner,* p. 15.

8   *Ibid.,* p. 85.

9   *Ibid.,* p. 86.

10   Hebrew title: *Be-Kur ha-Demamah* (Tel Aviv, 1948).

11   Hebrew title: *Mi-Lev El Lev* (Tel Aviv, 1954).

Notes to *Cultivators of*
Introspection:
Feierberg; Gnessin; Schoffmann

1   In Hebrew: *Ba-'Erev.*

2   For a slightly different version of the passage, see Solomon Goldman in his introduction to *Whither*—the English translation of Feierberg's *Le-An* by Ira Eisenstein (London-New York, 1959), pp. 10-11.

3   M.Z. Feierberg, *Kobez Sippurav u-Ketabav* (Cracow, 1904), p. 30 and 84. In Eisenstein's translation, p. 26 and p. 115. It is an interesting biographical fact: Feierberg was born a day before *Yom Kippur.* Its holiness, its gravity, its awe was thus brought to his attention and awareness on a personal and on an ethnic level. The offensive performance of the protagonist on *Yom Kippur* adds, perhaps, biological to psychological evidence for the identification of the author with the chief character of the novel. Conversely, the Jewish philosopher Franz Rosenzweig was so affected by the piety of Jews on *Yom Kippur* that, on the verge of conversion to Christianity, he changed the entire course of his life and became the deeply committed, Jewishly religious spokesman of his generation. On that fateful occurrence in the life of Rosenzweig, see Nahum N. Glatzer, *Franz Rosenzweig—His Life and Thought* (Philadelphia, 1953), pp. 17-20. On the significance of the Days of Awe, see Franz Rosenzweig, *The Star of Redemption* tr. by William W. Hallo (New York—Chicago—San Francisco, 1970), pp. 323-328.

4   M.Z. Feierberg, *op, cit.,* p. 90. For a different translation of the passage, see Eisenstein's *Whither,* p. 124.

5   There was a bond of sympathy between Bialik and Feierberg. Bialik's famous poem *"Ahare Moti"* is dedicated—in its original version in *Ha-Zofeh*—to the memory of Feierberg. See F. Lachower, *Toledot ha-Sifrut ha-'Ibrit ha-Hadashah* IV, (Tel Aviv, 1948), p. 71.

6   M.Z. Feierberg, *op. cit.,* p. 98.

7   In Hebrew: *"Sifrutenu ha-Yafah we-Hobotehah."*

8   M.Z. Feierberg, *op. cit.,* p. 136.

9   The monographs of Brandwein and Miron deserve to be singled out for their perspicacity and sensitivity, for the detailed analyses of their plots and structures and characters. See H. Brandwein, *Meshorer ha-Sheki'ah: Uri*

Nissan Gnessin u-Masseket Yezirato (Jerusalem, 1964); Dan Miron, *Gnessin Ahare Hamishim Shanah* in several issues of '*Akshab* (1962/63-1965/66) and "*Al Mekomo Shel ha-Sippur be-Bet Saba bi-Yezirat U.N. Gnessin"* in *Ha-Sifrut* I (Tel Aviv, 1968/69), pp. 319-336.

10   The titles in Hebrew: *ha-Ziddah, Bentayim, be-Terem, Ezel.* See *Kitbe Uri Nissan Gnessin* I (Merhavyah, 1946), pp. 87-348.

11   A Hebrew letter to his close friend Simon Bihovsky, the husband of the poetess Elisheva, begins with a casual, consciously sluggish phrase in Russian: "Warsaw, I don't know the date but I know it is 1900."(*Varshava, nye znayu chisla, no znayu chto 1900g*). See *Kitbe U.N. Gnessin* III, p. 21.

12   "The lie, beloved of men. . .because, to all appearances, it eases their burden of life." *Ibid.,* p. 38.

13   *Kitbe Uri Nissan Gnessin* I, p. 188.

14   *Ibid.,* pp. 103-104.

15   In an acute, one-page miniature essay with a semi-ironical title "*U.N. Gnessin we-Na'arotav*" Schoffmann stresses the affection of women for Gnessin. See *Kol Kitbe G. Schoffmann* V (Tel Aviv, 1960), p. 158.

16   *Kitbe U.N. Gnessin* I, p. 41.

17   *Ibid.,* p. 44.

18   Perhaps it is no accident that Genia is Gnessin's mouthpiece for his admiration of Feierberg. She remarks, in reference to the novel *Whither:* "It pays to learn Hebrew if only for the sake of reading this impassioned work in the original." *Ibid.,* p. 27.

19   In Hebrew: *Ba-Gannim.* First published in Frischmann's *Sifrut* I (Warsaw, 1909), p. 99-112.

20   *Kitbe Uri Nissan Gnessin* I, p. 358. My translation differs slightly from David Segal's in *Hebrew Short Stories* ed. S.Y. Penueli and A. Ukhmani (Tel Aviv, 1965), p. 99.

21   For an original interpretation of the stories, see Brandwein, *op. cit.,* pp. 192-258.

22   *Kitbe Uri Nissan Gnessin* II, p. 25.

23   In Hebrew: "*Adam ba-Arez.*" *Kol Kitbe G. Schoffmann* III (Tel Aviv, 1960), pp. 5-32.

24   *Ibid.,* II, p. 233.

25   The quotation is a translation of a passage from Simon Bernfeld's *Sefer Ha-Dema'ot* I (Berlin, 1923), p. 271.

26   "Deborah" in a translation by I. Halevy-Levin, the editor of *Israel Argosy* II (Jerusalem, 1953), p. 121. For the original, see *Kol Kitbe G, Schoffmann* III, p. 131.

27   The phrase is biblical. See *Judges* 5:7.

28   See *Israel Argosy* II, p. 122. For the original see *Kol Kitbe G. Schoffmann* III, p. 132.

29   Hebrew title was *Ba-Ma'agal*. In *Kol Kitbe G. Schoffmann* III, pp. 76-77: *Ba-'Iggul*. The translation by Milka Silberschlag appeared in *Jewish Frontier* (April, 1939), p. 21.

30   For the biblical episode, see *Samuel* 2, 3:15-16.

31   *Kil Kitbe G. Schoffmann* IV, p. 172.

32   See Peter Altenberg, *Ketabim Nibharim* tr. G. Schoffmann (New York, 1921). Schoffmann also translated Chekhov's *The Cherry Orchard* and *The Sea Gull*.

Notes to Hebrew Literature
Between Two World Wars

1   Thirty-five massive volumes of *ha-Tekufah* appeared between 1918 and 1950. The peregrinations of the periodical from Moscow to Warsaw, from Warsaw to Berlin, from Berlin to Tel Aviv, from Tel Aviv to New York reflect partly the personal peregrinations of the publisher Abraham Joseph Stybel and partly the ethnic vicissitudes of the Jewish people.

2   Maxim Gorky who knew and valued Bialik's poetry in the admirable Russian translation of Vladimir Jabotinsky—fourth edition, Petrograd 1917—interceded with the Russian government and succeeded in obtaining an exit permit for the poet and twelve other Hebrew writers. The group sailed from Odessa to Constantinople and separated in the Turkish metropolis. On the tedious difficulties which involved the negotiations for the permit, see especially Bialik's letters to his wife Mania in Hebrew translation from Yiddish and Russian in *Iggerot H.N. Bialik* II (Tel Aviv, 1938), pp. 199–208.

3   The title of the pamphlet—*Zilzele Shama'*—is based, conservatively, on *Psalms* 150:5. The editor, Matov, was also known as Yosippon and, in Israel, as Saaroni. A devastating review of the pamphlet by the poetess Elisheva appeared in *ha-Shiloah* XLIII (1925), pp. 471–474. Another Hebrew writer, M. Hayyug, complained about the lack of revolutionary ardor in the book. See *Bereshit* (Moscow, 1926), p. 200.

4   The volume was edited by Abraham Krivoruchko who had not yet acquired his abbreviated surname Kariv and M. Hayyug who wrote under numerous aliases: Z.S. Braun, S. Haron, M.Z. Plotkin. For attestation of the editors who are not mentioned by name in *Bereshit*, see Alfred A. Greenbaum, "Hebrew Literature in Soviet Russia," *Jewish Social Studies* XXX[3] (July, 1968), p. 141.

5   In Hebrew: *Ga'ash.*

6   In Hebrew: *'Ale 'Asor.* The title is based on *Psalms* 92:4.

7   In its first edition the novel consisted of two parts which were published by Abraham Joseph Stybel. The first part appeared in Berlin—Tel Aviv, 1929/30, the second part in Tel Aviv in 1934/5. In a recent edition—Tel Aviv, 1968—mistakes of the first edition have been eliminated, helpful notes have been added, minor revisions have been made and a third part has been added.

The fourth and final part—if it exists—still awaits publication. See the editorial remarks at the end of the new edition on p. 495.

8   See Eisig Silberschlag, *Saul Tschernichowsky: Poet of Revolt*, p. 62.

9   *Chłopi* in Polish. The four volumes of the novel correspond to the four seasons of the year.

10   On the Siberian exile, see S. Grodzensky's introduction to Lenski's volume of poems *Me-'Eber Nehar ha-Lethe* (Tel Aviv, 1960), pp. 6-12. The poet was arrested at the end of 1934. *Ibid.*, p. 225.

11   *Ibid.*, p. 97.

12   For the original version of the poem, see *Shire Hayyim Lenski* (Tel Aviv, 1938/9), p. 68; for an improved version *Me-'Eber Nehar ha-Lethe*, p. 75. Lenski's poetry achieved three editions: the first entitled *Shire Hayyim Lenski*; the second—a twin edition which embraced his and Rodin's poetry under the title *He-'Anaf ha-Gadu'a* (Jerusalem, 1954)—is augmented by ten poems, a story, an essay, a sheaf of letters to Hebrew writers and an appreciation of Lenski's work by Abraham Kariv; the third and best edition—*Me-'Eber Nehar ha-Lethe*—contains 131 new poems.

13   The Hebrew version of the epic is entitled *Sefer ha-Tundrah*. See *Shire Hayyim Lenski*, pp. 125–168.

14   *Me-'Eber Nehar ha-Lethe*, p. 28.

15   *He-'Anaf ha-Gadu'a*, p. 224.

16   *Ibid.*, p. 262.

17   *Ibid.*, p. 263.

18   To be exact: 10.5% according to the census of 1921, 9.8% according to the census of 1931. The chief reason for the drop in the percentage rates was emigration. See Raphael Mahler, *Yehude Polin Ben Shete Milhamot 'Olam* (Tel Aviv, 1968), p. 18. The book is indispensible for the study of the statistical, social and economic status of Jewry in Poland between the two world wars.

19   In Hebrew: *Zor wi-Yerushalayim*. See Israel Cohen's introduction to Matityahu Shoham, *Ketabim* (Jerusalem, 1964), pp. 17–18.

19a   William Butler Yeats, *Essays* (New York, 1924), p. 525.

20   Aaraon Zeitlin, *Shirim u-Poemot* (Jerusalem, 1949), pp. 110-111.

20a   *Ibid.*, p. 108.

21   "'Aniyim," *Ibid.*, p. 36.

22   *Ibid.*, pp. 113-114.

23   *Tarbut*, a cultural organization with a Zionist ideology, was established in 1921. On the eve of the Second World War it directed a vast educational network with Hebrew kindergartens and elementary schools, high schools and teachers' seminaries, evening classes for adults and dramatic groups. Hebrew was the language of instruction and Hebrew works dominated the libraries under the control of *Tarbut*. See Harry M. Rabinowicz, *The Legacy of Polish Jewry* (New York—London, 1965), pp. 93–94.

24   See Pomeranc's autobiographical letter of March 28, 1936 from Warsaw to Asher Barasch in *Yedi'ot Genazim* (Tammuz, 1968), p. 283.

25   In Hebrew: *Bi-Sefatayim El ha-Sela.*

26   In Hebrew: *Halon ba-Ya'ar* (Cracow, 1939). Both volumes, together with additional poetry, appeared in *Shirim* (Givatayim-Ramat Gan, 1966).

27   *Numbers* 20:11.

28   Ber Pomeranc, *Shirim*, p. 66.

29   Pomeranc made some interesting and enlightening remarks on the difficulties of translation after the end of his Hebrew version of Wyspiański's *Wesele* [Marriage]: It is possible to fill a box with fruit that grew under a southern sky and ship it for use to Eskimos in the north. But it is impossible to transport northward some southern earth that will nurture the fruit; it will freeze there. Language is. . . the original soil, the cement for the ideational structure. . . Stanisław Wyspiański, *Ha-Hatunah* tr. by B. Pomeranc (Warsaw, 1938), p. 213. The Hebrew poet faced insuperable problems in the rendition of the Polish text—from the translation of the *dramatis personae* to the translation of the sextet which was sung throughout Poland: "Boor, you had a horn of gold."

30   *Psalms* 102:1.

31   B. Pomeranc, *Halon ba-Ya'ar*, p. 25; *Shirim*, p. 127.

32   *Idem, Shirim*, p. 72.

33   *Ibid.*, p. 85.

34   Harold Shimel, *"Le-Ha'atik Aklim," Moznayim*, (June, 1971), p. 56.

35   B. Pomeranc, *Shirim*, p. 104.

36   *Ibid.*, p. 229.

37   B. Pomeranc, *Halon ba-Ya'ar*, p. 3; *Shirim*, p. 261.

38   *Halon ba-Ya'ar*, p. 13, *Shirim*, p. 115.

39   *Halon ba-Ya'ar*, p. 133; *Shirim*, p. 224.

40   *Halon ba-Ya'ar*, p. 39; *Shirim*, p. 141.

41   *Exodus* 28: 9-11.

42   M. Shoham, *Ketabim* (Jerusalem, 1964), p. 486.

43   *Ibid.*, p. 505.

44   *Ibid.*, p. 512.

45   *Ibid.*, p. 575.

46   *Ibid.*, p. 651.

47   M. Shoham, *Zor wi-Yerushalayim* (Tel Avis, 1933), p. 35.

48   *Ibid.*, p. 37.

49   In Hebrew: *Elohe Barzel Lo Ta'aseh Lak.*

50   In Hebrew: *"Kedem,"* *Ketabim*, pp. 275–296.

51   *Ketabim*, p. 341.

52   In Hebrew: *"Le-Zarot u-le-Haver."*

53   M. Shoham, *Ketabim*, p. 723.

54   M. Lusternick, *Tehumim* 2–3 (1936/7), pp. 126–127.

55   On the last issue of *Tehumim* which was salvaged by Lusternick, see reminiscences of one of its editors, Nathan Eck, *Ha-To'im be-Darke ha-Mawet*, pp. 195–196.

56   *Ibid.*, pp. 202–204. Hebrew writers in the ghetto included Hillel Zeitlin, Menahem Edmund Stein, Ber Pomeranc, Isaac Katzenelson. There were many others. A voluminous anthology of the ghetto writers was published under the title *Udim* and edited by Elhanan Indelman (Jerusalem—Tel Aviv, 1959/60). The co-sponsors were the Ogen Publishing House in America and M. Newman in Israel.

57   See Izhak Grinfeld, "A Hebrew Book That Appeared On The Eve Of The Holocaust," *Yad wa-Shem Bulletin* 21 (November, 1967), pp. 45–47.

58   In Latin: *De Vita Caesarum.*

Notes To Minor Center of
Hebrew Literature in America

1   When the Jews celebrated the two hundred and fiftieth anniversary of their settlement in America, they referred to the ship which brought twenty-three Jews to Manhattan by the name of St. Catarina. See addresses of Judge Mayer Sulzberger, Oscar S. Straus, Louis Marshall and others in *The Two Hundred and Fiftieth Anniversary of the Settlement of the Jews in the United States* (New York, 1906). But it was demonstrated convincingly on the basis of early records that the correct name of the ship was St. Charles. See Samuel Oppenheim, *The Early History of the Jews in New York, 1654–1664* (New York, 1909), pp. 41–42. Incidentally, the two hundred and fiftieth anniversary which commemorated the grant of settlement from the Dutch West India Company in 1655 was celebrated in 1905. The tercentenary was celebrated in 1954: the emphasis was on the arrival of Jews in New Amsterdam in 1654.

2   Mass immigration began in the 1880's and gained steady momentum till the First World War. It is not without interest that early immigrants from eastern Europe to the United States were encouraged by Joachim Heinrich Campe's book *Discovery of America (Die Entdeckung von Amerika* in German) which was translated into Hebrew in 1823 and into Yiddish in 1824 by Mordecai Aaron Günzburg. See Moses Rischin, *The Promised City* (Cambridge, 1962), pp. 19-20; also *Leksikon fun der Nayer Yidisher Literatur* II (New York, 1958), p. 235.

3   Benjamin Sheftall (1692–1765) may have recorded the story of early Jewish settlers in Savannah in Hebrew though he could have meant Yiddish when he said he wrote it in Hebrew. See Malcolm H. Stern, "New Light on the Jewish Settlement of Savannah," *American Jewish Historical Society* LII[3] (March, 1963), p. 172.

4   For a broadside of the congregation *Kahal Kadosh Bet Shalom,* see Edwin Wolf 2nd, "Some Unrecorded American Judaica Printed Before 1851," *Essays in American Jewish History* (Cincinnati, 1958), p. 231.

5   See Malcolm H. Stern, *ibid.,* p. 75.

6   Allan Tarshish, "The Economic Life of the American Jew," *ibid.,* pp. 264–265.

7   *American Jewish Archives* XIII[2] (November, 1961), pp. 190–191.

8   On the austerity of the Sabbath in colonial America, Samuel Eliot Morison, *Builders of the Bay Colony* (Cambridge, Mass., 1930), p. 129.

9   Perry Miller, *The New England Mind* (New York, 1939), p. 415.

10   Thomas Morton's book on New England was published under the title *New English Canaan or New Canaan* (Amsterdam, 1637). See the excellent edition of Charles Francis Adams, Jr. First published by The Prince Society as vol. XIV (Boston, 1883). Reprinted in New York in 1967.

11   Six centers of learning were established in America before 1760—Harvard College, William and Mary, Yale, the College of New Jersey (later Princeton), King's (later Columbia) and the Charity School of Philadelphia (later the Academy and College of Philadelphia, and eventually the University of Pennsylvania).

12   See Governor Bradford's *Of Plymouth Plantation* ed. by Samuel Eliot Morison, (New York, 1967), p. XXVIII.

13   *The American Language,* Fourth Edition (New York, 1936), p. 79; also *Supplement I* (New York, 1945), pp. 136–138.

14   For the reproduction of the title page of the 1803 edition, see A.S.W. Rosenbach, *An American Jewish Bibliography* (Baltimore, 1926), p. 123; for the reproduction of the title page of the 1810 edition, *ibid.*, p. 144.

15   For a reproduction of the title page, *ibid.*, p. 231.

16   *Ibid.*

17   For the title pages of the two editions, see *ibid.*, p. 291; 298–299.

18   William Chomsky, "Hebrew Grammar and Textbook Writing in Early Nineteenth Century America," *Essays in American Jewish History*, p. 131.

19   There is also a Hebrew title page. A.S.W. Rosenbach, *op. cit.*, p. 293.

20   *Ibid.*

21   *Ibid.*, p. 325; 327; 328; 367; 369.

22   On James Logan's studies of Hebrew see Edwin Wolf 2nd and Maxwell Whiteman, *The History of the Jews of Philadelphia from Colonial Times to the Age of Jackson* (Philadelphia, 1957), pp. 16–18.

23   In Hebrew: *Sefer ha-Gilgulim.*

24   William Chomsky, *op. cit.*, p. 126.

25   For a reproduction of the title page see A.S.W. Rosenbach, *op. cit.*, p. 159.

26   Edwin Wolf 2nd and Maxwell Whiteman, *op. cit.*, p. 312.

27   *Ibid.*, p. 142; 311. 309. The oft-repeated story that Rebecca Gratz is the model of Sir Walter Scott's Rebecca of York in *Ivanhoe* has never been substantiated. Washington Irving is supposed to have told Scott in 1818, when the latter planned the composition of his novel, that Rebecca Gratz and Samuel Ewing, a young lawyer and son of the Provost of the University of Pennsylvania, were in love but did not marry because of their religious

differences. But Rebecca Gratz never claimed identification with Scott's Rebecca. *Ibid.*, pp. 239; 313-314.

28 *Ibid.*, p. 373; see also the chapter on "The First American Jewish Theological Seminary: Maimonides College, *1867-1873*" in B.W. Korn, *Eventful Years and Experiences* (Cincinnati, 1954), pp. 151–213.

29 *Occident XI* (December, 1853), p. 432.

30 *Occident XXV* (1868), p. 601.

31 Israel Abrahams, *By-Paths in Hebraic Bookland* (Philadelphia, 1920), p. 259.

32 Hebrew title of the text: *Moreh Derek le-Lammed Et Na'are Bene Yisrael Darke Lashon 'Ibrit.*

33 On the translation and on Leeser's knowledge of Hebrew, see Matitiahu Tsevat, "A Retrospective View of Isaac Leeser's Biblical Work," *Essays in American Jewish History*, pp. 295–313.

34 For a reproduction of a page of James Logan's Hebrew vocabulary, see Edwin Wolf 2nd and Maxwell Whiteman, *op. cit.*, opposite p. 240.

35 On Monis, see Wolfson's brief article, written with his customary precision, in the *Dictionary of American Bibliography* 13 (1934), pp. 86–87. The earliest Hebrew grammar was published in 1735 and authored by Judah Monis who held an instructorship of Hebrew at Harvard University. It bristles with grammatical mistakes from the title page to the Hebrew translation of the Lord's Prayer at the end. Monis did not follow in the footsteps of a young Jew in England who, in 1613, refused to be converted, though encouraged to teach at Oxford University. A day before conversion "the Jew decamped!" See Samuel Eliot Morison, *The Founding of Harvard College* (Cambridge, 1935), p. 75. For a reproduction of the first page of the *Hebrew Nomenclator*, with the gracious permission of Harvard University, see Eisig Silberschlag, "Hebrew Literature in America: Record and Interpretation," *The Jewish Quarterly Review XLV* (April, 1955), opposite p. 432.

36 Hyman B. Grinstein, *The Rise of the Jewish Community of New York 1654-1860* (Philadelphia, 1945), Appendix XIII, p. 520.

37 David de Sola Pool, *Portraits Etched in Stone* (New York, 1952), p. 192.

38 *Ibid.*, p. 243.

39 A.S.W. Rosenbach *op. cit.*, pp. 196–198.

40 Hebrew title: *Sefer Abne Yehoshua.*

41 In Hebrew: *Binyan Yehoshua.*

42 In Hebrew: *Homat Yehoshua.*

43 Joshua Falk, *Sefer Abne Yehoshua* (New York, 1860), p. 3.

44 Not one hundred and twenty-eight pages as erroneously listed in E. Deinard, *Kohelet Amerikah* II (St. Louis, Mo., 1926), p. 5.

45 *Sefer Abne Yehoshua*, p. 3.

46 *Ibid.*, p. 4.

47 I.J. Benjamin, *Three Years in America* I tr. from the German by Charles Reznikoff with an introduction by Oscar Handlin (Philadelphia, 1956), p. 82.

48 *Panim El Panim* (December 5, 1969), p. 9; on R. Eliezer Bergman, David Tidhar, *Enziklopediyyah la-Haluze ha-Yishuv u-Bonav* XI (Tel Aviv, 1961), p. 3860.

49 I.J. Benjamin, *op. cit.*, pp. 324–333. The outbreak of the Civil War—not the negative opinions of the European authorities—prevented the erection of the monument. Rabbi Samson Raphael Hirsch counseled sagely: "Were you to devote. . . the interest of the amount which the erection of a monument would cost towards the annual bestowal of a physical, intellectual, or moral benefit upon a single human soul, you would honor his [Touro's] memory. . . in a more Jewish. . .manner than by the most magnificent monument which you may execute in bronze or marble." *Ibid.*, p. 329.

50 *Di Yidishe Zeitung*—an irregular Yiddish periodical in lithograph, which made its first appearance on March 1, 1870, carried Hebrew articles and *Di Post*, jointly edited by Bernstein and Gershuni, had a Hebrew supplement. See M. Starkman, "Yobel ha-'Ittonut ha-Idit ba-Amerikah," *Sefer ha-Shanah li-Yahadut Amerikah* VIII-IX (1946), pp. 560–561.

51 See Moshe Davis, "Ha-Zofeh be-Erez ha-Hadashah," *Alexander Marx Jubilee Volume, Hebrew Section* (New York, 1950) p. 118.

52 *Ibid.*, pp. 125–126, n.26.

53 *Megillah* 29 a.

54 Hebrew title: *Shir Zahav li-Kebod Yisrael ha-Zaken.*

55 Hebrew title: "*Hatan we-Kallah.*"

56 On Gershuni's apostasy and subsequent return to Judaism, see Jacob Kabakoff, *Haluze ha-Sifrut ha-'Ibrit ba-Amerikah* (Tel Aviv, 1966), pp. 79–80; Kabakoff also discusses Gershuni's conversion in his review of Davis's book, *Bet Yisrael ba-Amerikah. Mehkarim u-Mekorot* (Jerusalem, 1970) in *Judaism* XX³ (Summer, 1971), p. 373.

57 Jacob Kabakoff, *op. cit.*, p. 83.

57a *Kol Shire Naphtali Herz Imber* (Tel Aviv, 1950), p. 275.

58 This characterization is from the pen of one of them—J.L. Horowitz—in *Ner ha-Ma'aravi* 2 (1897), p. 214.

59 In *Kohelet Amerikah* I (St. Louis, 1926), p. 65. Simcha Berkowitz notes the assertion but makes no comment. See his study on "Ephraim Deinard: Bibliophile and Bookman," *Studies in Bibliography and Booklore* (Spring, 1971), p. 143.

60 *Kohelet Amerikah I*, pp. 6–9.

61 *The Colonial American Jew III* ed. Jacob R. Marcus (Detroit, 1970), pp. 1204–1205.

62 E.R. Malachi, *Iggerot Soferim* (New York, 1931), p. 133.

63   Idem, "Ozerot Ruah 'Alu be-Esh," Bizaron (May-June, 1966), p. 71.

64   Ibid., pp. 71–76.

65   Hebrew title: Nezah Yisrael (Chicago, 1896/7). On the book, see Jacob Kabakoff, op. cit., pp. 143–151. Idem, "The Role of Wolf Schur as Hebraist and Zionist," Essays in American Jewish History, pp. 433–439.

66   Hebrew title: "Minhat Yehudah."

67   The translation by F. De Sola Mendes in Bernard Drachman's "Neo-Hebraic Literature in America," Proceedings of the Seventh Biennial Convention of the Jewish Theological Seminary Association (New York, 1900), p. 106. The theme of immigration had also inspired Emma Lazarus (1849–1887) whose sonnet "The New Colossus"—in English, of course—was placed inside the Statue of Liberty at the entrance to the harbor of New York. Sabato Morais, the first president of the Jewish Theological Seminary, dedicated an admiring tribute to her—in Hebrew and in English—in American Hebrew (December 9, 1887). Reprinted in Drachman, op. cit., pp. 116–119.

68   Abraham Luria, Ha-Pa'amon (New York, 1897/8), p. 53. The title of the poem appears in English: The heroison [!] of Richmond Pierson Hobson.

69   It was published in Jerusalem in 1895 under the title Shoel ke-'Inyan.

70   M. Weinberger, Ha-Yehudim we-ha Yahadut be-New York (New York, 1887), p. 5. The allusion is to the talmudic dictum in Kiddushin 82 b: "The world cannot exist without a perfume-maker and without a tanner—happy is he whose craft is that of a perfume-maker and woe to him who is a tanner by trade."

70a   M.E. Holzman, Sefer 'Emek Refaim (New York, 1865), pp. 6–9. The author chose the word Refraim=shades,inhabitants of the netherworld as a pun on Reform.

71   Hebrew title: Ha-Mahanayim (New York, 1888).

72   Hebrew title: Nahal Abraham (New York, 1896).

73   Ibid., p. 81.

74   Shire Menahem (New York, 1899/1900), p. 3.

75   See Dolitzky's poem, "Shekel ha-Kodesh," ibid., p. 11.

75a   Ephraim E. Lisitzky, In the Grip of Cross-Currents tr. by Moshe Kohn and Jacob Sloan (New York, 1951), pp. 175–176.

76   M. Weinberger, op. cit., p. 36.

77   I. J. Benjamin, op. cit., p. 89.

78   Ibid., p. 97.

79   Ibid., p. 106.

80   M. Weinberger, op. cit., p. 31.

81   Ibid., pp. 17–18.

82 I. J. Benjamin, *op. cit.*, I, p. 108.

83 M. Weinberger, *op. cit.*, p. 19.

84 See his autobiography in *Genazim* I (Tel Aviv, 1961) ed. by G. Kressel, pp. 60–61; see also Lloyd P. Gartner, "From New York to Miedzyrecz: Immigrant Letters of Judah David Eisenstein, 1878–1886," *American Jewish Historical Society* LII³ (March, 1963), pp. 234–243.

85 *Genazim I*, p. 68.

86 The Constitution of the United States was also translated by Daniel Persky. See *Sefer ha-Shanah li-Yehude Amerikah* (New York, 1938), pp. 404–415.

87 A similar society by the name of *Hebrat Dorshe ha-Sifrut ha-'Ibrit* existed, according to the testimony of Peter Wiernik, in Chicago. See Joel S. Geffen, "America in the First European Hebrew Daily Newspaper: *Ha-Yom* (1886–1888)," *American Jewish Historical Quarterly* LI³ (March, 1962), p. 163.

88 A lecture by Ben Avigdor was published in New York in 1908 under the title *Ha-Sifrut ha-'Ibrit ha-Hadashah wa-'Atidotehah*. The author takes a dim view of the achievements of Hebrew writers and the status of the Hebrew language in America: "Our brethren did almost nothing for the Hebrew language and its literature. *Ibid.*, p. 29.

89 *Kitbe Hillel ben Zeev Malachowsky* II (Brooklyn, 1939/40), pp. 158–159.

90 Bernard Drachman, *op. cit.*, pp. 60–61.

91 *Ner ha-Ma'aravi* I³ (1895), p. 4.

92 *Ibid.*, II¹ (1897) pp. 16–19.

93 Hillel Malachowsky, *Ketabim ba-Sefer* (Philadelphia, 1902), p. 89.

94 *Ner ha-Ma'aravi* I, p. 3.

95 In imitation of *2 Samuel 23:1*.

96 Playing with another fanciful derivation of America from the Hebrew root *Marok*=cleanse, Rosenzweig asks: why is this country called America? Because it cleanses the sins of the people. The impure become pure, the disqualified become people of quality.

97 Hebrew title: *Talmud Yankai* (New York, 1909).

98 Hebrew title: *Masseket Purim*. On the authorship and date of composition, see Israel Davidson, *Parody in Jewish Literature* (New York, 1907), pp. 131–134.

99 It is still a favorite. M.J. Bar On castigates political and social life in Israel in *Masseket Yamim Tobim*—part and parcel of a satirical *Israeli Talmud*. It has been published in Tel Aviv in 1958/9.

100 Hebrew title: *"Beraitot de-Rabbi Yizhak"* in *Shire Yizhak Kaminer* (Odessa, 1905), pp. 233–236.

101 Gershon Rosenzweig, *"Masseket Amerikah," Talmud Yankai*, p. 5.

102 *Ibid.*, p. 14.

103   *Ibid.*, p. 28.

104   *Ibid.*, "*Masseket Masweh,*" p. 1.

105   *Ibid.*, "*Masseket Amerikah,*" p. *Gimmel* (opposite p. 4) and p. 6.

106   *Ibid.*, "*Masseket Amerikah,*" p. 1.

107   *Ibid.*, in *Masseket Hedyotot*, p. 3. At the end of the nineteenth and in the beginning of the twentieth century regeneration of humanity through anarchism—with its emphasis on ethnical asceticism and its cult of nature—was advocated by Charles Péguy and Georges Sorel, Gustav Landauer and Ernst Toller. See David Meakin, "Decadence and the Devaluation of Work: the Revolt of Sorel, Péguy and the German Expressionists," *European Studies Review* I (January, 1971), pp. 49-60.

108   *Ibid.*, "*Masseket Amerikah,*" p. *Zayin* opposite p. 12.

109   1 *Kings* 5:12.

110   Hebrew title: *Hamishah we-Elef Miktamim Mekoriyyim* (New York, 1903). Actually there are only five hundred and thirty-two epigrams.

111   *Ibid.*, p. 119.

112   The slender volume of three translations was published in a bilingual edition and dedicated to the man who had also befriended Naphtali Herz Imber—"Mayer Sulzberger embodying all that is good in American Judaism." Rosenzweig must have thought that the three patriotic poems would also be sung in Hebrew for he furnished them with musical notes and a transliterated translation.

113   *Proverbs* 18:20.

114   Hebrew Title: *Barkai.*

115   Imber wrote "Hatikvah" in the town of Yassy, in the home of Baron Moses Waldberg, before the end of 1878. The place and the date, authenticated by the poet himself, have been contested: Palestine has been given as the place and the eighties as the date of composition. This theory has also the poet's support: in *Barkai*, his first volume of verse, "Jerusalem 1884" is written at the end of the poem. Whatever the case may be, so much is certain: when the first colonies were founded in Palestine, the poem became the rage of the settlers. The melody was adapted from a well-known *motif* of Smetana by an anonymous cantor or by one of the farmers in Rishon le-Zion. There is a remote possibility that Imber himself imported it from Rumania to Palestine. See Eisig Silberschlag, "Naphtali Herz Imber," *Judaism* V (Spring, 1956), pp. 149-150.

116   Naphtali Herz Imber, *Barkai he-Hadash* (Złoczów, 1899/1900), p. 4. The volume was published by his brother Shemaryahu to whom he had dedicated two poems. Another brother, Mordecai, participated in the publishing venture. Of the 1000 copies 200 were sent to the poet, 800 were destroyed by fire in his native town. See Shemaryahu Imber's valuable but chronologically unreliable introduction to *Kol Shire Naphtali Herz Imber* (Tel Aviv, 1950), p. 29.

117   *Ibid.*, p. 254.

118   A whole section in Imber's collected poems is devoted to wine-songs. Purah, the Angel of Forgetfulness, is invoked in prayer; Omar Khayyam, lover of the cup, is lovingly resuscitated; the grapes of Rishon le-Ziyyon and the vats of the Land of Israel are singled out for special praise. *Ibid.*, pp. 299-327. In a poem *"Ha-Kos"* Imber declared that, had it not been for the cup, he would have preferred death. *Ibid.*, p. 298.

119   *Ibid.*, p. 280. The translation is by Milka Silberschlag.

120   *Barkai he-Hadash*, pp. 123-129.

121   Hebrew title: *Barkai ha-Shelishi* (New York, 1904).

122   The Yiddish title: *"Zu Di Yapanezer." Ibid.*, p. 46-47.

123   Hebrew title: *Temarim u-Zemarim.*

124   Hebrew title: *Ha-Kos.* It is a paraphrase of 101 quatrains of Omar Khayyam in Fitzgerald's version with a dedication to Mayer Sulzberger, an introduction by Joseph Jacobs, a panegyric in verse by George Alexander Kohut, two original poems and, not to leave a blank page, a translation of a poem by the Queen of Rumania under the title *"Ha-Gefen Bokiyyah."* Imber was attracted to the persianizing trends of the *fin de siècle* and translated some of Bodenstedt's *Lieder des Mirza Schaffy. Kol Shire Naphtali Herz Imber*, p. 279. Imber's dedicatory poem to Omar Khayyam is prefaced by a motto—omitted in the collected edition—of Mirza Schaffy. *Ha-Kos*, p. XI.

125   The other six graces: Hope, Faith, Love, Brotherhood, Knowledge, Song. See *Kol Shire Naphtali Herz Imber*, pp. 295-298.

126   Imber does not seem to have been aware of an English translation of *Sefer Yezirah* by W. Westcott in 1893.

127   In his essay on "The Music of the Psalms" (Chicago, 1894—a reprint from *Music* (September, 1894)—we read that David was the father of Hebrew music, that the Temple was a musical college and that three obscure *Hazanim*—composers in Imber's terminology—"are worthy of niches in the temple of fame along with Mozart, Beethoven and Wagner." *Ibid.*, p. 585. From his twenty-three page tract on the *History of Money*, which was published and copyrighted by Katie A. Imber in 1899 and which was pompously "dedicated to nobody to be read by anybody, for benefit of everybody," we learn that "the advent of the yellow metal on the market is shrouded in mystery, and we have no record when that yellow devil made his appearance among the sons of man. . .The first historical fame the metal won is recorded in Biblical history, when the Jews made a golden calf. . .From that time gold became the rival of silver." *Ibid.*, p. 11.

128   Naphtali Herz Imber, *Treasures of Two Worlds* (Los Angeles, Cal., 1910), p. 190.

129   Naphtali Herz Imber, *The Letters of Rabbi Akiba* (Washington, Government Printing Office, 1897), p. 701.

130   *Menahot* 29b.

131   Introduction to *Kol Shire Naphtali Herz Imber*, p. 34.

132	For early relationships between American and English literature with Hebrew literature, see my paper "Ha-Gorem ha-Anglo-Saksi be-Sifrutenu ha-Hadashah: Maga'im Rishonim" given at the Fourth World Congress of Jewish Studies and published in its second volume (Jerusalem, 1968), pp. 71-75; also my "American Classics in Hebrew Translation," Jewish Book Annual XXIV (New York, 1966/7), pp. 23-30.

133	On Hebrew translations of Byron's "Hebrew Melodies," see Jacob I. Dienstag, "Targumin 'Ivrim mi-Sifrut Anglit-Yehudit," Jewish Book Annual VIII (New York, 1949/50), p. 46.

134	Alexis de Tocqueville, Democracy in America, ed. by J.P. Mayer and Max Lerner, tr. by George Lawrence (New York, Evanston and London, 1966), p. 294.

135	In Hebrew: Mul Ohel Timmurah. Poemah mi-Zeman Shilton ha-Sefardim ba-Amerikah. The first edition was published in Jerusalem; it was reprinted in Silkiner's Shirim (Tel Aviv, 1926/7).

136	Ibid., p. 99.

137	Hebrew title: "U-Melek En be-Moab." The poem was published in Massad I ed. by Hillel Bavli (Tel Aviv, 1933), pp. 9-14.

138	See "Manoah Franko" in Massad II (Tel Aviv, 1935/6), pp. 9-54.

139	Ibid., p. 56.

140	Ibid., p. 44.

141	N.B. Silkiner, Shirim, p. 25.

142	Ibid., p. 60.

143	It was reprinted in the sumptuous edition of Shakespeare's Tragedies in Hebrew in Tel Aviv in 1959. Incidentally, all translations in that volume—with one exception—have been done by Hebrew poets who lived and created in America: Romeo and Juliet, King Lear and Antony and Cleopatra by Reuben Grossman-Avinoam; Julius Caesar by Ephraim E. Lisitzky; Hamlet, Timon of Athens, and Coriolanus by Israel Efros. Lisitzky also translated The Tempest which appeared as a separate book (New York, 1941). Halkin translated The Merchant of Venice (Berlin-Charlottenburg, 1929) and King John (Jerusalem, 1947). Antony and Cleopatra, translated by Hillel Bavli, first appeared in Hatekufah 32-33 (New York, 1947), pp. 315-392 and in Hatekufah 34-35 (New York, 1950), pp. 395-494; as a book it was published in Tel Aviv in 1952. Another translation of Antony and Cleopatra by Joseph G. Libes appeared in the same year in the same city. Julius Caesar was also partially translated by Bialik; and Hamlet had, beside Efros, three other translators: Bornstein, Davidowitz and Shlonsky. On these and older Shakespearean translations, see Joshua Bloch, "Shakespeare in Hebrew Garb," Jewish Book Annual XIV (New York, 1956/7), pp. 23-31.

144	Ephraim E. Lisitzky, Shirim (Tel Aviv, 1928), p. 29.

145	Hebrew title: "Ki-Teko'a Shofar," ibid., pp. 241-280.
146	Hebrew title: Naftule Elohim (Tel Aviv, 1934).

147   *Ibid.*, p. 92.

148   Hebrew title: *Medurot Do'akot* (New York, 1937).

149   *Ibid.*, p. 65.

150   *Ibid.*, p. 34.

151   Hebrew title: *Be-Ohale Kush* (Jerusalem, 1953).

152   *Ibid.*, p. 3.

153   Hebrew title: "*Yisrael ba-Shittim,*" *ibid.*, pp. 95-104.

154   Négritude is a Sénghorian coinage: it connotes Negro culture as an independent entity.

155   Alexis de Tocqueville, *Democracy in America*, p. 292.

156   Hebrew title: *Wigwamim Shotekim* (Tel Aviv, 1933); reprinted in the first volume of the eight-volume edition of Efros's collected works: *Kitbe Yisrael Efros* I (Tel Aviv, 1966), pp. 3-118.

157   Hebrew title: "*Halomo Shel Aman,*" *Kitbe Yisrael Efros* II, pp. 44-50.

158   Hebrew title: *Zahav* (New York, 1942). Reprinted in the first volume of *Kitbe Yisrael Efros*, pp. 119-249.

159   *Kitbe Israel Efros*, I, p. 86.

160   *Ibid.*, p. 69.

161   *Ibid.*, p.

162   The first published poem by Efros "*Pa'ame Halomot,*" written in 1911, begins with a *tête à tête* by the banks of the Hudson. *Kitbe Yisrael Efros* II, pp. 9-10.

163   Hebrew title: *Ha-Pilosofiyyiah ha-Yehudit ha-'Attikah* (Jerusalem, 1959).

164   The translations appeared originally in an essay "*Shirat ha-Kushim,*" *Nimim* (Berlin, 1923), edited by Bavli. It was reprinted in his book of essays *Ruhot Nifgashot* (Jerusalem-Tel Aviv, 1957/8), pp. 280-291.

165   Hillel Bavli, *Shirim* (Tel Aviv, 1938), pp. 211-221.

166   *Ibid.*, p. 235.

167   Bavli's essays on English and American literature in his *Ruhot Nifgashot*, pp. 223-279.

168   The ten poems "*Le-Helen*" in *Shirim*, pp. 98-105.

169   Hebrew title: "*Zeif Yegonim*" in *Shirim*, pp. 295-343.

170   *Ibid.*, p. 383.

171   *Ibid.*, p. 384.

172   *Ibid.*, pp. 155-171.

173   Simon Halkin, "*Derakim we-Zidde Derakim be-Sifrutenu*" I (Jerusalem, 1969), p. 42.

410   EISIG SILBERSCHLAG

174   *Idem, 'Al ha-I* (Jerusalem, 1945/6), pp. 28-44.

175   Hebrew title: *"Tefillot," ibid.*, pp. 24-27.

176   Hebrew title: *"'Al Hof Santa Barbara," ibid.*, pp. 177-188.

177   Hebrew title: *"Be-Yamim Shishshah we-Lelot Shiv'ah," ibid.*, pp. 117-154.

178   Hebrew title: *"Tarshishah," ibid.*, pp. 300-305.

179   Hebrew title: *"Baruch ben Neriyyah." Ibid.*, pp. 281-299.

180   The novel appeared in Berlin in 1928. The Hagrite is a *double entendre:* in Hebrew it alludes to a root, the meaning of which is: emigrate. In the Bible the Name *Hagri,* the Hagrite, occurs almost exclusively in the *Book of Chronicles.* He is mentioned among officials who "were the rulers of the substance which was King David's" (*Chronicles* 1, 27:31). It is no mere coincidence that the name Yehiel, son of Hachmoni, occurs in the same chapter in verse 32. And Hachmoni alludes to wisdom. Thus the title of Halkin's first novel—*Yehiel ha-Hagri*—is rich in theological and secular connotations.

181   Hebrew title: *'Ad Mashber* (Jerusalem, 1944/5).

181a   The stories—eleven of them—have been published under the title *Nekar* (Jerusalem, 1972). English title: *Adrift.*

182   *"Dimyon Hofshi we-Dimyon Meshubad," ha-Miklat III* (New York, 1920), p. 255.

183   Hebrew title: *"Gezel Ahavah," ibid.*, pp. 119-120.

184   In his book of poems *Hakukot Otiyyotayik* (Tel Aviv, 1963/4), p. 209.

185   *Ibid.*, pp. 217-218.

186   *Ibid.*, pp. 219-222.

187   *Ibid.*, pp. 113-134.

188   *Ibid.*, pp. 193-196.

189   Moses Feinstein, *"Kayin we-Hevel, Massad* I, pp. 221-229.

190   *Ha-Tekufah* XVI (1922), p. 395.

191   Hebrew title: *"Kallaniyyot,"* in *Hakukot Otiyyotayik*, p. 189.

192   Hebrew title: *Melo ha-Tallit 'Alim* (New York, 1941).

193   Some of the essays on contemporary thinkers have been reprinted in *Erele Mahashabah* (Tel Aviv, 1969). The essay on Rabbi Kook is a paean in praise of mystical thinking. *Ibid.*, pp. 171-195.

194   Hebrew title: *"Kabbezanim"* in *Melo ha-Tallit 'Alim*, p. 207.

195   Simon Ginzburg, *Shirim u-Poemot* (Tel Aviv, 1931), pp. 132-133.

196   *Ibid.*, (unpaginated): "To H.N.Bialik/The Guide and the illuminator of my youth/This lifework of mine is dedicated/In love and longing."/Ginzburg also wrote a poem *"Ahare Mot Bialik," Shirim u-Poemot* (Jerusalem-Tel Aviv, 1970), pp. 73-77, a poem *"Li-Bialik," ibid.*, p. 84 and *"Kinat David"* dedicated

to the memory of Bialik, *ibid.*, p. 85.

196a *Shirim u-Poemot,* p. 83.

197 *Ibid.*, p. 77.

198 Hebrew title: *Ahabat Hoshe'a* (Tel Aviv, 1935). The poem has been subjected to a searching analysis in a doctoral thesis submitted to Professor André Neher at the University of Strasbourg. See Janine Strauss, *Ahavat Hoshe'a* (Strasbourg, 1969).

199 The biography is Simon Ginzburg's doctoral thesis at Dropsie College under the title *The Life and Works of Moses Hayyim Luzzatto* (Philadelphia, 1931).

200 It first appeared in Moses Hayyim Luzzatto, *Sefer ha-Mahazot* ed. by Simon Ginzburg (Tel Aviv, 1927). On the discovery of the manuscript, see Ginzburg's introduction, *ibid.*, p. III.

201 The letters appeared under the title of *Rabbi Mosheh Hayyim Luzzatto u-Bene Doro* (Tel Aviv, 1937).

202 *Sefer ha-Shanah li-Yehude Amerikah* (New York, 1940), pp. 65-68.

203 The translation, with a brief introduction by David Ginzburg, the son of the poet, and a brief postscript by Sholom J. Kahn, appeared under the aegis of the M. Neuman Publishing House in Israel (Jerusalem-Tel Aviv, 1970).

204 Hebrew title: *"El Baruch Spinoza," Shirim we-Sonetot* (New York, 1935), pp. 36-38.

205 Hebrew title: *Halom we-Goral* (Tel Aviv, 1936); *Abraham Abulafia* appeared in Jerusalem in 1956.

206 H.A. Friedland, *Shirim* (Cleveland, Ohio, 1940). There is also a posthumous volume of folksongs translated from the Yiddish: *Shire Am.*

207 H.A. Friedland, *Sonetot* (Tel Aviv, 1939), p. 25.

208 Hebrew title: *"Adam we-Sefer"* in *Sonetot* (Tel Aviv, 1939), p. 43.

209 Hebrew title: *"Mot Safranit"* in *Shirim* (Tel Aviv, 1940), pp. 7-20.

210 Hebrew title: *"Lavlar," ibid.*, pp. 52-54.

211 Hebrew title: *"Sefarad"* in *Sonetot*, p. 33.

212 Hebrew title: *"Nadlikah Nerot"* in *Shirim*, p. 175.

213 Hebrew title: *"Be-Rivvevot Am"* in *Sippurim* (Tel Aviv, 1939), pp. 100-108.

214 Hebrew title: *"Mumhe Min ha-Huz, ibid.*, pp. 151-164.

215 Hebrew title: *"Miktavim," ibid.* pp. 1-11.

216 A.S. Schwartz, *Shirim* (Tel Aviv-Jerusalem, 1958/9), pp. 20-21.

217 *Ibid.*, p. 61.

218 Hebrew title: *"Dagah Ketanah," ibid.*, pp. 75-77.

219 *Ibid.*, p. 332.

219a Reuben Grossman-Avinoam, *Shirim u-Poemot* (Tel Aviv, 1950), pp. 11-54. The death of the son, who fell in the War of Independence in 1948, moved Grossman to edit a three-volume anthology of writings by young soldiers who fell in defense of Israel. The title: *Gevile Esh* (Jerusalem, 1951/2-1960/1).

220 Reuben Grossman, *Shirim* (Tel Aviv, 1930), p. 32.

221 Hebrew title: *"Ha-Semehot be-Helkan,"* *Shirim,* pp. 159-173.

222 See *"Dori"* in Aaron Domnitz, *Shirim we-Sippurim* (Baltimore, 1965/6), p. 66.

223 See *"Neginot 'Arev," ibid.,* p. 64.

224 Gabriel Preil, *Nof Shemesh u-Kefor* (New York 1944), p. 18.

224a From the poem "Van Gogh: Williamsburg" in *Ha-Esh we-ha-Demamah* (Tel Aviv, 1968), p. 80. For a different translation, see "Three Poems by Gabriel Preil" tr. by Robert Friend (*Midstream,* May, 1968).

224b A collection of short stories, translated by Hillel Halkin, under the title *In the Courtyards of Jerusalem,* appeared in Philadelphia in 1967.

225 Hebrew title: *"Talush"* in *Kitbe I. D. Berkowitz* I (Dvir, Tel Aviv, 1959), pp. 37-45.

226 Hebrew title: *"Mi-Merhakim," ibid.,* pp. 138-143.

227 Hebrew title: *"Yarok," ibid.,* pp. 144-146.

228 Hebrew title: *Ba-Arazot Rehokot, ibid.,* pp. 293-323.

229 Hebrew title: *"Amerikah 'Olah le-Erez Yisrael," ibid.,* pp. 181-198.

230 Hebrew title: *Menahem Mendel be-Erez Yisrael, ibid.* pp. 213-289.

231 Hebrew title: *"Ha-Nehag," ibid.,* pp. 199-203.

232 Hebrew title: *Yemot ha-Mashiah, ibid.,* pp. 378-519.

233 *Hatoren* appeared in New York between 1913 and 1925—first as a monthly, then as a weekly, and in the last four and a half years as a monthly again. Berkowitz was the editor from March 3, 1916 to February 23, 1917; co-editor with Shemaryahu Levin from March 2, 1917 to April 25, 1919. See Fannie M. Brody, "The Hebrew Periodical Press in America," 1871-1931, *Publications of the American Jewish Historical Society XXXIII* (Baltimore, 1934), p. 149.

234 Hebrew title: *Ben Erez we-Shamayim* (Tel Aviv, 1964).

235 Hebrew title: *Mashiah Nosah Amerikah* in *Sefer ha Mahazot* (New York, 1943), pp. 269-330.

236 Hebrew title: *Ketoret be-Af ha-Satan, ibid.,* pp. 331-366.

237 *Uriel Acosta* (Tel Aviv, 1932/3-1938).

238 *Rom u-Tehom* (Tel Aviv, 1950/51).

239 *Ahad Haam* (New York, 1941).

240   *Alfred Dreyfus* (Merhavya, 1946).

241   Hebrew title: *Ha-Betulah mi-Ludmir* (Jerusalem, 1956).

242   Hebrew title: *Ha-Lev we-ha-Herev* (Tel Aviv, 1954/5).

243   Hebrew title: *He-Hazer ha-Penimit* (Tel Aviv, 1954).

244   Hebrew title: *Ha-Hoze Roeh et Kallato, Sefer ha-Mahazot,* pp. 383-404.

245   Hebrew title: *Kelape Mizrah, ibid.,* pp. 405-416.

246   Hebrew title: *Nesi'at ha-Zaddik, ibid.,* pp. 199-268.

247   Originally composed in Russian, *The Dibbuk* was translated into Yiddish by the author and brilliantly done in Hebrew by Hayyim Nahman Bialik. It was first performed by the Vilna Ensemble in Yiddish in 1920 and by Habimah—the National Theater of Israel at the present time—in Moscow in 1922. The meagre plot—the exorcism of a *Dibbuk* from the body of a girl—is compensated by folklore in imaginative profusion. Brilliantly acted by both theatrical companies it became a classic in Europe and America. In the history of the theater it marked the end of naturalism as represented by Stanislavsky and the beginning of expressionism as represented by Evgeny Vakhtangov.

248   *Zon* (Berlin-Charlottenburg, 1929); *Adamah* (Tel Aviv, 1931); *Nahalah* (1932/3); *Moshavah* (Tel Aviv, 1935/6).

249   See A. Epstein, *Soferim 'Ibrim ba-Amerikah* I, p. 336.

250   Hebrew title: *Bi-she'at Herum* (Philadelphia, 1932).

251   *Mr. Koonis* (Tel Aviv, 1933/4).

252   Hebrew title: *I ha-Demaot* (New York, 1941).

253   First published in *ha-Doar* in 1929 and then reprinted under its original subtitle *"Yomano Shel Adam Boded"* in the collection of stories *le-Or ha-Venus* (Tel Aviv, 1954), pp. 193-232.

254   *Ibid.,* pp. 176-192.

255   Hebrew title: *Dor Holek* (New York—Tel Aviv, 1928).

256   Hebrew title: *Hizdamnut* in *Ba-Deyotah ha-Shelishit* (Tel Aviv, 1937), p. 130.

257   "Miflat." *Ibid.,* pp. 72-106.

258   Time and place of publication: New York and London, 1956.

259   *Shevilim be-Safrut Amerikah ha-Hadashah* (New York, 1939/40).

260   Hebrew title: *Derakim wa-Derek* (New York-Tel Aviv, 1950/1).

261   *Bavel wi-Yerushalayim* (London-Waltham, Mass., 1956/7).

262   Hebrew title: *Mahashavah we-Emet* (Tel Aviv, 1938/9). A condensation in English by Abraham Regelson appeared under the title: *Thought and Truth, A Critique of Philosophy: Its Source and Meaning* (New York, 1956).

263   Hebrew titles: *"Kibshonah Shel Battalah* and *'Al Devar ha-Groteskah* respectively in *Min ha-Safah we-li-Fenim* (Tel Aviv, 1933/4), pp. 163-197.

BIBLIOGRAPHICAL EPILOG

The literary texts—in the original Hebrew—have been used as the raw material of the book. The literary histories of Lachower and Klausner, Schapiro and Shaanan, Waxman and Zinberg, have been quoted in the notes. Earlier histories of literature by Franz Delitzsch and Moritz Steinschneider, Raisin and Slouschz—have also been utilized.

Since literary material is embedded in the massive histories of Jews—especially in the works of Graetz and Dubnow, Baer and Baron, Mahler and Katz—they have been consulted frequently and profitably.

For philosophical insights the monumental researches of Wolfson have been invaluable. For the mystic movements in the sixteenth and seventeenth centuries the specialized works of Gershom G. Scholem have revealed new vistas for every reader and scholar. And the monographs of Tishbi and Benayahu on messianic trends, the seminal books and articles of Dubnow and Buber, Dan and Weiss on hasidic literature have opened new avenues of evaluative judgments in neglected regions of Jewish life and letters.

For the period of enlightenment and the subsequent two hundred years the Hebrew periodicals from ha-Meassef and Bikkure ha-'Ittim to ha-Shiloah and ha-Tekufah have been a constant source and companion. Collections of documents like Dinur's [Dinaburg's] Yisrael ba-Golah and Hibbat Ziyyon as well as Asaf's Mekorot le-Toledot ha-Hinnuk ha-'Ivri also yielded material for the centuries between the expulsion from Spain and the present era.

The disproportionate length of the chapter on "Hebrew Literature in America" needs no apology: little has been done, much needs to be done in this untilled field. In the brief interval of peace between the two world wars Hebrew literature in America had a sudden flowering and a swift

414

decline. The essays of Malachi, Ribalow and Kabakoff have illumined this marginal region.

If the author has foregone the pleasure of a lengthy bibliography, it was because the book had reached bulkier proportions than he had anticipated. Besides, the ample notes contain a vast amount of bibliographical material.

*

The dot under the *Het, Zade* and *Kof* has been discarded for technical reasons.

INDEX

416